Imperialism and the development myth

Manchester University Press

PROGRESS IN
POLITICAL ECONOMY

Series editors: Andreas Bieler (School of Politics and International Relations, University of Nottingham), Gareth Bryant (Department of Political Economy at the University of Sydney), Mònica Clua-Losada (Department of Political Science, University of Texas Rio Grande Valley), Adam David Morton (Department of Political Economy, University of Sydney), and Angela Wigger (Department of Political Science, Radboud University, The Netherlands).

Since its launch in 2014, the blog Progress in Political Economy (PPE) – available at www.ppesydney.net/ – has become a central forum for the dissemination and debate of political economy research published in book and journal article forms with crossover appeal to academic, activist and public policy related audiences.

Now the Progress in Political Economy book series with Manchester University Press provides a new space for innovative and radical thinking in political economy, covering interdisciplinary scholarship from the perspectives of critical political economy, historical materialism, feminism, political ecology, critical geography, heterodox economics, decolonialism and racial capitalism.

The PPE book series combines the reputations and reach of the PPE blog and MUP as a publisher to launch critical political economy research and debates. We welcome manuscripts that realise the very best new research from established scholars and early-career scholars alike.

Imperialism and the development myth

How rich countries dominate in the twenty-first century

Sam King

MANCHESTER UNIVERSITY PRESS

The right of Sam King to be identified as the author of this work has been asserted by them in accordance with the Copyright, Designs and Patents Act 1988.

Published by Manchester University Press
Oxford Road, Manchester M13 9PL

www.manchesteruniversitypress.co.uk

British Library Cataloguing-in-Publication Data
A catalogue record for this book is available from the British Library

ISBN 978 1 5261 5901 4 hardback
ISBN 978 1 5261 7191 7 paperback

First published 2021
Paperback published 2023

Typeset by Newgen Publishing UK

Contents

Figures

Tables

Foreword

It is over a hundred years since the leader of the Bolshevik faction of the Russian Social Democrat Party, Vladimir Lenin, wrote *Imperialism: The Highest Stage of Capitalism*. Written in the spring of 1916 while the 'Great War' raged across Europe, Africa and Asia, Lenin used his time in exile from Russia to sum up his view on the nature of modern capitalism.

He defined what he called the 'highest stage' of capitalism as 'imperialism'. By this he meant that capitalism had reached a stage in its economic development at its apogee – either the capitalist mode of production would be replaced by socialist revolution, or capitalism would degenerate into war and disaster. That was because it could no longer develop the productive forces embodied in human labour and technology in order to raise the living standards and livelihoods of the world's billions of people.

Modern capitalism had become imperialism. The world had become dominated by just a few countries that monopolised the surplus value extracted from the world's labour power, stopping the rest of the capitalist world from developing, to use Marx's words, 'in its own image'.

Sam King's compelling book proposes that Lenin's thesis was correct in its fundamentals – namely, that capitalism had developed into what Lenin called 'monopoly finance capital'. The world has become polarised into rich and poor countries with no prospect of any of the major poor societies ever making it into the rich league anymore.

A hundred years later no country that was poor in 1916 has joined the exclusive imperialist club (save for the exception of Korea and Taiwan, which specifically benefited from the 'cold war blessings of US imperialism'). King presents a battery of empirical data to show this; in particular, that the gap between the per capita income of the top thirteen or so economies and the rest of the world that existed a hundred years ago is still there – indeed the gap has widened, not narrowed, even if you take into account China.

The great hope of the 1990s, as promoted by mainstream development economics that Brazil, Russia, India, China and South Africa (BRICS) would soon join the rich league by the twenty-first century, has proven to be a mirage. These countries remain also-rans and are still subordinated and exploited by the imperialist core. There are no middle-rank economies, halfway between, which could be considered as 'sub-imperialist' as some Marxist economists argue.

And it is not just per capita income gaps that reveal this. Recent studies by Marxist economists on international trade between imperialist economies and the rest show the huge and persistent transfer of value through 'unequal exchange' from the poor to the rich. And that includes China. This alone shows that China is not an imperialist country, as some Marxists claim.

Despite Lenin's *Imperialism* proving correct in its predictions, it has been ignored, dismissed, criticised and condemned as irrelevant to twenty-first-century capitalism. King examines the various criticisms that range from claiming that Lenin's work is out of date because colonies have disappeared; Lenin lacked rigour in concept; he relied on non-Marxist theories like those of Hobson; and even that imperialism, as Lenin described it, no longer exists in the twenty-first century.

King shows these criticisms are nonsense and often based on a misunder-standing or misrepresentation of what Lenin was arguing. The key concept in Lenin's *Imperialism* was of 'monopoly finance capital'. But monopoly finance capital did not mean competition had disappeared; on the con-trary, Lenin argues that it means intensified competition, but between more powerful actors – monopoly capitals. Lenin did not mean that capitalism had been 'financialised', as understood in the current heterodox theory where the finance sector supposedly dominates and controls the industrial sector, as though there were two 'classes' within capital. Lenin meant that capitalism had fused finance with industry into the form of 'monopolies' that now controlled the technology and the labour process, as Marx and Engels had observed and predicted (see Chapter 7).

According to King, this leads to competition for the domination of the labour process, which takes the form of a struggle for highest labour prod-uctivity. This competition produces winners and losers and therefore the creation of two types of capital – monopoly and non-monopoly capital. On an international level, this leads to a division between imperialist monopoly capital and Third World non-monopoly capital and therefore between rich and poor states, where the poor societies are exploited by the rich societies.

Although Lenin's *Imperialism* highlights the export of capital to the 'developing world', imperialist exploitation is not defined by this. As Lenin himself argued (see Chapter 5), it is defined by the monopoly of techno-logical superiority that enables the imperialist countries to extract surplus value from the 'non-monopoly' capitals through both trade and subsidiaries located abroad. That extraction does not mainly occur within transnational companies, as many modern heterodox analyses argue. According to the United Nations Conference on Trade and Development (UNCTAD) – a key data source about international trade and investment flows – only one-third of value transfers from poor to rich takes place from subsidiaries of transnational companies to the head office. More usually, independent Third World capitalists exploit their own labour force but then, in selling on the world market where international prices are set, much of the surplus value they have extracted domestically is transferred to the dominant higher-technology monopoly capitals in the imperialist economies.

Monopoly finance capital does not negate Marx's value theory and the transformation of values into prices of production. Total value still equals total prices globally, as per Marx's law of value. But through 'unequal exchange' in international trade, monopoly capitals (imperialism) achieve a higher rate of profit at the expense of non-monopoly capitals (the periphery or Third World), which get a lower rate of profit. King shows empirically how corporate profitability is higher across many sectors in imperialist countries.

There is one important omission from Lenin's analysis of imperialism, in my view. Why did imperialism emerge when it did in the late nineteenth century? Lenin says that it was due to the inexorable process of replacing human labour with machines and thus the increased concentration and centralisation of capital as the weak are gobbled up by the strong. But there is another factor that flows from this process.

As Marx showed, only human labour creates value and profit for capital, not machines. Therefore, these advances in the production process lead to a fall in the overall profitability of capital. Marx argued this was the most important law of political economy. Falling profitability in the late nineteenth-century depression in Europe and America forced capitalist companies to expand across the globe in the search for more cheap labour and higher profits. Marx recognised this as a key counteracting factor to the tendency for profitability to fall. Imperialism is the result.

King shows that imperialism is alive and not so well for the world's people. But he also deals with the issue of whether any of the poor countries of the world, under the heel of the imperialist few, can break out. King – correctly in my view – argues that cannot happen because monopoly capital with its domination over technology can persist in capturing more of the value created by workers in all countries, while the peripheral, non-monopoly capitalist countries are forced to eke out profits using cheap labour inputs and low-level technology – and that this polarisation cannot be broken while imperialism lasts.

But is that the case with China? Can it be an exception? Can China through its state-controlled and directed economic structure raise its technological level up to the levels monopolised by the imperialist countries? King thinks not because, although China has been the most successful of the non-monopoly capital countries globally in the last several decades, it now has essentially the same economic and social structure as the other BRICS. China is not imperialist, but it is capitalist and therefore in this world of imperialism, it is doomed to be exploited in the same way as all the rest, indeed even more quantitatively.

However, King recognises that China's relative success in development in part expressed the gains of the Chinese revolution. A legacy of that historic event was the continuing state ownership control of banks, investment and many of the most powerful corporations. And he quotes my own view that this effectively ameliorates or restricts the operation of the law of value – the basic law of motion of the capitalist system – in China.

Imperialism, or 'monopoly capitalism', as King's book shows, is effectively the modern form that the law of value takes in the world economy. Therefore, its amelioration, or its elimination from China, could mean a break from the grip of global monopoly capital. However, achieving that depends on China taking the direction of a democratically planned economy and not the 'capitalist road' as one faction in the communist bureaucracy strives for. Above all, it will depend on the expansion of socialist revolution internationally.

The rise of China may not be a threat to imperialist domination, but to the American ruling elite it does appear to be a rival to their economic and political hegemony. Thus, as from the days of Nixon and Mao, we have the switch in US strategy from the policy of 'engagement' in the hope and expectation that American multinationals would rule in Beijing; to the policy of 'containment' (the trade and technology war and military encirclement) now that the Chinese will not play the imperialist ball.

The age of 'globalisation' is over. This is the issue of twenty-first-century imperialism, proving Lenin's point that monopoly capital does not mean the end of competition, rivalry and war – on the contrary.

Imperialism may still be with us a hundred years since Lenin, but it is not permanent. It has two Achilles heels. First, as King argues, because only human labour creates value and profit for capital and machines do not, increasingly mechanised production displacing labour leads to falling overall profitability and thus to crises of production and investment. The imperialist system came about in order to counteract capital's falling profitability, but it cannot abolish that tendency. The end of 'globalisation' will intensify the class struggle between capital and labour globally.

And that brings up the second weak heel of capital: the proletariat. The global proletariat has never been larger in history, both in numbers and as a proportion of the potential human workforce. The labour process may be economically dominated by imperialist monopoly capital, but it is the working class that does all the work and runs all technology. It is in workers' power to end imperialist domination and replace it with a cooperative world of equality that is 'from each according to her ability and to each according to her need'.

Michael Roberts

Introduction

Contrary to the celebration and fear of the rise of China, 'the rise of the rest' and other apparent ascendancies, this book argues that the imperialism of the rich countries is alive and well. China does not threaten the global dominance of the rich countries and it cannot while under the global capitalist system – far from it. Indeed, China remains a poor country – with low per capita income and wealth – and is being held in that position by the scientific and productive monopolies of the rich countries. This is the essence of the imperialist stranglehold on China.

The same stranglehold grips not only China but almost every country in Asia, Africa and South America. The whole of what used to be called the 'Third World' – a term we are told is no longer relevant – is still poor and exploited. Despite carrying out a growing part of the world's work, the poor countries are not breaking free of imperialist domination. Nor do any of them, including China, threaten to topple, replace, outcompete or overtake the imperialist states. This book explains how the rich, imperialist countries are able to maintain their dominance decade after decade and why this situation will continue as long as the present system remains in place.

For years, to make such statements has invited not only ridicule but incomprehension. China's supposed threat to the imperialist countries appears so obvious to almost everyone. Most discussion is not about if China can catch up, but how long it might take, or what it will look like. This view is held by the huge majority of working people, scholars and intellectuals, including many on the Left. Callinicos expressed the dominant view when he said, 'One has only to utter the word "China" to indicate what's wrong with the Third Worldist understanding of imperialism'.[1] What he suggests is that China debunks the idea the world is divided into rich, imperialist and poor, exploited countries; that we should abandon such views, which are symbolised by the term 'Third World'.

Until recently, another popular talking point – the rise of the 'BRICS' countries (Brazil, Russia, India, China and South Africa) – was also supposed to debunk the 'Third Worldist' view that the world is divided between rich and poor countries. Yet this has already fallen out of fashion. The imagined rise of BRICS is now obviously false as all the others, besides China, are widely acknowledged as facing deep economic crises. But no rethink of what caused so many unrealistic expectations about their development is taking place. Without a rethink, it is hard to see how the outlook will change. The same thinking is still being applied to China.

Today a small core of rich countries – largely the same states as a hundred years ago – still dominate the international economy, securing the lion's share of total world income. It is easy to identify them because they are many, many times richer than all the other major societies. They are home to just 13 per cent of the world's people. These are the imperialist countries. Like a hundred years ago, the imperialist countries are principally Western Europe, North America and Japan – plus Australia and New Zealand. We can now add Israel, South Korea and Taiwan.

The world has become ever more polarised – especially since the collapse of the Soviet Union. The polarisation is between this small group of imperialist countries and the vast majority of countries that make up the 'Third World'. Today there is almost no middle ground or 'Second World' between the rich and poor states. China is exemplary of this pattern. China remains a poor country with per capita income less than 20 per cent of the imperialist states (see Chapter 1). This book shows that is where it and other countries will remain, so long as the world remains capitalist.

Readers who are old enough may find parts of the contemporary China hype sounds familiar. In the 1960s – long before anyone started talking about BRICS – it was claimed that Brazil was approaching something then called economic 'take-off', which would launch it into the orbit of the developed, imperialist states.[2] These expectations were disappointed. Brazil today languishes in the same position within the world hierarchy as it did six decades ago. It is still a relatively well-developed Third World state, richer than the worst off, but vastly poorer than the imperialist societies. Brazil's per capita income remains essentially unchanged relative to the imperialist world – just 19 per cent of the average imperialist country's per capita income.

The hype around the threat of competition from this or that Third World country that is 'catching up' or poised to 'overtake' imperialist countries is part of the propaganda offensives of the capitalist classes within the imperialist societies. Capitalists cutting wages or replacing workers with machines in such countries find it convenient to point their finger at competition from alien states and peoples as the cause. The foreign threat is exaggerated to make attacks on workers appear necessary, inevitable and not the fault or responsibility of the capital that actually carries them out. Denigrating these countries as failed states inhabited by inferior or threatening peoples and regimes is a part of making this sales pitch easier. This book focuses on critiquing the economic hype associated with this propaganda.

The real and imagined threat of Chinese economic competition has proven every bit as useful as the war on terror as a rallying cry for national chauvinism and racism in the post-Cold War world. It has greatly assisted US capitalists and capitalists in other rich countries to justify attacks on living conditions of working people in their own countries – necessary to safeguard capitalist profitability in the neoliberal period. The propaganda offensive against China is helped endlessly by the fact that large sections of the Left, including Marxists, have swallowed it whole. For example, US socialists like Ashley Smith argue that China is 'a new imperial power'.[3]

If China really was a threat to the world dominance of the United States and other imperialist societies, when US capitalists or their political representatives told workers they need to accept job losses and pay cuts due to overwhelming Chinese competition, this would have some basis. In reality it is marginal US producers that are seriously threatened by Chinese competition. Other companies have taken advantage of cheap Chinese labour to reduce their costs and increase their profits. For them the China threat provided a perfect cover.

We know large parts of the US working class have accepted these arguments and do view China as a threat, given their support for Trump's racist programme to 'Make America Great Again' or alternative America first programmes promoted by Biden, Sanders and others. The same situation exists in Europe, Australia and all the major imperialist states.

China cannot be a threat to the imperialist countries so long as it remains a second-tier economy that is subjugated and exploited by the imperialist ruling classes, backed by the national governments they control. It is also the reason why key imperialist propaganda outlets – like the *New York Times*, *Washington Post*, Australian ABC and seemingly every mainstream political party and major news outlet across the imperialist world – work so hard to convince us of the so-called threat.

On the other hand, continuing imperialist exploitation of China and other poor countries is *also* a powerful social basis for racism among working people. The imperialist system, as it stands, delivers wages in all the rich countries that are five or ten times higher than China and the rest of the Third World. Without doubt this is a powerful reason – or bribe – for workers to accept the current system, to support it, or at least not oppose it actively. Outsourcing of the most dangerous and environmentally destructive processes provides an additional benefit. Principally this goes to First World capital, but also it benefits the imperialist societies as a whole. This too is a powerful basis for acquiescence or passivity.

The global rich–poor divide is a financial confirmation that the peoples of First and Third World are not treated as equals – some are deemed by the system to be more deserving of a better life style than others. The divide will remain the principal basis of racism and national chauvinism unless working people can be convinced of an anti-imperialist perspective. For that to be possible we need to have a clear understanding of what the imperialist system is and how it fundamentally operates. The starting point is confronting the false narrative that the imperialist countries are collapsing under the weight of Chinese competition. They are not. If there is a threat of collapse it stems from internal contradictions of the whole system that is increasingly unable to secure dignified living conditions and a safe and sustainable environment for working people wherever they live.

An analysis of the considerable growth and development of the Chinese economy takes up a good part of this book. This growth and development is shown to be completely different to how it is presented in the imperialist propaganda and to what most people think. To understand China – the largest Third World society – we need to also understand its relationship to the imperialist societies, as well as to other poor countries. That is, we need an understanding of the worldwide imperialist system that we live in – the aim of this book.

China's underlying weakness, and that of all Third World states, is that its growth (including during the neoliberal period) is of a type of capitalist development that is qualitatively inferior to that which occurs in the imperialist societies. It is different to the type of development that would be necessary for China to compete with imperialism's most essential strength – its domination of the global labour process.

In contemporary capitalism – imperialism – domination at the highest levels of the labour process – that is, in the most complex, sophisticated and difficult types of labour – is the only path to 'catch up' with the high-income societies because such domination is, in turn, the basis of their domination of the world economy.

Imperialist monopoly capital dominates the highest aspects of the labour process, so that non-monopoly capital is relegated to the lowest level or ordinary levels of the labour process. This fact is the kernel of the development of an international division of labour as it now exists. On that basis we can see the development of two poles within the global division of labour – a pole of high-end labour and its opposite, a pole of low-end, ordinary labour.

Capitalist producers and countries are both divided and polarised on this basis. Some capitalists, primarily those based in the imperialist countries, produce commodities[4] under conditions reflecting their dominance of the technologically highest, most complex and productive production processes. These are the monopoly capitalists.

Other capitalists, primarily based in the Third World countries, produce commodities under conditions reflecting their very limited access to technologically complex and productive processes and as a consequence, are restricted to mostly more simple production processes – even if these are sometimes carried out on a massive scale. These are the non-monopoly capitalists. Monopoly capital dominates in the small handful of imperialist countries; non-monopoly capital operates everywhere else.

The book also shows that the path to transform themselves into a new group of monopolists is decisively closed off to the capitalist class of any large Third World society – including the largest one. The nature of Chinese and other Third World participation in the world market does not prepare them for or tend towards challenging the essential imperialist monopoly. Indeed, the polarised nature of the world division of labour ensures the opposite is true, that Third World participation in the global labour process is mostly restricted to simple low-end tasks, with only minor exceptions. Without being able to challenge imperialist monopoly over the labour process, no broader challenge is possible.

What China has achieved in the neoliberal period is highly significant. It is crucial to understand what has happened more precisely. China's rapid production growth and exports have reshaped the world economy. However, this does not mean that China is catching up with imperialist countries. China has achieved catch-up, more or less, with the other large Third World economies, like Brazil and Mexico. These countries and some others, together with China, occupy an intermediate position within the international division of labour. They are characterised by a relatively high level of development compared to other, poorer Third World societies, but far below the level of development of the imperialist societies. They are the most successful capitals only at the specific aspects of the global labour process that are allocated to the Third World. They are the most successful Third World societies at carrying out standard, or 'ordinary', non-monopoly labour processes.

Being the best at non-monopoly labour processes sets this group apart from other Third World societies, but it does not mean they are anywhere near being able to catch up and overtake the economies of the imperialist countries. They may be able to offer some resistance to the worst excesses of imperialist economic aggression for periods of time, but they are not in a position to threaten monopoly capital's dominant position at the apex of the global economy. They will continue to be the object of economic aggression and exploitation. Imperialist societies are characterised by the monopoly of the opposite type of labour processes – highest and high-end labour. Monopoly over high-end labour is the only type of monopoly possible based on the labour process itself. It is very difficult to establish a sustainable monopoly over something that is relatively easy to duplicate (i.e. ordinary, low-end labour processes).

During the neoliberal period, the shift of low-end production to the Third World has not and is not bringing about a convergence in the income,

wealth or social and economic development between rich and poor countries. Rather, the huge gap between the small club of imperialist states and
the vast majority of poor states has persisted and grown, even as the Third
World has contributed an increasing share of global labour.

The neoliberal period also witnessed the defeat and decline of most Third
World national liberation movements of various types. Their defeat, alongside the collapse of the Soviet Union, were critical factors that enabled capitalist imperialism to develop new forms – later dubbed neoliberalism – which
allowed it to emerge from the crisis of the 1970s and early 1980s.

With the decline of the Third World mass, anti-imperialist struggle, came
also a decline of the anti-imperialist intellectual work that characterised
earlier periods. This decline in anti-imperialist thought and action affected
not only the important intellectual currents often collectively referred to
as 'dependency theory' but also affected the overlapping field of Marxist
writing on imperialism. For the three decades, 1980–2011, new work on
the economics of imperialism virtually ceased among First World Marxist
academics. Marxists belonging to activist groups and parties in the rich,
English-speaking world hardly fared better. Today the empirical fact of
global income and social polarisation between rich and poor countries is –
with notable exceptions – hardly acknowledged or discussed by many First
World Marxists.

Theoretically the decline of Marxist work on imperialism occurred
alongside widespread rejection, especially by scholars, of Lenin's famous
book *Imperialism: The Highest Stage of Capitalism*. As little new work was
being written, rejection of Lenin was often based on little or no discussion
of the book itself besides shorthand reference or caricature. The few works
that did attempt to explain the contemporary imperialist world economy
have not developed any well-known Marxist theory that can account for the
dynamics seen in the neoliberal period.

Yet Lenin's *Imperialism* – and in particular its key concept, monopoly
finance capital – appears to provide a usable framework. This book argues
that contemporary world polarisation into rich and poor societies is based
upon imperialism's monopolistic dominance in the labour process. This is
not an original insight. Monopolisation of technical supremacy and thus
of labour productivity are given great emphasis by Lenin – something long
overlooked. This contrasts with contemporary explanations that tend to
emphasise factors other than the labour process itself – such as military
strength, institutional power, finance or price distortions.

By focusing on the labour process and the ways in which imperialist
monopoly intersects with the labour process, Lenin's theory also allows us
to outline the specific manner in which Marx's labour theory of value can be
applied to the conditions of contemporary monopoly capitalism (a Marxist

theory of unequal exchange). This Leninist application of Marx's economic theory provides a framework that allows the book to develop a simple, clear and empirically verifiable explanation of the economic core of contemporary imperialism.

In this labour conception of imperialism, the role of the imperialist state is also extended beyond those roles for which it is commonly noted: developing and enforcing laws, supressing workers, going to war or giving financial assistance to capital. In addition to these, the imperialist state is intimately involved in raising labour productivity. Capitalist firms are little able to independently carry out the broad social policies required to create highest labour productivity and find themselves fundamentally dependent for this on the imperialist state.

The key theoretical insight of this book – the development of the concept of non-monopoly capital – is shown to be a necessary component and theoretical extension of Lenin's broader theory of monopoly finance capital. Many contemporary heterodox researchers and mainstream press reports, at least when taken together, confirm the existence of monopoly and non-monopoly capital as well as the uneven and exploitative relationship between them. Researchers, like Steinfeld, Schwartz and many of the world-systems writers cannot help but describe the exploitative relationship between 'global lead firms' and Third World capital (even if they do not always call it this), nor fail to notice that the essential basis of this dominance is technological superiority. However, much of the research, conforming to mainstream views on development, tends to view exploitative relationships as temporary or incidental, and not systemic.

The significance of Lenin's work is that it gives the most useful and accurate definition of monopoly. First, Lenin's concept of monopoly is based in the labour process itself. Second, it remains inherently capitalist in character. He therefore emphasises privately owned production of commodities for the market. What this means is that the market establishes the arena where competition for technological and labour process supremacy is fought. As the widespread privatisations and 'free market' reforms of the neoliberal period testify, this appears to have been correct. Building on this basic Marxist definition, the rest of this book shows how imperialism's labour process monopoly constitutes the basis of its domination, exploitation and – under capitalism – its permanence.

In the conditions of capitalist imperialism, Third World societies developing new technologies – even where this is possible – is not sufficient on its own. To challenge imperialist dominance would require developing new technologies for the production of commodities sold on the capitalist world market. Therefore, it requires developing new technologies that can defeat the belligerent competition of incumbent technological leaders on the market – something entirely different to the incremental learning and improvement envisaged by multilateral development institutions such as the World Bank.

In monopolistic competition for control of markets, it is not enough to make certain advances and to achieve marginal improvements. This may be adequate for progress relative to other non-monopoly capital, or to gain a minor improvement in bargaining position relative to monopoly capital. It results only in marginal and temporary gains. To 'catch up' in monopolistic competition (i.e. to approach or equal the level of the advanced economies) would mean decisively breaking the stranglehold of the leading multinational corporations (MNCs) and do so while being at the same time attacked by them and by imperialist states. Imperialism's stranglehold can be broken only by decisively *surpassing* it technologically, by defeating the incumbent monopolies and replacing the imperialist societies as the driver of world development.

Incumbent imperialist monopolies can break the back of non-monopoly competitors and relegate them time and again to a subservient position, as Trump and the US Department of Commerce have shown in relation to Chinese telecommunications companies ZTE and Huawei. The reason these punitive sanctions were effective, or even possible, is because of the already existing US and broader imperialist domination in the production of the products the sanctions effected – otherwise China could simply work around them.

Societies suffering the legacy of colonial oppression and imperialist subjugation cannot consistently, and across a range of areas, develop groundbreaking scientific advances, nor apply these on a society-wide basis. To make real progress in raising the social-cultural level of a society is not quick or easy. Nor can it be achieved merely by correct policy settings, good luck or a technocratic, business-led development.

Genuine social progress to the degree needed cannot occur outside of and in opposition to the principal centres of scientific knowledge (the imperialist states) without involving mobilisation of the broad masses of the population. Yet that can hardly happen if the main purpose of development is merely to enrich local capitalist classes – and this remains the goal in countries dominated by non-monopoly capital. Moreover, not even the most revolutionary Third World society could conceivably *surpass* the technical and scientific level of modern imperialist states when operating under the blows of imperialist hostility and sabotage.

What is decisive is that Third World capitalism is prevented even from taking incremental steps that would eventually make possible a challenge to imperialism. This is because as capitalist societies they participate in production of commodities for the capitalist world market. Moreover, they are compelled to do so in accordance with an existing division of labour complete with its established technological and social polarisation. There is no entry point to this system, other than at the bottom.

Thus the very form of their participation in the global economy organically and continuously reproduces in these societies the same broadscale underdeveloped social foundation that makes catch-up impossible. This is why even well-meant policies (such as *Made in China 2025* or its various precursors), while they may have an impact, cannot fundamentally change the international position of the host society.

Imperialist monopoly over the labour process is the reason no large poor country has joined the imperialist camp for a hundred years – save for those special cases benefiting from the Cold War blessings of US imperialism, namely South Korea and Taiwan. This is also the reason that world income and world division of labour are starkly polarised into two distinct camps – high and low – as opposed to exhibiting a spectrum of variations, with many middle-income countries. In reality there are almost none.

The two poles of imperialist society have been given many different names over time: core and periphery, North and South, semi-colonial versus imperialist, metropolis and satellite or Third World and First World. It is more important to be clear about what we are referring to than the particular label used. Clarifying what these refer to is the task of this book. As such, any term might do. However, given the growing degree of polarisation between the rich and poor societies (outlined in Chapter 1) and the almost negligible presence of any middle-income societies in between the two poles, it seems the terms 'Third World' and 'First World' perhaps best express the ongoing relationships of oppression and exploitation of the poor countries. Some readers will be more familiar with using the terms 'Global North' and 'Global South' as these have become prevalent particularly among non-governmental organisations (NGOs) and academic writing in recent years. However, in many regions of the world, for example Indonesia and Latin America, the terms First World and Third World remain dominant or terms that more people understand or use.

Opponents of this book will contend that its arguments are too determinist, that they amount to concluding history has ended, that no further historical or social development is possible under capitalism. But the book does not imply this. The neoliberal period demonstrated an overall tendency towards rapid technological progress and social change. However, this does not mean that all possible development paths remain open.

Addressing this contention at the turn of the century, Lorimer argued:

> The assumption [is] that the possibilities of development open to a given historically conditioned social form of production [i.e. capitalism] are unlimited. The whole facts and processes analysed by Marx, and Lenin, show on the

contrary that only a specifically limited and conditioned development of the productive forces is possible to each historically determined social form of production.[5]

To be sure, China, Brazil, India, Indonesia, Nigeria, Egypt and the rest of the Third World can and will develop. These societies are home to the majority of humanity and occupy most of the Earth's surface. As strange as it might seem to the imperialist ruling classes and their racist ideologues, it is in the present-day Third World that resides the powerful creativity and as yet unknown potential of most human beings.

What will not and cannot happen is that this awesome human potential, this explosive power, will be unleashed via meek subjugation to the imperialist system and its masters; by obedient participation in the capitalist market, devoted and diligent toil for the production of commodities complementary to the advanced imperialist economies. Nor will liberation be achieved through social movements subordinate to these parameters. There is no possibility of Third World catch-up under capitalism. Though there is every possibility that imperialist oppression and exploitation of the great mass of humanity living in the Third World – and also in the First World – may be capitalism's undoing. Imperialism in the twenty-first century is expanding the army of its own gravediggers – the world working class – far beyond any it could have previously imagined.

Notes

1 A. Callinicos, *Imperialism and Global Political Economy* (Cambridge, UK, Polity, 2009), p. 5. For a liberal version, see T. Friedman, *The World Is Flat* (New York, Picador/Farrar, Straus and Giroux, 2005).

2 L. C. Bresser-Pereira, 'The Rise of Middle Class and Middle Management in Brazil', *Journal of Inter-American Studies*, 4:3 (1962), 313.

3 A. Smith, 'Deal or No Deal, the Rivalry Between the US and China Will Intensify', *Truth Out* (2019), 22 May.

4 Commodity production in this work refers to production for sale of both goods and services.

5 D. Lorimer, 'Introduction', in V. I. Lenin, *Imperialism: The Highest Stage of Capitalism* (Sydney, Resistance, 1999), p. 15.

Part I

Two worlds

1

Income polarisation in the neoliberal period

It is common for contemporary Marxist writers to argue that the neoliberal period increased the income and wealth gap – or the polarisation of income and wealth – between rich and poor people, or between the working class and capitalist class. It is less common to acknowledge the growing polarisation between the small group of imperialist societies and the much larger group of Third World societies.[1] Many First World Marxists argue that the terms 'First World' and 'Third World' are meaningless, dated terms that do not correspond to today's reality.[2] That the imperialist societies are almost the same group of countries, occupying almost the same position as a hundred years ago, is something rarely noted and even less analysed. Yet such international polarisation has not only persisted since the Second World War but has grown substantially – especially during the neoliberal period.

The international polarisation represents, alongside the polarisation of income and wealth between classes, a crucial form of the general trend towards the concentration and centralisation of capital that Marx anticipated.[3] It is also an important concrete form taken by the growing inequality between classes. As such, no accurate analysis of the international class struggle is possible today without taking the worldwide division and polarisation between societies into account.

At the second congress of the Communist International (Comintern) in 1920, Lenin emphasised the division of the world into a small minority of oppressor nations and 'the vast majority' of the world's population who lived in the oppressed societies. He estimated that 'about 70 percent of the world's population belongs to the oppressed nations'.[4] Since then polarisation has dramatically increased. By 2015 not 70 per cent but 85 per cent of the world's population lived in poor countries. The relative size of the rich country population – 13.6 per cent of the world's people – has halved compared with Lenin's estimate. Strikingly, today truly 'middle-income' or 'Second World' countries are almost non-existent, accounting for just 1.4 per cent of world population. The world's states are clearly divided into top and bottom parts, with a large, almost unpopulated gap in between (Table 1.1).

Table 1.1 First, Second and Third World population and income, USD, 2015

	First World: income above $25,000	Second World: income $15,700–$25,000	Third World: income below $15,700	World
Number of states and territories	32	14	148	194
Population (thousand)	996,667	100,412	6,239,386	7,336,465
GDP (trillion)	$44.24	$2.00	$27.74	$73.98
Share of world GDP	59.8%	2.7%	37.5%	
GDP per capita	$44,392	$19,909	$4,446	$10,084
GDP per capita – percentage of First World average	100%	44.9%	10%	22.7%
Share of world population	13.6%	1.4%	85%	

Sources: World Bank (2017); United Nations Department of Economic and Social Affairs: Population Division (2015).

Gross domestic product (GDP) in US dollars is the most meaningful measure of the current health and power of each national capitalist class. Unlike so-called purchasing power parity (PPP), which exists only as a statistical construction, USD GDP measures (however imperfectly) income that capitalists and workers actually receive for the sale of commodities they own. US dollars command purchasing power over goods sold on the world market.

By measuring national income in USD (or its exchange equivalent in other national currencies) we gain an indication of the quantity of goods that can be obtained on the world market in exchange for a given country's own labour product. This comparison of labour product for labour product is an objective measure not of a given country's value creation, but of how much value it can capture. Comparing *per capita* GDP is useful as it compares the world *market* value (i.e. price) of labour product per person. This has a rough equivalence to per worker and per hour, as there is a general correlation between the size of population and workforce. Gross GDP, on the other hand – that is, total national product – can simply indicate a large or small population or country but, unlike GDP per capita, has no correlation with the degree of concentration of capital, rates of profit or individual income.

Gross Indian GDP (over USD 2 trillion) for example, is very large, larger than Italy and not far off France. In a certain sense, this does correspond to power. The Indian state apparatus is certainly regionally powerful in relation to its smaller neighbours that have a similar level of development. However, the gross figure gives no indication of the competitive position of Indian capital on the international market.

World income polarisation can be visually represented by graphing the income level of the twenty most populous countries in the world (Figure 1.1). These countries, representing more than 5 billion people or 70 per cent of world population, are strikingly polarised into rich and poor countries, with no middle countries at all. If the graph were bigger, it would show that the largest fifty states in the world all fall into the same pattern. They achieve either First World or Third World per capita income. The largest middle-income or Second World state, Saudi Arabia (population 31.5 million), is the fifty-first country in the world by population. The next biggest, Taiwan (population 23.5 million), is the sixty-second, followed by Greece (population 11 million), the seventy-seventh largest country in the world.

This definition of the Third World (i.e. countries with low per capital income) includes 85 per cent of world population but just 38 per cent of

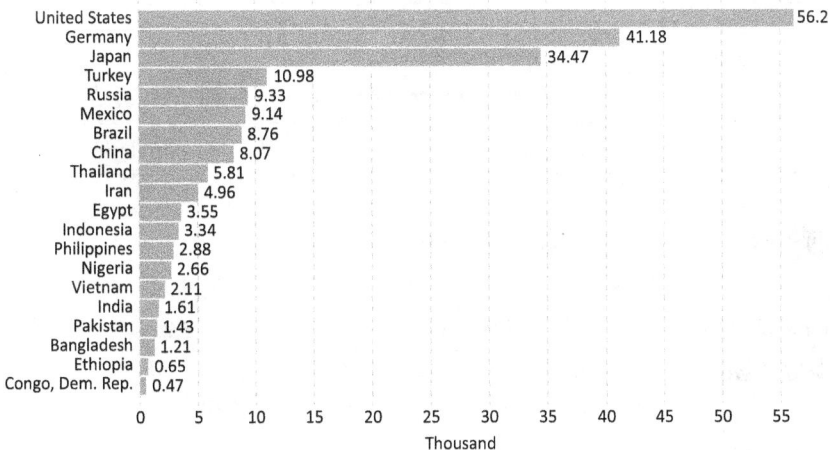

Figure 1.1 Twenty largest states (70 per cent of world population), GDP per capita, USD, 2015.

income, while the First World gets 59 per cent of income for just 13.5 per cent of population. Third World is defined as those countries whose per capita income (in 2015) was less than $15,700. First World countries earned above $25,000, so there is a large gap between them.

The income bracket corresponding to the 'Second World' or 'middle income', spans from $15,700 to $25,000 (Table 1.2). This is larger than any other income bracket, yet it has the smallest population. This can be seen if we compare the two brackets immediately below the Second World (i.e. 'Third World 1' and 'Third World 2') (Table 1.2). Combined, these have a smaller income bracket size than the Second World ($8,700 compared to $9,430), yet their population is nineteen times greater. Above the Second World sit the least rich imperialist societies; those contained in the income brackets 'First World 4'. This bracket has a smaller range of incomes than the Second World, but a population 38 per cent larger. 'First World 3' is also smaller but has a population over two and a half times larger than the Second World. The same is true for 'First World 2' and 'First World 1'. The First World vastly outnumbers the Second World by a ratio of more than 8:1. The Second World consists of a small number of mostly tiny societies.

The income categories, as defined here, are in accordance with the way countries are actually clustered. The figure taken as the upper limit of the Third World in 2015 ($15,700) is not arbitrary but represents the upper limit of a definite cluster of a relatively prosperous grouping, 'Third World 1'. Besides some micro-states, all these are in Latin America and Eastern Europe, the most important being Argentina (income $13,432), Venezuela ($12,625), Chile ($13,416), Panama ($13,268), Poland ($12,555) and

Table 1.2 World income brackets, current USD, 2015

Income group	Income bracket	Share of world population (%)
First World 1	$50,001+	5.1
First World 2	$42,001–$50,000	2.1
First World 3	$34,001–$42,000	4.2
First World 4	$25,001–$34,000	2.2
Second World	$15,701–$25,000	1.4
Third World 1	$11,351–$15,700	2.1
Third World 2	$7,001–$11,350	27.4
Third World 3	$3,001–$7,000	12.8
Third World 4	$1–$3000	42.8

Hungary ($12,617). The richest was Uruguay with an income of $15,574. As can also be seen in Figure 1.2, all these countries have a similar income and, according to World Bank statistics, have done so for a long time.

The figure of $15,700 takes in the upper limit of this definite grouping (Third World 1), which consists of two similar groupings, one in Latin America and another in Europe. Both are quite developed, yet clearly second rate in relation to the vastly more prosperous imperialist states. While the number of dollars defining this group must be adjusted each year, the countries in it remain largely unchanged over time. This relates to the characteristic they have in common: being more developed than most other Third World capitals, yet remaining non-monopolistic in relation to imperialism. The degree of coherence of this grouping can be seen when it is compared to the far more incoherent, eclectic and unstable Second World. It is fully justified to define Third World 1 as the top rung of a broader grouping called the Third World. This is further justified because it appears as the upper echelon of a larger subgroup of relatively developed Third World states (i.e. Third World 2 and Third World 1).

In Latin America the larger group of relatively developed Third World states (Third World 2) includes the populous states of Mexico (income $9,005) and Brazil ($8,539). Income in Chile and Argentina is not significantly higher. The nations in this group sometimes trade places. Yet on the whole they stick within a fairly tight income band. Third World 1, at

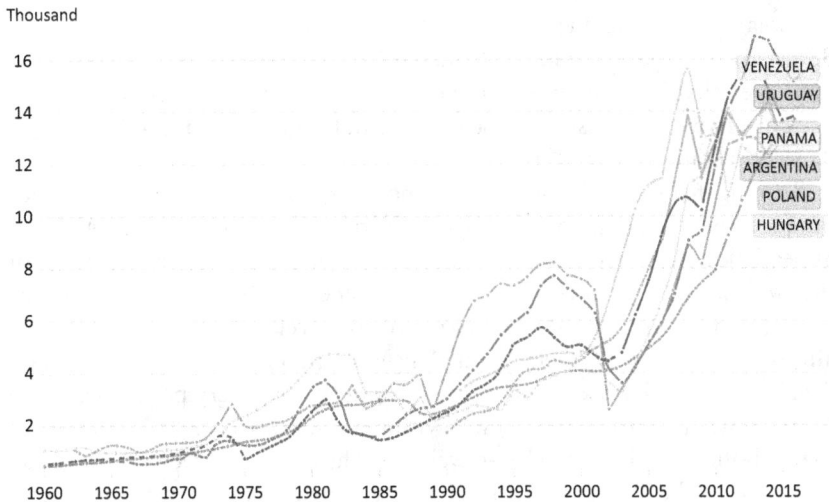

Figure 1.2 Top-income Third World states, GDP per capita, USD, 1960–2017. Includes: Uruguay, Argentina, Chile, Venezuela, Panama, Poland and Hungary.

Thousand

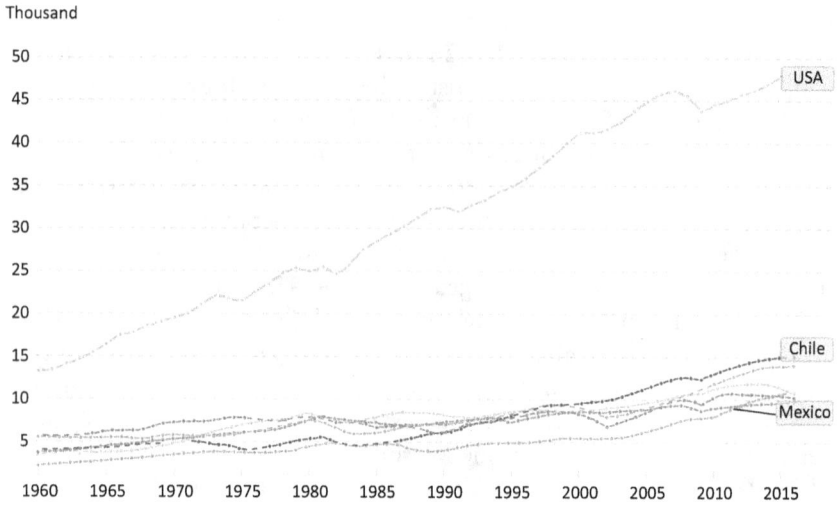

Figure 1.3 Latin America, Third World 1 and 2 versus United States, GDP per capita, constant 2010 USD, 1960–2017. Includes (top to bottom): United States, Chile, Uruguay, Panama, Brazil, Argentina and Mexico.

least since 1960, has not moved far from the much larger Third World 2 (Figure 1.3).

Looking at the 2016 income of all the largest North and South American states, the most pronounced gap is between the United States and Canada and the rest – between the First and Third Worlds. The only outliers in the polarised income division in the Americas are the Bahamas (population 388,000) and the US colony of Puerto Rico (population 3.7 million) – a tax haven that has been in economic crisis and losing population for over a decade.[5] However, these tiny societies do not register on a graph of major American states (Figure 1.4).

Turning to Third World income more broadly, Latin America is not unique. Rather, the major developed Third World states in Latin America appear alongside major developed Third World states in other parts of the world, most importantly China (income $8,000), Russia ($9,093[6]) and Turkey ($9,126). These large, relatively developed states have income almost identical with their Latin American peers Mexico ($9,005) and Brazil ($8,539). Thus a group of the most developed, very populous, Third World states ('Third World 2') fall within a remarkably tight income band that is both well above the less-developed Third World states such as India ($1,598) or the Philippines ($2,904) yet still far below even the lowest imperialist states (Figure 1.5).

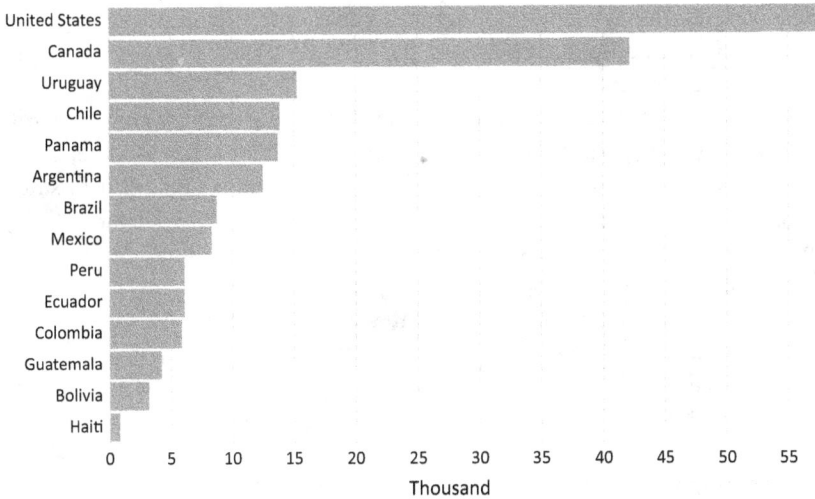

Figure 1.4 Largest states by population in the Americas, GDP per capita, USD, 2016 (figures for Venezuela are unavailable).

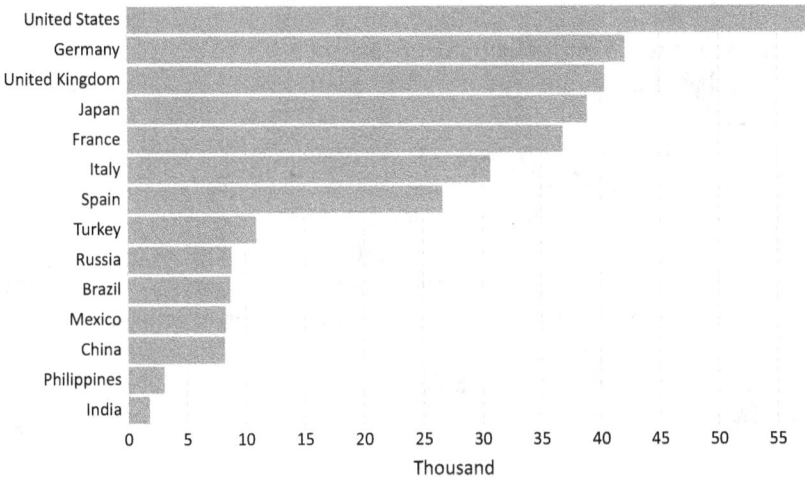

Figure 1.5 Selected large Third World and First World states, GDP per capita, USD, 2016.

Third World 2 groups some 28 per cent of the entire world population into the small income bracket of $7,001–$11,350. It should be expected that alongside this populous income bracket certain smaller states would appear as its outliers. Indeed, Third World 1 appears as a satellite of the much larger Third World 2. Uruguay, Chile and Argentina then can be understood as the upper echelon of the broader group of most developed Third World countries.

We can rank this grouping within the global economy by comparing its income to the imperialist states. Even the poorest imperialist state, Spain (income $25,832), earns nearly *double* the top-earning Third World states Argentina ($13,432) and Chile ($13,416) and *three times* Mexico, Brazil and China, Russia and Turkey. That is the size of the *smallest* gap between the two distinct worlds.

In Europe, there are eight small states between the richest major Third World state, Poland ($12,555), and the imperialist state with the lowest income, Spain ($25,832). These are Slovakia ($16,088), Estonia ($17,119), Czech Republic ($17,548), Greece ($18,002), Portugal ($19,222), Slovenia ($20,727), Malta ($22,596) and Cyprus ($23,243).

Most important European ex-socialist states, except the former German Democratic Republic (GDR), have Third World income levels. Russia ($9,093), Ukraine ($2,115), Poland ($12,555), Romania ($8,973) and Hungary ($12,617) are the largest. Besides the Ukraine, these have comparable income to the most developed Latin American states. The most populous state – Russia – has a per capita income almost identical with Brazil and Mexico, the most populous Latin American states. Similarly, the largest top-level Third World European states – Poland and Hungary – have incomes similar to Argentina and Chile.

Besides ex-socialist states, the other European part of the Second World is Portugal and Greece. Uniquely, Portuguese income appears to have tracked the imperialist world, but at a lower level, for more than fifty years. Greek income, on the other hand, has historically been around or above Spain and Italy. As such, it was a part of the imperialist pole until its recent crisis and might be expected to return in the future. If not, it will be the only non-oil producing state to fall from the First World group since 1960 at least.[7] While certainly presenting a variation within the bipolar world, these Second World European states account for only 0.6 per cent of world population – forty million people (Figure 1.6).

So far we have outlined the top-income Third World countries, which together account for 30 per cent of world population, as well as the Second World, which accounts for 1.6 per cent.

The imperialist pole is delimited at its bottom by its poorest member, Spain ($25,832). Spanish income paralleled the richer European states since 1960, albeit at a slightly lower level (Figure 1.7). Admittedly there was a divergence after the 2008–9 crisis between Spain (and Italy) and the stronger Northern European states. Yet divergence between stronger and weaker states should be expected during a crisis. Since around 2013, that

Thousand

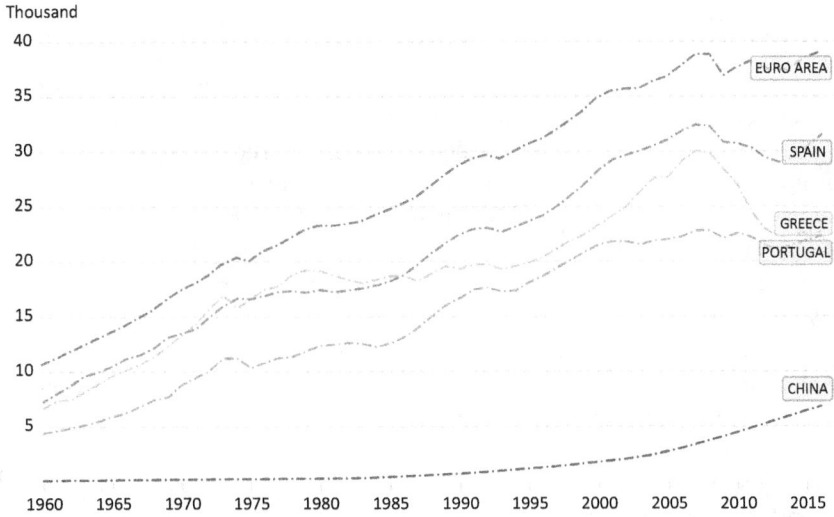

Figure 1.6 Portugal, Greece and Spain, GDP per capita, constant 2010 USD, 1960–2016.

Thousand

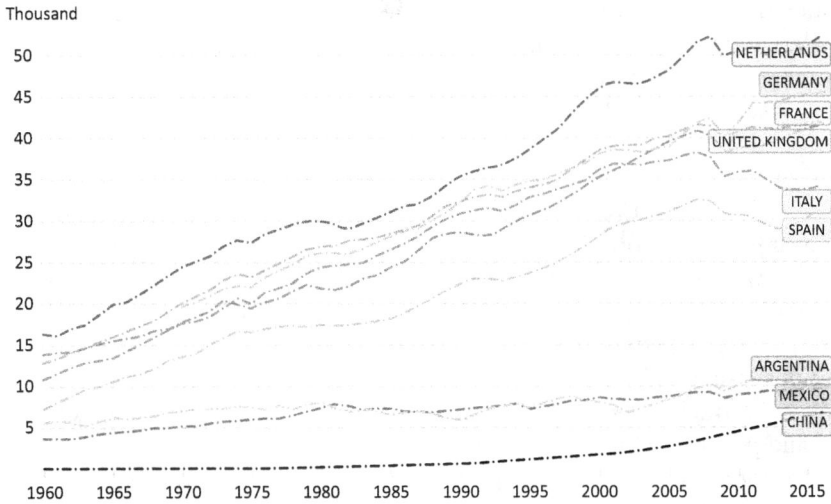

Figure 1.7 Selected states, GDP per capita, constant 2010 USD, 1960–2016.

began to reverse as Spanish multinational corporations (MNCs) such as Banco Santander, Repsol and Zara continue to benefit from their monopolistic global positions. The large and powerful Spanish state forms a solid floor of the imperialist world while, besides some smaller oil exporters, all the states above it are part of the imperialist club.[8]

Inequality

The data so far demonstrates the existence of the two principal economic groupings and outlines their delimitation as well as showing how barren is the space between them. However, to demonstrate the distance between the two groups, we had to focus on the highest Third World and lowest First World income countries. As such, the discussion has vastly understated the extent of inequality between the two camps as a whole. To more fully express this, we need to compare various Third World incomes to First World income as a whole (average $44,428). Compared with this income level, Argentina and Chile earn around 33 per cent, Poland 29 per cent, Russia, Mexico, Brazil and Turkey around 20 per cent and China 18 per cent. That is a comparison of *top* Third World income to the *average* imperialist income.

In the *richest region* of the Third World, 122 million Colombians, Peruvians, Ecuadorians, Cubans and Dominicans all average from one-seventh to one-ninth of First World income. Still in the richest region, a further 65 million residents of Guatemala, Bolivia, Haiti, Honduras, Paraguay, El Salvador and Nicaragua mostly earn around half that. If we look at Asia and Africa, *where most people live*, the comparisons are more extreme. Indonesia – not an absolutely low-income country – earns 8 per cent of the imperialist average. This compares favourably to India (4 per cent), Pakistan and Bangladesh (3 per cent) and Nigeria (6 per cent).

Those are the really big countries. The Philippines and Ethiopia, each home to 100 million people, earn 7 per cent and 1 per cent respectively. Vietnam and Egypt, each home to more than 90 million people, earn 5 per cent and 8 per cent respectively, while 79 million Iranians earn 12 per cent of average First World income.

The whole Third World averages just 10 per cent of average First World income and 17 per cent of Spain, the poorest First World country. Thus, while the gap between the richest Third World and poorest First World nations stands at 1 to 2, average Third World to average First World income is 1 to 10 and it is 1 to 6 with Spain. Of course inequality between the richest and poorest individuals is greater still.

To argue the world is not polarised, one must do as the World Bank does and define extremely poor countries as 'middle income'. The World Bank, absurdly, defined 'middle income' for 2015 as GDP per capita between $1,026 and $12,475 – covering most of the world's population. Accordingly, Cambodia, Zambia, India, Timor Leste and Bangladesh were all 'lower middle income' while Poland, Argentina, Chile and Equatorial Guinea, for example, were all considered 'high income'.[9]

Even without taking such an offensive stance, to make any reduction in the size of the population said to be living in poor countries, it would be necessary to define China and its peers as middle income. Yet this too would be an absurd procedure. Chinese 2015 income ($8,000) was just a fraction of states like the United States, Japan, Australia and Israel and less than one-third of Spain (Table 1.2). China's income peers, like Mexico, Brazil, Russia and Turkey – all of which fall into 'Third World 2' in Table 1.2 – are hardly better off.

An objection may be raised that the cases of South Korea, Taiwan, Hong Kong and Singapore contradict the stark global polarisation. However South Korea, Hong Kong and Singapore have all converged with the income of the imperialist states, and as such, form a part of the imperialist core, confirming not contradicting, world polarisation. While data is difficult to obtain for Taiwan, its 2011 income (around $21,000) was already close to Spain's 2015 level. It may soon follow South Korea ($27,222) and enter the high-income club if it has not already.

The exceptional nature of these countries is that they have moved from one pole to the other. As such, if our world income snapshot was taken not in 2015 but in, say, 2000, the picture would not be so neat. Then, Hong Kong, Taiwan and South Korea (but not Singapore) would still have been well below Spain. It is true these societies represent exceptions to the stability of the North and South poles, as they have moved from the Third to First World income level. However, to believe they represent an example that can be replicated by any large section of the Third World is incorrect. To focus on them and ignore the overarching reality of a starkly divided world misses the principal problem.

All four are not historical nations but pieces of larger nations broken off by imperialist annexation or anti-communist war. In the context of the Chinese revolution and the threat of more revolutions in Asia, these states were given preferential development assistance and opportunities.[10] Strong alliances between the United States and South Korea, Taiwan and Singapore remain today.

Taken together, these regions come to just over 1 per cent of world population. They are so small that their catch-up has been more than offset by population growth, meaning the Third World is a growing part of world population even without them. All four are located in East Asia, the world's most rapidly growing area. Rapid growth in China, the Philippines, Indonesia and elsewhere during the neoliberal period provided the basis for a more advanced type of development in these much smaller fragments of Asian capitalism. Their entry into the imperialist camp would not have been possible had they not been able to develop the type of parasitical relationship between themselves and China (and other Third World countries) that the rest of the imperialist states had already developed. To view these areas as a model for the development of the Third World more broadly misunderstands the type of development that has taken place. In short, they are now imperialist economies sitting within the top echelons of the global division of labour – though still below the leading imperialist societies like the United States, Germany and Japan.

Increasing polarisation

It is common to accept that imperialism divided rich from poor societies *historically* yet contend that division is now rapidly changing, especially during the neoliberal period. The perceived rise of China or increasing weight of the BRICS countries or Third World industrialisation more generally, are seen as undermining the historical domination of the imperialist powers.

As such, much of the discussion above, which proceeded from a snapshot of a recent year – 2015 – might be viewed as inconclusive. Indeed, it *would* be inconclusive if it could be shown that even the wide income polarisation of 2015 was being undermined by progressively rising income in parts of the Third World, particularly China. In other words, it might be argued that, while the world was still polarised in 2015, this could soon be overturned or is already being overturned.

If this were true, the income gap between the First and Third Worlds should be shrinking. However, the gap grew rapidly and consistently from 1980 through to 2015. As can be seen (Table 1.3), per capita income in the imperialist societies grew, on average, by $19,428 over this period measured in constant 2010 USD. In the thirty-six largest Third World societies, growth averaged just $2,561 or 13 per cent of the imperialist world. Chinese income grew faster than other Third World countries, but not as fast as the imperialist societies. At $6,150 it grew less than the imperialist camp's increase.

Rapid increase in polarisation can be seen graphically when we plot the income growth of the largest twenty societies in the world since 1960 (Figures 1.8 and 1.9).

Figure 1.9 represents the seventy-five largest societies in the world, or 93 per cent of world population. As can be seen, it still clearly conforms to the pattern of stark polarisation. There are very few societies that do not conform to one or another of the principal bands.

Saudi Arabia is represented by the line that looks like a mountain towering above all other societies in the 1970s, but then falls through the First World band in the 1980s before ending in the middle of the graph. Venezuela is the line that emerges from within the First World band in 1960 and stagnates or falls slightly, converging with the upper echelon of the Third World this century. The position of these two oil exporters in the middle of the

Table 1.3 Aggregate growth in GDP, constant 2010 USD, 1980–2015

	1980			2015			Income growth per capita
	Population (billion)	GDP (trillion)	GDP per capita	Population (billion)	GDP (trillion)	GDP per capita	
24 largest First World economies	0.74	$19.6	$26,494	0.98	$45	$45,922	$19,428
36 largest Third World economies by population	3.58	$6.2	$2,065	5.39	$24.9	$4,626	$2,561
China	0.98	$0.3	$348	1.38	$8.9	$6,498	$6,150
35 largest Third World excluding China	2.18	$6.2	$2,839	4.01	$16	$3,991	$1,152

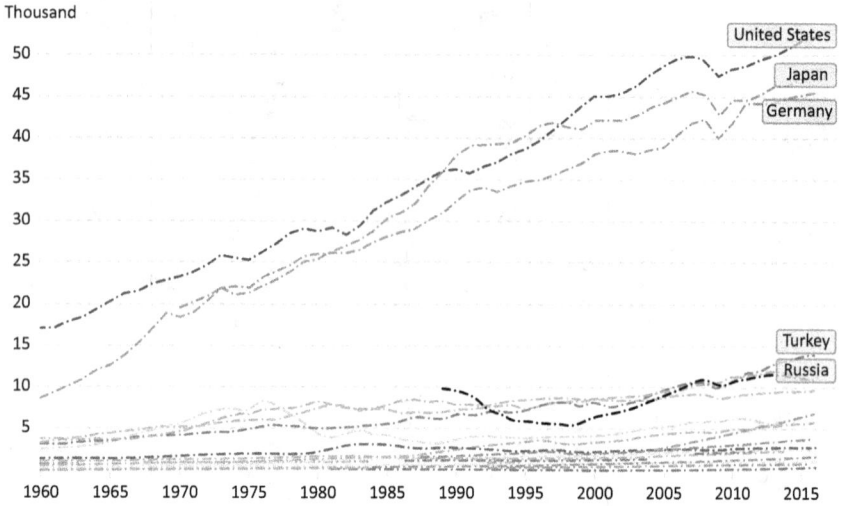

Figure 1.8 Twenty largest states, GDP per capita, constant 2010 USD, 1960–2016. From highest to lowest according to 2016 income: United States, Japan, Germany, Turkey, Russia, Brazil, Mexico, China, Iran (2015), Thailand, Indonesia, the Philippines, Egypt, Nigeria, India, Vietnam, Pakistan, Bangladesh, Ethiopia and the Democratic Republic of the Congo.

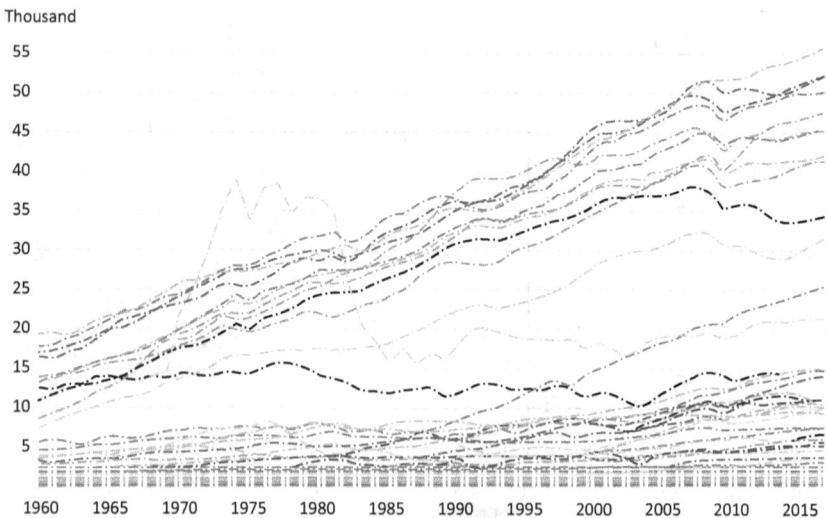

Figure 1.9 Seventy-five largest states, GDP per capita, constant 2010 USD, 1960–2016 (excluding Taiwan – no data available).

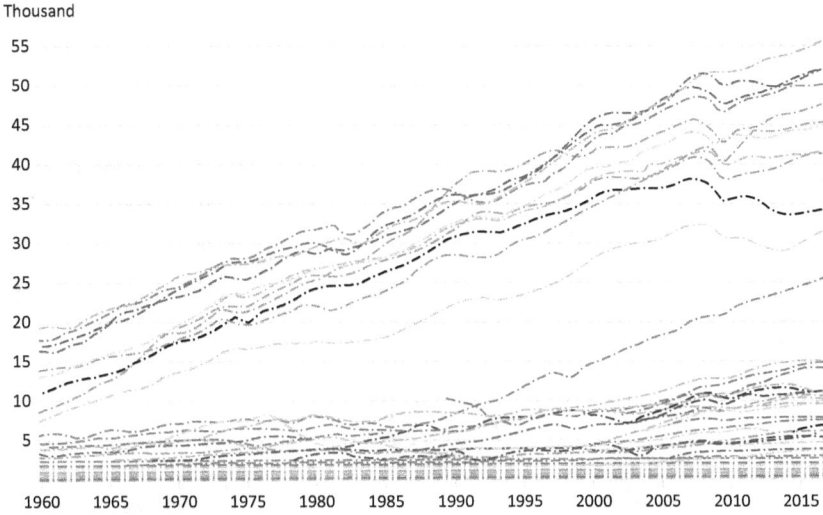

Figure 1.10 Seventy-five largest states, GDP per capita, constant 2010 USD, 1960–2016 (excluding Saudi Arabia, Venezuela and Taiwan).

chart expresses more about oil prices and production than their general level of development. If we exclude them from the chart, we get what is a more essential picture of the general, dominant world development trajectory over the period (Figure 1.10).

This remarkable chart – representing 92 per cent of world population – shows few deviations from the principal bands. The line that starts just above the Third World in the late 1980s and then dives into it represents Russia's return to capitalism. The line that parallels the rest of the imperialist band, albeit at a distance below it, is Spain. The single line to emerge from the Third World band represents South Korea.[11] If the World Bank included Taiwan in its charts, its line would also emerge from the Third World, parallel to South Korea, albeit a little bit later and lower.

An almost identical picture emerges in the current dollar version of the chart for the same data (Figure 1.11). In this case South Korea overtakes Spain. Each band has several nations that briefly soar above it before returning to the main group – expressing, in part, currency fluctuations. The lines briefly leaving the imperialist band are Japan (until 1995), the Netherlands (until 2008) and Australia (until 2013–14). Those leaving the Third World before returning are Argentina (1990–2001), Mexico (1993–94 and 1999–2003) and Poland (peaked in 2008). The line abruptly jutting out of the Third World before disappearing entirely represents the failed Iraqi occupation of Kuwait.

Thousand

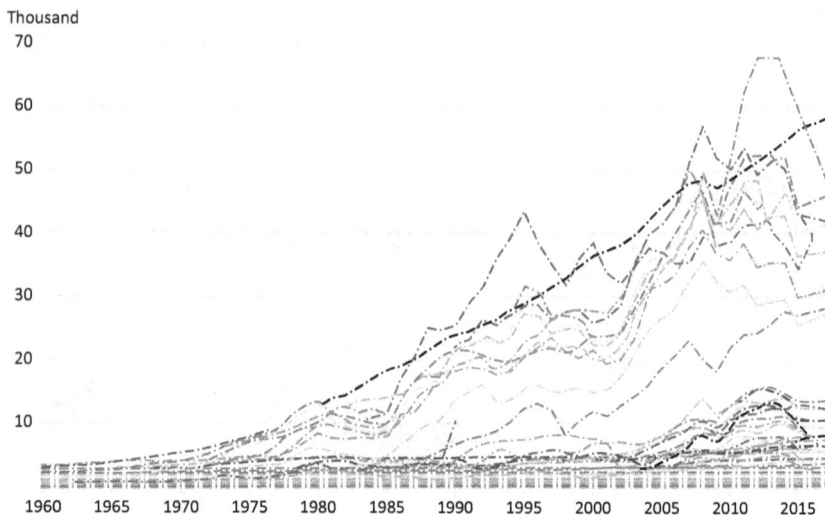

Figure 1.11 Seventy-five largest states, GDP per capita, USD, 1960–2016 (excluding Saudi Arabia, Venezuela and Taiwan).

These telling graphics provide much needed perspective on the idea that China and the Third World are rapidly catching up to the imperialist states. Notably, Chinese income nowhere emerges from the Third World band. Chinese per capita income grew $6,150 (2010 constant) during 1980–2015 compared with $19,428 for the imperialist core. In current dollars it grew $7,874, compared with $43,609 in the United States, $29,085 in Germany, $25,057 in Japan and $19,492 in Spain. Thus, China's gap with the First World *increased*; even its distance from the lowest-income imperialist state increased. It is the sort of 'catch-up' that leaves one further behind – not unlike having coffee with your manager.

Growth rate as percentage of prior income

It might be argued that even though the Third World as a whole, and also China taken alone, fell further behind in aggregate terms since 1960, and again since 1980, one or both might still be expected to catch up in the future. The main argument given for this position is the high rate of income growth in the Third World measured as a percentage of a country's own previous income. This particular measure is constantly emphasised in bourgeois financial reportage – typically abbreviated simply as GDP growth, though rarely per capita.

As shown in Table 1.4, the aggregate growth of income for the period 1980–2015 was seven and half times higher in the imperialist core than

Table 1.4 GDP growth rate, constant 2010 USD, 1980–2015

		First World economies (24 most populous)	Third World economies (36 most populous)
1980	Population (million)	740,947	3,158,163
	GDP	$19,630,327	$6,521,833
	GDP per capita	$26,494	$2,065
2015	Population (million)	979,406	5,385,103
	GDP	$44,976,674	$24,911,830
	GDP Per capita	$45,922	$4,626
	Per capita income growth	$19,428	$2,561
	Rate of per capita income growth	x 1.73	x 2.24

Source: World Bank (2017).

in the largest thirty-six Third World countries. If we convert the figures for income growth to a percentage of previous income, we find imperialist income grew at a rate of 173 per cent over the period, while that of the Third World grew faster at 224 per cent (Table 1.4).

On this basis we can say that *if* these rates of income growth continue, the Third World will catch up – *eventually* – but it will take a very long time. If the same percentage growth rates were to repeat over the next 35 years (2015–50), the aggregate gap between the Third and First World average income would again not shrink but grow (Table 1.5). Even the aggregate *rate of growth* of the gap would increase. Between 1980 and 2015, the gap increased by $17,000. It would increase to $69,000 by 2050, $115,000 by 2085, $188,000 by 2120, $288,000 by 2155, $457,000 by 2190, $650,000 by 2225 and $846,000 by the year 2260. This all assumes the same trajectory as occurred in the neoliberal period. Only after that does it begin to close. Even the gap between the Third World and (crisis-ridden) Spain would continue expanding for the next 200 years!

The absurdity of such 'projections' is obvious. However, it is telling to draw this common argument to its conclusion.

It might be objected that relying on data from the period 1980–2015 makes these conclusions out of date. However if we look at the most up-to-date data, there is no change in the trends. For example (in 2020 USD) China's per capita income rose from $8,067 in 2015 to $10,262 in 2019.

Table 1.5 'Projected growth' based on historical growth rates, constant 2010 USD

	First World (24)	Spain	Third World (36)
1980 GDP per capita	$26,494	$17,442	$2,065
2015 GDP per capita	$45,922	$30,587	$4,626
Growth rate in period	x 1.73	x 1.75	x 2.24
'Projected' growth			
Year 2050	$79,583	$53,650	$10,362
Year 2085	$137,917	$94,101	$23,211
Year 2120	$239,010	$165,054	$51,994
Year 2155	$414,205	$289,504	$116,466
Year 2190	$717,817	$507,791	$260,883
Year 2225	$1243,976	$890,665	$584,378
Year 2260	$2,155,811	$1,562,227	$1,309,006
Year 2295	$3,736,021	$2,740,145	$2,932,174
Year 2330	$6,474,524	$4,806,215	$6,568,070

Over the same period US income rose from $56,756 to $65,118 (four times faster). Spanish income – $25,732 to $29,614 – also rose far faster than China.

The discussion has so far focused on global incomes. Yet, a similar or more dramatic picture could easily be drawn about global wealth. A society with less wealth per capita can hardly be expected to catch up to wealthier societies if it secures a radically lower income. Credit Suisse reportage on global wealth per adult seems to conclude no catch-up is occurring.

According to Credit Suisse, 'Africa, India, Latin America, and most notably China, all increased their share of world wealth between 2000 and 2007, hinting at the possibility that global wealth inequality was on a long-term downward trend'.[12] However, this trend reversed with the economic crisis. Since 2007, China increased wealth faster than any other Third World state, but the United States dwarfs these gains. As shown (Table 1.6), US wealth gains post-crisis are both faster than China's as a percentage and close to ten times faster in aggregate gains per person. Thus, even if we add together the average gains for all 1 billion Chinese adults, this is less than half that of 246 million adults in the United States.

Table 1.6 China versus United States, wealth per adult, USD, 2000–16

Year	China	United States
2000	$5,672	$206,116
2007	$16,643	$287,096
2016	$22,864	$344,692

Source: Credit Suisse (2016).

China's income growth

The principal view, however, is not that the Third World as a whole is catching up, but that only parts of it are, or most commonly, that only China is. The Chinese economy experienced tempestuous growth in the neoliberal period. The phenomenal growth of capitalist production in China since the early 1980s, and particularly since China joined the World Trade Organisation in 2001, is enormously significant to any study of contemporary imperialism.

Chinese growth was so rapid that income in 2015 was almost nineteen times higher than in 1980. This compares to just 1.4 times higher for the thirty-five other largest Third World societies (excluding China) and 1.7 times for the imperialist states. Hence, if such a percentage rate of growth were sustainable, China would easily surpass the average income of the imperialist camp within the next thirty-five years.

The problem is, expanding the Chinese income by a factor of nineteen between 2015 and 2050 would require an *aggregate* dollar-income expansion 1,867 per cent *greater* than its growth in the neoliberal period. Put another way, aggregate 1980–2015 Chinese income growth was only 32 per cent as great as that of the imperialist states. To repeat its *percentage* growth rate in the next period, Chinese aggregate income expansion would need to be over three times greater than the imperialist states on a per capita basis. As China's population is greater than all imperialist states combined, it would need to raise income over four times more than the entire imperialist world. Obviously nothing approaching that can happen in the context of the imperialist world monopoly.

To sustain the same percentage growth rate, China would have to repeat its historical performance (i.e. grow to nineteen times its present size in thirty-five years!) To put that in perspective, China in 1980 had 23 per cent of world population and 1.22 per cent of its income. In 2015, it had 18.8 per cent of world population and 14.9 per cent of world income. It is clear

China cannot grow its income nineteen times without fundamentally changing the entire organisation of the world economy.

Perhaps we do not need to set the bar so high. If China is not projected to catch up with average rich-country income by 2050 but only with 'projected' Spanish income, its economy needs to expand *only* 826 per cent! (constant 2010 USD). Still, try to imagine what an eightfold expansion of the Chinese economy might look like.

According to *The Economist*, in 2017 China 'produces nearly as much coal and steel as the rest of the world combined, and even more aluminium and cement'.[13] Yet this enormous expansion of production has created such a degree of excess capacity that the government is constantly forced to curtail production. Recent plans involve cuts to capacity in coal, steel and aluminium by 25 per cent, 20 per cent and 30 per cent respectively by 2020 in big production centres.[14] As soon as we put down the calculator and think about real-world implications, the notion that Chinese production – as it currently exists – could conceivably be multiplied by *eight* is revealed as unreal.

Of course if the Chinese capitalists could position themselves at the top of the global division of labour – just as the First World capitalists do presently – then they would not need to expand production volumes so much because they would be able to produce different commodities and sell them at a higher price. This would give Chinese capitalists (and therefore potentially workers too) a higher income from the same labour hours employed. A popular belief seems to be that China will do this almost inevitably.

It is true that during the neoliberal period, China did raise its relative position within the global division of labour. Because Chinese capital made this transition rapidly, and it is a large state home to much of world labour, many commentators appear to have concluded that some sort of 'momentum' will continue for a considerable period of time. Hence, there appears to be a certain common-sense rationality to this view. What it ignores is the monopoly position held within the global division of labour by the most powerful First World capitalists, as will be shown.

China's still incomplete movement from low towards highest Third World income can be seen in Figures 1.12 and 1.13. While it still has not reached the income level of highest-income Third World states (Figure 1.12), the current dollar measure shows a convergence with the other largest top Third World states – Russia, Brazil and Mexico.

If the Chinese bourgeoisie is generally unable to move into higher-value labour processes, it is unlikely to raise income significantly faster than the world average. There is also the added dynamic (already commenced) of

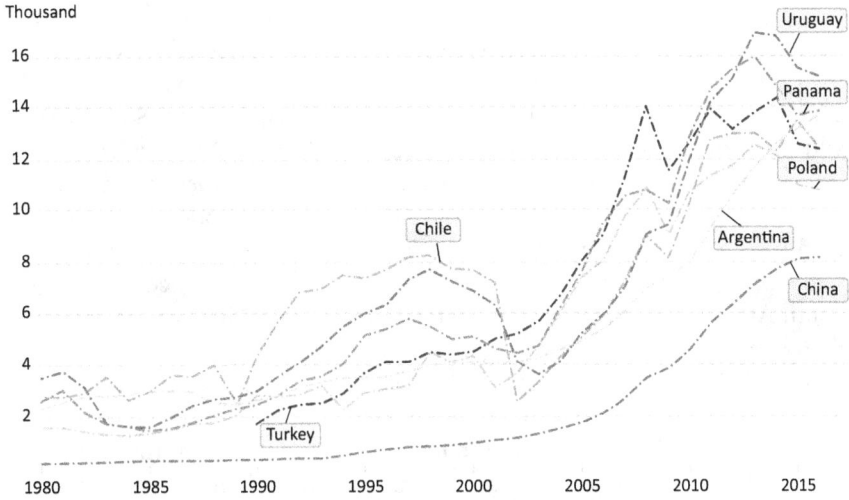

Figure 1.12 China versus highest-income Third World states, GDP per capita, USD, 1980–2016. Top to bottom according to position in 2016: Uruguay, Chile, Panama, Argentina, Poland, Turkey and China.

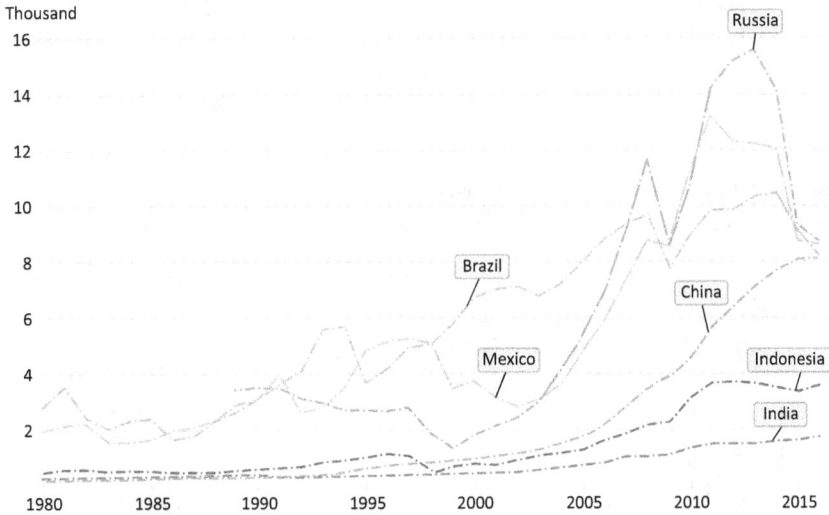

Figure 1.13 Selected large Third World states, GDP per capita, USD, 1980–2015. Top to bottom in order of 2016 position: Russia, Brazil, Mexico, China, Indonesia and India.

loss of low-value industries to cheaper labour societies. The combination of these tendencies may mean the more relevant historical precedent for the future of Chinese income is not China of 1980–2015, but Third World countries with the highest income in 1980 – Brazil, Mexico, South Africa and Argentina. All those societies, as well as Turkey and Malaysia, that now have comparable income, are crowded into a highly competitive space.

It was widely held in the 1960s that Brazil and other poor societies would eventually reach a stage of economic 'take-off'. Yet over the past thirty-five years, Brazil grew just 35 per cent on a per capita basis, Mexico 27 per cent, South Africa 15 per cent and Argentina 31 per cent. This growth is slower than either the Third World or imperialist average.

Table 1.7 divides the thirty-six largest Third World economies into six income brackets according to their income in 1980. It can be seen that the higher the starting income, the lower the growth rate in the neoliberal period. Notably, India, Vietnam, Thailand and Myanmar all achieved growth between 400 per cent and 650 per cent over the period – the highest growth of any major countries besides China and South Korea. Like China, they started from a 1980 GDP per capita of less than $500.[15] Thus, China's growth appears as an extreme example of the generally rapid growth among very low-income countries in Asia. When China is excluded from the figures, the overall pattern remains: higher income = lower growth rate.

In part, Table 1.7 simply expresses a mathematical tendency.[16] However, it also reflects something more real. As suggested, competition from imperialist capital bears down on higher-income Third World economies,

Table 1.7 Growth rates of thirty-six largest Third World states by population, grouped according to their 1980 GDP per capita. Figures given in constant 2010 USD, 1980–2015

1980 GDP per capita	Growth rate 1980–2015
Oil exporters, average 1980 GDP per capita $10,023 (5 economies)	x 1.074
$7,501–10,000 (3 economies)	x 1.387
$5,001–7,500 (3 economies)	x 1.957
$3,001–5,000 (7 economies incl. South Korea)	x 2.528
$1,001–3,000 (5 economies)	x 2.686
$1–1,000 (excluding China, 12 economies)	x 2.991
$1–1,000 (13 economies)	x 4.198

Source: World Bank (2017).

Note: Oil exporters are excluded from the general income brackets.

preventing them from raising income – the 'middle-income trap' appears to be alive and well. As is known, China's recent growth rates also seem to be conforming to this pattern. From 2015 to 2019 growth had already fallen to 6 per cent from previous rates of 10 per cent or more.

The counterposed phenomenon, also well known in heterodox economics, is so-called easy first stage or early industrialisation in which societies in transition to capitalist production relations can generate rapid economic development for a time.[17] This growth is 'easy' if capitalist production is in competition with petty commodity producers. Ruined peasants and artisans formed an expanding army of cheap labour in post-war Asia, Latin America and Africa, just as they had during capitalism's early career in Europe – while their former markets are colonised by a few rapidly expanding capitalist businesses. This is a general phenomenon for societies in transition to capitalist production relations. It is caused by the superiority of capitalist productive relations over petty commodity production.

Rapid expansion is possible because the capitalist class can capture and convert into capital pre-existing societal social resources. Existing bankrupt farms can be bought and made profitable with the investment of less new labour than creating farmland from scratch on virgin soil. The bankrupted farm already contains (congealed) human labour in the form of fences, buildings, clearings, etc. These useful things can be appropriated by the capitalist class and added to its own stock of productive capital. Similarly, a capitalist manufacturing enterprise may be able to rapidly capture a national market if its competition consists of traditional producers using less labour-efficient techniques. As these are impoverished by their competition with more advanced labour processes, they are forced to staff the factories of the emergent bourgeoisie, a process associated in modern times with the rapid urbanisation across the Third World. Marx called this process the primitive accumulation of capital.

Much that was previously not monetised becomes monetised or is revalued higher since it is contributing to capital accumulation. As such, it will show up (using current terms) in the GDP figures. What was already there is only now counted, or counts for more, contributing to a high growth *figure*. However, once the transition is over (i.e. once the petty producers have been dispossessed and their wealth appropriated), rapid 'easy' growth ends. Competition is no longer against petty producers but now between different capitalists – with a far less certain result. This general phenomenon significantly contributed to the rapid growth in the neoliberal period of not only China, but also Indonesia, Thailand, India and many other poor countries.

Additionally, in China, there were significant social-political advantages the emergent bourgeoisie could appropriate as a result of its unique history. The Chinese revolution not only expropriated the landlord class (thus removing a fetter on capitalist development) but also broke the political power of imperialism inside the country, replacing it with a relatively strong and centralised state apparatus able to implement national economic policy to a greater degree than comparable Third World states like India and Indonesia.[18]

While not identical to Marx's primitive accumulation of capital, similarities exist with the process of reintroduction of capitalism in China by the Chinese Communist Party (CCP). The ascendant capitalist class benefited from its ability to capture and convert into capital pre-existing social resources, especially the already educated and disciplined workforce, industrial establishments and means of communication.

It is significant that the only large area of the Third World with exceptionally rapid development – China – is also where imperialism was politically defeated and expelled from the country. It is also significant that the other, smaller areas of exceptionally rapid development – Taiwan, South Korea, Hong Kong and Singapore – were all states in close political alliance with imperialism and given special treatment during imperialism's Cold War struggle against communism. These developmental exceptions form a ring around China's eastern seaboard and were consciously developed with special assistance from the United States and Britain as bulwarks against communist expansion. These exceptions might also therefore be considered, in part, an indirect achievement of the Chinese revolution. This suggests the greatest success in capitalist development comes through overthrowing capitalism and expelling the imperialists (as in China), partially doing so (Korea) or existing in the immediate vicinity of such struggles and gaining special treatment (Taiwan) or being small port-city statelets, benefiting from a combination of all these factors (Hong Kong and Singapore).

While many very poor countries experienced rapid income growth from 1980 to 2015, the exceptional growth in China can be viewed as resulting, on the one hand, from the social achievements of the Chinese revolution and, on the other hand, from the ability of the emergent Chinese capitalist class, under the leadership of the CCP, both to convert these achievements into capital and at the same time to deliver to the world economy the greatest of all sources of value – Chinese labour. An exceptional achievement indeed, and one that has paid off handsomely for both Chinese capital and, most of all, for imperialism – though much less so for Chinese workers.

China's *past* exceptionalism (i.e. its capitalist achievement above and beyond other previously lowest-income countries) may be explainable by a combination of these factors. However, the principal argument made in this book is that the *character* of Chinese capital remains non-monopoly in a global context, and its future development, growth and relationship to imperialism will be governed by that fact.

It has been shown that the world is divided into two economic groups, and there is a vast gulf in income levels between the two. Income is polarised (as opposed to simply scattered or dispersed with no clear gulf in the middle). It will be shown this income polarisation parallels polarisation between monopoly and non-monopoly capital on the capitalist world market (Chapters 9–11). The two poles represent the winners and losers in international competition. The cut-throat nature of competition on the capitalist market explains why there is almost no centre. States where the bourgeoisie can establish some significant monopoly gravitate towards the top. States where this is not possible are repelled far below. The size of the gap reflects the antagonistic, exploitative and dominant relationship between monopoly and non-monopoly capital.

As UNCTAD observed in 2016, 'the absence of ... a general convergence trend ... has been a striking feature of economic history over the past century'.[19] A small posse of imperialist states – largely the same states as a hundred years ago – dominate the international economy and gain the lion's share of income from it.

Notes

1 J. Lees, 'Growing Wealth Inequality Reaching Breaking Point', *Socialist Appeal* (2017), 4 December. An exception is M. Yates, 'Measuring Global Inequality', *Monthly Review*, 68:6 (2016).

2 For example, P. Weiniger, 'Understanding Imperialism: A Reply to Sam King', *Marxist Left Review*, 9 (2015).

3 K. Marx, *Capital: A Critique of Political Economy*, vol. 1, *The Process of Production of Capital* [1867] (Moscow, Progress, [n.d.]), chap. 25. This and most other work referenced to Marx, Lenin and other classical Marxist writers is available through the Marxist Internet Archive at www.marxists.org.

4 V. I. Lenin, 'Report on National and Colonial Questions to the Second Comintern Conference July 26, 1920', in J. Riddell (ed.), *The Communist International in Lenin's Time: Workers of the World and Oppressed Peoples, Unite! Proceedings and Documents of the Second Congress, 1920* (New York, Pathfinder, 1991), vol. 1, p. 212.

5 Data is scarce. In 2013, Puerto Rico's GDP per capita was almost as high as Spain. Since then, this poorest region of US-controlled territory has been undergoing an economic crisis comparable to that of Greece in the European Union. M. Roberts, 'Puerto Rico: When It Rains, It Pours', *Michael Roberts Blog* (2017) 17 October, https://thenextrecession.wordpress.com/2017/10/17/puerto-rico-when-it-rains-it-pours/.

6 Russian income clearly falls within the Third World. This is not intended as an intervention into debates around whether the Russian state, with its unique history and characteristics, is imperialist or not.

7 Unless Chile and Argentina are considered to have been part of the core group prior to 1973–74, when their incomes briefly peaked.

8 The richest oil producers – United Arab Emirates ($40,439), Kuwait ($29,301), Qatar ($73,653) and Brunei ($30,555) – have a combined population of less than sixteen million.

9 World Bank Data Team, 'New Country Classifications by Income Level', *Data Blog* (2016), 7 January, blogs.worldbank.org/opendata/new-country-classifications-2016.

10 M. C. Howard and J. E. King, 'Whatever Happened to Imperialism?' in R. M. Chilcote (ed.), *The Political Economy of Imperialism: Critical Appraisals* (New York, Kluwer, 1999), p. 34.

11 South Korean 2016 income was still below Spain if measured in constant 2010 USD.

12 Credit Suisse, *Global Wealth Report 2016* (Zurich, Credit Suisse, 2016), p. 136. From 1994 to 2006, the US share of Morgan Stanley MSCI All Country World (ex. US market) index rose from 10 per cent to 24 per cent. See H. Schwartz, *Subprime Nation: American Power, Global Capital, and the Housing Bubble* (New York, Cornell University Press, 2009), pp. 203, 221.

13 *The Economist*, 'Great Leap Backward: Capacity Cuts in China Fuel a Commodity Rally and a Debate' (2017), 7 September.

14 *The Economist*, 'Great Leap Backward'.

15 See S. T. King, *Lenin's Theory of Imperialism Today: The Global Divide Between Monopoly and Non-Monopoly Capital* (PhD thesis) (Melbourne, Victoria University, 2018).

16 Growth as a percentage of previous income will tend to be higher when starting from a lower base because any growth is compared to a lower denominator.

17 M. Ariff and H. Hill, *Export-Oriented Industrialisation: The ASEAN Experience* (Sydney, Allen and Unwin, 1985), p. 3.

18 J. Petras, 'Rising and Declining Economic Powers: The Sino–US Conflict Deepens', *Journal of Contemporary Asia*, 41:1 (2011), 120.

19 UNCTAD, *Trade and Development Report 2016* (New York and Geneva, 2016), p. 40.

Part II

Contemporary Marxist analysis

Chapter 2 – which outlines the historical decline of Marxist writing on imperialism – is essential to understanding the central arguments put forward in this book. Chapters 3 and 4 add to this understanding but are less essential. They prove that most contemporary Marxist writing on imperialism rejects Lenin's theory (or is not familiar with it); minimises or does not focus on economic imperialism and Third World exploitation; or can't adequately explain how, exactly, imperialism works. For readers unfamiliar with other contemporary works or less interested in examining the key writers criticised – which include Harvey, Callinicos, Bellamy Foster (as well as Amin, Baran and Sweezy) and Smith – it would be possible to skip directly from the end of Chapter 2 to the start of Chapter 5. Alternatively the reader could choose to read only the sections of Chapters 3 and 4 most relevant to them, or return to them after completing the book.

2

Decline of Marxist analysis of imperialism

Amsden's 1990 comment that, 'In modern times, just to use the word [imperialism] is to label what is said as Marxist'[1] may have been a little late. There had been little new Marxist work on imperialism since Mandel's and Amin's work in the 1970s.

The spread of the Marxist theory of imperialism and its later decline parallel the rise and decline of anti-imperialist mass struggle (and the class struggle more broadly). Anti-imperialist mass struggle in the twentieth century occurred principally in two waves triggered by the first and second inter-imperialist world wars. Lenin's *Imperialism* is a product of the first of these waves. During the second wave large national liberation movements in China, India, Indonesia and elsewhere gained political independence for their countries. The newly formed governments then came to focus on the question of 'development'. As Lane argues, the class struggle in these countries turned to the question of what type of development, or what type of society, the newly independent nations should become.[2]

Owen pointed out,

> Just as the first wave of interest [in imperialism theory] took place during the early decades of this century when the world was finally being divided up among the empires of the European powers, so too the second wave, beginning in the 1950s, was in large measure a reflection of the new situation produced by the dismantling of these same imperial structures.[3]

Freeman later observed,

> The desperate plight of the peoples of North Africa, of Central and Southern America, of South East Asia, led to assault after assault on the established 'peaceful' order both colonial and post-colonial which provided the backdrop to the formation of the Marxist generation of the 1960s. Our generation was formed as much by the Battle of Algiers and the Tet Offensive as by the 1968 student revolts.[4]

The 1966 Tri-Continental Conference, representing left-wing social movements and independent Third World governments, declared from Havana:

> The nations of Asia, Africa and Latin America which have won their political independence are realizing that formal sovereignty is not enough to ensure

full liberation … to obtain this it is vital to eliminate all the causes of imperialist oppression and exploitation and to carry out profound changes in the social and economic structure … economic liberation must be added to political liberation.[5]

Economically, the post-war capitalist world was marked by rapid capitalist expansion in the imperialist countries, alongside relative stagnation in the new Third World states, or economic growth that was too slow to rapidly resolve crushing social problems. Nor did it enable catch-up with the imperialist world. Mandel thought this was because 'endemic movements of rebellion and liberation among the peoples of the so-called Third World … together with the rise of new branches of industry in the metropolitan countries' reduced the rate of capital export to the poor countries in this period.[6] This crisis of capitalist expansion further fuelled the social rebellion in what Mandel characterised as a 'permanent pre-revolutionary crisis in the dependent countries'.[7]

The development problems and class conflict between the weak or embryonic capitalist classes, different classes of working people and imperialist bourgeoisie found a general expression in the contradictions of what Prashad describes as the 'Third World project'.[8] This was manifested in the conferences, declarations and policies of such gatherings as the Bandung Conference (1955), the Non-Aligned Movement (founded 1961) and the Tri-Continental Conference in Havana (1966). The Tri-Continental Conference represented both socialist and non-socialist forces. As the Moroccan president of the Conference Preparatory Council, Medhi Ben Barka put it, the conference represented 'two currents of the world revolution': the 'current born with the October Revolution and the national liberation revolutions currents'.[9]

The threat to imperialist domination represented by these formations and the mass movements behind them influenced the perspectives of John F. Kennedy's Alliance for Progress in Latin America, which aimed to co-opt them. In what appears a radical stance by today's standards, Kennedy aimed to concede certain basic reforms in order to develop a broader basis of support for capitalist development. In Kennedy's view, 'Those who possess wealth and power in poor nations [must] accept their own responsibilities. They must lead the fight for those basic reforms *which alone can preserve the fabric of their societies.*'[10] The Alliance for Progress did not last into the 1970s. However, the later formation within the United Nations of the Brandt Commission, the South Commission, UNCTAD and the diplomatic-political campaign for a New International Economic Order (NIEO) may be viewed as later reformist attempts to address the causes of the ongoing anti-imperialist mass movements.

In this environment of radical ideological ferment, English-language Marxism adopted, in general, a far more anti-imperialist stance and focus than has been the case since. Under the pressure of anti-imperialist mass movements, key aspects of imperialism theory, such as monopoly, value transfer and industrialisation, appear to have enjoyed a far richer discussion in the 1970s than today. The radicalisation and upsurge were the source of the major modern works on imperialism such as Mandel's *Late Capitalism* (1972) and Amin's *Unequal Development* (1976).[11]

Writers like Hymer, or heterodox writers such as Emmanuel, appear far more familiar with or influenced by Lenin and those parts of Marx relating to imperialism than some avowedly Marxist contemporary writers.[12] The heterodox anti-imperialist 'dependency' school, which began as an intellectual current in Latin America, also had an important positive impact on Marxist writing inside the United States and the imperialist states more generally – particularly with the Marxian current around *Monthly Review*, which has retained anti-imperialist politics to this day.

In retrospect, the Declaration of Havana in 1966 may have been the crest of this anti-imperialist wave. Later, Nixon's 1972 normalisation of relations with China, the winding down of the Vietnam War (and aerial destruction of much of Indochina), the consolidation of reactionary pro-imperialist military dictatorships in Indonesia, Chile, Brazil, Argentina and the Congo, the rise of Sadat in Egypt, Israel's second defeat of Arab armies in the October War of 1973 and the subjugation of the Palestinians all contributed to demobilisation and defeat of the post-Second World War wave of mass struggle – though this was never uniform. These defeats – together with the decline and fall of the Soviet Union – were crucial in opening the way in the Third World for capitalist development policies later dubbed 'neoliberalism' and 'globalisation'.

The sharp rise in US interest rates in 1980–81 – the 'Volker Shock' – made much Third World debt unpayable and accelerated the final collapse of the remaining examples of import substitution industrialisation (ISI) capitalist development, most dramatically in Mexico. Besides US interest rates as a trigger for neoliberal policies, Prashad also emphasises 'enthusiastic commitment' to the ideology of neoliberalism from 'emergent elites in the "global cities" of Africa, Asia, and Latin America'.[13]

The economic and political success of the neoliberal period (in capitalist terms) in contrast to post-war 'permanent pre-revolutionary crisis' in the Third World, can be summarised as its greater capacity to integrate Third World labour into production for the world market. This provided the impetus (and *value*) for a new period of world capitalist expansion and gave Third World labour (and therefore also Third World capitalists) a more prominent and central role than it had hitherto enjoyed. In this sense, the neoliberal expansion occurred in a more balanced way than the post-war boom. Both First and Third World capitalist economies experienced a prolonged period of relatively stable growth for around twenty-five years from the early 1980s until 2008–9. Neoliberalism – in this way closer to classical imperialism than the post-war boom – may be characterised as having successfully developed the degree to which the Third World was exploited, as opposed to oppressed, by imperialism.

Intensified exploitation of the rapidly growing Third World labour force began to provide a far more solid social basis for an economic and political alliance of First and Third World capitalist classes. By bringing an enlarged Third World bourgeoisie to the table of profitability (albeit as junior partners), and expanding the Third World middle class, neoliberal globalisation resolved, for a time, the question of the national liberation and capitalist development of major Third World nations – at least from the perspective of their capitalist rulers. The 'permanent pre-revolutionary crisis' was over (in most countries), and the wave of national liberation struggles that characterised the post-war period was not matched by a new wave of equal strength in the neoliberal period.

Added to this, the stagnation and collapse of the Soviet economy in the 1970s and 1980s were major factors that not only shifted politics to the right, but also removed a supportive factor making some sort of resistance to imperialism more feasible for many poor countries. The decline of Marxist anti-imperialism *theory* was a function of this objective retreat of class forces. The principal overall effect of these changes for anti-imperialist theory and writing in the First World countries was straightforward – there was far less of it. The second impact, which amounts to the same thing, was that the few anti-imperialist works written often accommodated essentially pro-imperialist positions – particularly in economics.

In the realm of intellectual struggle, the path from the previous status quo, where imperialism was central to much Marxist thinking in the 1960s and 1970s, to the new situation, where it is all but absent, had to overcome the influence of Lenin's Marxist theory of imperialism and the political orientation adopted by Lenin and the early Comintern, which emphasised the crucial importance of the distinction between oppressor and oppressed nations. The most influential self-identified Marxist in both of these struggles was the First World, *pro-imperialist* writer Bill Warren.

Warren and his contemporary influence

Warren is relevant because of his widespread contemporary influence and openly pro-imperialist positions. Incredibly, Warren appears to have written the most recent, well-known critique of Lenin's *Imperialism*.[14] His work – published at the dawn of the neoliberal period – ushered in a new era of First World Marxist consensus against Lenin. Warren's principal argument was that imperialism is progressive and should be embraced. The main progressive aspect, according to Warren, is economic. Yet he relies on economic arguments – and these are adopted by his contemporary sympathisers – which can hardly be distinguished from mainstream capitalist economics. According to Warren, 'Marx's notes on the effects of British rule in India ... leave no room for doubt that [Marx and Engels] held that the overall effect of imperialism ... would be to accelerate the creation of a world market and thereby not only to unite humanity but also to bring the backward societies the material and cultural benefits of Western civilisation.'[15] Warren spends a considerable part of his book arguing that 'the colonial record, considering the immense numbers of people involved, was remarkably free of widespread brutality'.[16] Against Marx, but following Marx's opponent Malthus, Warren thought 'mass unemployment, chronic underemployment, shanty towns, gross overcrowding, pressure on the land and so on' in the Third World are not a result of capitalism but 'stem from population growth'.[17] Lenin, we are told, had 'underestimate[d] the genuineness of Western bourgeois democracy'[18] because 'capitalism and democracy are ... linked virtually as Siamese twins'.[19] Rather surprisingly for a 'Marxist', we are told, 'in the last analysis the material welfare of the population [not profits as Marx argued] is the aim of [capitalist] economic growth'.[20] Logically therefore, according to Warren, we should seek 'a more efficient and humane capitalist development instead of the inappropriate imposition of a welfare approach and a Soviet-style model on countries lacking both the requisite advanced economic basis for the welfare state and the communist leadership required for the soviet model'.[21] Warren rejected Lenin's thesis that a qualitative change occurred in capitalism around the turn of the last century, creating a new stage of development – imperialism. He views capitalism as continuing to spread advanced productive forces and relations, much as it did in its youth. For this reason, Warren argues, imperialism is a historically progressive form of capitalism.

Warren's pro-capitalist critique of imperialism remains broadly influential particularly among First World Marxist academics. Howard and King's highly regarded *History of Marxian Economics* viewed Warren's thesis as 're-asserting the coherence of the original Marxian position', 'a return to Marx' and 'basically sound'.[22] Following Warren, they thought, 'as genuinely capitalist extensions to new territories is taking place, a duplication of European achievement will occur, including sustainable economic growth'[23] and that 'it is now increasingly apparent that the principal barrier to global development is not the incorporation of the periphery into the world economy, but whether advanced capitalist countries will continue to ... allow this incorporation to continue'.[24] Harvey, confusingly, equates Warren with Marx when writing that Marx

> took the view that there was something progressive about capitalist development and that this was true even for British imperialism in India (a position that did not command much respect in the anti-imperialist movements of the post-Second World War period, as the icy reception of Bill Warren's work on imperialism as the pioneer of capitalism showed).[25]

Callinicos criticises Warren's reactionary political positions while giving detailed, sympathetic consideration to his economic view of imperialism. He too presents Warren as responsible for some sort of return to Marx and quotes Warren in refutation of what he calls 'the larger Lenin-Bukharin synthesis'. He accepts Warren's caricature of Lenin's monopoly as eliminating competition (see Chapter 7) and follows Warren in viewing capitalist development in the Third World as refuting dependency theory. 'A related problem with the larger Lenin–Bukharin synthesis is its association of imperialism with "monopoly capitalism", since, strictly speaking, monopoly implies the absence of competition, but competition is an essential mechanism in both disproportionality theories of crisis and Marx's own theory of the tendency of the rate of profit to fall.'[26] These follow Amsden's suggestion that 'the intellectual antecedents of Warren's view are traceable directly to Marx, so to suggest that Warren missed the point about economic development is also to suggest that Marx himself missed the point'.[27] Yet Warren argued imperialism was progressive in the 1970s, not the 1870s. As famously expressed in Marx's preface to *A Contribution to a Critique of Political Economy*, it is a fundamental tenet of Marxism that every social system plays a historically progressive role in its earlier stages before, at a certain point, it turns into a 'fetter' that stunts further development until it is overthrown by a new system:

> At a certain stage of development, the material productive forces of society come into conflict with the existing relations of production or – this merely expresses the same thing in legal terms – with the property relations within the framework of which they have operated hitherto. From forms of development of the productive forces these relations turn into their fetters. Then begins an era of social revolution.[28]

For Warren's view that modern capitalist imperialism remained historically progressive in 1980, to be Marxist he needed to show 'material productive forces of society' had not *yet* 'come into conflict with the existing relations of production', that is, capitalist property relations had not come to constitute a 'fetter' on social development. A fetter is a factor that slows down or inhibits progress. That is to say, he should show that material productive forces could not be *more* rapidly developed under more advanced social relations (i.e. under socialism). However, completely against Marx's concept of social relations as 'fetters', the entire framework of Warren's book is premised on the assertion that *any* human social progress under capitalism shows the social system continues to possess a progressive historical character.

Warren makes no attempt to show that this framework is based in Marx's theory. Much Third World human social progress in the twentieth century could be argued to have taken place in opposition to imperialist fetters. In short Warren assumes but does not prove social progress occurs, to the extent it has, principally as a result of, not in spite of, imperialism. Warren dismissed those who perceived the possibility of *more* rapid social progress as 'normative-utopian' and 'ahistorical' – effectively arguing for the legitimacy and continuation of bourgeois rule and the impossibility or undesirability of social revolution.[29]

For Warren's arguments to have scientific validity, he would have had to demonstrate that social-productive development in backward societies was not, as Baran argued, already beginning to accelerate in parallel with accelerating social progress in Europe. That is, he would have had to show that human development was not generally accelerating alongside the generalised increasing intensity of human interaction that was occurring (albeit unevenly) around the era of early capitalism.[30] It would be necessary to show such a trend would and could not have accelerated more than actually occurred, had these regions not succumbed to foreign imperialist control. Many Marxists have argued that independence from foreign imperialism was critical to the development of Japan, Russia and even Germany.[31] Finally, Warren would have needed to show that the contemporary situation had not subsequently matured to the point where a more advanced social system (i.e. socialism, or steps towards it by workers and farmers' states) could be adopted and bring about a more rapid development of the social productive forces than is (or was in 1980) occurring under imperialist domination.

Unless some or all of these conditions are shown to be true, then Warren's 'evidence' in comparing one epoch to another does not prove what he claims. Warren does not attempt to show any of these things and hence a major part of his book is devoted to 'proving' what is, for Marxists, an obvious truism: capitalism – which represents a higher form of social development than *pre*-capitalist social systems – can and does achieve higher levels of human social and cultural development than was possible in pre-capitalist societies. Fifty years earlier Lenin had already stated, 'On the whole, [imperialist] capitalism is growing far more rapidly than before'.[32] Though unlike his Menshevik political opponents (and Warren), Lenin did not conclude that revolutionaries should therefore allow imperialism to continue its work.

Warren selectively quotes Marx on British India. Yet by 1881, Marx's perspective on the role of the British in India was strongly negative, arguing they 'pushed the indigenous people not forward but backward'.[33] Writing in *Capital*, well after the short articles that Warren quotes, Marx says,

> By ruining handicraft production in other countries, machinery forcibly converts them into fields for the supply of its raw material. In this way East India was compelled to produce cotton, wool, hemp, jute, and indigo for Great Britain ... A new and international division of labour, a division suited to the requirements of the chief centres of modern industry springs up, and converts one part of the globe into a chiefly agricultural field of production, for supplying the other part which remains a chiefly industrial field.[34]

Marx actively and enthusiastically supported Indian, Chinese and Irish struggles against Britain. According to Lewis, 'A renewal of the Irish national struggle in the 1860s led Marx and Engels to modify their views. In fact they began to approach the national question less from the angle of the struggle between capitalism and feudalism and more from the angle of the struggle between the imperialist powers and the colonized nations.'[35] Marx concluded, 'Every time Ireland was about to develop industrially, she was crushed and reconverted into a purely agricultural land'.[36] Marx and Engel's mature view of English colonialism and imperialism as a reactionary force was the reason the pair strongly supported national liberation struggles from Ireland and China to the Sepoy uprising of 1857 that began in Meerut, India.

As Renton has argued, 'Almost alone among his contemporaries in Britain, Marx sided with the victims of Empire against its instigators. At each stage he blamed the British for violence which accompanied resistance to their rule.'[37] In relation to Ireland, the oppressed country he was most familiar with and for which his views were the most developed, Marx raised a three-point programme against British domination: '(1) self-determination and independence, (2) an agrarian revolution by the Irish themselves, and (3) protective tariffs against England'.[38] These views are completely inexplicable within Warren's framework.

In his critique of Lenin's work Warren counterposed Lenin's early book *The Development of Capitalism in Russia* to his later *Imperialism*.[39] *Imperialism* held that the onset of capitalism's imperialist period modifies the development of backward nations and the capitalist world system. For Warren, no such real-world change occurred. As such, *The Development of Capitalism in Russia* is held up as an example of the canon of healthy original Marxism, subsequently overturned by Lenin's erroneous *Imperialism*.

Yet Warren does not attempt to argue why *The Development of Capitalism in Russia* negates *Imperialism*. He merely takes quotations from the former emphasising capitalism's development of the productive forces, assumes these statements to be timeless and, therefore, to prove that Lenin later abandoned his earlier Marxist position. On this basis Warren's own assertion that capitalism was progressive in the 1970s is supposedly substantiated by Lenin's work from the 1890s.[40]

Warren suggests Lenin's *Imperialism* argued that 'the vigorous competitive incentive to innovate had vanished … the monopolists would eventually find all profitable spheres of domestic investment exhausted'[41] and that the 'general thrust of [Lenin's] argument [was] that monopoly capitalism was … stagnant compared to competitive capitalism.[42] In 'the Leninist assessment', imperialism was 'unable to modernize backward societies'.[43] Yet none of these assertions can be found in Lenin's work. Lenin explicitly contradicts them, writing, for example, that 'main railways have either been or are being built in those countries, elementary conditions for industrial development have been created, etc.'[44]

GDP growth equals development: Warren's apparent innovation

Warren's work, in effect, argues that all types of capitalist growth are the same or will become so in time: 'Successful capitalist development is here understood as that development which provides the appropriate economic, social and political conditions for the continuing reproduction of capital, as a social system representing the highest form of commodity production.'[45] That is, 'successful capitalist development' is that which reproduces capitalism. This position is held in common with contemporary writers who view GDP growth in Third World capitalism as indistinguishable from economic development in imperialist states.[46]

For Warren, the new productive forces in the Third World were 'becoming remarkably like that of the developed economies'.[47] Predating contemporary rising China arguments, Warren stated,

> International economic change has been so rapid and sweeping … The present situation could more appropriately be conceptualized as a spectrum of varying levels, rates, and structures of national development, one in which the positions of individual countries are constantly shifting. [This was] rapidly dissolving conceptual division of the world into developed and underdeveloped countries.[48]

On this basis, Warren held wildly inaccurate development expectations. He argued that 'the prospects for successful capitalist economic development (implying industrialization) of a significant number of major underdeveloped countries are quite good'.[49] Brazil, Zaire, Colombia, South Korea,

Taiwan and Peru were all named in this context. Four decades later, the Democratic Republic of the Congo (formerly Zaire), Peru, Brazil and Colombia can hardly be said to have escaped underdevelopment and cannot be fairly equated with the special cases of South Korea and Taiwan. Nor can most of the other nations in the world.

Yet equating growth of capitalist commodity production with social progress is not a theoretical innovation. That capitalism *equals* progress is a bourgeois outlook by definition. Warren's innovation was only to provide a 'Marxist' justification for such a position. This was the reason Frank dismissed Warren as 'part and parcel of a reactionary counter-offensive, not only from the right, but unfortunately also on the part of much of the left'.[50] Warren's 'Marxism' appears as a version of modernisation theory, not even necessarily a social democratic version, hardly distinguishable, at least in broad outline, from the stages of growth espoused by Rostow.[51] It is significant therefore if Warren's economic outlook now permeates Marxist thinking.

Something similar to what Rostow once called economic 'take-off' is now a widely held expectation among contemporary Marxists, especially regarding China (see Chapter 4). Harman, for example, approvingly quoted Warren's view that the countries in the Third World 'could catch up with the West without breaking with capitalism'.[52] One First World blogger even suggests that, 'from a Marxist perspective', we 'cannot rule out a future Indian imperialism, or even a future imperialism centred in sub-Saharan Africa'![53]

As Kiely points out, such 'views concerning the equalization of accumulation sound suspiciously like neo-liberal interpretations of the global economy, in which convergence takes place through liberalization policies'.[54] Rapid GDP growth in the world's largest country – China – is seen from this perspective as irrefutable evidence that world power *must* be shifting. That GDP growth rates are seen to equal development means there is a never-ending stream of 'evidence' to confirm the convergence thesis.

Agreement with Warren stems not from the bold flamboyance or theoretical seriousness of his argument but from the near universal failure of contemporary writers themselves to decisively break from the view that capitalist commodity production leads to the development of advanced capitalism.

Contemporary Marxism's rejection of Lenin

Parallel to the decline of anti-imperialist mass struggle, in academic writing Lenin had already become marginal by the early 1980s. Marshal describes how, by the early 1980s, a 'new consensus' had developed, according to which Lenin's work was seen as previously having been treated with a 'reverence it does not deserve'.[55]

Quite a number of Lenin's Marxist detractors have published their views, and based on what they have said, if Lenin's *Imperialism* were a film, you would not go to see it. His work was found to be 'disturbing',[56] 'defective'[57] and 'bickering'.[58] It was seen as 'not original at all and borrows practically everything from Bukharin'.[59]

Written from 'a dogmatic and rigidly deterministic standpoint',[60] Lenin's work is viewed as 'crude' and 'buttressed by superficial observations by the bourgeois liberal propagandist Hobson'. It became 'obsolete ... as soon as it appeared' and has been 'clouding the issues in ambiguity', 'distorting history' and 'rejecting some fundamental precepts of Marxist economics' in a 'logically and analytically lamentable' manner![61]

A 'minor'[62] and 'marginal work that never had any scientific pretensions',[63] *Imperialism* supposedly exemplifies the 'subordination of scientific exigencies to those of political activity'.[64] The pamphlet was a 'political polemic not a theoretical analysis' that 'adds nothing new to the discussion of the concept'.[65]

Lenin 'makes little or no contribution to the development of a theory of imperialism'.[66] *Imperialism* 'could hardly be termed a real theoretical advance',[67] but may be a 'theoretical failure'.[68] Not 'a theoretical piece, even though it attempts a rather grand statement', but a 'Ricardian step backwards'.[69] Founded on a 'fundamental mistake that has, ever since, continued to plague proper understanding',[70] Lenin's 'pamphleteering'[71] is essentially a 'popularisation of earlier writing',[72] yet somehow still 'monumentally confusing'.[73]

'Underconsumptionist',[74] and 'following the reductionist logic of the early twentieth-century theorists',[75] Lenin elaborated a 'linear analysis'[76] involving a 'confusion of the rules of scientific work with those of political activity'.[77] Without 'much to say about what was then considered the undeveloped world',[78] *Imperialism* cannot 'adequately describe contemporary capitalist developments'.[79] In fact, according to Callinicos, it was 'completely at odds with the economic patterns that developed after 1945'.[80]

Almost all of this was published after Warren's work, during a period when no substantial critique of Lenin's *Imperialism* has been produced. The exception is Barone, who still defended Lenin in 1985 – though he subsequently shifted focus to class structure inside the imperialist world.[81] Yet even in 2016, Shaikh still found Lenin's work to be an 'imprimatur'[82] (i.e. received wisdom). Later Mohandesi opined that Lenin's 'very loose writing ... has sown much confusion ... This was especially unfortunate'.[83]

The historical career of important works of art and science suggest bitter hostility – such as that against Lenin's *Imperialism* – might be understood as testament not to weakness but strength. The severity of hostility shows its potency in hitting on the raw nerves of accepted wisdom, and especially of those ideas most important to the ruling ideology. Galileo received some poor reviews too.

But it is tricky for purported supporters of the October Revolution to openly condemn the perspectives of its leaders. Gasper is therefore more polite. He finds Bukharin and Lenin 'did a remarkably good job' at explaining the *first half* of the twentieth century.[84] For Harman the 'enduring power' of Lenin and Bukharin's writings 'lies in the way in which they still provide an explanation, like no other, of the whole of what has been called the "30 years' war" of the twentieth century … [1914–45]'.[85] The 'enduring power' in other words, did not endure.[86]

Imperialism, Callinicos reassures us, is 'more than an outdated pamphlet' and Marxists must 'continue to engage with [Lenin's] arguments, even if we may choose to criticize or even reject many of his assumptions and conclusions'.[87] Following Brewer and Harvey, Callinicos reasons that '*Imperialism* was not intended to be a definitive scientific study but rather, as its subtitle declares, a "popular outline" '.[88]

The upturn in writing that occurred around the 2003 Iraq invasion, including Harvey's *New Imperialism*, saw no need to rethink Lenin's *Imperialism*. Chibber compared this work with the 1970s, which he says 'was the occasion for a rediscovery of Lenin, Luxemburg, Bukharin and other thinkers of the Third International, much of the current body of work is moving toward a rejection, or at any rate drastic modification, of leading elements of their legacy'.[89] For Harvey, contemporary developments go beyond the scope of Lenin's theory.[90] Thus *New Imperialism* draws theoretically from the non-Marxists Arendt and Arrighi as well as Rosa Luxemburg – but not Lenin. In a symposium discussing Harvey's work, Ashman pointed out that there is now 'general agreement that the classical theorists of *Imperialism*, whose accounts are now nearly 100 years old, may be important reference points but they are not an adequate guide to the contemporary world'.[91] Yet no post-war Marxist could conceivably ever have held the classics as 'an adequate guide to the contemporary world'. Such a counterposition serves to obscure the disconnect between contemporary and classical theory and the absence of any contemporary critique of Lenin.

In 2004, Panitch and Gindin counterposed their own 'extension of the theory of the capitalist state' to Lenin's *Imperialism*.[92] In his 2007 discussion on imperialism theory, Foster suggested that 'the concept of the imperialist world system in today's predominant sense of the extreme economic exploitation of periphery by center, creating a widening gap between rich and poor countries, was largely absent from the classical Marxist critique of capitalism'.[93] Perhaps aware that Lenin, Bukharin and Luxemburg's classical Marxist critiques of imperialism can easily be shown to have emphasised 'extreme economic exploitation of periphery by center', Foster concedes that Lenin in fact did acknowledge 'aspects of dependency and non-linear development',[94] but only in 'traces'.[95]

Commemorating fifty years since the publication of Baran and Sweezy's *Monopoly Capital*, Foster makes no reference to Lenin except to portray Baran and Sweezy's work as seeking 'to give a sharper meaning to what thinkers like Rudolf Hilferding and V. I. Lenin had referred to as "finance capitalism" and "the monopoly stage of capitalism"'.[96] Notably, neither Foster's year 2000 commemoration of Baran and Sweezy's *Monopoly Capital* nor his 2006 (fortieth year) version mention Lenin at all.[97] Evidently, for Foster, Baran and Sweezy's work is itself the modern articulation and/or successor of Lenin's *Imperialism* – though nowhere in Foster's work is the relationship explained.

Baran and Sweezy's book mentions Lenin only twice, and there is no engagement with his theory of imperialism. The first mention asserts without explanation that 'neither Lenin nor any of his followers attempted to explore the consequences of the predominance of monopoly for the working principles and "laws of motion" of the underlying capitalist economy'.[98]

With individual exceptions, it appears an academic consensus against *Imperialism* held good for four decades.[99] It is thought that Lenin's *Imperialism* must be rejected owing to its theoretical weakness or limitations. Yet it is difficult to find substantive criticism of his work. None of Lenin's ostensible supporters who advocate a different or modified theory have offered a critique. Among Lenin's opponents, by far the most detailed critique is Warren. Given the controversy, it is surprising to observe the paucity of actual discussion of, or even familiarity with *Imperialism* (let alone with Lenin's other relevant works, especially during the early Comintern period) beyond a few often quoted passages.

For example, a 2018 issue of *Viewpoint Magazine* was devoted to the question of imperialism. In attempting to give a contemporary definition, Mohandesi, though he provides no direct quotations, rejects Lenin's theory as economically determinist, before advancing his own view that 'in the 21st century, we see a whole host of developed capitalist countries outside the conventional metropolitan core: India, China, Turkey, or Thailand, to name only a few'.[100] No explanation is given as to what the writer means in describing these countries as 'developed'.

Lenin's central theoretical concept – monopoly finance capital – is erroneously presented by Brewer, for example, as representing the 'dominance of bank capital over industrial capital'.[101] This is contrary to Lenin's explicit statements (see Chapter 6). Proceeding from this error, Brewer confuses Lenin's references to imperialism's 'parasitism' with the parasitism of the finance sector, bank or money capital (that is – finance capital as Brewer, not Lenin, understands it).[102]

Modern opponents of Lenin generally reference other modern opponents of Lenin to substantiate their claims when purportedly dealing with Lenin's work itself. Article after book tends succinctly to repeat the same common points of rejection familiar to many academic works. For example, McNally's *Understanding Imperialism: Old and New Dominion* contains no references to Lenin or other classical writers. Only Wood, Harvey and Panitch and Gindin are referenced, all of whom reject Lenin's contemporary relevance. McNally makes the unreferenced claim that 'the biggest flaw in these [classical] theories of imperialism is that they saw territorial occupation by the major powers as a necessary feature of global capitalism'.[103] Yet, as will be shown, Lenin explicitly argued the opposite.

Another conflation of 'classical theories' comes from Panitch and Gindin, who, following Brewer, argue simultaneously against what they believe to constitute both Hobson's and Lenin's theories, asserting them to be fundamentally similar.[104] Willoughby critiques Bukharin while referring to 'the Leninists' and their 'economic reductionist methodology'.[105]

Harvey's 1982 book, *The Limits to Capital*, makes multiple references to Lenin, but from the outset these are marred by terrible caricature. For example, the first reference to Lenin is an unattributed apparent misquotation where Lenin supposedly wrote of 'the highest stage of monopoly capitalism' and 'shortly thereafter coined the expression "state-monopoly capitalism"'.[106]

A surprising number of contemporary scholars are apparently reluctant even to read, let alone engage with, Lenin's work. No well-known contemporary writer uses Lenin's work as a theoretical starting point, even critically.[107] There is no widely known influential elaboration, sustained defence or application of Lenin's imperialism in academic or non-academic literature. Nor is there any popular explanation of contemporary imperialism that incorporates Lenin's framework. No well-known journal, magazine or book defends Lenin's theory. It is mostly left to *Monthly Review* and a small number of individuals to defend Lenin's central proposition of imperialist exploitation. However, none do so in a manner consistent with Lenin's theory.

The new consensus against Lenin coincides with the collapse of new academic Marxist work on imperialism of any variety. Between Warren's *Imperialism* (1980) and Harvey's *New Imperialism* (2003), there was no important new work. Chilcote observed in the late 1990s that 'few contemporary writers explicitly search for earlier ideas and build [imperialism] theory on past debates'.[108] Today there can be no serious talk of 'reverence' for Lenin in academia.

If Lenin's *Imperialism* had been replaced with another Marxist theory, a more rigorous debate could have been expected. Yet no well-known Marxist theory has even been suggested as a replacement, let alone debated or widely adopted.[109] The absence of any accepted Marxist theory, it has been shown, coincides with both a long downturn in writing on imperialism and a downturn in struggle underlying that. The weakness of First World Marxism explains its divorce from imperialism theory, not the other way around. Rejection of Lenin's *Imperialism* therefore appears as part of the broader collapse of anti-imperialist movements and social struggle. It was in this context that Marxists tried to understand the important economic developments of the neoliberal period.

Notes

1 A. Amsden, 'Imperialism', in J. Eatwell, M. Milgate and P. Newman (eds), *Marxian Economics* (Basingstoke, Palgrave Macmillan, 1990), p. 205.
2 M. Lane, *Unfinished Nation: Indonesia Before and After Suharto* (London, Verso, 2008), pp. 22–8.
3 R. Owen, 'Introduction', in R. Owen and B. Sutcliffe (eds), *Studies in the Theory of Imperialism* [1972] (London, Longman, 1978), p. 1.
4 A. Freeman, 'Ernest Mandel's Contribution to Economic Dynamics', *MPRA Paper No. 64974*, University of Manitoba, 1996, p. 15.
5 General Declaration of the Tri-Continental Conference, Havana, 1966, cited in D. Horowitz, *Imperialism and Revolution* (London, Allen Lane, 1969), p. 250.
6 E. Mandel, *Late Capitalism* [1972] (London, Verso, 1978), p. 64.
7 Mandel, *Late Capitalism*, p. 61; E. Mandel, *The Meaning of the Second World War* (London, Verso, 1986).
8 V. Prashad, *The Poorer Nations: A Possible History of the Global South* (London, Verso, 2014).
9 J. B. Perdue, *The War of All the People: The Nexus of Latin American Radicalism and Middle Eastern Terrorism* (Sterling, VA, Potomac, 2012), p. 31.
10 Cited in Horowitz, *Imperialism and Revolution*, p. 251 (emphasis added).
11 Mandel, *Late Capitalism*; S. Amin, *Unequal Development: An Essay on the Social Formations of Peripheral Capitalism* (Sussex, Harvester, 1976).
12 S. H. Hymer, 'The Internationalization of Capital', *Journal of Economic Issues*, 6:1 (1972), 91–111.
13 Prashad, *Poorer Nations*, p. 134.
14 B. Warren, *Imperialism: Pioneer of Capitalism* (London, New Left, 1980). A similar critique of Lenin, which also remains influential, is A. Brewer, *Marxist Theories of Imperialism: A Critical Survey* [1980] (London, Routledge and Kegan Paul, 1990).

15 Warren, *Imperialism*, p. 84; G. Kitching, 'The Theory of Imperialism and Its Consequences', *Middle East Research and Information Project* (1981), p. 41; C. Kay, *Latin American Theories of Development and Underdevelopment* (London and New York, Routledge 1989), p. 143.
16 Warren, *Imperialism*, p. 128.
17 Warren, *Imperialism*, p. 113.
18 Warren, *Imperialism*, p. 100.
19 Warren, *Imperialism*, p. 28.
20 Warren, *Imperialism*, p. 129.
21 Warren, *Imperialism*, pp. 254–5.
22 M. C. Howard and J. E. King, *A History of Marxian Economics*, vol. 2, *1929–1990* (London, Macmillan, 1992), pp. 216–17, 218.
23 Howard and King, 'Whatever Happened to Imperialism?' p. 24; M. C. Howard and J. E. King, *A History of Marxian Economics*, vol. 1, *1883–1929* (London, Macmillan, 1989), p. 79.
24 Howard and King, *Marxian Economics*, vol. 1, p. 219.
25 D. Harvey, *The New Imperialism* (New York, Oxford University Press, 2003), p. 163.
26 Callinicos, *Imperialism and Global Political Economy*, pp. 58, 5. Brewer, says, 'In most of his argument, Warren followed Marx.' See Brewer, *Marxist Theories*, pp. 279–80.
27 Amsden, 'Imperialism', p. 215; B. Milanovic, 'Is "Neo-Imperialism" the Only Path to Development?' *globalinequality* (2017), 18 May.
28 K. Marx, *Contribution to a Critique of Political Economy* [1859] (Moscow, Progress, 1977), preface.
29 Warren, *Imperialism*, p. 166.
30 Baran argued, 'There is ample evidence in the history of all countries in question to indicate the nature of its general trend. Regardless of their national peculiarities, the pre-capitalist orders in Western Europe and in Japan, in Russia and in Asia were reaching at different times and in different ways their common historical destiny.' See P. A. Baran, *The Political Economy of Growth* [1957] (New York, Monthly Review, 1973), p. 298; Mandel, *Late Capitalism*, p. 54; F. S. Weaver, 'The Limits of Inerrant Marxism', *Latin American Perspectives*, 13:4 (1986), 103.
31 Baran says, 'The rapidity of Japan's transformation into a capitalist, industrialized country was due to a large extent to the military and economic threat from the West.' See Baran, *Political Economy of Growth*, p. 298.
32 V. I. Lenin, *Imperialism: The Highest Stage of Capitalism* [1917], vol. 1, *Selected Works* (Moscow, Progress, 1963), chap. 10.
33 K. Marx, 'Marx on Social Relations in Russia' [March 1881], in *Late Marx and the Russian Road, Marx and the Peripheries of Capitalism*, ed. S. Teodor (New York, Monthly Review, 1983), marxists.org/archive/marx/works/1881/zasulich/draft-3.htm.
34 Marx, *Capital*, vol. 1, chap. 15.

35 T. Lewis, 'Marxism and Nationalism', *International Socialist Review*, 13 (2000).

36 K. Marx, 'Outline of a Report on the Irish Question to the Communist Educational Association of German Workers in London' [1867], in *Marx and Engels on Ireland* (Moscow, Progress, 1971), marxists.org/archive/marx/works/1867/12/16.htm.

37 D. Renton (ed.), *Marx on Globalisation* (London, Lawrence and Wishart, 2001), p. 79–80; L. Pradella, 'Imperialism and Capitalist Development in Marx's Capital', *Historical Materialism*, 21:2 (2013), 117–47.

38 K. Mohri, 'Progressive and Negative Perspectives on Capitalism and Imperialism', in R. M. Chilcote (ed.), *Imperialism: Theoretical Directions* (Amherst, NY, Humanity, 2000), p. 139.

39 V. I. Lenin, *The Development of Capitalism in Russia: The Process of the Formation of a Home Market for Large-Scale Industry* [1899], vol. 3, *Collected Works* (Moscow, Progress, 1960).

40 Warren, *Imperialism*, p. 48.

41 Warren, *Imperialism*, p. 51.

42 Warren, *Imperialism*, p. 82. The word 'stagnant' appears only once. That is in Lenin's paraphrase of Lysis's assessment of France as 'the usurers of Europe', not Lenin's treatment of monopoly capitalism in general. Lenin also uses the word 'stagnation' twice, but on both occasions it appears in the phrase '*tendency* to stagnation and decay' [original emphasis].

43 Warren, *Imperialism*, p. 110; V. G. Kiernan, *Marxism and Imperialism* (London, Edward Arnold, 1974), p. 47; J. Willoughby, 'Evaluating the Leninist Theory of Imperialism', *Science and Society*, 59:3 (1995), 331; Callinicos, *Imperialism and Global Political Economy*, p. 42; J. Milios and D. P. Sotiropoulos, *Rethinking Imperialism: A Study of Capitalist Rule* (London and New York, Palgrave Macmillan, 2009), p. 23.

44 Lenin, *Imperialism*, chap. 4.

45 B. Warren, 'Imperialism and Capitalist Industrialization', *New Left Review*, 81 (1973), 2.

46 As early as 1974, McMichael et al. already responded to Warren, that the presence of 'industrial growth in the Third World is clearly not at issue – rather the problem is the character of this industrial growth, and what it expresses about international capitalist development, and the structural contradictions inherent in the process of (worldwide) capital accumulation'. See P. McMichael, J. Petras and R. R. Rhodes, 'Imperialism and the Contradictions of Development', *New Left Review*, 85 (1974), 84. As is explicit in Frank's seminal concept, 'the development of underdevelopment', the position of dependency theorists such as Frank was not about whether Third World societies were capitalist but the specific character of post-war Third World capitalist development. See A. G. Frank, *Capitalism and Underdevelopment in Latin America: Historical Studies of Chile and Brazil* [1967] (New York, Monthly Review, 2009).

47 Warren, *Imperialism*, p. 151.

48 Warren, *Imperialism*, pp. 190, 170. This conclusion concurs with N. Harris, *The End of the Third World: Newly Industrializing Countries and the Decline of an Ideology* (London, Penguin, 1987), p. 202; J. Willoughby, *Capitalist Imperialism, Crisis and the State* (London, Harwood, 1986), p. 54. For a critique, see McMichael et al., 'Imperialism and the Contradictions of Development', p. 85.

49 Warren, 'Imperialism and Capitalist Industrialization', p. 3.

50 A. G. Frank, 'Dependence Is Dead, Long Live Dependence and the Class Struggle: An Answer to Critics', *World Development*, 5:4 (1974), 102, cited in Kay, *Latin American Theories*, p. 180.

51 Rostow, *Stages of Growth*; Warren, *Imperialism*, p. 134.

52 C. Harman, *Zombie Capitalism: Global Crisis and the Relevance of Marx* (Chicago, Haymarket, 2009), p. 189; Callinicos, *Imperialism and Global Political Economy*, p. 5.

53 S. Williams, 'Is Russia Imperialist?' *A Critique of Crisis Theory* (2014), https://critiqueofcrisistheory.wordpress.com/is-russia-imperialist/.

54 R. Kiely, *Rethinking Imperialism* (London, Palgrave, 2010), p. 172.

55 A. Marshall, 'Lenin's Imperialism Nearly 100 Years On: An Outdated Paradigm?' *Critique: Journal of Socialist Theory*, 42:3 (2014), 317–18.

56 Brewer, *Marxist Theories*, pp. 110–11.

57 L. Panitch and S. Gindin, 'Global Capitalism and American Empire', *Socialist Register*, 40 (2004), 5.

58 D. Harvey, *A Brief History of Neoliberalism* (New York, Oxford University Press, 2007), p. 59.

59 T. Cliff, *Lenin 2: All Power to the Soviets* [1976] (Chicago, Haymarket, 2004), chap. 4.

60 G. Arrighi, *The Geometry of Imperialism: The Limits of Hobson's Paradigm* (London, New Left, 1978), p. 20, cited in Callinicos, *Imperialism and Global Political Economy*, p. 44.

61 Warren, *Imperialism*, pp. 4, 67, 48–9.

62 Brewer, *Marxist Theories*, p. 116.

63 A. Emmanuel, 'White-Settler Colonialism and the Myth of Investment Imperialism', *New Left Review*, 73 (1972), 36.

64 Arrighi, *Geometry of Imperialism*, cited in Warren, *Imperialism*, p. 91.

65 J. Tomlinson, 'Finance Capital', in Eatwell et al., *Marxian Economics*, p. 190.

66 Brewer, *Marxist Theories*, p. 116.

67 G. N. Howe, 'Dependency Theory, Imperialism, and the Production of Surplus Value on a World Scale', *Latin American Perspectives*, 8:3–4 (1981), 99.

68 Harvey, *A Brief History of Neoliberalism*, p. 59.

69 P. Zarembka, 'Lenin as Economist of Production: A Ricardian Step Backwards', *Science and Society*, 67:3 (2003), 279.

70 Panitch and Gindin, 'Global Capitalism', p. 5.

71 Harvey, *A Brief History of Neoliberalism*, p. 59.

72 R. Chilcote, 'Imperialism: The Highest Stage of Capitalism – VI Lenin', in Chilcote, *Imperialism*, p. 85.

73 Willoughby, 'Evaluating the Leninist Theory', p. 332.
74 Brewer, *Marxist Theories*, pp. 118–19; Callinicos, *Imperialism and Global Political Economy*, pp. 47, 52.
75 J. Willoughby, 'Assessing Lenin's Theory', in Chilcote, *Imperialism*, p. 173.
76 S. Avineri, 'The Roots of Imperialist Theory in Marx', in Chilcote, *Imperialism*, p. 129.
77 Arrighi, *Geometry of Imperialism*, cited in B. Semmel, 'On [Arrighi's] "The Geometry of Imperialism" ', *New Left Review*, 118 (1979), 73.
78 R. Munck, 'Dependency and Imperialism in Latin America: New Horizons', in Chilcote, *Political Economy of Imperialism*, p. 142.
79 J. Willoughby, 'Early Marxist Critiques of Capitalist Development', in Chilcote, *Political Economy of Imperialism*, p. 126.
80 Callinicos, *Imperialism and Global Political Economy*, p. 179.
81 C. A. Barone, *Marxist Thought on Imperialism: Survey and Critique* (London, Macmillan, 1985).
82 A. Shaikh, *Capitalism: Competition, Conflict, Crises* (New York, Oxford University Press, 2016), p. 353.
83 S. Mohandesi, 'The Specificity of Imperialism', *Viewpoint*, 6 (2018).
84 P. Gasper, 'Imperialism: Lenin and Bukharin' [speech presented at the Socialism 2008 Conference, Chicago], 2008, www.youtube.com/watch?v=kWRrd8I1gUU; C. Harman, 'Analysing Imperialism', *International Socialism*, 2:99 (2003); Callinicos, *Imperialism and Global Political Economy*, pp. 50–2.
85 Harman, 'Analysing Imperialism'; J. B. Foster, 'Late Imperialism: Fifty Years After Harry Magdoff's The Age of Imperialism', *Monthly Review*, 71:3 (2019).
86 P. Gasper, 'Obama, Imperialism and Capitalism', *International Socialist Review*, 78 (2011).
87 Callinicos, *Imperialism and Global Political Economy*, p. 66.
88 Callinicos, *Imperialism and Global Political Economy*, p. 43. This is a restatement of Brewer, *Marxist Theories*, p. 108.
89 V. Chibber, 'Capital Outbound', *New Left Review*, 36 (2005), 151.
90 Harvey, *The New Imperialism*, p. 46.
91 S. Ashman, 'Symposium on David Harvey's The New Imperialism: Editorial Introduction', *Historical Materialism*, 14:4 (2006), 3.
92 L. Panitch and S. Gindin, *The Making of Global Capitalism: The Political Economy of the American Empire* (London and New York, Verso, 2013), p. 7.
93 J. B. Foster, 'The Imperialist World System: Paul Baran's Political Economy of Growth After Fifty Years', *Monthly Review*, 59:1 (2007).
94 Foster, 'Imperialist World System'.
95 Foster, 'Imperialist World System'; J. B. Foster, 'The New Imperialism of Globalized Monopoly-Finance Capital', *Monthly Review*, 67:3 (2015). This follows Brewer (*Marxist Theories*, p. 113) who says that Lenin 'does not stress the obstacles which this development meets, nor does he stress its one sided and limited effects'.

96 J. B. Foster, 'Monopoly Capital at the Half-Century Mark', *Monthly Review*, 68:3 (2016).

97 J. B. Foster, 'Monopoly Capital at the Turn of the Millennium', *Monthly Review*, 51:11 (2000); J. B. Foster, 'Monopoly-Finance Capital', *Monthly Review*, 58:7 (2006).

98 P. Baran and P. Sweezy, *Monopoly Capital: An Essay on the American Economic and Social Order* (New York, Monthly Review, 1966), p. 4.

99 Sakellaropoulos and Sotiris advocate a fresh look at Lenin's *Imperialism*. See S. Sakellaropoulos and P. Sotiris, 'From Territorial to Nonterritorial Capitalist Imperialism: Lenin and the Possibility of a Marxist Theory of Imperialism', *Rethinking Marxism*, 27:1 (2015), 104. Marshall argues that to do so requires that Lenin's work must be 'removed from a 1960s–1970s era "north–south" debate over underdevelopment to which it never belonged'. See Marshall, 'Lenin's Imperialism', p. 328.

100 Mohandesi, 'The Specificity of Imperialism'.

101 Brewer, *Marxist Theories*, p. 118.

102 Brewer, *Marxist Theories*, p. 118.

103 D. McNally, 'Understanding Imperialism: Old and New Dominion', *Against the Current*, 117 (2005).

104 Panitch and Gindin, argue: 'The classical theories of imperialism developed at the time, from Hobson's to Lenin's, were founded on a theorization of capitalist economic stages and crises. This was a fundamental mistake that has, ever since, continued to plague proper understanding. The classical theories were defective in their historical reading of imperialism.' See Panitch and Gindin, *The Making of Global Capitalism*, p. 5.

105 Willoughby, *Capitalist Imperialism*, pp. 17, 19. Milios and Sotiropoulos reject Lenin's theory, though suggest Lenin's work did prefigure a concept they call 'Lenin's notion of the imperialist chain'. See Milios and Sotiropoulos, *Rethinking Imperialism*, p. 32.

106 D. Harvey, *The Limits to Capital* (Oxford, Basil Blackwell, 1982), pp. 138, 283, 289.

107 These views stand in stark contrast to previous generations of Marxists. Trotsky, for example, argued that 'it was Lenin who gave a scientific characterisation of monopoly capitalism in his Imperialism'. See L. Trotsky, *Ninety Years of the Communist Manifesto* [1938] (New York, Fourth International, 1948); T. Kemp, 'The Marxist Theory of Imperialism', in Owen and Sutcliffe, *Studies in the Theory of Imperialism*, p. 26.

108 Chilcote, *Political Economy of Imperialism*, p. 6.

109 Wood, for example, defines modern imperialism as a 'unique mode of economic domination managed by a system of multiple states led by the United States'. Drop the mention of the United States and that definition could have applied to the Ottoman, Roman or Portuguese empires. See E. M. Wood, *Empire of Capital* (London and New York, Verso, 2005), p. 152.

3

Contemporary Marxist response to world polarisation

> The net drain of wealth from East to West that had prevailed for over two centuries has been reversed as East Asia in particular has risen to prominence as a powerhouse in the global economy (Harvey, 2014).

Having long rejected Lenin and embraced something like Warren's (or Rostow's) modernisation theory, influential Marxist work in this century either ignores the global polarisation or acknowledges it only weakly and partially. No major work adequately explains how the global social divide is maintained and reproduced.

Patnaik, returning to the United States in 1990 after fifteen years abroad, observed 'a remarkable transformation that has taken place in the Marxist discourse in America over the last decade or more, namely, hardly anybody talks of imperialism any more'.[1] After the 1991 Gulf War, Cumings argued that to discover the word 'imperialism' used to describe the United States would require an 'electron microscope'.[2] For Munck, at the turn of century, 'the discourse of imperialism has faded from view'.[3] Explaining, in 2016, why he had chosen to do his PhD on British imperialism, Norfield commented that 'nothing had been done on this topic relating to the UK since the 1980s'.[4]

Chilcote wrote:

> During the 1990s the language of development and imperialism began to assimilate the term 'globalization' to express the pervasive and expansive world economy ... debate around the idea of globalization has directed attention away from imperialism and left the general impression that the rapidly advancing capitalist world is emerging unified and harmonious.[5]

This tendency within Marxist writing was an adaptation to the broader ideological climate. Referring not only to Marxists, Kiely observed that before 2003 'amongst most Western academics, imperialism as a concept began to be viewed with almost antiquarian irony'.[6]

There was a small surge of publishing before and after the second US-led invasion of Iraq in 2003.[7] Renewed interest in imperialism came from US conservatives who, after 9/11, in major capitalist publications

like the *New York Times* and *Washington Post*, began explicitly to advocate an 'imperialist' US global role. In *Foreign Affairs* magazine, one neo-
conservative ideologue argued, 'The chaos in the world is too threatening to
ignore, and existing methods for dealing with that chaos have been tried and
found wanting ... But a new imperial moment has arrived, and by virtue of
its power America is bound to play the leading role.'[8] This wave of public
thinking generated by neo-conservatives is the context for new Marxist
work on imperialism of that period. *Socialist Register* devoted consecutive
volumes to imperialism in 2004 and 2005, while *Historical Materialism* ran
a symposium on Harvey in 2006. Commenting on this upturn in output,
Chibber thought he 'may be seeing the most fertile spurt of thinking about
imperialism on the left since the 1970s'.[9] Yet soon, concern about imperialism receded once more.

Imperialism gets barely half a page of consideration in Duménil and Lévy's
The Crisis of Neoliberalism. Their book defines imperialism so loosely it
could occur in any class society, not only capitalism.[10] Robinson's *Global
Capitalism and the Crisis of Humanity* suggests Marxism must 'go beyond'
the theory of imperialism.[11] Harvey's *Seventeen Contradictions*[12] does not
even rank imperialism among capital's top *seventeen* contradictions!

Popular Marxist accounts of contemporary economic changes use some
combination of the concepts of 'financialisation', 'globalisation' and First
World 'deindustrialisation'. The starting point for Harvey and others is
the movement to the Third World of aspects of bulk production. This is
generally viewed as manifesting US or imperialist 'deindustrialisation' and
decline. Still, the reality of continued greater capital accumulation and
income in the imperialist states, despite this supposed industrial decline, is
what must be analysed. Most often this was done via the popular notion of
'financialisation'.[13]

Harvey's 'new imperialism' to no imperialism

The most influential, ostensibly anti-imperialist, new theoretical work
this century is Harvey's 2003 book, *The New Imperialism*. Harvey's key
concepts – 'accumulation by dispossession', discrete duel 'logics' of power
attributed to state and private capital respectively – and capital's 'geo-
spatial' or 'spatial temporal dynamics' and 'spatial-fix' crisis theory, which
collectively constitute Harvey's new imperialism theory, do not explain
Third World exploitation or the reproduction of imperialist dominance. In
2003, Harvey acknowledged Third World exploitation and attempted to
use these theoretical tools – especially 'accumulation by dispossession' – to
explain it. Yet his 2014 book, *Seventeen Contradictions*, retains the same

theoretical tools while dropping any reference to exploitation of poor countries or imperialism.

Harvey's 'spatial-fix' framework is *opposed* to any thesis of rich–poor national exploitation. For Harvey, 'above all, uneven geographical development serves' not to maintain the position of specific privileged or monopolistic capitalist groups but 'to move capital's systemic failings around from place to place'.[14]
According to Harvey, 'the world is a much more equal place than it once was. Millions of people have escaped from poverty. Much of this has been due to the phenomenal growth of China … Disparities in the global distribution of wealth and income between countries have been much reduced with rising per capita incomes in many developing parts of the world.'[15] Harvey says, 'Anti-capitalist movements must abandon all thoughts of regional equality and convergence', which would amount to 'unacceptable and unachievable global monotony'![16] He does not explain what he means by these comments. However, it is doubtful equality would seem unacceptably monotonous to most of the world's people who, unlike the professor, cannot 'eat vegetables from California in Paris and drink imported beers from all over the world in Pittsburgh', as Harvey claims to do.[17] He says that 'the salient conflicts in the world today are class conflicts within states, including the American ones, rather than conflicts between them'.[18]

Harvey did not need to modify his accumulation by dispossession/financialisation thesis in order to move from new imperialism to 'no imperialism' – he simply changes who he says is parasitic. In 2003, accumulation by dispossession was Harvey's explanation for the pillage of Asian countries during the 1998 economic crisis, led by the International Monetary Fund (IMF). By 2014, it had morphed into the response of US capital to its own supposed long-term productive decline in relation to rising China and 'the East'. Such a malleable tool can apparently explain anything and everything.

How *Monthly Review* explains imperialism

The *Monthly Review* tendency, by contrast, rightly emphasises Third World oppression and exploitation, Third World struggles and anti-imperialism – including by strongly opposing imperialist attacks on China.[19] Foster has long placed imperialist exploitation of the Third World at the centre of his work. He points out that 'the inner logic of imperialism [is] most evident in the rising gap in income and wealth between rich and poor countries, and in net transfers of economic surplus from periphery to center that make this possible. The growing polarization of wealth and poverty between nations … is the system's crowning achievement on the world stage.'[20] Yet this cannot easily be explained using the theoretical framework of 'monopoly capital' as understood by the *Monthly Review* tendency (see also Chapter 7). The leading *Monthly Review* theorist, Paul Sweezy, argued:

> Under conditions of monopoly, exchange ratios do not conform to labor-time ratios, nor do they stand in a theoretically demonstrable relation to labor-time ratios ... it appears to be obvious, as Hilferding said, that 'the realization of Marx's theory of concentration, of monopolistic merger, seems to result in the invalidation of Marx's value theory.'[21]

Foster is thus forced to search for an explanation of imperialist exploitation outside of the Marx's value theory. For this reason he ends up looking outside of the labour process for answers.

> Third World countries have long experienced an enormous net outflow of surplus in the form of net payments to foreign investors and lenders located in the center of the world system. These and other payments for services (for example freight charges owed to capital in the rich countries) have a negative effect on the current account balances of underdeveloped countries and tend to pull them into the red irrespective of the trade balance, which is also normally stacked against them.[22]

The formulation poses but does not answer the essential theoretical question: by what precise mechanism are poor countries continuously forced to pay high prices – whether for freight or any other commodities they must buy?

The absence of a focus on investigating the labour process means that while Suwandi and Foster describe 'global labor arbitrage' – the search for cheap labour – as the 'key element of the contemporary imperialist system',[23] they are unable to explain why imperialism disproportionately benefits from labour arbitrage while Third World capital does not. Suwandi and Foster pertinently ask 'how the system has been able to shift production to those parts of the globe with the lowest unit labor costs, while maintaining, and in some ways even increasing, the overall centre–periphery division within the capitalist world economy'.[24] They answer, following Baran, by citing a non-labour contractual factor: 'new international trade agreements designed to perpetuate the power of the present imperial core'.[25] Baran's earlier explanation of Third World exploitation also makes the non-labour argument that 'plunder [which] has been rationalized and routinized by a mechanism of impeccably "correct" contractual relations' is what determines prices.[26] Because Suwandi and Foster do not perceive an imperialist monopoly over the labour process, they suggest it is possible that the extra surplus value created in the South will begin to be usurped, not predominantly by the imperialist capital after all – but by Third World capital: 'growth of emerging economies [threatens] to destabilize the domination of the global

North over the world economy'.[27] They ask, 'What if emerging economies and their states become strong enough to assert some control over production, over the information systems governing production, over legal and trade conditions, and so on? ... How can the multinational retain control of technology under these circumstances?'[28] This is a very good question. Though a better one might be, 'Can so-called emerging economies do this?' Suwandi and Foster do not give evidence either way, yet make the wild, unsubstantiated claim that 'much of the most advanced production – is now being carried out in the Global South'.[29]

Separately, Foster, again following Sweezy, proposed 'financialisation' as the mechanism of exploitation of the Third World, arguing that what he called 'monopoly-finance capital' represented a 'new hybrid phase of the system'.[30] Despite using Lenin's exact formulation (i.e. monopoly finance capital), Foster never evaluates where his view converges or differs with Lenin's. In the most recent iteration of Foster's financialisation, we are told 'center economies no longer constitut[e] to the same extent as before the global centers of industrial production and capital accumulation'. Rather, they rely 'more and more on their role as the centers of financial control and asset accumulation'.[31] So once again production is presented as going south.

But how is centre economy 'asset accumulation' a mechanism and not a result of value transfer? And what does Foster consider different between traditional 'capital accumulation' and new financialised 'asset accumulation'? Accumulation of financial 'assets' (i.e. financial paper) certainly constitutes an important aspect of imperialist monopolistic advantage today. But that has long been the case. How exactly finance, conceived as a separate section of capital, can exert control over non-financial capital (which such a formulation must assume) remains a mystery.

In overlooking unequal exchange in trade based on monopoly in the labour process itself, Foster is consistent with Sweezy, who rejected it explicitly:

> It should be particularly noted that trade between two countries can affect the distribution of the value produced within either one or both of them ... but that it cannot transfer value from one to the other. A more advanced country, for example, cannot extract value from a less advanced country by trade alone; it can do so only through the ownership of capital in the latter.[32]

From around 2011, a modest upturn in the output of Marxist articles and books on imperialism brought a change in emphasis to contemporary Marxist writing. A part of this new work was published through *Monthly Review*. The upturn included writing that incorporated important insights of heterodox literature on global value chains (GVCs) and global production networks. It was from this time that Foster, McChesney and Jonna, for example, argued that 'imperialist rent' was 'extracted from the South through the integration of low-wage, highly exploited workers into capitalist production'.[33] Lauesen and Cope noted 'the change in the international division of labor' as well as an 'enormous growth in the number of proletarians integrated into the capitalist world system'.[34]

Books published since 2012 on the imperialist system, the economics of imperialism or the international division of labour include Cope, *Divided World, Divided Class* (2012), Panitch and Gindin, *The Making of Global Capitalism* (2013), Norfield, *The City* (2016), Smith, *Imperialism in the Twenty-First Century* (2016), Patnaik and Patnaik, *A Theory of Imperialism* (2017) and Suwandi, *Value Chains: The New Economic Imperialism* (2019).[35]

Unlike the earlier uptick that was provoked by US conservatives, the latest wave is motivated by opposition to imperialist economic exploitation of the Third World. Norfield, for example, points out that not only the United States but a 'small group of countries' with enormous advantages possess the 'ability to siphon off value created elsewhere'.[36] He says that 'there is no accounting for how the low-cost imported cheap labour products boosted the recorded profits of US corporations'.[37] However, no writer has yet resolved the most important issue – exactly how the labour process itself is controlled in ways that reproduces imperialist monopolistic supremacy via capitalist commodity production.

Panitch and Gindin investigate how the United States created and maintains its hegemony. They argue 'the crucial question' of which state will be dominant in the future turns on state 'capacity to take on extensive responsibilities for managing global capitalism'.[38] The book also contains perhaps the fullest brief summary statement of the global labour division in the neoliberal period within any Marxist work:

> The development of new networks of integrated production. Far from the shift of productive activity from the developed core leading to a fragmentation of production, [this] was part and parcel of a much greater global coordination of production through a broad range of subsidiaries, suppliers and distributers. The growing tendency on the part of the multinational corporations to centralize their key strategic and administrative functions in their home country, while decentralizing labor-intensive production abroad, already discerned by Stephen Hymer in the early 1970s, had become pronounced by the mid-1980s. It especially accelerated through the 1990s in response to the pressures and opportunities brought on by the liberalization of trade and capital flows, the application of new information technologies, the development of infrastructures, and, above all, the growth of new proletarians in the developing world.[39]

Indeed! We should add also that this is a crucial way that the imperialist countries as a whole (not just its MNCs) monopolise the overall production process in the neoliberal period. However, owing to the institutional and legal focus of their work, this brief statement is neither elaborated nor incorporated into the book's main argument, which, as said, focuses on state 'capacity to take on extensive responsibilities for managing global capitalism'.[40] What is not covered in their main argument is imperialist state capacity to assist private monopoly capital to create and maintain monopoly over the 'key strategic' functions in the labour process. In contradiction to the above summary, Panitch and Gindin argue that, since the 1970s, 'capitalist globalization produces tendencies towards a narrowing of the differences in wages and conditions between developed and developing countries'.[41]

John Smith's *Imperialism in the Twenty-First Century*

Smith's book does a great job of outlining empirically how the production of certain global commodities – T-shirts, coffee and iPhones – causes value transfers from Third to First World economies.[42] This empirical work helps provide the basis to begin theoretically answering the question of value transfer through trade (i.e. unequal exchange).

Yet key parts of this evidence – which help lay bare both the monopolistic position of First World capital in relation to Third World producers and how that position is secured – is excluded from Smith's theoretical explanation of value transfer. The latter turns on the issue of super-exploitation of Third World labour. But super-exploitation alone cannot explain unequal exchange.

Quoting Higginbottom, Smith proposes that 'the idea of super-exploitation needs to be conceptually generalised at the necessary level of abstraction and incorporated into the theory of imperialism. Super-exploitation is ... the hidden common essence defining imperialism.'[43]

It is true that super-exploitation of cheap Third World labour is central to imperialism. The problem, however, is explaining exactly how MNCs and imperialist states make sure they are the primary beneficiaries. Given that most Third World labour is employed by Third World capitalists, what force prevents these direct employers themselves capturing most of the extra surplus value created by super-exploitation of the workers in their own factories, mines and farms?

Even if we accept Smith's view that super-exploitation has become the increasingly dominant form of increasing surplus-value extraction in the modern world,[44] this would mean only that we accept the large contribution of super-exploitation to total world surplus value, as opposed to imperialist

super-profits. The latter require not just the creation of surplus value some-
where in the world, but its capture by definite individual capitals based in
the imperialist states. Smith's so-called third form of surplus value, which is
what he calls super-exploitation, in other words, even if a correct theoretical discovery, would bring us no closer to a theory of imperialism. Super-
exploitation, taken alone, can explain neither unequal exchange nor how
imperialist societies reproduce their dominance.

Smith's given reason for excluding his empirical evidence of the domination of the world market by MNCs is that an explanation of imperialism cannot be found in monopoly. Smith contends that monopoly – as
Lenin understood it – cannot help us understand the global economic divide
between rich and poor countries:

> Most strands of western Marxism, including many claiming adherence to
> Lenin's legacy, have disregarded Lenin's insistence on the economic and pol-
> itical centrality of the division of the world into oppressed and oppressor
> nations, dwelling instead on Lenin's argument that in its economic essence
> imperialism is monopoly capitalism. Compounding the problem, neither of
> these antithetical definitions seems to be consistent with the concepts and cat-
> egories developed by Marx in *Capital*.[45]

Smith presents his own theoretical work as aiming to overcome an 'inevitable disconnection, persisting right to this day, between Lenin's theory of
imperialism and Marxist value theory'.[46] The supposed disconnection seems
to emanate from Lenin's concept of monopoly, which in Smith's view does
not apply to Marx's law of value. According to Smith, 'above average profits resulting from some sort of monopoly ... implies a violation of the law
of value ... a departure from the law'; monopoly 'negate[s] the law of value'
and stands as its 'antithesis'.[47]

Yet Smith's understanding of monopoly is in contradiction to Lenin's.
Smith considers that 'a technological innovation can become an insurmountable barrier when the innovator is given a legal monopoly over its
use. Here, the source of monopoly power is not the technological innovation itself but the legal protection given to the innovator against potential competitors.'[48] 'Apple's fat profits arise', we are told, not from not its
designs and product development, but 'from *patented* technology as well as
branding and retailing'.[49]

Thus for Smith the monopoly possessed by the world's leading MNCs on
the world market is not technological or productive but *legal*. This is presumably the reason he views monopoly as negating the law of value. Smith
does not substantiate his view that legal papers constitute the most important
form of monopoly by explaining how that would actually work to maintain
imperialism. Yet the related claim – denial that productive superiority is the

basis of imperialist monopoly – is the central premise of Smith's account of how value is transferred. Lenin gives essentially the opposite definition of monopoly to Smith (see Chapter 7).

As we saw, Smith defines monopoly as a legal, not productive, category. Therefore, in his pursuit of a 'value theory of imperialism',[50] he must exclude monopoly as a central concept – because legal papers are not central to Marx's labour theory of value.

In order to explain unequal exchange in trade between rich and poor countries, it is necessary to show why rich countries can sell their commodities dear and poor countries are forced to sell cheap (or to show why one of these occurs). Smith in his empirical work justifiably states that Third World countries must sell cheap because of 'race-to-the-bottom competition' among themselves. So why – if not a superior productive position – does this race-to-the-bottom competition not also afflict imperialist capital?

Following Emmanuel, Smith argues that the reason is *lack of competition* between First and Third World capitals. The two authors' formulations on this are almost identical. For Smith:

> A most striking feature of the imperialist world economy is that, as we have seen, Northern firms do not compete with Southern firms, they compete with other Northern firms ... We therefore have North–North competition, and we have cutthroat South–South competition, but no North–South competition – that is between firms, if not between workers.[51]

In Emmanuel's 1972 version: 'In general ... the two groups, that of the developed countries and that of the underdeveloped ones, do not export the same products, and the problem of competition between the groups on the commodity market does not arise. What does arise is competition within a group, i.e. within the North and within the South.'[52] Why does only South–South competition cause its participants to race to the bottom if not their relatively weak productive capacity? According to both authors, the relative productive capacities or productivities of the two groups are not compared by the market, because they do not export the same products.[53] Thus for Smith and Emmanuel, 'competition' is limited to capitals producing the same commodities.

But if it were true that imperialist monopoly is not based in productive dominance (i.e. if First and Third World societies had similar labour productivity and similar ability to carry out high-technology labour processes), what would stop Third World capital from investing in the same areas as First World capital? If they could do this successfully, it would deliver them a level of profitability comparable to the imperialist states (or higher, given cheaper labour), hence completely overturning incumbent imperialist control. Smith's answer, given the above, is that patents or other legal barriers prevent this, but such an answer cannot be a 'value theory of imperialism' because patents are not labour.

The principal theoretical mistake in Smith's work is following Emmanuel and Amin in assuming imperialism should not be analysed as a form of capitalist competition. For this reason, Smith treats differential profits as *somehow* part of the sphere of production and not distribution. In other words, Smith's 'value theory of imperialism' conflates Marx's theory of value in its inner essential (abstract) form (with one capital) and the modified form this essence takes under monopoly capitalism today (especially the competition between many capitals). In this vein, following Higginbottom, Smith suggests that 'imperialist division of the world' has 'become a property of the capital relation itself'.[54] 'The development of the international division of labour in the neoliberal period "manifests an evolution of the capital–labor relation, which increasingly takes the form of a relation between Northern capital and Southern labor"'.[55] Notably, in the above formulation, the Third World capitalist is abolished, something that has no basis in reality. The nature of outsourcing is not to abolish the Third World capitalist but to contract them. Only where Third World labour is directly employed by an MNC – the opposite of outsourcing – is the Third World capitalist abolished (or prevented from forming). Imperialism's increasing use of outsourcing and 'arm's length' arrangements in the neoliberal period means that in the actual concrete functioning of the capitalist market, value produced by Third World workers must first be appropriated by their employer – the Third World capitalist – via appropriation and ownership of the products produced in Third World factories. Only after the capitalist has appropriated the value product as commodities they own can that same value then be forfeited (in part) on the market by selling those commodities below their value to First World capital that enjoys a superior market power. Plainly, the value must be *redistributed* via a process of intercapitalist competition (which involves the changing hands of the products of labour at variance to their value) – precisely the opposite of how Smith attempts to account theoretically for the transfers.

Rather than seeking to develop a theory of imperialism as an aspect of capitalist competition, Smith tries partially to maintain the assumptions of *Capital* volumes 1–3 that commodities are sold at their value.[56] Thus Smith's level of abstraction in examining world trade is higher than Marx had intended for his own planned examination of world trade and capitalist competition. Smith misses this, arguing instead that his own theory 'relaxes' Marx's assumptions. In fact it only *partially* relaxes the level of abstraction Marx used for his abstracted 'general analysis of capital'. That is the basic reason why Smith's work cannot explain how the imperialist system operates and reproduces itself. For the same reason, its theoretical core lacks logical coherence.

Smith's work – especially empirically – is a significant advance on other work of the period, which is why it has been engaged in detail here. However, as shown, its theoretical limitation flows from what has been common to the period – it is unable to show how the imperialist domination is reproduced via domination over the labour process itself, nor how this is expressed in its domination of the world market. Yet that focus is the only way to apply Marx's law of value to the contemporary world economy.

Notes

1 P. Patnaik, 'Whatever Has Happened to Imperialism?' *Social Scientist*, 18:6–7 (1990), 73.
2 B. Cumings, 'Global Realm with No Limit, Global Realm with No Name', *Radical History Review*, 57 (1993), 47–8, cited in G. Arrighi, 'Hegemony Unravelling – 1', *New Left Review*, 32 (2005).
3 R. Munck, 'Dependency and Imperialism in Latin America: New Horizons', in Chilcote, *Political Economy of Imperialism*, p. 147.
4 T. Norfield, 'Finance and the Imperialist World Today' [interview by Philip Ferguson], *Redline* (2016), 29 February.
5 Chilcote, *Political Economy of Imperialism* pp. 2, 13.
6 M. Cox, 'Foreword', in Kiely, *Rethinking Imperialism*, p. viii.
7 See, for example, M. Hardt and A. Negri, *Empire* (Cambridge, MA, Harvard University Press, 2000); Wood, *Empire of Capital*; G. Balakrishnan (ed.), *Debating Empire* (London and New York, Verso), 2003; A. Boron, *Empire and Imperialism: A Critical Reading of Michael Hardt and Antonio Negri* (London, Zed, 2005); L. Panitch and C. Leys (eds), *The New Imperial Challenge: Socialist Register*, vol. 40 (London, Merlin, 2004); L. Panitch and C. Leys (eds), *The Empire Reloaded: Socialist Register*, vol. 41 (London, Merlin, 2005); A. Callinicos, *The New Mandarins of American Power* (Cambridge, UK, Polity, 2003); Harman, 'Analysing Imperialism'. From a world-systems perspective, see I. Wallerstein, *Decline of American Power: The US in a Chaotic World* (New York, New Press, 2003).
8 S. Mallaby, 'The Reluctant Imperialist: Terrorism, Failed States, and the Case for American Empire', *Foreign Affairs*, 81:2 (2002). The *New York Times Magazine* cover announcing its feature in March 1999 declared: 'For globalization to work, America can't be afraid to act like the almighty superpower that it is.' See T. Friedman, 'Manifesto for a Fast World', *New York Times Magazine* (1999), 28 March; M. Ignatieff, 'The American Empire: The Burden', *New York Times Magazine* (2003), 5 January. In 2003, Daalder and Lindsay observed: 'In the last six months alone, as debate on Iraq peaked, the phrase "American empire" was mentioned nearly 1,000 times in news stories,

while bookstores have been quickly filling their shelves with freshly minted tomes on the subject.' I. H. Daalder and J. M. Lindsay, 'American Empire, Not "If" but "What Kind"', *New York Times* (2003), 10 May. For analysis of this trend, see B. Bowden, *The Empire of Civilization: The Evolution of an Imperial Idea* (Chicago, University of Chicago Press, 2009); Kiely, *Rethinking Imperialism*, p. 1.

9 Chibber, 'Capital Outbound', p. 151.
10 According to Duménil and Lévy, 'in any stage of imperialism, the major instruments of these international power relations, beyond straightforward economic violence, are corruption, subversion, and war'. See G. Duménil and D. Lévy, *The Crisis of Neoliberalism* (Cambridge, MA, Harvard University Press, 2011), p. 9.
11 W. I. Robinson, *Global Capitalism and the Crisis of Humanity* (New York, Cambridge University Press. 2014), pp. 99–112.
12 Harvey, *Seventeen Contradictions*.
13 Roberts aptly commented on the 'endless' number of papers on financialisation. See M. Roberts, 'China: A Weird Beast', *Michael Roberts Blog* (2015), 17 September, https://thenextrecession.wordpress.com/2015/09/17/china-a-weird-beast/.
14 Harvey, *Seventeen Contradictions*, p. 228. The word 'spatiotemporal' adds no specific or clear meaning. For example, when Harvey writes the sentence, 'growing resentments of being locked into a spatiotemporal situation of perpetual subservience to the centre did, however, spark anti-dependency and national liberation movements' (Harvey, *The New Imperialism*, pp. 59–60), he would have conveyed an identical meaning if the word 'spatiotemporal' were removed. Where Harvey defines imperialism as 'a certain form of the production of space' (Harvey, *The New Imperialism*, p. 87), we might ask, what then is the difference between modern capitalist imperialism and that of the Romans? Or that of beavers? Ants?
15 Harvey, *Seventeen Contradictions*, p. 239.
16 Harvey, *Seventeen Contradictions*, p. 162.
17 Harvey, *The New Imperialism*, p. 97.
18 Harvey, *Seventeen Contradictions*, p. 26. This follows Kidron's 1965 comment that 'the growing uniformity in the conditions of exploitation, the growing irrelevance of national struggles as such, the growing fusion of national and class struggles and the growing similarity in the immediate aims of the working class the world over', were among the important reasons why 'we don't have imperialism but we still have capitalism'. See M. Kidron, 'International Capitalism', *International Socialism*, 1:20 (1965).
19 Baran and Sweezy, *Monopoly Capital*, pp. 12, 206. See *Monthly Review* special edition, 'China 2020', *Monthly Review*, 72:5 (2020).
20 Foster in H. Magdoff and J. B. Foster, *Imperialism Without Colonies* (New York, Monthly Review, 2003), p. 18; J. B. Foster, R. W. McChesney and J. R. Jonna, 'The Global Reserve Army of Labor and the New Imperialism', *Monthly Review*, 63:6 (2011).

21 P. M. Sweezy, *The Theory of Capitalist Development* [1942] (New York, Monthly Review, 1970), pp. 270, 55. Suwandi quotes Baran and Sweezy thus: 'Corporations "can and do choose what prices to charge for their products", as the system bans the practice of "price cutting" under the assumption that it would lead to "economic warfare" among oligopolies.' See I. Suwandi, 'Labor-Value Commodity Chains, The Hidden Abode of Global Production', *Monthly Review*, 71:3 (2019); I. Suwandi, *Value Chains: The New Economic Imperialism* (New York, Monthly Review, 2019), p. 29.

22 J. B. Foster, 'Monopoly-Finance Capital', *Monthly Review*, 58:7 (2006).

23 I. Suwandi and J. B. Foster, 'Multinational Corporations and the Globalization of Monopoly Capital: From the 1960s to the Present', *Monthly Review*, 68:3 (2016); Foster, 'The New Imperialism'.

24 Suwandi and Foster, 'Multinational Corporations'.

25 Suwandi and Foster, 'Multinational Corporations'.

26 Baran, *Political Economy of Growth*, pp. 339, 232; Suwandi, *Value Chains*, pp. 162–3; For a study of the origin of Baran and Sweezy's views, see J. Brolin, *The Bias of the World: Theories of Unequal Exchange in History* (PhD thesis) (Finland, Lund University, 2007).

27 Suwandi and Foster, 'Multinational Corporations'.

28 Suwandi and Foster, 'Multinational Corporations'.

29 Suwandi and Foster, 'Multinational Corporations'.

30 Foster, 'Monopoly-Finance Capital'.

31 Foster, 'The New Imperialism'.

32 Sweezy, *The Theory of Capitalist Development*, p. 290.

33 Foster et al., 'Global Reserve Army of Labor'.

34 T. Lauesen and Z. Cope, 'Imperialism and the Transformation of Values into Prices', *Monthly Review*, 67:3 (2015); Z. Cope, 'Global Wage Scaling and Left Ideology: A Critique of Charles Post on the "Labour Aristocracy"', in *Research in Political Economy*, 28 (2013), 100.

35 Z. Cope, *Divided World Divided Class, Global Political Economy and the Stratification of Labour Under Capitalism* [2012] (Montreal, Kersplebedeb, 2015); Panitch and Gindin, *The Making of Global Capitalism*; T. Norfield, *The City: London and the Global Power of Finance* (London and New York, Verso, 2016); J. Smith, *Imperialism in the Twenty-First Century: Globalization, Super-Exploitation and Capitalism's Final Crisis* (New York, Monthly Review, 2016); U. Patnaik and P. Patnaik, *A Theory of Imperialism* (New York, Columbia University Press, 2017); Suwandi, Value Chains.

36 Norfield, *The City*, p. 183–4.

37 Norfield, *The City*, p. 155.

38 Panitch and Gindin, *The Making of Global Capitalism*, p. 336.

39 Panitch and Gindin, *The Making of Global Capitalism*, p. 287.

40 Panitch and Gindin, *The Making of Global Capitalism*, p. 336.

41 Panitch and Gindin, *The Making of Global Capitalism*, p. 337.

42 Smith, *Imperialism in the Twenty-First Century*.

43 Smith, *Imperialism in the Twenty-First Century*, p. 239. For Smith, 'global

labor arbitrage – super-exploitation – that is, forcing down the value of labor-power, the third form of surplus value increase, is now the increasingly pre-dominant form of the capital-labour relation' (p. 250).

44 Smith, *Imperialism in the Twenty-First Century*, p. 250.
45 Smith, *Imperialism in the Twenty-First Century*, p. 228.
46 Smith, *Imperialism in the Twenty-First Century*, pp. 225–6.
47 Smith, *Imperialism in the Twenty-First Century*, pp. 205, 217, 222.
48 Smith, *Imperialism in the Twenty-First Century*, pp. 230, 34.
49 Smith, *Imperialism in the Twenty-First Century*, pp. 230, 34 (emphasis added).
50 Smith, *Imperialism in the Twenty-First Century*, p. 240.
51 Smith, *Imperialism in the Twenty-First Century*, p. 84.
52 A. Emmanuel, *Unequal Exchange: A Study of Imperialism in Trade* (New York and London, Monthly Review, 1972), p. 135.
53 Smith, *Imperialism in the Twenty-First Century*, p. 86.
54 Smith, *Imperialism in the Twenty-First Century*, pp. 225, 235.
55 Smith, *Imperialism in the Twenty-First Century*, p. 50.
56 Except for deviation according to *prices of production* – see Marx, *Capital*, vol. 3, chaps 8–10.

4

The idea of China as a rising threat

It is an undeniable fact that contemporary China has risen in many highly important senses. Its weight in world trade and the increased income and consumption are obvious examples. It is also a fact that the emergence of Chinese competition has bankrupted certain individual capitals in the First World and made certain lines of production unviable in the imperialist world or parts of it. Some weakest First World capitalists who could neither exploit the dynamic of offshoring and labour specialisation to their own advantage, nor transition to other production spheres, went bankrupt. It is this dying or redundant capital, and the destruction of sections of the working class tied to it – in some cases whole communities or regions – that form a solid social basis for the rising China discourse inside the imperialist countries. There are also sections of capital, or more often labour, that are bankrupt or redundant for reasons that have nothing or little to do with China, but – reflecting the dominant anti-China ideas – they view their decline as being caused by China's so-called rise.

Capital that is being suffocated perhaps has a natural affinity for hyperbolic discourse against competitors. For weakest imperialist capital locked out of globalisation and bankrupted by it, the changes appear simply as a loss of production to overseas competition, especially to China. The history of racist nationalism in the imperialist working classes has made many workers receptive to such ideas. The rising China idea enjoys a broad following among every stratum within the imperialist societies.

Pew Research Center's spring 2018 Global Attitudes Survey asked, 'How serious a problem is the loss of US jobs to China?' Some 83 per cent of the US-based respondents rated this as either somewhat serious (32 per cent) or very serious (51 per cent). Somewhat or very serious was also how 82 per cent of respondents rated the US bilateral trade deficit with China. Fully 89 per cent of respondents said the same about Chinese ownership of US debt. Some 88 per cent believe it is 'better if the US, not China, is the world's leading power'.[1]

The spread of capitalist commodity production in China and across much of the Third World roughly coincides with the period of neoliberalism internationally. Thus the period of 'offshoring' and its associated job losses for workers in the imperialist economies coincides historically with other deprivations inflicted on working classes inside the rich countries in the neoliberal period. For this reason, some of the attacks on the living standards of First World working people carried out by their capitalist rulers can be falsely presented as an inevitable part of imperial decline and China's rise.

Rising China discourse helps undermine labour confidence and organisation inside imperialist states. Capital's political representatives can plausibly deny responsibility for declining living conditions of affected communities. These are presented as necessary to ward off the threat to national or regional competitiveness. The phenomenon is not new. Marchlewski argued in 1904 that 'the "decline of British industry" has become a slogan for the imperialist agitators to bait the masses. For England's working class, the decline of English industry would undoubtedly be a fearful danger, and that is why the slogan is very dangerous.'[2] The same is true today, except that imperialism is not declining in relation to the Third World. Yet the political danger is clear. The response of many workers to capitalist austerity in the neoliberal period has been not to seek to replace capitalism, but to rally around the flag under right or left protectionist programmes such as those of Trump, Sanders or Johnson.

The rising China discourse and the confidence it projects in the prospects of Third World capitalist development also lends implicit ideological support to Third World capitalist ruling classes and their political representatives such as Xi Jinping, Modi and Duterte, who present themselves as leaders of national revival against imperialist domination and national shame, or at least as the architects of social progress.

As Starrs points out, 'it has become a staple of conventional wisdom that global economic power is shifting inexorably towards the East and the South'.[3] Because the other supposed contenders have fallen away, attention now falls principally on one place – China. The *New York Times*, for example, casually refers to 'the industrial might of an emerging superpower'[4] – of course this is China – while the Hong Kong-based *South China Morning Post*, a little closer to the action, trips up on contradictory language, like arguing 'the nation seeks to catch up as a technology leader'.[5]

It is the overwhelming view, among mainstream commentators, that China is rising in a way that is somehow imperialist or ultimately will challenge the imperialist monopoly on wealth and power.[6] Most First World Marxist writing sees China as either 'a new imperial power', as Ashley Smith puts it, or developing in that direction.[7] As Panitch and Gindin pointed out,

Given the severity and duration of the latest crisis [i.e. 2008–9] in a global capitalist economy that the American state had been so central in constructing, it was hardly surprising to see a resurgence of pronouncements that US hegemony was coming to an end ... [because] pundits of every persuasion once again blur the lines between a capitalist crisis and a decline of US empire.[8]

The virtual consensus brings together thinkers who are opponents on other issues. For Callinicos and Probsting, China today parallels late nineteenth- to early twentieth-century Germany.[9] Petras et al., echoing Harvey, perceive a 'shift in economic power from North America and Western Europe towards Asia – China and India'.[10] Foster and McChesney detect a 'declining hegemony' of US power vis-à-vis China.[11] 'The relative "deindustrialization" in the Global North is now too clear a tendency to be altogether denied.'[12] Norfield suggests that 'China presents a far more important challenge to the US domination of the world economy and world finance than do European countries'.[13] For Amin, in 2010, 'the crisis *of the late imperialist countries* of generalized, financialized, and globalized oligopolies is patent ... [while] the ruling classes of the Southern states – or at least of those of them termed "emerging" – have regained the initiative and entered into accelerated industrialization and agricultural "modernization".'[14] Wood and Callinicos present their own view of China's rise as consistent with Lenin's. They suggest China's rise as an imperialist power will trigger inter-imperialist conflict or war with the United States – supposedly fulfilling Lenin's expectation.[15] Yet nowhere does Lenin predict the rise of a former colonial country to the rank of imperialist power. He does say that in the *pre-monopoly* era, Germany and the United States were able to surpass Britain. But to equate the nineteenth century with China in the twenty-first is to equate pre-monopoly conditions with monopoly – hardly Lenin's argument.

Roberts considers the Chinese economy possesses 'good long-term catch-up potential' – though he says it is not capitalist.[16] Other writers, such as Long et al. view China as 'market socialist', or socialist.[17]

The perception of US decline is an ongoing theme. Brewer claimed in 1990 that 'US hegemony in the capitalist world is clearly over'.[18] Ferrer argued in 1979 that the bargaining position of underdeveloped countries had improved while power among the imperialist states had been dispersed.[19] She was predated by Warren's 1973 article, among many others, that made similar arguments.[20] By the 1980s, it was already a mainstream idea that the United States was in decline.[21] Among Marxists too, by the mid-1980s it had become 'commonplace' to assume that 'the erosion of American economic, political, and military power [was] unmistakable'.[22]

Hung draws a parallel between contemporary China boosters and eighteenth-century enlightenment intellectuals whose infatuation with China 'reflected cursory, exotic, and sometimes deliberately distorted information about China', while 'the latest celebration of the Chinese miracle [has] been informed by superficial understanding of China's political economy'.[23] Inside China itself, he says, 'the prospect of endless economic growth has long been offset by anxiety about a looming economic crisis'.[24]

China's rise as an imperialist power would be historically unprecedented in the imperialist era. It would demand a detailed and clear analysis of its causes, precise character and significance. However, there is no well-known Marxist attempt to do this. Typically, China's supposed rise is simply noted in passing with a brief unsubstantiated assertion. Or even just implied, such as in Suwandi and Foster's comment that 'much of the most advanced production – is now being carried out in the global South'.[25] I can find No Marxist who explores in detail what China's supposed new imperialist or elevated status means or how it got there.

Perhaps the closest any work comes to that is a section of Norfield's valuable book on imperialism and finance. Norfield argues that China is the world's third imperialist power, behind the United States and the United Kingdom. This is based on aggregate statistics indicating economic size and financial and military assets but not detailed analysis of China or its role in the international labour division.[26] Norfield's country ranking system does not make a qualitative assessment of production, military effectiveness or even the relative strength of financial assets held – though he does the latter elsewhere in his book. The five criteria are the size of a country's economy, its ownership of foreign assets, the international prominence of its banking sector, the status of its currency in foreign exchange trading and its level of military spending.

For others, the basic argument among those who consider China capitalist seems to boil down to rehashing Warren's position: all capitalist growth ultimately points towards advanced capitalism. Therefore a lot of growth – as in China – will ultimately equal very advanced capitalism (i.e. imperialism).

Against this dominant view, important Marxist or Marxian China experts like Zhang, Hung, Starrs and Nolan are far more cautious. Nolan's powerful 2012 book and the work of Starrs are among the most important. Panitch, Gindin and Ahmad also reject the rising China thesis, if briefly.[27] Notably there is no well-known Marxist China expert writing in English from the rising China perspective. There is a complete dichotomy between the views of China coming from area specialists compared to others.

Callinicos's 2009 book proceeds by asserting China's rise as a given: 'One has only to utter the word "China" to indicate what's wrong with the Third Worldist understanding of Imperialism.'[28] His justification, given two hundred pages later, boils down to aggregate GDP size and annual rate of GDP growth. Callinicos refers to China's then 'average annual growth rate of 8–10 per cent for thirty years'.[29] He adds, 'five out of the fifteen biggest economies in the world in 2007 were in the global South'.[30] However, given that thirteen of the fifteen biggest states by population are in the Global South, this is hardly surprising.

Conflating the spread of capitalist commodity production with a new imperialism represents the principal concrete manifestation of Marxian adaption to Warren's version of modernisation theory. Aggregate GDP, annual growth of GDP and the aggregate size of China's economy are examples of quantitative growth of capitalist commodity production but do not reveal the concrete function of Chinese labour within the international labour division – nor its prospects.

Harman claimed that 'there can be no argument about the massive industrial growth of China. Since 1978 China's growth rate has been 9.5 percent.'[31] Notice how Harman here conflates GDP growth (i.e. growth of capitalist commodity production in general) with *industrial* production. When Harman tells us, 'the vast industrial developments around Shanghai have few comparisons in Western Europe',[32] we are left to imagine in what specific ways these are incomparable, or indeed comparable. For Harman, apparently, their greater size was awesome enough to demonstrate superiority.[33]

A variation of the 'capitalism equals imperialism' outlook is the argument that foreign investment equals imperialism. Probsting comments that 'one of the most important characteristics of an imperialist bourgeoisie is its formation of monopolies which export capital. Indeed such a development happened in China during the last decade.'[34] But today foreign direct investment (FDI) is a common trait not just of China but of even the poorest Third World economies. Papua New Guinea, Guatemala and Timor Leste all engage in FDI.[35]

It might be assumed from the preceding chapters that contemporary First World Marxist scholars got nothing right. That is not the argument made here. The reviews prove only that contemporary work has not yet accounted for the current world polarisation or explained how capitalist imperialism reproduces itself. This crucial shortcoming is necessary to point out clearly and should not be papered over. In doing so, the chapters engaged principally with what authors are seen to have got wrong. For that reason it is likely they presented an incomplete and distorted picture of the authors that appeared.

Other aspects of imperialism such as debt dependency, trade policy, environmental plunder, foreign aid, the role of multilateral institutions, political intrigue and war are addressed in works not discussed here. These are important. But all of these aspects, even in combination, cannot adequately explain imperialism's continued dominance. For that we need to look at its most central and essential mechanism, one that is also at the centre of

Marxist theory – imperialist monopoly in the labour process – and this has not been systematically addressed in recent work. Its omission is the reason there is no adequate contemporary theory of imperialism and why we do not yet know how the rich countries rule.

Notes

1 K. Devlin, 'Americans Leery of China as Trump Prepares to Meet Xi at G20', *Pew Research* (2018), 30 November.

2 J. B. Marchlewski, 'English Imperialism', *Leipziger Volkszeitung*, 240 (1904), cited in R. B. Day and D. Gaido (eds), *Discovering Imperialism: Social Democracy to World War I* (Chicago, Haymarket, 2012), p. 305.

3 S. Starrs, 'The Chimera of Global Convergence', *New Left Review*, 87 (2014).

4 K. Bradsher, 'China's New Jetliner, the Comac C919, Takes Flight for First Time', *New York Times* (2017), 5 May.

5 M. Jing, C. Chen and J. Cai, 'China Calls on Private Sector to Beef Up Investment in Basic Science as It Seeks to Become Tech Powerhouse', *South China Morning Post* (2019), 11 March.

6 *Fortune* ran a cover 'China Buys the World', with the subhead: 'The Chinese Have $2 Trillion and Are Going Shopping. Is your Company – and Your Country – On Their List?' *Fortune*, 160:8 (2009). See also K. Mahbubani, 'While America Slept: How the United States Botched China's Rise', *Foreign Policy* (2013), 27 February; M. Fisher and A. Carlsen, 'How China Is Challenging American Dominance in Asia', *New York Times* (2018), 9 March; E. Wong, 'U.S. Versus China: A New Era of Great Power Competition, But Without Boundaries', *New York Times* (2019), 26, June.

7 For example, Smith, 'Deal or No Deal'; J. Lees, 'Australian Imperialism in an Era of US–China Tensions', *Red Flag* (2019), 8 August; R. Delizo, 'US Imperialist Aggression in the Early 21st Century', *Links* (2010) 27 November; McNally, 'Understanding Imperialism'; B. Fine, 'Debating the New Imperialism', *Historical Materialism*, 14:4 (2006), 133–56; M. Probsting, *The Great Robbery of the South: Continuity and Changes in the Super-Exploitation of the Semi-Colonial World by Monopoly Capital. Consequences for the Marxist Theory of Imperialism* (Vienna, Revolutionary Communist International Tendency, 2013), pp. 248, 255–63, 289.

8 Panitch and Gindin, *The Making of Global Capitalism*, p. 331.

9 M. Probsting, 'China's Emergence as an Imperialist Power', *New Politics*, 15:57 (2014), 102; Callinicos, *Imperialism and Global Political Economy*, p. 220.

10 J. Petras and H. Veltmeyer, *Imperialism and Capitalism in the Twenty-First Century: A System in Crisis* [2013] (New York, Routledge, 2016), p. 212; Petras, 'Rising and Declining Economic Powers', p. 118; A. Smith, 'Obama's New Imperialist Strategy', *International Socialist Review*, 83 (2012); C. Fuchs, 'Critical Globalization Studies and the New Imperialism', *Critical Sociology*, 36:6 (2010), 864.

11 J. B. Foster and R. W. McChesney, *The Endless Crisis: How Monopoly-Finance Capital Produces Stagnation and Upheaval from the USA to China* (New York, Monthly Review, 2012), p. 16.

12 Foster et al., 'The Global Reserve Army'; M. Itoh, 'Unequal Exchange Reconsidered in Our Age of Globalization' [talk presented at the Rebellious Macroeconomics: Marx, Keynes and Crotty Conference, Amherst, MA, Political Economy Research Institute], (2007), p. 11–12; R. Rowthorn, and R. Ramaswany, 'Deindustrialization: Causes and Implications', *IMF Working Paper 97/42* (1997); J. Narayan and L. Sealey-Huggins, 'Whatever Happened to the Idea of Imperialism?' *Third World Quarterly*, 38:11 (2017), 2390.

13 Norfield, *The City*, p. 17.

14 S. Amin, *The Law of Worldwide Value* (New York, Monthly Review, 2010), pp. 125, 108 (emphasis added). Chinese threat to imperialism is also perceived by Day and Gaido, *Discovering Imperialism*, p. 93; G. Achcar, 'Rethinking Imperialism: Past, Present and Future', *International Socialism*, 2:126 (2010); Wood, *Empire of Capital*, pp. 156–7; P. Gowan, 'Industrial Development and International Political Conflict in Contemporary Capitalism', in A. Anievas (ed.), *Marxism and World Politics* (New York, Taylor and Francis, 2012), p. 142.

15 Wood, *Empire of Capital*, p. 126; Callinicos, *Imperialism and Global Political Economy*, pp. 207–8.

16 M. Roberts, *The Long Depression: Marxism and the Global Crisis of Capitalism* (Chicago, Haymarket, 2016), p. 215; M. Roberts, 'Xi Takes Full Control of China's Future', *Michael Roberts Blog* (2017), 25 October, https://thenextre-cession.wordpress.com/2017/10/25/xi-takes-full-control-of-chinas-future/.

17 Z. Long, R. Herrera and T. Andréani, 'On the Nature of the Chinese Economic System', *Monthly Review*, 72:5 (2018).

18 Brewer, *Marxist Theories*, p. 282.

19 A. Ferrer, 'Notas de una Theoria de la Dependencia', *Comercio Exterior*, 29:8, 1979, cited in Kay, *Latin American Theories*, p. 183.

20 Warren, 'Imperialism and Capitalist Industrialization'.

21 For example, P. Kennedy, *The Rise and Fall of the Great Powers: Economic Change and Military Conflict from 1500 to 2000* (London, Vintage, 1989).

22 Panitch and Gindin, *The Making of Global Capitalism*, p. 3. The issue was already significant enough that Grossman felt the need to comment in 1929 that 'far from signifying the impending doom of European capitalism, as Hildebrand and others forecast, the industrialisation of the more backward countries signifies an expansion of world exports'. H. Grossman, *The Law of the Accumulation and Breakdown: Being Also a Theory of Crises* [1929], trans. J. Banaji (London, Pluto, 1991), chap. 3.

23 H. Hung, 'Sinomania: Global Crisis, China's Crisis?' *Socialist Register*, 48 (2012), 217.

24 Hung, 'Sinomania', p. 217; H. Hung, *The China Boom: Why China Will Not Rule the World* (New York, Colombia University Press, 2015).

25 Suwandi and Foster, 'Multinational Corporations'; Smith, *Imperialism in the Twenty-First Century*, pp. 49, 85.

26 Norfield's 'world hierarchy' of imperialist nations views China as the world number three behind only the United States and Great Britain. See Norfield, *The City*, p. 111.

27 Panitch and Gindin, *The Making of Global Capitalism*, p. xi; A. Ahmad, 'Imperialism of Our Time', *Socialist Register*, 40 (2004), 51. Brenner considered only other rich countries as competitors to the United States. See R. Brenner, *The Boom and the Bubble: The US in the World Economy* (London, Verso, 2002), p. 61.

28 Callinicos, *Imperialism and Global Political Economy*, p. 5.

29 Callinicos, *Imperialism and Global Political Economy*, p. 210.

30 Callinicos, *Imperialism and Global Political Economy*, p. 210; Achcar, 'Rethinking Imperialism'.

31 C. Harman, 'China's Economy and Europe's Crisis', *International Socialism*, 2:109 (2006).

32 Harman, 'China's Economy and Europe's Crisis'; Harman, *Zombie Capitalism*, p. 243.

33 Saull, by contrast, at least poses the question of the 'material basis of American hegemony'. See R. Saull, 'Rethinking Hegemony: Uneven Development, Historical Blocs, and the World Economic Crisis', *International Studies Quarterly*, 56 (2012), 324.

34 Probsting, *Great Robbery of the South*, p. 264; F. Chesnais, 'The Economic Foundations of Contemporary Imperialism', *Historical Materialism*, 15:3 (2007), 125; G. Bailey, 'Accumulation by Dispossession: A Critical Assessment', *International Socialist Review*, 95 (2014–15).

35 UNCTAD, *World Investment Report 2017* (New York and Geneva, 2017), pp. 226–8.

Part III

Lenin's theory of imperialism and its
contemporary application

5

What Lenin's book does *not* say

The word 'imperialism' came into popular usage in Europe to describe the intensified 'carving up' of Africa and Asia by the European powers. This scramble for colonies and increasing inter-state rivalry were the main development in international politics from the mid-1880s, culminating in the outbreak of the First World War.

Profound social and material changes in capitalism and the crises this transition provoked provided the social conditions that made Lenin's study possible and necessary. It is usual for pivotal scientific work to emerge out of profound crisis. Marxists defend the relevance of Marx's major works on the basis that important scientific work will have a lasting value for its subject. However, Lenin's classical Marxist work on imperialism has not been offered the same defence inside the rich countries.

Lenin aimed to give a Marxist explanation of the cause of this change that could stand against competing bourgeois or reformist explanations. These tended to view imperialism as a policy of military aggression, colonialism or war, which was counterposed to another possible policy – a return to supposedly freely competitive capitalism or some form of it, or to a more peaceful 'ultra-imperialism'. Arguing at the time against the principal rival socialist explanation, given by leading German Social Democrat Karl Kautsky, Lenin argued that 'Kautsky detaches the politics of imperialism from its economics'.[1] Against this, Lenin argued imperialist aggression was an inherent tendency of the capitalist system in its new form. 'Monopoly finance capital' (which he variously abbreviated as 'monopoly capital', 'finance capital' or simply 'imperialism') was the key concept Lenin advanced.[2]

With the onset of the First World War, the Social Democratic movement lurched to the right and split. An overwhelming majority of socialist leaders and workers in Europe supported their own governments' war efforts. This completely divided workers along nationalist lines, isolating Lenin and his co-thinkers as a tiny minority. That every major Social Democratic Party split along similar lines indicated the phenomenon must have been grounded in a powerful material basis within the capitalism of the period.

Contra Harvey's depiction, Lenin was aware that no amount of 'pamphleteering' (i.e. agitation), against the political leadership of this great class-collaborationist wave could have any hope of success unless it was well grounded in an accurate appraisal of the underlying material-social basis of the phenomenon. It would also need to outline a course of action for the working class that was equally based in material-social realities. Such an accurate assessment of material realities is what Lenin aimed to achieve in his theoretical study of imperialism. To this end, in 1915–16 he undertook a systematic study of bourgeois and Marxist sources related to imperialism, concurrently with extensive study of Marxist philosophy and political economy.

In doing so, Lenin had three political objectives: prove that the First World War was 'an annexationist, predatory war of plunder on the part of both sides';[3] prove that Kautsky's theoretical arguments were 'obscuring the profundity of the contradictions of imperialism and the inevitable revolutionary crisis to which it gives rise';[4] and show a 'causal connection' between the new imperialist stage of capitalism and the emergence of a 'relatively stable opportunist, pro-imperialist, trend within the working-class movement of the "advanced" capitalist countries'.[5] Lenin sought to achieve the first two objectives by proving the scientific validity of the concept of 'monopoly finance capital' as capitalism's highest and last possible stage.[6]

Lenin's manner of expressing theoretical conclusions in *Imperialism* is highly cautious. Only the most abstract, essential characteristics of the imperialist system – such as monopoly, parasitism, decay, exploitation, continuing commodity production, political reaction and increasingly acute social contradiction and conflict – were stated as essential features. His method involves considering in detail the concrete totality of the multiple and sometimes contradictory tendencies of his own time to arrive at a 'composite picture' of the system. The contemporary reader wishing to use Lenin's work as a tool to help understand our own period therefore finds no ready answers. Rather it is necessary to draw another composite picture, a contemporary one, based on new concrete study. *Imperialism* provides only a general guide for that study. As Kemp noted, Lenin's 'claims are modest and carefully qualified'.[7]

This cautious manner perhaps disappoints many modern readers. Lenin's opponents mistake it as 'untheoretical' or 'almost meaningless logically', etc., as outlined.[8] But had Lenin attempted to draw more *specific* conclusions about the nature of imperialism beyond what he considered incontrovertibly proven (i.e. had he made guesses), the work would likely have suffered from the wrong generalisations of contemporary conditions that afflicts, for example, aspects of Bukharin's work (see Chapter 7).

Given the substantial posse of Marxist writers and academic specialists who have for decades declared Lenin's *Imperialism* to be wrong and anti-quated, it could be expected that countless errors and wrong expectations would have been uncovered in the text. Yet no such list appears to exist. Lenin's opponents have discovered no categorical, wrong prediction or per-spective. In place of that, various caricatures are popularised and repeated. Most commonly it is argued that Lenin viewed colonialism as a necessary form of imperialist domination, that *Imperialism* is 'all about' capital export or else that he was wrong to characterise imperialism as capitalism's high-est stage.

Lenin's key working concept – monopoly finance capital – is also rou-tinely caricatured. Critiques ostensibly aimed at Lenin in fact use contem-porary writers' own understandings of those words. Typically the word monopoly is dropped so 'finance capital' can be presented in various ways inconsistent with Lenin, but reflecting contemporary views influenced by 'financialisation' (Chapter 6). Where monopoly is mentioned, this often involves the assumption that it is counterposed to competition, or, as for Sweezy, Shaikh and Smith, counterposed to Marx's law of value.

The same is true for the widespread rejection of Lenin's view of imperi-alism as capitalism's highest stage. Most writers do not see that Lenin's concept of a 'highest stage' of capitalism is taken directly from volume 3 of Marx's *Capital*. It tends to be erroneously viewed instead as simple agita-tion or as a prediction of imminent capitalist collapse. It will be shown that Lenin's 'monopoly finance capital' in fact sticks closely to the framework established by Marx in *Capital*. Thus, while theoretically formulating the arrival of a new capitalist epoch, Lenin's work is one of orthodox Marxism.

Lenin's central concept – monopoly finance capital – and his detailed concrete elaboration of this concept, especially in chapter 1 of *Imperialism*, shows two things. First, that monopoly over the labour process is the most essential basis of monopoly in general. Second, that imperialism's monopoly must ultimately remain capitalist in form and therefore involves the capit-alist production of commodities for the market. This dual essence of Lenin's work gives it a powerful explanatory power that is relevant to many crucial modern phenomena, as will be outlined.

Imperialism also articulates or strongly anticipates a range of important phenomena so well known today that many are now taken for granted. These include the increasing domination of monopolies, the rise of what have now become MNCs, the increasing importance of finance capital, the confluence between the state and capital, the increasing role of the state, the transition of the bourgeoisie to a *wholly* parasitic class and the consolida-tion of a labour aristocracy in the imperialist countries. However, because

Imperialism has been so maligned for so long, before examining what it says, it is necessary to first clarify what it does not say.

To begin to peel back some of the layers preventing Lenin's book from seeing much daylight, it is necessary to counter directly some common caricatures and refute these with direct quotations from Lenin's writings.

Export of capital

Among the most pervasive caricatures of Lenin's work is the view that it is *predominantly* about the export of capital, or what is today called foreign investment. The overwhelming majority of writers from the 1970s onwards, especially those opposed to Lenin's theory, subscribe to this view.[9] Where evidence is given, it is usually a single isolated quotation without discussion about how capital export fits into Lenin's broader theory. I cannot find any writer who *shows* how exactly 'capital export' forms the centrepiece of Lenin's theory or even how it fits within his theory.

Kidron popularised attacks on Lenin on this basis in the 1960s. He made, for example, the unsubstantiated claim that Lenin thought 'capital exports were the prime index of modern capitalism'.[10] Kidron argued, 'In broadest outline, Lenin's thesis was that capitalism's maturity compels it to export capital on a large scale'.[11] Kiernan also saw capital export as the 'entire thesis' advanced by Lenin.[12] Barrat-Brown tells us Lenin had argued that 'it is the export of capital that is typical of monopoly capitalism and that requires the division and redivision of the world'.[13] For Shaikh, 'The export of capital is the lynchpin of [the Marxist] theory of imperialism'.[14] Warren makes the unattributed claim, 'Lenin held that imperialism was essentially an economic relationship governed by the necessity for capital export',[15] defining Lenin's theory as 'the over-ripe, capital-export theory of imperialism'.[16] Howard and King argue that 'the entire Leninist conception of imperialism as a stage of capitalism [was] dominated by export of capital',[17] which was 'among the weakest aspects of accepted theory'.[18]

Callinicos, without reference, claims, 'the picture that Lenin had painted [was] of an imperialist system based on the export of capital to the colonies'.[19] Panitch and Gindin say that 'early 20th-century theories of imperialism' saw export of capital as itself imperialist.[20] Contemporary *defenders* of Lenin's theory, Clarke and Annis, have adopted the position that capital export represents 'the quintessential imperialist activity'.[21]

Export of capital was and remains *one* indispensable and characteristic feature of imperialism. However it is not 'the lynchpin' of Lenin's theory. In outlining his 'conditional and relative' list of five 'basic features' of imperialism, it is monopoly, not capital export, which appears at the core of all five. Export of capital is not first, but third on the list, which is ordered causally. Each of the five features is the subject of one of the ten chapters in Lenin's book. The chapter entitled 'Export of Capital' is the shortest of all, containing fewer than 1,500 words (compared with 15,000 words devoted to explaining the concentration of capital and formation of finance capital).[22] Elsewhere, Lenin gives the 'briefest possible definition of imperialism' not as 'capital export'. Rather, 'imperialism is the monopoly stage of capitalism. Such a definition would include what is most important'.[23]

In the chapter entitled 'The Parasitism and Decay of Capitalism', Lenin argues that 'the export of capital, [is] *one of* the most essential economic bases of imperialism'.[24] In 'The Place of Imperialism in History', Lenin's only reference to capital export is this sentence: 'To the numerous "old" motives of colonial policy, finance capital has added the struggle for the sources of raw materials, for the export of capital, for spheres of influence, i.e., for spheres for profitable deals, concessions, monopoly profits and so on, *economic territory in general*.'[25] Capital export had greatly accelerated in Lenin's time. For this reason, it was a point of emphasis not only for Lenin but for most Marxists writing about imperialism before the First World War, as can be seen in multiple instances published by Day and Gaido's compilation.[26] Karski, for example, argued that 'capital exports have become *the most important* economic means for the conquest of the world by capital'.[27]

In debating revisions to the Bolsheviks' programme in 1917, Lenin emphatically rejected the idea that export of capital is *the* central question in understanding imperialism. He opposed a change to the programme proposed by Sokolnikov that would have defined imperialism principally as 'export of capital'. In Lenin's view, 'we must begin with the characterisation of imperialism as a whole – and in that case we must not single out only the "export of capital" ', complaining that 'comrade Sokolnikov inserted *a bit* of the definition of imperialism (the export of capital)'.[28]

True, capital export is a principal *example* given in *Imperialism* of exploitation of the colonies. However, this may have been simply that it was convenient as an example, because one can find figures in bourgeois sources stating the magnitude of imperialist profits on this basis. Unlike unequal exchange, capital export is visible. As a way to prove the exploitative character of the imperialist economies, against opportunist indifference, capital export provided a clear case.

If profits on capital exports and 'coupon clipping' (bonds) represented the principal or most transparent form of imperialist exploitation in Lenin's era, then he was more than justified in emphasising these. Lenin's work (and Bukharin's) also emphasise the particular role of capital export in the initial establishment and early development of capitalist relations of production abroad – an important point in imperialism's early career. Lenin argued, 'It is particularly important to examine the part which the export of capital plays in creating the international network of dependence and connections of finance capital'.[29] As Lenin says, 'The export of capital thus becomes a means of encouraging the export of commodities'.[30]

Colonialism

Falsely presenting Lenin as having thought imperialism synonymous with colonialism, Kidron argued, 'Taking Lenin's "last stage" literally, colonial independence and the continuation of capitalism are incompatible. And yet we have both – in increasing quantities. Moreover, opposition to colonial independence, has had in most cases little of the spirit of the "last ditch stand" one would expect from a society fighting for its existence.'[31] In his influential 1979 survey, *Theories of Underdevelopment*, Roxborough, too, incorrectly claims Lenin saw a 'necessary connection between colonies and monopoly capital'.[32] The following year, Warren claimed 'the theory of imperialism as elaborated by Lenin in 1916 had stressed that the entire system of exploitation on which modern (i.e. monopoly) capitalism was based rested on colonial exploitation'.[33] A decade later, in their seminal work, *A History of Marxian Economic Thought*, Howard and King repeated the claim Lenin saw colonialism as vital for imperialism.[34]

For Callinicos, 'the picture that Lenin had painted [was] of an imperialist system based on the export of capital to the colonies'.[35] Panitch and Gindin argue that 'early 20th-century theories of imperialism' did not understand the importance of informal empire.[36] Ghosh thought Lenin took colonialism as a given.[37] In a welcome exception, Foster, following Magdoff, acknowledges Lenin did *not* see formal political control as necessary for imperialism.[38]

It is true Lenin emphasised colonialism as one important aspect of imperialism, and in his era this was both justified and common.[39] However, if he had viewed colonies as necessary to imperialism he probably would have said so. Notably, in his famous five features provisionally defining imperialism, 'colonialism' is not mentioned. The fifth feature, which does not refer only to colonialism, is this: '(5) the territorial division of the whole world among the biggest capitalist powers is completed'.

In the corresponding chapter, Lenin wrote: 'Finance capital is such a great, such a decisive, you might say, force in all economic and in all international relations, that it is capable of subjecting, and actually does subject, to itself even states enjoying the fullest political independence.'[40] Lenin uses the term, 'division of the world', which is evidently interpreted by some contemporary readers as denoting colonialism. However, as Lenin himself notes, the term was in fact the prevailing term in bourgeois economic literature of his time:

> Since we are speaking of colonial policy in the epoch of capitalist imperialism, it must be observed that finance capital and its foreign policy, which is the struggle of the great powers for the economic and political division of the world, give rise to a number of transitional forms of state dependence. Not only are the two main groups of countries, those owning colonies, and the colonies themselves, but also the diverse forms of dependent countries which, politically, are formally independent, but in fact, are enmeshed in the net of financial and diplomatic dependence, typical of this epoch. We have already referred to one form of dependence – the semi-colony. An example of another is provided by Argentina ... A somewhat different form of financial and diplomatic dependence, accompanied by political independence, is presented by Portugal.[41]

Lenin opposed the view of Bukharin and others that national self-determination is impossible under imperialism. He says:

> It would be no less mistaken to delete any of the points of the democratic programme, for example, the point of self-determination of nations, on the ground that it is 'infeasible', or that it is 'illusory' under imperialism. The assertion that the right of nations to self-determination cannot be achieved within the framework of capitalism ... is fundamentally wrong in theory ... it would be ridiculous to deny that, with a slight change in political and strategical relationships, for example, between Germany and England, the formation of new states, Polish, Indian, etc., would be quite 'feasible' very soon ... finance capital, in its striving towards expansion, will 'freely' buy and bribe the freest, most democratic and republican government and the elected officials of any country, however 'independent' it may be.[42]

For Lenin,

> The imperialist tendency towards big empires is fully achievable, and in practice is often achieved, in the form of an imperialist alliance of sovereign and independent – politically independent – states.

> Norway 'achieved' the supposedly unachievable right to self-determination in 1905, in the era of the most rampant imperialism. It is therefore not only absurd, but ludicrous, from the theoretical standpoint, to speak of 'unachievability' ... British finance capital was 'at work' in Norway before and after secession. German finance capital was 'at work' in Poland prior to her secession from Russia and will continue to 'work' there no matter what political status Poland enjoys. That is so elementary that it is embarrassing to have to repeat it. But what can one do if the ABC is forgotten?[43]

It is worth quoting further due to the accuracy with which Lenin's insights on this question anticipated much later developments.

> National struggle, national insurrection, national secession are fully 'achievable' and are met with in practice under imperialism. They are even more pronounced, for imperialism does not halt the development of capitalism and the growth of democratic tendencies among the mass of the population. On the contrary, it accentuates the antagonism between their democratic aspirations and the anti-democratic tendency of the trusts.[44]

> [Yet] The domination of finance capital, as of capital in general, cannot be abolished by any kind of reforms in the realm of political democracy, and self-determination belongs wholly and exclusively to this realm.[45]

> The imperialist era does not destroy either the striving for national political independence or its 'achievability' within the bounds of world imperialist relationships. Outside these bounds, however, a republican Russia, or in general any major democratic transformations anywhere else in the world are 'unachievable' without a series of revolutions and are unstable without socialism.[46]

Supporting such a revolutionary (bourgeois-democratic) course, Lenin wrote that socialists must 'demand the unconditional and immediate liberation of the colonies without compensation – and this demand in its political expression signifies nothing more nor less than the recognition of the right to self-determination'.[47] Far from being refuted by achievement of national independence, Lenin's perspective clearly anticipated and strongly supported the anti-colonial revolutions that occurred in India, China, Indonesia and elsewhere after the second inter-imperialist world war.

This chapter, by quoting Lenin's writing, has already taken a hammer to two of the most pervasive and long-held misconceptions preventing contemporary thinkers from reading and engaging Lenin's work. But besides capital export and colonialism there is another major aspect of Lenin's work commonly seen as evidence that Lenin was wrong. Showing that imperialism is capitalism's 'highest and last possible stage' – while easily caricatured – represented a major theoretical breakthrough with far-reaching implications for clarifying crucial contemporary issues – especially so-called financialisation. Undoubtedly among the slipperiest theoretical problems of the modern economy, financialisation seems really able to be clarified only with reference to how the issue is dealt with at the dawn of finance capital. One little known aspect is that the concept of capitalism's highest stage is not original to *Imperialism*. This and financialisation are both concepts that are clearly taken from volume 3 of Marx's *Capital*.

Notes

1 Lenin, *Imperialism*, chap. 7.
2 Lenin gave little importance to which words were used to designate the new period, so long as their meaning was clear: 'The argument about words which Kautsky raises as to whether the latest stage of capitalism should be called imperialism or the stage of finance capital is not worth serious attention. Call it what you will, it makes no difference'. Lenin, *Imperialism*, chap. 7.
3 Lenin, preface to the French and German editions of *Imperialism* [1920].
4 Lenin, *Imperialism*, preface [1920].
5 Lorimer in Lenin, *Imperialism* [1999], pp. 8–9.
6 The third claim – that of the labour aristocracy – is also derived from the monopoly super-profits made possible on this basis.
7 Kemp, 'The Marxist Theory of Imperialism', in Owen and Sutcliffe, *Studies in the Theory of Imperialism*, p. 27.
8 Warren, *Imperialism*, p. 71; Brewer, *Marxist Theories*, p. 116; Callinicos, *Imperialism and Global Political Economy*, p. 43.
9 Even writers sympathetic to Lenin appear to take for granted the received view that Lenin saw capital export as the most fundamental aspect of his theory. For example, see Smith, *Imperialism in the Twenty-First Century*, p. 232.
10 M. Kidron, 'Imperialism, Highest Stage But One', *International Socialism*, 1:9 (1962).
11 Kidron, 'Highest Stage But One'. A mainstream version of the same attack on Lenin written the previous year in almost identical terms. See D. K. Fieldhouse, '"Imperialism": An Historiographical Revision', *Economic History Review*, 14:2 (1961), 195.
12 Kiernan, *Marxism and Imperialism*, pp. 42, 46.
13 M. Barrat-Brown, *Essays on Imperialism* (Nottingham, Spokesman, 1972), p. 53.
14 A. Shaikh, 'The Laws of International Exchange', in E. J. Nell (ed.), *Growth, Profits and Property* (Cambridge, UK, Cambridge University Press, 1980), p. 211. Chilcote also overstated Lenin's emphasis on capital export, see Chilcote, 'VI Lenin', in Chilcote, *Imperialism: Theoretical Directions*, p. 85.
15 Warren, *Imperialism*, p. 125.
16 Warren, *Imperialism*, p. 55; Emmanuel, 'White-Settler Colonialism', p. 48.
17 Howard and King, *Marxian Economics*, vol. 2, p. 191.
18 Howard and King, *Marxian Economics*, vol. 2, p. 121; Kay, *Latin American Theories*, p. 142.
19 Callinicos, *Imperialism and Global Political Economy*, pp. 179, 153.
20 Panitch and Gindin, *The Making of Global Capitalism*, pp. 5–6; L. Panitch, 'Rethinking Marxism and Imperialism for the Twenty-First Century', *New Labour Forum*, 23:2 (2014), p. 23; Marshal, 'Lenin's Imperialism', p. 322; Amsden, 'Imperialism', in Eatwell et al., *Marxian Economics*, p. 208; Smith, *Imperialism in the Twenty-First Century*, p. 232.

21 R. Clarke and R. Annis, 'The Myth of "Russian Imperialism": In Defence of Lenin's Analyses', *Links: International Journal of Socialist Renewal* (2016), 29 February.

22 In *Imperialism* Lenin makes twenty-five references to 'capital export', 'exporting capital', etc. These are mostly contained in the short chapter on that topic. By comparison, there are 208 mentions of 'monopoly', 'monopolies', etc.

23 Lenin, *Imperialism*, chap. 7.

24 Lenin, *Imperialism*, chap. 8 (emphasis added).

25 Lenin, *Imperialism*, chap. 10 (emphasis added).

26 Day and Gaido, *Discovering Imperialism*.

27 J. B. Marchlewski (Karski), 'Imperialism or Socialism? Imperialismus oder Sozialismus? Arbeiten uber die Entwicklung des Imperialismus und den antimonopolistischen Kampf der Arbeiterklasse' [1919], in Day and Gaido, *Discovering Imperialism*, p. 506 (emphasis added); K. Radek, 'German Imperialism and the Working Class', in K. Wolff, 'In den Reinhen der Deutschen Revolution 1909–1919: Gesammelte Aufsatze und Abhandlungen von K. Radek', in Day and Gaido, *Discovering Imperialism*, p. 532; P. Lench, 'Militia and Disarmament', *Die Neue Zeit*, 30:2 (1912), in Day and Gaido, *Discovering Imperialism*, p. 573; O. Bauer, *The Question of Nationalities and Social Democracy* [1907] (Minneapolis, University of Minnesota, 2000), p. 385; H. Cunow, 'Trade Agreements and Imperialist Expansion Policy', *Die Neue Zeit*, 18:2 (1900), in Day and Gaido, *Discovering Imperialism*, pp. 190–1; H. Cunow, 'American Expansion Policy in East Asia', *Die Neue Zeit*, 20:2 (1902), in Day and Gaido, *Discovering Imperialism*, p. 209; Parvus (A. Helphand) 'Before the "Hottentot Elections"', in Parvus, *Die Kolonialpolitikund der Zusammenbruch* (Leipzig, Leipziger Buchdruckerei Aktiengesellschaft, 1907), in Day and Gaido, *Discovering Imperialism*, p. 329. Parvus (A. Helphand), 'Colonies and Capitalism in the 20th Century', in Parvus, *Die Kolonialpolitikund*, in Day and Gaido, *Discovering Imperialism*, p. 345; N. Bukharin, *Imperialism and World Economy* [1915–17] (London, Martin Lawrence, n.d.), pp. 102–3.

28 V. I. Lenin, *Revision of the Party Programme* [1917], vol. 26, *Collected Works* (Moscow, Progress, 1964) (emphasis added).

29 Lenin, *Imperialism*, chap. 3.

30 Lenin, *Imperialism*, chap. 4.

31 Kidron, 'Highest Stage But One'; Kidron, 'International Capitalism'.

32 I. Roxborough, *Theories of Underdevelopment* (London, Macmillan, 1979), p. 56.

33 Warren, *Imperialism*, p. 108.

34 Howard and King, *Marxian Economics*, vol. 2, p. 77.

35 Callinicos, *Imperialism and Global Political Economy*, p. 179.

36 Panitch and Gindin, *The Making of Global Capitalism*, pp. 5–6.

37 J. Ghosh, 'The Creation of the Next Imperialism: The Institutional Architecture', *Monthly Review*, 67:3 (2015).

38 Foster in Magdoff and Foster, *Imperialism Without Colonies*. Magdoff said, 'The oversimplification which identifies imperialism with colonialism pure and simple neither resembles Lenin's theory nor the facts of the case' (p. 45).

39 Similarly, in 1920 Roy argued: 'The economic interrelation between Europe and the colonies is at the present time the foundation of the entire system of capitalism. Surplus value, which was in the past produced in England, is at the present time produced in the colonies.' See M. N. Roy, 'Supplementary Report on National and Colonial Questions to the Second Comintern Conference July, 26, 1920', in Riddell, *The Communist International in Lenin's Time*, p. 222.

40 Lenin, *Imperialism*, chap. 6.

41 Lenin, *Imperialism*, chap. 5.

42 Lenin, *Theses: The Socialist Revolution and the Right of Nations to Self-Determination* [1916], vol. 22, *Collected Works* (Moscow, Progress, 1966).

43 Lenin, *A Caricature of Marxism and Imperialist Economism* [1916–17], vol. 23, *Collected Works* (Moscow, Progress, 1964), chap. 4.

44 Lenin, *Caricature of Marxism and Imperialist Economism*, chap. 4.

45 Lenin, *Theses: Right of Nations to Self-Determination*.

46 Lenin, *Caricature of Marxism and Imperialist Economism*, chap. 4.

47 Lenin, *Theses: Right of Nations to Self-Determination*.

6

Is imperialism the 'highest stage of capitalism'?

> One capitalist always kills many. Hand in hand with this centralisation, or this expropriation of many capitalists by few, develop, on an ever-extending scale, the cooperative form of the labour process, the conscious technical application of science, the methodical cultivation of the soil, the transformation of the instruments of labour into instruments of labour only usable in common, the economising of all means of production by their use as means of production of combined, socialised labour, the entanglement of all peoples in the net of the world market, and with this, the international character of the capitalistic regime (Marx, 1867).

It is often assumed that in describing imperialism as 'the highest stage of capitalism', Lenin thought the system would imminently collapse. Alternatively, he is believed to have viewed one or another of the forms of imperialist rule present in his own period – such as colonialism or inter-imperialist war – as essential and permanent characteristics of imperialism. Starting from these caricatures, the dramatic changes that have taken place since Lenin's time are assumed to so thoroughly rebuke his 'highest stage' that no further evidence is needed. However, common perceptions misunderstand what Lenin meant by capitalism's 'highest stage'. Sutcliff argued Lenin's stages are 'not so useful when the problem is not to explain the genesis of imperialist war (the First World War) but to observe the status of the underdeveloped countries [or the] laws of motion of modern imperialism as they affect the Third World'.[1] Howe wrote that 'the imperialist structure of the late nineteenth and early twentieth century was, sadly, not the highest stage of capitalism, and Lenin gives us little indication of the essential dynamics of a [future] stage that [for Lenin] could not exist'.[2] According to Brewer, Lenin 'led Marxists astray for a long time. Since they thought capitalism was in the last throes of decay and dissolution',[3] such Marxists could not explain its survival. Fuchs says, 'When Lenin spoke of imperialism as "parasitic decaying capitalism" or of imperialism as "already dying capitalism", he meant that the end of capitalism is near'.[4]

Wood thought the 'final stage' of capitalism 'meant that capitalism would end before the non-capitalist victims of imperialism were finally and completely swallowed up by capitalism … [and] where the main axis of international conflict and military confrontation would run between imperialist states'.[5] Amin also understood Lenin's 'highest stage' to mean the capitalist crisis he witnessed would be the last crisis.[6] Panitch and Gindin portray Lenin as having contended 'the process of globalization' is 'impossible to sustain'.[7]

Kiernan considered Lenin thought capitalism was 'ready in short to give up the ghost', something that made him unable to grasp the prospect of 'welfare or prosperity capitalism' after the Second World War.[8] Callinicos argues the original Russian title of Lenin's pamphlet was the 'latest' not 'highest' stage of capitalism and that it was changed only after his death.[9] However, the reference Callinicos gives for this claim is an article by Foster that nevertheless admits that Lenin's handwritten manuscript of 1916 *was* entitled *Imperialism, the Highest Stage of Capitalism* after all.[10] In fact Hilferding's not Lenin's thesis was entitled 'The Latest Phase of Capitalism'.[11]

Multiplying new 'stages'

Certainly a lot has changed since Lenin's time, and it is popular for academic writers to 'periodise' the various eras according to their own criteria. These efforts often overemphasise phenomena that are prevalent or novel at the time of writing.

In 2006, Foster quotes Sweezy to argue, 'I will provisionally call this new hybrid phase of the system "monopoly-finance capital" '.[12] Patnaik coins a new stage called 'international finance capital'.[13] Screpanti proposes that a new form, 'global imperialism' (the last of five stages) has transpired.[14] Amin said 'generalized-monopoly capitalism' ran from 1975 to 2000.[15] Smith concludes that 'neoliberal globalization must therefore be recognized as a new, imperialist stage of capitalist development',[16] while for Petras and Veltmeyer, neoliberalism was replaced by 'extractive capitalism'.[17]

Foster was perhaps justified in claiming that 'it is now a universal belief on the left that the world has entered a new imperialist phase'.[18] Less clear is what that phase is called, when it started or what it consists of. A multiplying collection of stages implies many are arbitrary – like the proverbial two sociology professors debating whether there are five or seven distinct social classes in capitalist society. Any good student can argue either case.

There will always be important *changes* between any one time and another.[19] Under capitalist imperialism these occur rapidly, perhaps increasingly so. As Lenin pointed out, 'the forms of the struggle may and do constantly change in accordance with varying, relatively particular and temporary causes'.[20] However, when Lenin wrote of the 'highest stage' of capitalism, he was talking about a specific concept from volume 3 of Marx's *Capital*.

The dizzying array of choice offered by contemporary Marxism contrasts with what appears to have been a Social Democratic consensus in Lenin's time that, as Karski put it, 'a new period characterised by the deepest changes in the internal structure of capitalist production and in property relations'[21] had come into being: 'The organisational forms of industry have also changed completely. The independent capitalist, owning his own enterprise, is steadily disappearing. His place is taken by the corporation, in which employees are paid by capital to manage production.'[22] This observation was not unique to Social Democrats. As Schulze-Gaevernitz also observed, 'Thirty years ago, businessmen, freely competing against one another, performed nine-tenths of the work connected with their business other than manual labor. At the present time, nine-tenths of this "brain work" is performed by officials.'[23] Commenting on the political sphere from a Marxist perspective, Rothstein argued that the new era of imperialism signalled a fundamental change. The South African war 'represents a dividing line in English History'; 'Liberalism was doomed as a political principle the moment the first rivals entered the world-industrial arena'.[24]

Bauer thought:

> The whole ideology of the capitalist class changes. The liberal bourgeoisie, which struggled against absolutist oppression, against feudal exploitation, against mercantilist constraint, loved liberty [for some] ... The modern bourgeoisie is different. It fears the working class of its own country and is determined to defend its property and its power, with force if necessary.[25]

Hilferding prefigured Lenin's later formulation in 1903 when he argued that modern commercial policy had 'ushered in the last phase of capitalism', which had become 'the immediate precursor of socialist society because it is the complete negation of that [capitalist] society; a conscious socialisation of all economic potentialities of modern society'.[26] It was also a general practice of both Social Democratic and bourgeois writers to refer to the new period as 'imperialism'.[27] Debate at the time revolved around the characterisation of this new stage.

Marx's concept of 'capitalist production in its highest development'

As Lorimer pointed out,

> Lenin did not have to invent a new theory to arrive at the conclusion that monopoly finance capitalism was the highest stage of development of capitalism. He merely had to show that the features that Marx had described as characteristic of this stage [in *Capital*, volume 3] had become the dominant and typical form of capitalist business activity at the beginning of the twentieth century.[28]

This was not at all marginal in Marx's theory of social revolution. As Marx also said in volume 3 of *Capital*:

> The monopoly of capital becomes a fetter upon the mode of production, which has sprung up and flourished along with, and under it. Centralisation of the means of production and socialisation of labour at last reach a point where they become incompatible with their capitalist integument. This integument is burst asunder. The knell of capitalist private property sounds. The expropriators are expropriated.[29]

Marx too is wrongly accused by hostile writers of assuming revolution was imminent when he was in fact expressing a general theoretical point on the transition from one social system to another – that the development of the new social system begins embryonically within the old. Marx's concept of 'capitalist production in its highest development' provides his fullest formulation of this point. With the formation of joint stock companies (that is, the precursor to modern day MNCs), Marx argued:

> The capital, which in itself rests on a social mode of production and presupposes a social concentration of means of production and labour-power, is here directly endowed with the form of social capital (capital of directly associated individuals) as distinct from private capital, and its undertakings assume the form of social undertakings as distinct from private undertakings. It is the abolition of capital as private property within the framework of capitalist production itself.[30]

This involved, 'transformation of the actual functioning capitalist [active in production] into a mere manager, administrator of other people's capital, and of the owner of capital into a mere owner, a mere money-capitalist … profit thus appears as a mere appropriation of the surplus-labour of others'.[31] This now purely parasitical capitalist, the 'mere money capitalist' whose former role in the production process is replaced with professional management, is the 'finance capitalist' that Hilferding and Lenin later refer to. They may own factories, mines, banks or any other form of capital. Their characterisation as 'finance capitalist' has nothing to do with whether such ownership is in the financial sector or not. Capitalist ownership in every sector will always be financial in its form – such as ownership of stocks or bonds.

Marx says,

> In stock companies the function is divorced from capital ownership, hence also labour is entirely divorced from ownership of means of production and surplus-labour. This result of the ultimate development of capitalist production is a necessary transitional phase towards the reconversion of capital into the property of producers, although no longer as the private property of the individual producers, but rather as the property of associated producers, as

outright social property. On the other hand, the stock company is a transition toward the conversion of all functions in the reproduction process which still remain linked with capitalist property, into mere functions of associated producers, into social functions.[32]

This is the abolition of the capitalist mode of production within the capitalist mode of production itself, and hence a self-dissolving contradiction, which prima facie represents a mere phase of transition to a new form of production. It manifests itself as such a contradiction in its effects. It establishes a monopoly in certain spheres and thereby requires state interference. It reproduces a new financial aristocracy, a new variety of parasites in the shape of promoters, speculators and simply nominal directors; a whole system of swindling and cheating by means of corporation promotion, stock issuance, and stock speculation. It is private production without the control of private property.[33]

The reader familiar with Lenin will recognise the closeness of Lenin's arguments (both of 'highest stage' and the 'financial aristocracy') to these passages.

Lenin's application of Marx's concept

Lenin sought to demonstrate the degree of socialisation already reached in capitalist production in his time provided the basis for social ownership and control:

When a big enterprise assumes gigantic proportions, and, on the basis of an exact computation of mass data, organises according to plan the supply of primary raw materials to the extent of two-thirds, or three-fourths, of all that is necessary for tens of millions of people; when the raw materials are transported in a systematic and organised manner to the most suitable places of production, sometimes situated hundreds or thousands of miles from each other; when a single centre directs all the consecutive stages of processing the material right up to the manufacture of numerous varieties of finished articles; when these products are distributed according to a single plan among tens and hundreds of millions of consumers (the marketing of oil in America and Germany by the American oil trust) – then it becomes evident that we have socialisation of production ... that private economic and private property relations constitute a shell which no longer fits its contents.[34]

Lenin makes a similar point about monopoly: 'We have seen that in its economic essence imperialism is monopoly capitalism. This in itself determines its place in history, for monopoly that grows out of the soil of free competition, and precisely out of free competition, is the transition from the capitalist system to a higher socio-economic order.'[35] Taking over Marx's conception of the financial aristocracy, Lenin says:

> It is characteristic of capitalism in general that the ownership of capital is separated from the application of capital to production, that money capital is separated from industrial or productive capital, and that the rentier who lives entirely on income obtained from money capital, is separated from the entrepreneur and from all who are directly concerned in the management of capital. Imperialism, or the domination of finance capital, is that highest stage of capitalism in which this separation reaches vast proportions.[36]

The large capitalists are completely removed from productive activity and replaced by boards of directors, professional managers and technical staff. This is the concrete historical sense in which such unflattering descriptors as 'rentier', 'financial oligarchy', 'parasite' and 'coupon clipper', when used by Lenin, are not mere terms of abuse but attempts at scientific characterisation of a social class that has already fulfilled its historical function and since become redundant.

The idea that any of this indicates Lenin thought capitalism would necessarily be overthrown in the short term is contradicted both in *Imperialism* and Lenin's other works. The 'shell' of capitalist social relations referred to above, Lenin says, 'may remain in a state of decay for a fairly long period (if, at the worst, the cure of the opportunist abscess is protracted)'.[37] Indeed!

Lorimer explains why this contradictory social formation necessarily constitutes the last possible stage in the development of capitalist social relations:

> Alienation of producers from ownership of the means of production is the inner relation which constitutes the essence of the capitalist form of commodity production. When, therefore, from being the inner relation connecting individual workers and individual capitalists in the production process, it becomes outwardly expressed as a fully-developed social antagonism – as a social conflict between the actual producers, associated by the production process into a collective individuality on one side, and the exploiting non-producers, equally associated by their ownership into a collective individuality opposite to theirs – it is obvious that (a) no further development of capitalist relations of production is possible; (b) that the social antagonism has become the starting point for a transition to a new social form of the productive process; and (c) that this starting point has its material basis and its general form in the positive and negative poles of the social antagonism itself, i.e., in associated production by associated owners for the satisfaction of their individual and common needs.[38]

The origin of Lenin's 'highest stage of capitalism' in Marx's 'capitalist production in its highest development', and their closeness, has been almost completely lost in contemporary Marxist writing.[39] For example, Marshal

observes that 'there are generally taken to be three classical direct influ-
ences on Lenin's *Imperialism* – J. A. Hobson's (1902) *Imperialism*, Rudolf
Hilferding's (1910) *Finance Capital* and Bukharin's (1915) *Imperialism and
World Economy*'[40] – while Marx is overlooked.

Understanding Lenin's 'highest stage' is important not only because it
removes a reason to disregard Lenin's work. The significance of the discovery of capitalism having entered its highest and last possible stage of
development is enormous. Much of the content of this now not so new
stage, such as permanent militarism, political reaction, the high degree of
socialisation of the production process, parasitism of the bourgeoisie and
objective ripeness for social ownership, is taken for granted. However, only
by understanding the origin of these phenomena so characteristic of contemporary capitalism is it possible to fully understand their inner connections and essential character.

A Marxist definition of 'finance capital'

The concentration of production; the monopolies arising therefrom; the merging or coalescence of the banks with industry – such is the history of the rise
of finance capital and such is the content of that concept (Lenin, 1917).

Rather than being like a cancer that surgery might remove to restore the capitalist body to health, it is more like a central nervous system: without finance,
modern capitalism is dead (Norfield, 2016).

It would be simple to caricature Marx as having overemphasised the importance of finance by selecting just a few quotations. He wrote, for example,
in what was obviously an exaggerated manner: 'The whole state machinery
of France transformed into one immense swindling and stockjobbing concern.'[41] We might retort that the French state's intimate involvement with
industries such as Aerospace and nuclear power shows Marx to have been
dead wrong and his work irrelevant in the modern world. Of course, this
exaggerated comment does not represent Marx's whole view. Yet similar
partial and simplistic misreading of Lenin permeates modern work.

The terms 'finance capital', 'monopoly capital' and 'monopoly finance
capital' are used interchangeably in *Imperialism*. Lenin's Marxist opponents
almost invariably select the term 'finance capital' for criticism. However,
'finance capital' abbreviates the fullest formulation – 'monopoly finance
capital'. Predilection for the incomplete form relates to a common misun-
derstanding and caricature: Lenin's 'finance capital' is replaced in the mind
of the modern reader as 'finance' in the common ways that term is understood today, such as the banks, the finance, insurance and real estate (FIRE)
sector, or merely money and financial paper ('securities').

If Lenin's readers do not grasp the changes in the social relations outlined above pertaining to capitalism's highest stage, specifically if they do not see the development of the collective, parasitical 'mere money capitalist', they tend also not to grasp Lenin's characterisation of the *whole* big bourgeoisie as 'parasitic', 'rentiers', etc. Lenin's words on parasitism are then misread as pertaining to only a section of the bourgeois – those owing financial sector firms. However, to attribute this position to Lenin contradicts what Lenin actually wrote. He unambiguously endorses Hilferding's observation of the increasing closeness of banking and industry. He defines finance capital as their 'coalescence'.

In 1942, Sweezy already sensed 'it is doubtful whether the term 'finance capital' can be divested of the connotation of banker dominance'.[42] While prescient, Sweezy does not say what causes the confusion. However, his own career seems to provide a clue. His 1968 book, *Monopoly Capital* viewed productive corporations as dominant over, or independent of the banks. By the 1990s, Sweezy concluded the opposite: he said finance had become dominant over industry.[43] Theoretically the premise of each position must be that these two class sections are distinct and antagonistic. That is the opposite to 'finance capital' defined as coalescence of previously separate class sections. Separation of the two à la Sweezy appears to be the common view.

Brewer attributes to Lenin his own conflation of rentiers with banks. According to Brewer, Lenin 'even more noticeably than Hilferding, stressed the dominance of the banks, and hence of rentiers',[44] and this 'foreshadows [Lenin's] discussion of "parasitism" '.[45] Therefore, when Brewer reads Lenin's discussion on parasitism, he reads it as an account of parasitism of the banks. Brewer thus concludes, contrary to what Lenin actually says, that Lenin 'described the development of monopoly in banking, and the dominance of bank capital over industrial capital'.[46] 'Coalescence' is transformed into 'dominance'.

Similarly, the reason Brewer found Lenin's treatment of 'financial swindles' to be 'disturbing'[47] is because, once Brewer superimposed on to Lenin the view that parasitic capital is only one section of the class, it became difficult to distinguish Lenin from Kautsky's reformist outlook: 'where the financier is rash, extravagant and violent the industrial manager is frugal, timid and peace-loving'.[48]

Harman presented Lenin as thinking 'finance capital (the banks) ... very much subordinated industrial capital to their needs'.[49] Chesnais attributes to Lenin and Hilferding the view that the 'global oligopoly' meant 'the banks'.[50] For Patsoura, Lenin's 'finance capital' was, again 'the banks'.[51] Sutton argues that Lenin understood 'the financiers of capital' as 'sectional interests'.[52]

Harvey's sole direct reference to Lenin in *Seventeen Contradictions* tends to confuse his position, arguing, 'Lenin famously saw capital moving into a new phase of monopoly power associated with imperialism at the turn of the twentieth century when the big industrial cartels combined with finance capital'[53] – not as Lenin had actually argued, that the merger of industrial and bank capital formed 'finance capital' as a new entity. McNally favours Lenin's view of the fusion between bank and industrial capital but credits it only to Hilferding.[54]

Lenin's 'finance capital'

Many of Lenin's formulations about the character of finance capital, with minor edits, could easily be passed off as modern work. The following description might just as easily have been written about the turn of last century as the previous century:

> The typical ruler of the world became finance capital, a power that is peculiarly mobile and flexible, peculiarly intertwined at home and internationally, peculiarly devoid of individuality and divorced from the immediate processes of production, peculiarly easy to concentrate, a power that has already made peculiarly large strides on the road of concentration, so that literally several hundred billionaires and millionaires hold in their hands the fate of the whole world.[55]

To give another example, the following statement would need only a few words changed to make it accurate a hundred years later: 'Finance capital, concentrated in a few hands and exercising a virtual monopoly, exacts enormous and ever-increasing profits from the floating of companies, issue of stock, state loans, etc., strengthens the domination of the financial oligarchy and levies tribute upon the whole of society for the benefit of monopolists.'[56] Further, Lenin says that 'speculation in land situated in the suburbs of rapidly growing big towns is a particularly profitable operation for finance capital'. If we change the words 'big towns' to 'cities' we get another modern comment. Moreover, who would disagree today with Lenin's observation that 'the bulk of the profits go to the "geniuses" of financial manipulation'?[57] Or with Lenin's contention (quoting Schulze-Gaevernitz) that Great Britain

> is gradually becoming transformed from an industrial into a creditor state. Notwithstanding the absolute increase in industrial output and the export of manufactured goods, there is an increase in the relative importance of income from interest and dividends, issues of securities, commissions and speculation in the whole of the national economy.[58]

Lenin was clearly alert to aspects of the growing power of finance capital that capture the attention of modern writers concerned with 'financialisation'. However, he had a fundamentally different understanding of these phenomena.

In defining finance capital, Lenin starts by quoting Hilferding:

> 'A steadily increasing proportion of capital in industry,' writes Hilferding, 'ceases to belong to the industrialists who employ it. They obtain the use of it only through the medium of the banks which, in relation to them, represent the owners of the capital. On the other hand, the bank is forced to sink an increasing share of its funds in industry. Thus, to an ever greater degree the banker is being transformed into an industrial capitalist. This bank capital, i.e., capital in money form, *which is thus actually transformed into industrial capital*, I call "finance capital". Finance capital is capital controlled by banks and employed by industrialists.'[59]

Lenin says,

> This definition is incomplete insofar as it is silent on one extremely important fact – on the increase of concentration of production and of capital to such an extent that concentration is leading, and has led, to monopoly ... The concentration of production; the monopolies arising therefrom; the merging or coalescence of the banks with industry – such is the history of the rise of finance capital and such is the content of that concept.[60]

> At the same time a personal link-up, so to speak, is established between the banks and the biggest industrial and commercial enterprises, the merging of one with another through the acquisition of shares, through the appointment of bank directors to the Supervisory Boards (or Boards of Directors) of industrial and commercial enterprises, and vice versa.[61]

Lenin repeatedly refers to the powerful monopolistic position of the big banks, even 'increasing the dependence of big industry upon a small number of banking groups'.[62] However, these are qualified by other references to the dependence of banks on industry for its profits, as is inevitable if, as Lenin argues, the two are increasingly fused, interlocked and mutually dependent. 'The result is, on the one hand, the ever-growing merger, or, as N.I. Bukharin aptly calls it, coalescence, of bank and industrial capital and, on the other hand, the growth of the banks into institutions of a truly "universal character".'[63] On the other hand, Lenin describes the competing view that perceives the 'omnipotence of the banks, [and of] the financial oligarchy' as separate from industry as a 'petty-bourgeois point of view in the critique of imperialism', one adopted by 'authors who make no claim to be Marxists'.[64]

To confirm what Lenin meant by the coalescence of banking with industry, one can check the names Lenin gives for the finance capitalist firms. They include Siemens, General Electric (GE), the Sugar Trust, US

Steel Corporation, Egyptian Sugar Refineries, Union Mining Company of Dortmund and the Steel Syndicate of Germany, none of which were banks or finance sector firms. In another instance, Lenin measured 'finance capital' by kilometres of railway line.[65] In defending Lenin's concept, Lorimer was able to take as his example the largest capitalist families in the United States at the time:

> The Morgan banking family, which made its initial fortune in [the] early 19th century out of the slave trade, provided the financing in 1901 for the merger of a number of steel companies into the US Steel Corporation. The Morgans' banking company JP Morgan & Co also took a controlling interest in US Steel, which immediately became and remains the biggest US steel maker ... By the end of the 1890s the Standard Oil Trust, a conglomeration of state-based oil companies controlled by the Rockefeller's Standard Oil Company of New Jersey, controlled 88% of US oil refining ... In 1891 the Rockefellers took a controlling interest in the National City Bank of NY ... [which by 1894] was the largest bank in the US. In 1955, National City Bank, then headed by James Stillman Rockefeller, merged with the Morgan-dominated First National Bank of New York ... which in 1976 renamed itself Citibank then Citigroup.[66]

Thus, for Lenin, the finance capitalist is not a banker or securities trader but 'a social stratum ... who live by "clipping coupons", who *take no part in any enterprise whatever*, whose profession is idleness'.[67] This description of the modern ruling class today represents the dominant view among contemporary Marxists. No Marxist sees the capitalist as fulfilling a necessary, active role in the labour process of any large enterprise (though they may be active in financial speculation). So dominant is this aspect of Lenin's view today that readers appear not to notice the significance of its original formulations in Marx's and Lenin's work or its contrast to the pre-monopoly period, when many capitalist owner managers would do the accounting and management tasks for their own factory or mine.

Contemporary 'financialisation' literature

Insufficiently understanding the fusion or 'coalescence' of banking with industry in the sense Marx and Lenin outlined leads writers to conceptually separate banking and the finance sectors, or just 'finance' itself (i.e. credit or money) from industrial capital. Once the two are separated in the mind of the observer, the increasing prevalence taken by the financial or fictitious form of *all* capital (such as a rise in stock market activity and trading of financial papers) tends to be interpreted as the increasing importance of 'finance capital' understood in the non-Leninist sense (i.e. the increasing dominance of finance over industry).

The problem arises because all capital inevitably takes on a money form at a certain point in the capitalist cycle and therefore also takes the form of finance (in the general sense of the term) as one of its necessary forms.[68] This is confusing when finance capital's more essential character remains insufficiently defined. The words used to describe it – 'finance capital' – also have long-established, well-known non-Marxist meanings, and these coincide with one real form of capital – money. In this context, some confusion seems inevitable. Based on the premise of separate and conflicting finance and industrial sections of capital, some writers tend to view the growth of the financial sector as the motor of capitalist development and signifying a qualitative change in the social system.

Harvey's version of financialisation is the most detailed and influential. There are many other versions.[69] Yet all attempts to separate industry from finance tend to become unworkable. As Norfield states, 'the owners of industrial companies are the owners of its equity capital, usually in the form of quoted financial securities that are fictitious capital' in the sense Marx outlined.[70] Moreover, 'a "productive" company, especially a large one aiming to boost its market position, will also get heavily involved in financial dealing. Typically this means merging with or taking over its rivals in stock market deals, or using the equity and bond markets to increase its financial strength.'[71] That is to say, financial power becomes the *expression* of the strength of *all* capitalists and firms.[72]

Panitch and Gindin also point out,

> It is a mistake to see the dominance of finance in terms of speculation displacing industrial activity ... the broadening and deepening of US financial markets, including their ability to attract so much capital from abroad, expanded the availability of relatively cheap credit for US firms ... [including] what has been called the 'financialization' of non-financial corporations. Without this usually becoming the foundation for their central activities or even their profits, large corporations increasingly engaged in financial arbitrage themselves.[73]

Searching Harvey's work for an explanation of how financial capital might exert power over some sort of contemporary version of 'industrial capital' the answer is not easy to find. We are taken back to the US dustbowl of the Great Depression years. The eviction of Oklahoma family tenant farmers (immortalised in Steinbeck's *The Grapes of Wrath*) is given as an early example of what Harvey calls 'accumulation by dispossession'. Harvey proposes that 'the prime lever for this transition [eviction] has always been the credit system'.[74] But one needs to ask, 'Transition to what?'

The productive transition in Great Depression Oklahoma, as Steinbeck documented, was from small, labour-intensive family tenant farming to large, mechanised monoculture in cotton. The actual revolutionising factor was not the banks but the tractor. Without this 'revolutionising the instruments of production' as Marx called it,[75] there would have been no sense in the banks foreclosing on the small family farms. Without the new productive techniques, the banks would be unable to gain a greater income from the land than their existing mortgage payments from the impoverished tenant families because they would have no way to use the land more productively (of value).

Harvey refers only to 'the prime lever', which might be understood to mean the superficial, not essential, cause of the evictions. Yet, even at a superficial level, the causes – as depicted by Steinbeck – contradict the elevated position Harvey gives to the credit system. In *The Grapes of Wrath*, police guns, quiescent, relatively privileged workers and the tractor itself, which physically destroys the Joad family's land and house, are more important. Steinbeck wrote: 'The tractors which throw men out of work, the belt lines which carry loads, the machines which produce, all were increased; and more and more families scampered on the highways ... the machines pushed them out.'[76] Steinbeck was emphatic about this. He noted to himself in 1938, while writing the book: 'The overtone of the tractors, the men who run them, the men they displace, the sound of them, the smell of them. I've got to get this over [to the reader]. Got to because this one's tone is very important – this is the eviction sound and the tonal reason for movement. Must do it well.'[77] Frustratingly, Harvey gives no explanation for how or in what sense he thinks 'the credit system' works as an independent mechanism standing above productive capital. In later iterations, Harvey's list of bad, parasitical capital is expanded. We are told that 'rentiers, the merchants, the media and communications moguls' and 'corporate monopolies like Apple, Monsanto, the big energy companies, pharmaceuticals' join the financiers to 'ruthlessly squeeze the lifeblood out of productive industrial capital' (i.e. to usurp a portion of their profits).[78] But how? The category of parasites is so eclectic Harvey can neither settle on a name for it nor designate its boundaries or criteria.[79] It is never explained, for example, why Monsanto, the big energy companies and pharmaceuticals are considered non-productive or non-industrial. All produce use values in the Marxist sense and do so using advanced industrial facilities.

Apple produces product designs. Its enormous cash reserves result from its enormous sales and price markups on products it has designed and engineered. A characterisation of Apple as principally a parasitical *non-productive* company would be justified only if the labour that Apple workers perform is superfluous to production. But if that were the case, what then is the basis of that company's monopolistic ability to extract value produced by its Chinese-based contractors? Why, for example, can't Foxconn oust Apple as the pre-eminent consumer electronics monopoly? This is the real question that Harvey's credit-system squeeze explanation obscures. Contra Harvey, it is not only financiers and merchants and (bad) producers like Monsanto that squeeze (good) direct producers. Direct producers populate the lists of the largest and most profitable companies in the world: for example, Microsoft and Samsung (see Chapter 11).

In Harvey's scenario, the financiers appear to have access to more or less infinite liquidity, while productive capital is for some reason neither able to generate its own finance nor to forge alliances with others to provide it. We are told, 'when the credit system operates a squeeze, when liquidity dries up and enterprises are forced into bankruptcy', there 'is no way for owners to hang on to assets and they have to relinquish them at a very low price to capitalists who have the liquidity to take over'.[80] Yet, plainly, banks or financiers cannot take assets at will. The debtor must first default, which depends on their profitability.

In supporting his accumulation by dispossession/financialisation theory, Harvey suggests 'the East and the global South became centres for industrial *value production*', while the imperialist countries 'focused on rent extraction' (i.e. *value extraction*).[81] If this were true, it completely contradicts his claim that value now flows West to East.

Politically, if an industrial bourgeoisie existed separately to the financial bourgeoisie, it might be expected to have made some noise about the largesse accruing to its putative competitors as a result of imperialist state bailouts of financial institutions after the great recession of 2008–9. Yet there was no campaign by 'productive capitalists' against this gravy train for finance. For example, the 2013 decision of the Basel Committee on Banking Supervision, tasked with responding to the global 'financial' crisis, recommended no punitive new regulation of the large banks. This was greeted with only muted discussion in the financial press and certainly none of the heat that could be expected from capitalists having their 'lifeblood' squeezed.[82]

Showing the coalescence of all big capital into a unified productive and financial monopoly allows us to better appreciate the essential character of the imperialist system that humanity faces: not a monopoly of money but of the social conditions for earning it.

Notes

1 B. Sutcliffe, 'Imperialism and Industrialisation in the Third World', in Owen and Sutcliffe, *Studies in the Theory of Imperialism*, p. 172; Warren, *Imperialism*, p. 4.

2 Howe, 'Dependency Theory and Imperialism', p. 88.

3 Brewer, *Marxist Theories*, p. 122.

4 Fuchs, 'Critical Globalization Studies', p. 864.

5 Wood, *Empire of Capital*, p. 126.

6 Amin, *The* Law of Worldwide Value, p. 116; S. Amin, 'Contemporary Imperialism', *Monthly Review*, 67:3 (2015).

7 Panitch and Gindin, *The Making of Global Capitalism*, pp. 5–6.

8 Kiernan, *Marxism and Imperialism*, p. 41.

9 Callinicos, *Imperialism and Global Political Economy*, p. 44; Harman, *Zombie Capitalism*, p. 93.

10 J. B. Foster, 'January 2004' [Editorial note], *Monthly Review*, 55:8 (2004).

11 R. Hilferding, *Finance Capital: A Study of the Latest Phase of Capitalist Development* [1910], ed. T. Bottomore (London, Routledge and Kegan Paul, 1981).

12 Foster, 'Monopoly-Finance Capital'; P. Sweezy, 'The Triumph of Financial Capital', *Monthly Review*, 46:2 (1994); J. B. Foster, 'The Age of Monopoly-Finance Capital', *Monthly Review*, 61:9 (2010); J. B. Foster, 'The Financialization of Accumulation', *Monthly Review*, 62:5 (2010).

13 P. Patnaik, 'Notes on Contemporary Imperialism', *MRonline* (2010), 20 December.

14 E. Screpanti, *Global Imperialism and the Great Crisis: The Uncertain Future of Capitalism* (New York, Monthly Review, 2014), pp. 9, 44.

15 Amin, 'Contemporary Imperialism'; Amin, *The Law of Worldwide Value*, p. 118.

16 J. Smith, 'Imperialism in the Twenty-First Century', *Monthly Review*, 67:3 (2015). Other versions are given by Harvey, *The New Imperialism*, pp. 42–9; C. Harman, *Explaining The Crisis: A Marxist Reappraisal* (London, Bookmarks, 1984), pp. 55, 62, 74; C. Harman, 'The State and Capitalism Today', *International Socialism*, 2:51 (1991); Callinicos, *Imperialism and Global Political Economy*, p. vi; Patnaik, 'Notes on Contemporary Imperialism'.

17 J. Petras and H. Veltmeyer, 'Imperialism and Capitalism: Rethinking an Intimate Relationship', *Global Research* (2015), 16 December.

18 Foster, 'The New Imperialism'.

19 E. H. Carr, *What Is History?* (London, Penguin, 1961).

20 Lenin, *Imperialism*, chap. 5.

21 Marchlewski, 'Imperialism or Socialism?' in Day and Gaido, *Discovering Imperialism*, p. 499; T. Rothstein, 'The South African War and the Decadence of English Liberalism', *Die Neue Zeit*, 19:2 (1901), in Day and Gaido, *Discovering Imperialism*, p. 234.

22 Marchlewski, 'Imperialism or Socialism?' in Day and Gaido, *Discovering Imperialism*, p. 500.

23 Schulze-Gaevernitz, 'Die deutsche Kreditbank', in *Grundriss der Socialekonomik, Tübingen* (1915), p. 151, cited in Lenin, *Imperialism*, chap. 2.

24 Rothstein, 'The South African War', in Day and Gaido, *Discovering Imperialism*, p. 235–6.

25 Bauer, *The Question of Nationalities*, p. 380; O. Bauer, 'National and International Viewpoints on Foreign Policy' (1909), in Day and Gaido, *Discovering Imperialism*, p. 50.

26 R. Hilferding, 'Der Funktionswechsel des Schutzzolles', *Die Neue Zeit*, 21:2 (1903), in Day and Gaido, *Discovering Imperialism*, p. 349.

27 For example, K. Kautsky, 'Germany, England and World Policy' (1900), in Day and Gaido, *Discovering Imperialism*, p. 175.

28 Lorimer in Lenin, *Imperialism* [1999], p. 17; S. Dobbs, 'Centenary of Lenin's Theory of Imperialism: A Reply to Pete Glover', *Marxist World* (2017), April.

29 Marx, *Capital*, vol. 1, chap. 32.

30 K. Marx, *Capital: A Critique of Political Economy*, vol. 3, *The Process of Capitalist Production as a Whole* [1894], ed. F. Engels (International Publishers, New York, n.d.), chap. 27.

31 Marx, *Capital*, vol. 3, chap. 27.

32 Marx, *Capital*, vol. 3, chap. 27.

33 Marx, *Capital*, vol. 3, chap. 27.

34 Lenin, *Imperialism*, chap. 10. Schumpeter argued: 'Since capitalist enterprise, by its very achievements, tends to automatize progress, we conclude that it tends to make itself superfluous – to break to pieces under the pressure of its own success. The perfectly bureaucratized giant industrial unit not only ousts the small or medium-sized firm and "expropriates" its owners, but in the end it also ousts the entrepreneur and expropriates the bourgeoisie as a class which in the process stands to lose not only its income but also what is infinitely more important, its function.' J. Schumpeter, *Capitalism, Socialism and Democracy* [1942] (New York, Taylor and Francis, 2003), p. 134.

35 Lenin, *Imperialism*, chap. 10.

36 Lenin, *Imperialism*, chap. 3.

37 Lenin, *Imperialism*, chap. 10; Lenin, *The Position and Tasks of the Socialist International* [1914], vol. 21, *Collected Works* (Moscow, Progress, 1964).

38 Lorimer in Lenin, *Imperialism* [1999], pp. 17–18.

39 Panitch commented: 'We cannot know what Marx would have made of the way Lenin identified imperialism with "the highest stage of capitalism".' See Panitch, 'Rethinking Marxism', p. 23; Pradella, 'Imperialism and Capitalist Development', p. 127. J. Smith highlights similarities between Lenin's highest stage with a comment Marx made in *Grundrisse*, but not with Marx's systematic outline of this concept in *Capital*, vol. 3 – see Smith, *Imperialism in the Twenty-First Century*, pp. 249–50. For a positive overview of Lenin's stages see T. Mcdonough, 'Lenin, Imperialism, and the Stages of Capitalist Development', *Science and Society*, 59:3 (1995), 352.

40 Marshal, Lenin's Imperialism', p. 318.

41 K. Marx, 'Revolution in China and in Europe', *New York Daily Tribune* (1853), 14 June.

42 Sweezy, *The Theory of Capitalist Development*, p. 269.

43 Baran and Sweezy, *Monopoly Capital*, p. 18; Sweezy, 'The Triumph of Financial Capital'.

44 Brewer, *Marxist Theories*, p. 118.

45 Brewer, *Marxist Theories*, p. 118.

46 Brewer, *Marxist Theories*, p. 118.

47 Brewer, *Marxist Theories*, p. 110–11.
48 K. Kautsky, *The Social Revolution*, vol. 1 [1902] (unknown location, Charles Kerr, 1903), part 2, section 5; Kautsky, 'Germany, England and World Policy' (1900), in Day and Gaido, *Discovering Imperialism*, p. 174.
49 C. Harman, 'Imperialism, East and West', *Socialist Review*, 2 (1980); Sutcliffe, 'Imperialism and Industrialisation in the Third World', in Owen and Sutcliffe, *Studies in the Theory of Imperialism*, p. 171; Howe, 'Dependency Theory and Imperialism', p. 88.
50 Chesnais, 'Economic Foundations of Imperialism', p. 126.
51 L. Patsoura, *Marx in Context* (New York, iUniverse, 2005), p. 255. For a heterodox version, see Amsden, 'Imperialism', in Eatwell et al., *Marxian Economics*, p. 208.
52 A. Sutton, 'Towards an Open Marxist Theory of Imperialism', *Capital and Class*, 37:2 (2013), 221.
53 Harvey, *Seventeen Contradictions*, p. 135; Clarke and Annis, 'The Myth of "Russian Imperialism"'; Probsting, *The Great Robbery of the South*.
54 D. McNally, 'From Financial Crisis to World-Slump: Accumulation, Financialisation and the Global Slowdown', *Historical Materialism*, 17:2 (2009), 56.
55 Lenin, 'Introduction', in Bukharin, *Imperialism and World Economy*.
56 Lenin, *Imperialism*, chap. 3.
57 Lenin, *Imperialism*, chap. 1. The same modern relevance is present in Marx's work where he argued capitalist production in its highest development 'reproduces a new financial aristocracy, a new kind of parasite in the guise of company promoters, speculators and merely nominal directors; an entire system of swindling and cheating with respect to the promotion of companies, issues of shares and share dealings. It is private production unchecked by private ownership.' See Marx, *Capital*, vol. 3, chap. 27.
58 Schulze-Gaevernitz, 'Die deutsche Kreditbank', quoted in Lenin, *Imperialism*, chap. 8.
59 Lenin, *Imperialism*, chap. 3 (emphasis added).
60 Lenin, *Imperialism*, chap. 3.
61 Lenin, *Imperialism*, chap. 2.
62 Lenin, *Imperialism*, chap. 2.
63 Lenin, *Imperialism*, chap. 2.
64 Lenin, *Imperialism*, chap. 9.
65 Lenin, *Imperialism*, chap. 7.
66 D. Lorimer, 'Capitalist Economic Crisis and Finance Capital' [paper presented to the RSP Marxist Education Conference], 2–5 January (2010).
67 Lenin, *Imperialism*, chap. 8 (emphasis added).
68 Marx, *Capital*, vol. 1, chap. 4.
69 Foster, 'Monopoly-Finance Capital'; Foster and McChesney, *The Endless Crisis*, pp. 19–21. In an earlier version, Foster's financialisation attempted to account for Third World exploitation without reference to production: 'Neoliberal financialization' through the Third World debt crisis, Foster said, 'attempts

to create a new "financial architecture" in underdeveloped countries, lead-
ing to new financial dependencies'. See Foster, 'Monopoly-Finance Capital';
Chesnais, 'Economic Foundations of Contemporary Imperialism', pp. 126,
134; U. Patnaik and P. Patnaik, 'Imperialism in the Era of Globalization',
Monthly Review, 67:3 (2015); Ahmad, 'Imperialism of Our Time', p. 44; A.
Higginbottom, '"Imperialist Rent" in Practice and Theory', *Globalizations*,
11:1 (2014), 28; Smith, *Imperialism in the Twenty-First Century*, p. 75.
According to Smith, 'increased profits delivered by outsourcing are not invested
in production ... and can be entirely devoted to leveraging asset values ... to
reap speculative profits thereby feeding the financialization of the imperialist
economies'. Smith, *Imperialism in the Twenty-First Century*, pp. 82, 75.

70 Norfield, *The City*, p. 93.
71 Norfield, *The City*, p. xiii, 74; Panitch and Gindin, *The Making of Global
Capitalism*, pp. 290, 188. However, in the same work, Panitch and Gindin separate the two thus: 'industrial as well as finance capital' (p. 90).
72 Norfield, *The City*, p. 90; Schwartz, *Subprime Nation*, pp. 115, 126.
73 Panitch and Gindin, *The Making of Global Capitalism*, p. 188; McNally also
points out that the so-called Asian financial crisis of the late 1990s, not coinci-
dentally, was concentrated where excess capacity 'in labour-intensive manufacturing and assembly' was also concentrated. See McNally, 'Financial Crisis to
World-Slump', p. 62.
74 Harvey, *The New Imperialism*, p. 156.
75 K. Marx and F. Engels, *Manifesto of the Communist Party* [1848], vol. 1,
Selected Works (Moscow, Progress, 1969), chap. 1.
76 J. Steinbeck, *The Grapes of Wrath* (New York, Penguin, 1992), pp. 249, 295.
77 Cited in R. Demott, 'Introduction', in Steinbeck, *The Grapes of Wrath*, p. xiv.
78 Harvey, *Seventeen Contradictions*, pp. 251–2.
79 Alternatively, 'The bankers, the Hollywood producers and the high-tech
community' is a slightly different presentation of the 'bad' capitalist. The latter list comes from Steve Bannon's 2010 far-right conspiracy documentary
Generation Zero.
80 Harvey, *The New Imperialism*, p. 155. For similar treatment of the Indonesian
crisis, see Harvey, *The New Imperialism*, p. 164.
81 Harvey, *Seventeen Contradictions*, p. 125 (emphasis added).
82 M. Roberts, 'Banking: Business as Usual', *Michael Roberts Blog* (2013), 7
January, https://thenextrecession.wordpress.com/2013/01/07/banking-business-
as-usual/.

7

Lenin's monopoly *capitalist* competition

The old boasted freedom of competition has reached the end of its tether and must itself announce its obvious, scandalous bankruptcy (Marx, 1894).

Competition becomes transformed into monopoly. The result is immense progress in the socialisation of production. In particular, the process of technical invention and improvement becomes socialised (Lenin, 1917).

This chapter is divided into two parts. First is a critique of contemporary Marxist literature on monopoly and competition; second is an outline of the strength and limits of Lenin's view. The contemporary critique begins with an overview of how contemporary writers have dealt with this aspect of Lenin's work, followed by an examination of two prominent contemporary views.

It has already been shown that 'finance capital', for Lenin, means the monopolistic merger of banking and industry, while the 'highest stage of capitalism' refers to the highest possible development of the social relations of production short of social revolution. However, Lenin's fullest expression for dominant capital at this stage – 'monopoly finance capital' – is hardly ever critiqued. Insofar as Lenin's opponents directly criticise his theory of monopoly, this is usually levelled against the abbreviated expression 'finance capital' and its caricature – even though Lenin spells out that 'monopoly' is the key to his theory.

There is no recent critique of Lenin's views on 'monopoly' that I can find. This is remiss because many of Lenin's opponents agree on the analytical centrality of monopoly to contemporary capitalism. Only Shaikh outlines a detailed argument that monopoly is not central to Third World exploitation.[1] The International Socialist Tendency's key concept historically has been 'state capitalism' – a form of state monopoly. For *Monthly Review* the key was 'monopoly capital' (the monopoly of corporations) and later 'monopoly finance capitalism' (of finance over industry). Monopoly is also implicit in most 'financialisation' writing. The perceived financial wing of capital could not 'squeeze' productive capital unless it held some type of monopolistic position. Where Lenin's monopoly is mentioned, it is falsely suggested that Lenin counterposed monopoly to competition as mutually exclusive.

Warren's presentation of Lenin's monopoly, as 'the vigorous competitive incentive to innovate had vanished'[2] was a caricature (see Chapter 2). Yet, Warren continues, 'the reasons why Lenin's thesis that monopoly capitalism was parasitic and decadent is invalid are not difficult to enumerate. The rise of oligopolistic market structure – or monopolistic firms, as they are popularly called – has not reduced competition but on the contrary has intensified it.'[3] Far from being a reason Lenin's theory is invalid, intensified competition is what Lenin argued monopoly entailed, though a series of writers followed Warren's example in caricaturing Lenin.[4] Panitch and Gindin frame their *Making of Global Capitalism* as having been written not about the 'unyielding economic laws and the development of a so-called monopoly capitalism', but rather about 'continuing competition and class conflict, and the contradictions to which they gave rise'.[5]

Smith's core thesis is premised on rejecting Lenin's monopoly as the analytical tool that can explain imperialism, though he says so in a roundabout way: 'insistence on the economic and political centrality of the division of the world into oppressed and oppressor nations' (the part Smith agrees with) is 'antithetical' to 'Lenin's argument that in its economic essence imperialism is monopoly capitalism'.[6] He asks, 'How, then, can we achieve a theoretical concept of monopoly that *is* firmly based on the categories of capital?'[7] Presumably Lenin was seen to not have done this already, or it would not remain for Smith to try to achieve it. Smith also falsely associates Lenin's monopoly with that of the *Monthly Review*.[8]

Shaikh's *Capitalism: Competition, Conflict, Crisis* is easily the most detailed Marxian critique of contemporary competition (which he calls 'real competition'). In important respects, Shaikh's 'real competition' is consistent with Lenin's monopoly competition: 'Competition pits seller against seller, seller against buyer, buyer against buyer, capital against capital, capital against labor and labor against labor ... the relevant profit must be defensible in the medium term ... Monopolistic industries ... must have regulating rates of profit that are persistently higher than the average regulating rate.'[9] Lenin might agree. But Shaikh does not think so. His book proceeds as an extended critique of neoclassical 'perfect competition' and does not engage Lenin. Yet Shaikh seems to claim this critique is also valid against all Marxist writing on monopoly: 'All branches of the Marxian monopoly capitalism school share the central premise that competition declines as firms become larger, more varied, and fewer in number. This is the foundation of their argument.'[10] According to Shaikh, 'Marxian' writers in this category think monopoly supersedes competition and ushers in a new stage of capitalism … Marx's argument about the concentration and centralisation of capital is said to ultimately negate his own analysis [of] the competitive laws of value. Hilferding was the first to advance this view but it was Lenin's imprimatur that made it central to Marxist discourse.[11]

Shaikh thus conflates Lenin's view with those of Hilferding, Baran, Sweezy and Amin, some of whom he references to substantiate his claim. But Shaikh provides no reference to Lenin's work.[12] Instead of a critique of Lenin's key concept, monopoly, Shaikh repeats the popular notion that Lenin 'based his own theory of imperialism on the enhanced need for capital exports in the monopoly stage'.[13] Thus in writing a 979-page Marxian book on competition, Shaikh still avoided a critique of Lenin's monopoly.

A reader of *Imperialism* can find direct refutation of these caricatures of Lenin's work. As Barone pointed out thirty years ago, an 'important difference between Lenin's analysis of monopoly and finance capital and both Hilferding's and Bukharin's analysis' is that for Lenin 'monopoly and the rise of finance capital do not negate competition or the contradictions of capitalism, but rather heighten competition and intensify contradictions'.[14]

Monthly Review's monopoly capital theory is commonly associated with Lenin. This starts with the *Monthly Review* writers themselves. In his 1942 work on monopoly, Sweezy claimed of his own work that, 'with minor qualifications, this is the definition of imperialism proposed by Lenin'.[15] Foster too claims the *Monthly Review*'s view on monopoly is a continuation of the monopoly of 'Hilferding and Lenin'.[16]

However, Sweezy's early book, while sympathetic to Lenin and granting him a few short mentions and quotations, takes little from Lenin in either its monopoly or imperialism sections. By contrast, Hilferding is repeatedly quoted. Sweezy follows Hilferding in falsely viewing tariff walls as a necessary and characteristic policy of monopolies and imperialism: 'monopoly capital demands tariffs'.[17] In contrast, tariffs are not at all central for Lenin, who points out, for example, 'it is extremely important to note that in free-trade England, concentration also leads to monopoly' just as in Germany.[18]

Baran and Sweezy's premise in writing *Monopoly Capital* was that 'neither Lenin nor any of his followers attempted to explore the consequences of the predominance of monopoly for the working principles and "laws of motion" of the underlying capitalist economy'.[19] Yet their book does not critique Lenin's monopoly to show this, merely asserting it in their introduction. Sweezy's 1990 account of the historical development of his and Baran's concept of monopoly capital confirms their difference with Lenin. He describes *Monopoly Capital* as descending from a 'direct line from Marx through Kalecki and Steindl' and then to Baran.[20]

Contra Lenin, Baran and Sweezy's *Monopoly Capital* begins: 'We must recognise that competition, which was the predominant form of market relations in 19th-century Britain, has ceased to occupy that position, not only in Britain but everywhere else in the capitalist world.'[21] This is different from Lenin, who does not refer to a decline in competition but of 'free competition' and its transformation into a higher form of monopoly competition.

Marx, they argue, 'treated monopolies not as essential elements of capitalism but rather as elements of the feudal and mercantilist past which had to be abstracted from in order to attain the clearest possible view of the basic structure and tendencies of capitalism'.[22] However this misrepresents Marx, who was aware, as we have seen, that the outcome of competition was increasing concentration and centralisation of capital resulting in monopoly and ultimately in 'capitalism in its highest stage of development'.[23]

As Magdoff later observed, 'in Marxist literature, the terms competition and monopoly are used to designate different phases of capitalist society. In neither of these phases is there either pure competition or pure monopoly. Indeed, it is the essence of the theory of imperialism to recognize that competition exists within the monopoly phase.'[24] While admitting monopoly and competition coexist, Foster tends to describe a 'spectrum' where the economic situation is sometimes closer to competition and sometimes 'closer to the monopoly side of the spectrum'.[25] That is to say, for Foster the two are still counterposed and they partially displace one another, even if monopoly does not completely eradicate competition. This is different from viewing monopoly as a new form of competition, in which case the two can simultaneously intensify.

Harvey develops essentially the same view. His critique of monopoly, like Shaikh's, proceeds from a critique of heterodox work and does not engage Lenin. He then caricatures Marx: 'the founding myth of liberal economic theory', a 'pure and perfect competitive market', 'surprisingly ... is accepted as gospel in Marx's *Capital*'.[26] Against Marx's 'gospel', Harvey sensibly points out, 'monopoly power is foundational rather than aberrational to the functioning of capital and that it exists in a contradictory unity with competition'. He presents this as 'a rather unusual stance to take', going further, he says, than *even* Stiglitz,[27] but appears unaware that an understanding of the connection between monopoly and competition is neither new nor 'aberrational' to either Marxism or heterodox economics.[28]

What Harvey discovered quite recently, Marx formulated more deeply in 1847:

> In practical life we find not only competition, monopoly and the antagonism between them, but also the synthesis of the two, which is not a formula, but

a movement. Monopoly produces competition, competition produces monopoly. Monopolists are made from competition; competitors become monopolists. If the monopolists restrict their mutual competition by means of partial associations, competition increases among the workers; and the more the mass of the proletarians grows as against the monopolists of one nation, the more desperate competition becomes between the monopolists of different nations. The synthesis is of such a character that monopoly can only maintain itself by continually entering into the struggle of competition.[29]

Lenin also noted:

Half a century ago, when Marx was writing *Capital*, free competition appeared to the overwhelming majority of economists to be a 'natural law'. Official science tried, by a conspiracy of silence, to kill the works of Marx, who by a theoretical and historical analysis of capitalism had proved that free competition gives rise to the concentration of production, which, in turn, at a certain stage of development, leads to monopoly. Today, monopoly has become a fact.[30]

Yet Harvey still does not fully arrive at a 'synthesis'. Instead he writes that 'capital *oscillates*, as Giovanni Arrighi pointed out, between the two extremes of the supposedly ruinous effects of unregulated competition and the excessive centralising powers of monopolies and oligopolies'.[31] For Harvey, like Foster, the two are not unified but mutually exclusive in the sense that the growth of one displaces a part of the other, albeit while still coexisting.

Therefore, Harvey says, 'the state of the contradictory unity between monopoly and competition at any one historical phase has to be established, not presumed'.[32] Yet Harvey cannot formulate their unity, only their 'oscillation' (i.e. their substitution one for another). The 1930s are taken to be competitive and the 1960s–1970s more monopolistic. In the neoliberal period, however, Harvey only identifies the *need* for Marxist writing to establish 'the state of the contradictory unity' but does not do it. This must be because *both* competition and monopoly are so clearly prevalent that Harvey's oscillating formula does not allow him to arrive at any specific conclusion.

Lenin's view, as shown in what follows, is that monopoly negates only 'free competition' but brings a new and higher form of competition into play. Further, this new form is not limited to state policies like colonialism and war, but also permeates the labour process itself, a point emphasised in *Imperialism*.

Monopoly seen to be separate from the labour process

We saw that Warren caricatured Lenin's *Imperialism* as predicated on stagnation (while holding that the poor countries were catching up). In making this claim of catch-up, he adopts a definition of monopoly outside of production and the labour process. Warren argued that 'the peculiar character of "know-how"', by which he means productive technology, is 'that its *allegedly* heavy costs to the purchaser reflect various forms of monopoly power rather than *real* costs'. Consequently, 'such costs are liable to decline considerably as the bargaining power of many Third World countries grows'.[33] Clearly, Warren counterposed monopoly to 'real' costs (i.e. those justified by necessary labour time).

Baran and Sweezy tended to portray monopoly capital's interest in the Third World as being to obtain especially 'privileged terms' through off-market deals.[34] This is counterposed to a view that emphasises monopolistic labour superiority, because the latter can achieve surplus profit *on* the market. Against 'Schumpeter's perennial gale of creative destruction' that was based, for Schumpeter, in technological development born of competition, Foster, following Baran and Sweezy, emphasises that 'the giant corporations often held back on the development and release of new technologies'.[35] Something that, *if it were the typical feature*, would tend to undermine their long-term technical superiority. Smith, as we have seen, says that 'the source of monopoly power derives not from the technology itself but the legal protection power given to the innovator'.[36]

Harvey's *The New Imperialism* largely ignored productivity, production technology and division of labour. His 2013 book *does* consider productive division of labour, but it disavows imperialism and does not consider competition. Its purpose in considering the division of labour is to critique the capital–labour relation from the point of view of capital *in general*, without considering the competition between different capitals and national economies. Hence he can develop no insight into productive monopoly because competition and monopoly are not investigated in this context.

Harvey thus argues capital *in general* assumes an agenda of deskilling of labour and thus bringing down the cost of that labour,

> What is on capital's agenda is not the eradication of skills per se but the abolition of *monopolisable* skills. When new skills become important, such as computer programming, then the issue for capital is not necessarily the abolition of those skills (which it may ultimately achieve through artificial intelligence) but the undermining of their potential monopoly character by opening up abundant avenues for training in them.[37]

While this may have some truth for capital *in general*, individual and national *monopoly* capitalist groups do the opposite – they monopolise highly skilled labour for themselves in order to defeat their competitors on the market.

The one-sidedness of Harvey's formulation is evident because the development of new technology that replaces labour in the production process can come into existence only as a result of still more highly skilled work (some by salaried professionals) in design, research, development and engineering. Hence deskilling and automation can proceed only via the actual process of capitalist competition, which results also in the creation of yet higher-level monopolistic positions for other new capital and labour; hence the continuous reproduction of a new, increasingly hierarchical, division of labour.[38]

As Braverman suggested,

> Every step in the labor process is divorced, so far as possible, from special knowledge and training and reduced to simple labor. Meanwhile, the relatively few persons for whom special knowledge and training are reserved are freed so far as possible from the obligations of simple labor. In this way, a structure is given to all labor processes that at its extremes polarizes those whose time is infinitely valuable and those whose time is worth almost nothing. This might even be called the general law of the capitalist division of labor.[39]

Precisely! This highly insightful observation anticipates the general movement that indeed transpired in the neoliberal period (see Chapter 9). Braverman erred only when arguing, 'over the long run it creates that mass of simple labor which is the primary feature of populations in *developed capitalist countries*'.[40] He could have said 'underdeveloped countries' but evidently did not anticipate the modern international division of labour that would later develop.

Paradoxically, Harvey draws a brief yet brilliant outline of monopoly as an impetus for capitalist commodification of culture, nature, the biosphere and even just the incidentally peculiar, all in pursuit of above-average profits through 'product differentiation', exclusivity and the like. This lucid exposition lays bare a whole series of key mechanisms of monopoly advantage and price setting. Yet, excruciatingly, he omits the most important of all categories from this examination – monopolisation of labour process.[41]

As will be seen in the next section, Lenin's theory solves the problem in Harvey and Foster's work of the counterposition or oscillation between monopoly and competition by showing monopoly is a new form of competition.

Lenin's theory of monopoly capitalist competition

Lenin argued that competition is not ultimately diminished by monopoly but changes in form. Owing to the higher level of organisation and greater resources of competing monopolist groups compared to the competition among smaller isolated producers in the period of free competition, monopoly competition tends to increase in intensity and reach into ever higher and more destructive social spheres.[42] This results in the enlisting of the highest social organism in capitalist society – state power – in aid of monopolist groups. Yet the character of competition for Lenin – and this is one of his most accurate, yet little understood, contributions – ultimately remains capitalist. This means it must involve the capitalist (privately owned) production of commodities for the market. The enlisting of, for example, state power, is principally in direct or indirect aid to such capitalist ends.

In another crucial aspect of Lenin's theory, the presence of *capitalist* monopolies, Lenin argued, also implies the immutable existence of capitalist non-monopoly producers and therefore a relation of dominance and exploitation between the two classes of capital. Lenin, it is commonly acknowledged, also outlined another aspect of capitalism's monopoly stage – monopoly of the few rich nations over the rest – as in fact has transpired. It will be shown in the following chapters that the monopoly of the imperialist nations over the Third World in fact represents the international manifestation of the domination of monopoly capital over non-monopoly capital. 'Imperialism' of the rich, monopoly capitalist nations therefore appears as an inevitable and organic part of Lenin's theory of monopoly finance capital as a whole.

There are at least six aspects of Lenin's theory of monopoly competition, which are outlined as follows: (1) competition between the various capitalist producers changes form and *intensifies* (not stagnates or diminishes) under conditions of generalised monopoly and tends to enlist all social spheres into that competition; (2) competition remains *capitalist* in character and therefore is still governed by the general laws that govern capitalist development; (3) the primary arena of competition, as in all periods of capitalism, remains the labour process; (4) competition for domination of the labour process takes the form of a struggle for *highest labour productivity*, which ultimately becomes a struggle to dominate the *highest aspects of the labour process*; (5) the outcome of this struggle, which produces winners and losers, is the creation and consolidation of two types of capital – *monopoly and non-monopoly capital*, which constantly compete, both within and between each group; and (6) on an international level, the consolidation of monopoly and non-monopoly capital takes the form or a division between imperialist monopoly capital and Third World non-monopoly capital and therefore rich and poor states and societies where the poor societies are exploited by the rich societies.

These six aspects give Lenin's theory of monopoly competition – the essence of his broader theory of imperialism – a coherence and potency. Almost all of these aspects are more or less explicit in *Imperialism*.

Intensification and generalisation of capitalist competition

Lenin tends to view monopoly as not only changing the forms of competition but intensifying it by raising it to ever higher levels, commensurate with the higher degree of development of monopoly capital. As Lenin says, 'A monopoly, once it is formed and controls thousands of millions, inevitably penetrates into *every* sphere of public life.'[43] It therefore must take competition with it into all public spheres; in other words, it enlists the various spheres – including the state – in its struggle against competing capitalist groups.

As suggested, Lenin resolves the counterposition or oscillation between monopoly and competition by showing monopoly is a new form of competition. Because the economy as a whole is dominated by monopolies, any increase in competition is not the displacement of monopoly but the result of intensification of the struggle between monopolist groups (or intensification of their struggle with non-monopoly capital). The breaking of one type of monopoly results in the strengthening of another. This change is carried out via competition and does not end it. In short, monopoly is competition – albeit in a new form.

Lenin better concretises Marx's initial synthesis of monopoly and competition. He does this by broadening the concept of competition beyond 'free competition'. As suggested, Lenin's view of monopoly competition continuously returns to commodity production and hence the labour process, yet adding new monopolistic forms to it:

> The deepest economic foundation of imperialism is monopoly. This is capitalist monopoly, i.e., monopoly which has grown out of capitalism and which exists in the general environment of capitalism, commodity production and competition, in permanent and insoluble contradiction to this general environment ... Monopoly under capitalism can never completely, and for a very long period of time, eliminate competition in the world market.[44]

> It is highly important to have in mind that this change [to the imperialist era] was caused by nothing but the direct development, growth, continuation of the deep-seated and fundamental tendencies of capitalism and production of commodities in general.[45]

At first glance, some of Lenin's formulations may appear contradictory. For example, he says,

> Imperialism emerged as the development and direct continuation of the fundamental characteristics of capitalism in general. But capitalism only became capitalist imperialism at a definite and very high stage of its development, when certain of its fundamental characteristics began to change into their opposites, when the features of the epoch of transition from capitalism to a higher social and economic system had taken shape and revealed themselves in all spheres.[46]

It might be argued that by 'change into their opposites' Lenin in fact concedes a lessening of capitalist competition. However, this tendency is arrested (or can only express itself partially and in a contradictory manner) because the system is not permitted to develop into 'a higher social and economic system' (i.e. into socialism). Short of revolution, which would resolve these contradictions, Lenin viewed imperialism as remaining a form of 'capitalist monopoly' that is characterised therefore by antagonism between private owners.[47]

To illustrate some of the forms of monopoly competition in his own time, Lenin quotes Kestner, who mentions stopping supplies of raw materials to rival concerns, agreements between capitalists and the trade unions in which unions allow members to work only for a cartel, stopping deliveries, closing trade outlets, agreements with buyers to trade only with the cartels, systematic price cutting, stopping credits and boycott.[48]

Lenin's own depiction of struggles and agreements between electricity, oil, shipping and rail monopolies provides a richer and more nuanced picture of monopoly competition (as it then existed). In what he calls 'the comedy of oil', Lenin brings together market warfare across different branches of production, the use of state legal provisions and even patriotic political campaigns as part of competition between different national capitalist groups and industries tied to the big banks.[49]

Yet, the most important transformation, and that which Lenin gives greatest emphasis to, is monopolistic domination of the labour process: highest labour productivity in the production of commodities through the systematic application of scientific research and development (R & D) (see Chapter 9). That Lenin emphasised R & D – in the production of commodities for the *consumer* market as opposed to war goods – suggests Lenin's overall conception of imperialism is bound by his view that so long as it remains capitalist in character (and it must), imperialism, in the long term, must also remain capitalist in form.

This reads like a tautology. Capitalism must remain capitalist. Of course! Yet this is what has been forgotten. It was understandable that during the war, Bukharin could falsely believe that state capitalist forms then assumed by belligerent states had become the new essential forms of capitalist imperialism, not temporary war measures, and hence had become permanent. Lenin, however, by a historical and theoretical investigation, concluded that, while the ever-increasing role of the state is an essential feature of imperialism, its forms and the forms of competition between monopolist groups are ultimately subordinate to the need to produce commodities and sell them on the market for a profit. While war can destroy commodities, the winners, if they are capitalists, must ultimately turn the conditions of their victory into the conditions for the production of commodities.

If monopoly competition ultimately remains about capitalist production of commodities, it must, for Marxists, also conform to the laws governing capitalist commodity production in general, as outlined in *Capital*. It was Lenin's refusal to forget or throw away the basic theoretical tenets established by Marx that arguably explains the longevity of his work.

Lenin's foresight about the continuation of capitalist commodity production derives from his awareness of the basic contradiction of the imperialist period as depicted in the concept of capitalism's highest stage: increasingly socialised production in the context of continued capitalist private ownership of the means of production. The outright merger of state and private property, by contrast, would mean abolition of private property and class rule in its capitalist form. As Lenin says, in bourgeois society, 'private property is sacred, and no one can be prohibited from buying, selling, exchanging or mortgaging shares, etc.'[50]

Lenin's grasp on the specifically capitalist nature of imperialism and monopoly accounts for the superior predictive ability of *Imperialism* compared with both Hilferding and Bukharin's work. Lenin's 'general framework [where] formally recognized *free* competition remains'[51] is clearly different to (and today more accurate than) Hilferding's 'general cartel' in which 'the entire capitalist production is consciously controlled from one center which determines the amount of production in all its spheres'.[52] Likewise Bukharin's concept of the 'state-capitalist trust' in which vertical integration tends to turn the entire national economy into a 'single combined enterprise' has not aged well.[53] Bukharin viewed imperialism as moving beyond the bounds of a system governed by Marx's law of value: 'State power absorbs virtually every branch of production. Not only does it preserve the general conditions of the exploitative process but, in addition, the state increasingly becomes a direct exploiter, organizing and directing production as a collective, joint capitalist.'[54] Both Hilferding and Bukharin's formulations made the mistake of overgeneralising from then prevailing forms of capitalist monopoly. During the First World War, these tended towards centralised command economies under direct state control.

Today, 'state-capitalist trusts' have mostly been supplanted by privately owned MNCs (i.e. state-*supported* privately owned monopoly capital). This is a higher form of monopoly than the trusts and cartels of a hundred years ago. The indirect form of state assistance does not make it less essential. National imperialist economies today can be described as a 'single combined enterprise' only in the most abstract sense (i.e. abstracting from prevailing competition between different capitalist groups). Lenin's expectations were more accurate. Even the most social-democratic, post-war, imperialist economies such as 'socialist' Sweden never abolished private property. Nor did European fascist regimes. Capitalist commodity production was abolished only where capitalist class rule was defeated by revolutions, as in Russia and China.

As suggested, Lenin's view of the continuing competitive nature of capitalist monopoly derives from the broader social contradiction of monopoly capitalism as a whole as described by Lenin, following Marx as capitalism's 'highest stage'. The contradictory totality of this new stage was described by Lenin as 'monopoly finance capital'. This conceptually unites the principal, contradictory historical tendencies inherent within capitalist social relations in the imperialist period – that is, deepening of the social character of the production process (and therefore steps towards socialism) constrained by private ownership of the means of production. In doing so, 'monopoly finance capital' develops Marx's synthesis of competition and monopoly to provide a general historical foundation for understanding imperialist competition today. The form of this competition takes is *primarily* monopoly domination of the labour process.

Monopolistic domination of the labour process, its highest aspects and productivity

Monopoly outside of the labour process is certainly important in Lenin's work (and Marx's). Political connections, war and the 'squeezing' of concessions through treaties or trade agreements are all named as forms of monopoly; however, these are viewed not as a substitute but a supplement to domination of commodity production. As shown, Lenin rejected Hilferding's emphasis on tariffs as a necessary form of monopoly. Instead he outlined a monopolistic intensification of what was the most essential element of capitalist competition for Marx: the revolutionising of the means of production.

To this end, Lenin quotes the American Government Commission on Trusts to argue: 'The [trust's] superiority over competitors is due to the magnitude of its enterprises and their excellent technical equipment.'[55]

In fact, he cites similar examples from every major imperialist power at the time (i.e. the United States, France, England and Germany). For Lenin, monopoly power emanated principally from the labour process itself. For a work written during inter-imperialist world war, the degree of emphasis Lenin gives to apparently obscure developments in technology for the production of consumption goods (not war goods) is striking. For example, detailing the US Tobacco Trust's 'inventions concerning the manufacture of cigarettes, cheroots, snuff, tinfoil for packing, boxes, etc.' might have been ridiculed had *Imperialism* been published prior to the Russian revolution. However, from a contemporary perspective, particularly in the neoliberal period, it seems emphasis on such apparently minute detail was justified.

In Marx's theory, capitalism's chief advantage over pre-capitalist commodity production was superior labour productivity.[56] This advantage was intensified over time because capitalist competition occurred via the constant 'revolutionising of the instruments of production' and thus constant improvement in labour productivity.[57] *Imperialism* does not deny this fundamental characteristic of capitalism but shows that the process of 'revolutionising' production has taken on a monopolistic, higher and more powerful form due to the more social manner in which big monopoly capital could carry it forward: 'It stands to reason that the big banks' enterprises, worth many millions, can accelerate technical progress with means that cannot possibly be compared with those of the past. The banks, for example, set up special technical research societies, and, of course, only "friendly" industrial enterprises benefit from their work.'[58] This aspect of *Imperialism* provides the kernel to understanding what contemporary theory does not explain – namely how the historical imperialist states are able continuously to reproduce their monopolistic position in the context of rapid spread of commodity production across many of the largest Third World societies. The reason is that under monopoly conditions, the position of productive pre-eminence is monopolised.

Lenin quoted the US Government Commission on Trusts to explain how this operated in his time:

> Since its inception, the Tobacco Trust has devoted all its efforts to the universal substitution of mechanical for manual labour ... With this end in view it has bought up all patents that have anything to do with the manufacture of tobacco and has spent enormous sums for this purpose ... With the same object in view, the trust has built its own foundries, machine shops and repair shops. One of these establishments, that in Brooklyn, employs on the average 300 workers; here experiments are carried out on inventions concerning the manufacture of cigarettes, cheroots, snuff, tinfoil for packing, boxes, etc. Here, also, inventions are perfected.

> Other trusts also employ what are called development engineers whose business it is to devise new methods of production and to test technical improvements. The United States Steel Corporation grants big bonuses to its workers and engineers for all inventions that raise technical efficiency, or reduce cost of production.[59]

Lenin comments: 'In German large-scale industry, e.g., in the chemical industry, which has developed so enormously during these last few decades, the promotion of technical improvement is organized in the same way.'[60] He quotes Jeidels to argue that '*durable* monopoly exists to a high degree in the gigantic enterprises in the modern iron and steel and electrical industries owing to their very *complicated technique, far-reaching organization and magnitude of capital*'. Even in France, which had the least concentrated

capital of the European imperialist powers at the time, socialisation of R &
D is highlighted, while 'in Great Britain it is the size of the enterprise and its
high technical level which harbor a monopolist tendency'.[61]

Successful monopolisation of R & D that develops the labour process
guarantees, by definition, a renewal of monopoly over advanced productive
techniques and thereby (it will be argued) over the labour process as a whole.

Lenin's outline does not constitute a full explanation of the monopolistic
domination of highest labour productivity as it has subsequently unfolded,
since it does not show the role of the imperialist state and of imperialist
society more broadly (i.e. beyond the activities of the trusts themselves) in
the reproduction of highest labour productivity within the imperialist countries. However, the examples he gives are prescient and show the embryonic
form of what later developed.

Monopolistic domination of non-monopoly capital

Far from arguing that competition is abolished, Lenin holds that not even
'*free* competition' is abolished in monopoly capitalism:

> Monopolies, which have grown out of free competition, do not eliminate the
> latter, but exist above it and alongside it, and thereby give rise to a number of
> very acute, intense antagonisms, frictions and conflicts.[62]

> Not in every branch of industry are there large-scale enterprises ... On the
> contrary, the monopoly created in certain branches of industry increases and
> intensifies the anarchy inherent in capitalist production as a whole ... The
> privileged position of the most highly cartelised, so-called heavy industry,
> especially coal and iron, causes 'a still greater lack of co-ordination' in other
> branches of industry.[63]

By describing in this way the simultaneous and permanent presence on
the world market of both monopolies and non-monopoly capital, Lenin's
Imperialism outlined a centrally important feature of the imperialist period,
crucial to understanding the dynamics of contemporary capitalism – the
simultaneous development and polarisation between monopoly and non-
monopoly capital.

Once the distinction between monopoly and non-monopoly capital is
made, we can discern three distinct forms of competition: among monopolies, among non-monopoly capitals and between monopolies and
non-monopoly capitals. On the competition between monopoly and non-
monopoly capital, Lenin says, 'The general framework of formally recognised free competition remains, and the yoke of a few monopolists on
the rest of the population becomes a hundred times heavier'[64] and 'the
old struggle between small and big capital is being resumed at a new and

immeasurably higher stage of development'.[65] This is a logical position because monopolistic 'revolutionising' of the means of production could not lead to an *overall* increase in profits for the monopoly sector unless it coexists with non-monopoly capital, from which extra surplus value can be usurped. The higher average rate of profit for monopolies (see Chapter 11) could not occur without a corresponding lower rate of profit for non-monopolies. As outlined in what follows, for Marx, the source of monopoly profits must always be the redistribution of a portion of total surplus value from other capital to the monopoly (i.e. from non-monopoly to monopoly capital).

'The prolonged raising of prices', Lenin quotes Kestner to say,

> has hitherto been observed only in respect of the most important means of pro-
> duction, particularly coal, iron and potassium, but never in respect of manu-
> factured goods. Similarly, the increase in profits resulting from this raising of
> prices has been limited only to the industries which produce means of produc-
> tion. To this observation we must add that the industries which process raw
> materials (and not semi-manufactures) not only secure advantages from the
> cartel formation in the shape of high profits, to the detriment of the finished
> goods industry, but have also secured a dominating position over the latter,
> which did not exist under free competition.[66]

Thus while the specific forms of this relationship have changed – it is no longer principally raw materials and processing industries that exert monopolistic dominance – Lenin's *Imperialism* had already observed that high monopoly profits cause lower profits in the non-monopolised sectors. This binary relationship flows inevitably from Lenin's insistence on the capitalist nature of monopoly and its continued competitive character. The monopolies cannot extort others on the market unless they have some victims.

Division between monopoly and non-monopoly states: exploitation of the poor countries

Lenin's emphasis on exploitation of the poor countries was integral to his overall theory. It is integrated into his definition of monopoly capitalism when he says: 'On the threshold of the twentieth century we see the forma-tion of a new type of monopoly: firstly, monopolist associations of capi-talists in all capitalistically developed countries; secondly, the monopolist position of a few very rich countries.'[67] He goes on to argue that 'capitalism has grown into a world system of colonial oppression and of the financial strangulation of the overwhelming majority of the population of the world by a handful of "advanced" countries'.[68] Between 1915 and 1917 Lenin made exposing imperialist exploitation of the poor countries central to his fight against Kautsky and opportunism. He continued emphasising it until his death. In 1915 he made the poignant observation:

> Imperialism means the progressively mounting oppression of the nations of the world by a handful of Great Powers; it means a period of wars between the latter to extend and consolidate the oppression of nations; it means a period in which the masses of the people are deceived by hypocritical social-patriots, i.e., individuals who, under the pretext of the 'freedom of nations', 'the right of nations to self-determination', and 'defence of the fatherland', justify and defend the oppression of the majority of the world's nations by the Great Powers.

> That is why the focal point in the Social-Democratic programme must be that division of nations into oppressor and oppressed which forms the essence of imperialism, and is deceitfully evaded by the social-chauvinists and Kautsky.[69]

In 1916, 'The programme of Social-Democracy must point out that under imperialism the division of nations into oppressing and oppressed ones is a fundamental, most important and inevitable fact'.[70] And in 1917, 'It would be expedient, perhaps, to emphasise more strongly and to express more vividly in our programme the prominence of the handful of the richest imperialist countries which prosper parasitically by robbing colonies and weaker nations. This is an extremely important feature of imperialism.'[71] Lenin investigates the question of the future of the poor countries under imperialism through his examination of the prospect of the 'partition' of China. It is striking just how close Lenin, and also Hobson from a liberal perspective, come to describing many of the realities of the relations between contemporary China and the imperialist countries. The example demonstrates perhaps most powerfully of all the contemporary relevance as well as the limitations of Lenin's work. With typical caution, Lenin again introduces his idea by quoting other writers, yet makes clear his own thinking. He quotes Schulze-Gaevernitz: 'The "danger" of imperialism lies in that "Europe will shift the burden of physical toil – first agricultural and mining, then the rougher work in industry – on to the coloured races, and itself be content with the role of rentier, and in this way, perhaps, pave the way for the economic, and later, the political emancipation of the coloured races".'[72] Lenin criticises Schultz-Gaevernitz racist, chauvinist outlook. He also approvingly compiles the following quotation from Hobson on the prospect of the 'partitioning' China:

> The greater part of Western Europe might then assume the appearance and character already exhibited by tracts of country in the South of England, in the Riviera and in the tourist-ridden or residential parts of Italy and Switzerland, little clusters of wealthy aristocrats drawing dividends and pensions from the Far East, with a somewhat larger group of professional retainers and tradesmen and a larger body of personal servants and workers in the transport trade

and in the final stages of production of the more perishable goods; all the main arterial industries would have disappeared, the staple foods and manufactures flowing in as tribute from Asia and Africa. ... We have foreshadowed the possibility of even a larger alliance of Western states, a European federation of great powers which, so far from forwarding the cause of world civilisation, might introduce the gigantic peril of a Western parasitism, a group of advanced industrial nations, whose upper classes drew vast tribute from Asia and Africa, with which they supported great tame masses of retainers, no longer engaged in the staple industries of agriculture and manufacture, but kept in the performance of personal or minor industrial services under the control of a new financial aristocracy ... examine the economic and social condition of districts in Southern England today which are already reduced to this condition, and reflect upon the vast extension of such a system which might be rendered feasible by the subjection of China to the economic control of similar groups of financiers, investors, and political and business officials, draining the greatest potential reservoir of profit the world has ever known, in order to consume it in Europe. The situation is far too complex, the play of world forces far too incalculable, to render this or any other single interpretation of the future very probable; but the influences which govern the imperialism of Western Europe today are moving in this direction, and, unless counteracted or diverted, make towards some such consummation.[73]

In his fight against the opportunism of the Second International, Lenin clearly sought to highlight this parasitic aspect of imperialism. That during the First World War, and in the context of his polemic against Kautsky's 'ultra-imperialism', Lenin would introduce into his own work the possibility of an 'alliance of Western states, a European federation of great powers' and 'the gigantic peril of a Western parasitism' shows the degree to which he considered this a real prospect and danger.

The modern neoliberal period did, in many respects, progress along lines generally indicated by Schulze-Gaevernitz and Hobson. Certainly the 'rougher work' in industry (as well as the most dangerous, toxic, mind-numbing and soul-destroying work) as far as possible, has been passed on to 'coloured races'.

It would also be difficult to deny that the imperialist centres are now characterised by a proportionately increased number of 'workers in the transport [and logistics], trade and in the final stages of production of the more perishable goods'. We could add marketing, finance, leisure and entertainment. It is also true of the neoliberal period that manufactures are flowing into the imperialist countries 'as tribute from Asia and Africa', or at least partially 'as tribute', though we should add Eastern Europe, Mexico and other Third World regions as tributaries.

Yet Schulze-Gaevernitz's fear of *economic* emancipation – has not eventuated and is not eventuating today. Such emancipation from imperialist domination could have been expected if the First World proletariat were in fact reduced *only or principally* to 'performance of personal or minor industrial services', etc. If that were the case, the Chinese bourgeoisie, for example, would no longer be obliged by any market compulsion to exchange its products with the imperialists at unfavourable prices. Imperialist compulsion would have to take principally extra-economic forms.

It is only when imperialist parasitism (the appropriation of surplus value produced by Third World workers) is combined conceptually with another aspect of Lenin's theory – monopolisation of highest labour productivity – that a highly contradictory characteristic of contemporary imperialism, perhaps its most important aspect – its sustainable parasitism upon the Third World – can be understood.

Certainly, the burden of physical toil (and undesirable work in general) is offloaded as far as practical (or alternatively mechanised), yet what has been retained is not only minor duties but also the highest forms of scientific and skilled labour. This tends to be the most important and interesting brainwork, the most sophisticated and capital-intensive production processes as well as high-end R & D. High-end labour, R & D and scientific work are increasingly *concentrated* in the imperialist states. To the extent that 'bulk production' and menial work have been abandoned or lost to Third World capitalist competitors imperialism specialises in their opposite.

The vitality (so far) of this system lies in this combination. A pure and gigantic parasite must die or kill its host. Monopoly finance capital by contrast remains productive (including of value) but only in certain technically advanced aspects of the labour process. To the extent it can monopolise the highest forms of the necessary labour, it can parasitically appropriate value from other parts of the labour process. Today monopoly of the highest spheres is secured, as Lenin tended to anticipate, by imperialist dominance of R & D and of scientific development writ large.

In this way Lenin's book on imperialism, written over a century ago, still provides the theoretical kernel with which we can explain contemporary imperialism in terms that are more or less straightforward, intuitive and empirically verifiable. Before applying this in the contemporary period, however, the final theoretical step necessary to make possible a Marxist explanation of the imperialist world economy today is to link this concept with Marx's labour theory of value.

Notes

1 Shaikh, *Capitalism*.
2 Warren, *Imperialism*, p. 51.

3 Warren says, 'The development of oligarchy and various forms of association and combination (in individual economies) has been associated with the disappearance of monopoly on a world scale and its replacement by competition – the disappearance that is, of the British world monopoly of manufacturing with the rise of vigorous competitors towards the end of the nineteenth century.' See Warren, *Imperialism*, p. 79. But Lenin had already made the same point: 'In the last quarter of the nineteenth century, this [British] monopoly was already undermined ... we see the formation of a new type of monopoly: first, monopolist capitalist combines in all capitalistically developed countries; second, the monopolist position of a few very rich countries.' See Lenin, *Imperialism*, chap. 4. Lenin's formulation can only be misread as reducing competition if the reader views monopoly and competition as counterposed.

4 Howard and King, *Marxian Economics*, vol. 2, p. 121; Foster and McChesney, *The Endless Crisis*, p. 109.

5 Panitch and Gindin, *The Making of Global Capitalism*, p. ix; Screpanti, *Imperialism and the Great Crisis*, p. 48.

6 Smith, *Imperialism in the Twenty-First Century*, p. 228.

7 Smith, *Imperialism in the Twenty-First Century*, p. 229.

8 Smith, *Imperialism in the Twenty-First Century*, p. 231; Brolin, *The Bias of the World*, p. 71.

9 Shaikh, *Capitalism*, pp. 260, 15, 272.

10 Shaikh, *Capitalism*, p. 355.

11 Shaikh, *Capitalism*, p. 353; Shaikh, 'The Laws of International Exchange', in Nell, *Growth, Profits and Property*, p. 227.

12 Shaikh, *Capitalism*, pp. 354–5.

13 Shaikh, *Capitalism*, p. 354.

14 Barone, *Marxist Thought on Imperialism*, p. 48; E. Dussel Peters and A. Yanez, 'Marx's Economic Manuscripts of 1861–63 and the "Concept" of Dependency', *Latin American Perspectives*, 17:2 (1990), 64.

15 Sweezy, *The Theory of Capitalist Development*, p. 307.

16 J. B. Foster, R. W. McChesney and R. Jonna, 'Monopoly and Competition in Twenty-First Century Capitalism', *Monthly Review*, 62:11 (2011).

17 Sweezy, *The Theory of Capitalist Development*, p. 299.

18 Lenin also comments: 'Differences between capitalist countries, e.g., in the matter of protection or free trade, only give rise to insignificant variations in the form of monopolies or in the moment of their appearance; and that the rise of monopolies, as the result of the concentration of production, is a general and fundamental law of the present stage of development of capitalism.' See Lenin, *Imperialism*, chap. 1.

19 Baran and Sweezy, *Monopoly Capital*, p. 4.

20 Sweezy, 'Monopoly Capitalism', in Eatwell et al., *Marxian Economics*, pp. 299–301.

21 Baran and Sweezy, *Monopoly Capital*, p. 6. According to Sweezy, capitalism's 'decline in competition, which began in the late 19th century, proceeded at an

accelerated pace' in the twentieth century, Sweezy in Eatwell et al., *Marxian Economics*, p. 300.

22 Baran and Sweezy, *Monopoly Capital*, p. 4.

23 Marx, *Capital*, vol. 3, chap. 27; Barone, *Marxist Thought on Imperialism*, p. 193.

24 Magdoff and Foster, *Imperialism Without Colonies*, p. 135.

25 Foster et al., 'Monopoly and Competition'.

26 Harvey, *Seventeen Contradictions*, p. 132. Harvey himself contradicts this claim when he notes that 'Marx thought that the end point of competition was bound to be monopoly power'. Harvey, *Seventeen Contradictions*, p. 135.

27 Harvey, *Seventeen Contradictions*, p. 134.

28 Schumpeter, *Capitalism, Socialism and Democracy*, pp. 89, 99, 101; E. J. Nell, 'Competition and Price Taking Behaviour', in Nell, *Growth, Profits and Property*, p. 103.

29 K. Marx, *The Poverty of Philosophy: Answer to the Philosophy of Poverty by M. Proudhon* [1847] (Moscow, Progress, 1955), chap. 2; Kemp, 'The Marxist Theory of Imperialism', in Owen and Sutcliffe, *Studies in the Theory of Imperialism*, p. 19.

30 Lenin, *Imperialism*, chap. 1.

31 Harvey, *Seventeen Contradictions*, p. 136 (emphasis added).

32 Harvey, *Seventeen Contradictions*, p. 136.

33 Warren, 'Imperialism and Capitalist Industrialization', p. 32.

34 Baran and Sweezy, *Monopoly Capital*, p. 201.

35 Foster et al., 'Monopoly and Competition'.

36 Smith, *Imperialism in the Twenty-First Century*, p. 230. This follows, among others, Amin who says technology is 'firmly protected' by the World Trade Organisation. See Amin, *The Law of Worldwide Value*, p. 110.

37 Harvey, *Seventeen Contradictions*, pp. 119–20.

38 Harvey too senses the contradiction when he admits, 'new technologies have often called for redefinitions of skill' (though it would be accurate to say creation of new skills) and 'technological change was and is not uniquely directed to labour control'. Though the latter is his main argument and Harvey does not outline to what other ends it is directed, see Harvey, *Seventeen Contradictions*, pp. 112–29.

39 H. Braverman, *Labor and Monopoly Capital: The Degradation of Work in the Twentieth Century* [1974] (New York, Monthly Review, 1998), pp. 57–8.

40 Braverman, *Labor and Monopoly Capital*, pp. 57–8 (emphasis added).

41 Harvey, *Seventeen Contradictions*, pp. 138–41. Productive technology enters the discussion only in another context: as a trigger for Harvey's 'spatial fix' to the over accumulation problem. Yet, the 'spatial fix' itself is presented as part of power moving to 'the East'. Thus technological innovation tends to appear in Harvey, not as a crucial mechanism for the reproduction of imperialist domination, but the catalyst for imperial decline.

42 Dussel Peters and Yanez, 'Marx's Economic Manuscripts', p. 64; Day and Gaido *Discovering Imperialism*, p. 87.

43 Lenin, *Imperialism*, chap. 3.

44 Lenin, *Imperialism*, chap. 8.

45 Lenin, 'Introduction', in Bukharin, *Imperialism and World Economy*.

46 Lenin, *Imperialism*, chap. 7.

47 Lenin, *Imperialism*, chap. 8.

48 F. Kestner, *Der Organisationszwang. Eine Untersuchung über die Kämpfe zwischen Kartellen und Aussenseitern* (Berlin, 1912), quoted in Lenin, *Imperialism*, chap. 1.

49 Lenin, *Imperialism*, chap. 5.

50 Lenin, *Imperialism*, chap. 3.

51 Lenin, *Imperialism*, chap. 1 (emphasis added).

52 Hilferding: 'If we now pose the question as to the real limits of cartelization, the answer must be that there are no absolute limits … The ultimate outcome of this process would be the formation of a general cartel. The whole of capitalist production would then be consciously regulated by a single body which would determine the volume of production in all branches of industry. Price determination would become a purely nominal matter.' See Hilferding, *Finance Capital*, chap. 15. Lenin, considered 'the statement that cartels can abolish crises is a fable spread by bourgeois economists'. See Lenin, *Imperialism*, chap. 1.

53 Bukharin, *Imperialism and World Economy*, p. 70. Bukharin's term 'state capitalist trusts' is sometimes wrongly attributed to Lenin. Lenin does not use it in *Imperialism* or anywhere I can find. Lenin does refer to 'state-monopoly capitalism' three times in the preface to *The State and Revolution* [1917], vol. 25, *Collected Works* (Moscow, Progress, 1964).

54 N. Bukharin, *Toward a Theory of the Imperialist State* [1915] (New York, M. E. Sharpe, 1982).

55 *Report of the Commissioner of Corporations on the Tobacco Industry* (Washington, DC, 1909), quoted in Lenin *Imperialism*, chap. 1.

56 For example, 'British steam and science uprooted, over the whole surface of Hindostan, the union between agriculture and manufacturing industry'. See K. Marx, 'The British Rule in India', *New York Daily Tribune* (1853), 25 June.

57 Marx and Engels, *Communist Manifesto*, chap. 1.

58 Lenin, *Imperialism*, chap. 2.

59 *Report on the Tobacco Industry*, quoted in Lenin, *Imperialism*, chap. 1.

60 Lenin, *Imperialism*, chap. 1.

61 O. Jeidels, *Das Verhaltnis der deutschen Grossbanken zur Industrie mit besonderer Berucksichtigung der Eisenindustrie* (Leipzig, 1905), p. 108, quoted in Lenin, *Imperialism*, chap. 1 (emphasis added).

62 Lenin, *Imperialism*, chap. 7.

63 Lenin, *Imperialism*, chap. 1.

64 Lenin, *Imperialism*, chap. 1.

65 Lenin, *Imperialism*, chap. 2.

66 Kestner, *Der Organisationszwang*, quoted in Lenin, *Imperialism*, chap. 1.

67 Lenin, *Imperialism*, chap. 4.

68 Lenin, *Imperialism* [1920], preface.

69 V. I. Lenin, *The Revolutionary Proletariat and the Right of Nations to Self-Determination [1915], vol. 21, Collected Works* (Moscow, Progress, 1974).

70 Lenin, *Theses: Right of Self-Determination*.

71 Lenin, *Revision of the Party Programme*; V. I. Lenin, 'The Question of Nationalities or "Autonomisation"', in *'Last Testament' Letters to the Congress* [1923], vol. 36, *Collected Works* (Moscow, Progress, 1966).

72 Schulze-Gaevernitz, *Die deutsche Kreditbank*, quoted in Lenin, *Imperialism*, chap. 8.

73 J. A. Hobson, *Imperialism: A Study* (London, James Pott, 1902), quoted in Lenin, *Imperialism*, chap. 8.

8

Monopoly and Marx's labour theory of value

It is not true that Lenin's theory of imperialism is disconnected from the Marxist theory of value, even though the link is not made explicit in his work. That would be true if monopoly, as Lenin understood it, had no connection to value transfer or if he saw monopoly as tending to abolish Marx's law of value (meaning that value transfers that result from monopoly have no relationship to Marx's theory). It has been shown that was not Lenin's view. In fact Lenin's theory, which involves the transfer of value from non-monopoly capital to monopoly capital, as well as among monopolies, develops how Marx said his law of value would operate in monopoly conditions. Marx said:

> If equalisation of surplus-value into average profit meets with obstacles in the various spheres of production in the form of artificial or natural monopolies, and particularly monopoly in landed property, so that a monopoly price becomes possible, which rises above the price of production and above the value of the commodities affected by such a monopoly, then the limits imposed by the value of the commodities would not thereby be removed. The monopoly price of certain commodities would merely transfer a portion of the profit of the other commodity-producers to the commodities having the monopoly price.[1]

Marx's comments here are limited to the general effect of monopoly and do not explain what factors determine the degree of extra profitability of a monopoly. This is because Marx's level of abstraction in volume 3 of *Capital* mostly does not deal with market competition.[2] Though notably Marx's comment above already clearly indicates the categories of monopoly and non-monopoly capital and surplus-value transfer between them.

The argument of the *Monthly Review* tendency is that, while a monopoly profit implies a transfer of surplus value from other producers, the actual size of this transfer cannot be reckoned or explained using Marx's law of value. Hence the law's redundancy under monopoly conditions. Sweezy says,

> Under conditions of monopoly, exchange ratios do not conform to labor-time ratios, nor do they stand in a theoretically demonstrable relation to labor-time ratios ... it appears to be obvious, as Hilferding said, that 'the realization of

Marx's theory of concentration, of monopolistic merger, seems to result in the invalidation of Marx's value theory.'[3]

> In so far as the allocation of productive activity is brought under conscious control, the law of value loses its relevance and importance; its place is taken by the principle of planning.[4]

This may be true of society-wide planning. However, fully social planning requires the abolition of private property. Until such a time, the various planning entities – monopolist groupings controlled by private capitalist owners – are in mutual competition and for that reason can never engage in truly collaborative and long-term planning (as opposed to various pacts). The limitation of monopoly capitalist planning is expressed, for example, in the continuation of boom–bust cycles – a fundamental feature of the capitalist system.

Following Sweezy, Amin argues,

> Monopoly is above all a hindrance to the equalisation of profit. Prices therefore cease to be determined by a general law based on values. The field of operation of the law of value contracts. There is no longer any rationality, even apparent, in the price system. Prices are determined by social relations of strength within the dominant class, between the financial groups that dominate the various sectors of economic activity.[5]

'Social relations of strength' may be an apt description of monopoly competition. Yet it only poses but does not answer the question of on what lawful basis 'strength' is built and what are its characteristics if monopoly competition in fact retains the character of capitalist private property.

John Smith and Shaikh reject *Monthly Review*'s view of monopoly. Yet, falsely assuming it to be the only possible Marxist view of monopoly, both writers, as shown, conflate *Monthly Review*'s monopoly with Lenin's and reject monopoly altogether on this basis. Smith, following Amin, holds that monopoly 'implies a violation of the law of value … a departure from the law'.[6] It 'negate[s] the law of value',[7] stands as its 'antithesis':[8] 'A value theory of imperialism [therefore] must … recognize that the source of imperialist profits is not to be found in any form of monopoly – however big a role monopolistic corporations may play in helping to generate these conditions.'[9] For Shaikh,

> In the case of monopoly, it is widely accepted by Marxists and non-Marxists alike that laws of price formation must be abandoned … Of course, once the laws of price formation in general are thrown out, the laws of international price formation necessarily follow. The focus shifts instead to the domestic and international rivalries of giant monopolies, to their political interaction with various capitalist states, and to the antagonisms and conflicts between these states themselves – in other words, to imperialism as an aspect of monopoly

capitalism. The law of value, like competitive capitalism itself, fades into history.[10]

All these writers proceed from a theoretical understanding of monopoly as the negation of competition. This view stems ultimately from rejecting Lenin's classical Marxist theory of *capitalist* monopoly as a new form of *capitalist* competition. Understood as capitalist competition, monopoly must be a new form of struggle by each capitalist group to increase its own portion of the total value *through sale of commodities on the market*. Struggle for the capitalist production of commodities for sale on the capitalist market to increase profits can hardly amount to the 'antithesis' of Marx's theory of value. The parameters of this struggle are determined by Marx's theory – albeit with certain modification owing to the new monopolistic form that competition now takes.

The continuity between pre-monopoly and monopoly forms of capitalist competition can be seen also in that both ultimately revolve around competition for superiority in the labour process and hence result in the same continuous revolutionising of the means of production that was identified in the *Communist Manifesto* as the great historical contribution of the capitalist system. Far from negating this tendency, capitalism's monopoly stage draws greater social resources into this process. Something that becomes all the more important because, as Marx observed, an increased rate of surplus value raises the level of labour-saving required before new machinery can be economically introduced by capitalists.[11]

Determination of profits

Marx's law of value has never and can never be expressed in the real world in a pure form because it is always subject to conditioning factors. On the other hand, the ways and degree that monopoly, or any other conditioning factor, can affect the operation of the law is restricted by the definite limitations set down in the law. As Marx infers above, the total surplus value available to capital as a whole is determined by the total magnitude of socially necessary labour carried out (beyond that necessary to provide for workers' consumption). Monopoly can only redistribute actually existing surplus value among the competing capitalist groups. Of course monopoly producers also produce surplus value. But this is in their capacity as producers not redistributors.

The amount of extra surplus value accruing to an individual monopoly capital (i.e. that above the average rate) is determined by the *degree* of monopoly that capital possesses. Likewise, the degree of appropriation of surplus value by monopoly capital as a whole from non-monopoly capital as a whole is also determined by the degree of monopoly it possesses. This is expressed as the difference between the average monopoly rate of profit and the average non-monopoly rate of profit.

Once it is accepted that the labour process is the underlying essential form of monopoly, it follows that the degree of monopoly is fundamentally determined by the degree of domination in the labour process. Hence the degree of appropriation of other capital's surplus value is also determined by the degree of *labour process* domination.

The degree of superiority is measured in capitalist practice by the cost to other capitals of the production of a given monopoly commodity (i.e. how much money would need to be invested to achieve the production of that commodity).[12] If other capitals would require a huge investment to achieve the production of a commodity that a monopoly has achieved with a relatively small investment, then its capacity for monopolistic price markup is high.

This parallels the way Marx showed that an individual capital with superior labour productivity in the same branch of industry gains above-average profit in pre-monopoly conditions.[13] There is no reason to think, as Smith argues, that Marx's law should not apply across branches, or in the production of different use values. Actually it does apply, as can be seen from the following contemporary example.

At a general level, there are two types of technical domination in the labour process. One is the cheaper production than competitors of the same commodities (i.e. ultimately with less labour). The other is production of commodities that few others can produce, or do so easily and well.[14] Both result in surplus profits because, in either case, it is possible to sell products for prices well above what it costs capitalists to produce them. Each of these is a different form of monopolistic superiority on the market that is based on dominance over the labour process.

Both forms necessitate superiority in the most sophisticated – and therefore highest – labour processes within an overall division of labour. This is even the case for monopolistic production of standard, undifferentiated commodities more cheaply than competitors. Abstracting from advantageous access to natural resources, or access to cheaper labour or other commodities, the monopolistic production of standard commodities results from higher labour productivity (i.e. from the use of less labour for a given magnitude of production). This comes about through the development of better technique (in other words, development of a higher or more sophisticated technique). While the product may be the same, the process of its formation is not.

Without better technique, the other way to cheapen production is by pushing down the cost of labour power or increasing the intensity of labour,

both of which, Marx argued, soon come up against definite natural limitations.[15] Owing to these natural limitations and the relative abundance of the
commodity of ordinary labour power in the Third World, the use of cheaper
labour power to carry out common or standardised production processes
cannot generally result in a monopoly. This is due to the ease with which
non-monopoly Third World capitals can replicate such labour processes.
Hence it is not generally possible to raise the price of such commodities
above the average *price of production* of *non*-monopoly capital, and thus to
gain profits above the average for *non*-monopoly capital.

Both forms of monopolistic domination in the labour process are recognised on the market as equivalent to each other because the price a capitalist
can get for the sale of either commodity is governed by the medium-term
cost to other capitals of producing it, including the cost of breaking incumbent monopoly to do so. The cost ultimately refers to the quantity of labour
that would have to be expended.

Hence the unique product sells on the market with a markup governed by
the degree of the technical superiority of the labour that produced it. This
is the same for uniquely productive labour producing undifferentiated commodities more quickly. The difference is that in the case of identical commodities, the degree of labour superiority can be measured by counting or
weighing the produce directly. In the case of unique commodities, the degree
of superiority can be calculated only approximately by an estimation of the
cost of investing in the production of that commodity – an estimation that
monopoly capital, in practice, makes on a routine basis. In both cases it is
the degree of labour productivity that dictates the size of monopoly profit.
This is the Marxist labour theory of unequal exchange.

The case of Google versus Samsung via Motorola

In 2014 Samsung produced the handsets for 81 per cent of the Android
segment of the global mobile-phone market. Google, being the producer of
Android, provided the operating system for 100 per cent of these. A great
synergy on paper perhaps, but the two giants fell out over the division of
revenues from phones containing both of their products. Samsung attempted

> to hide Android – and consequently Google's role in its achievement. It did
> this using 'TouchWiz', the company's proprietary skin which painted over all
> aspects of Android leaving it unrecognisable … Samsung began degrading
> Android performance by switching out vast parts of the software – phone
> dialler, calendar, email client, contacts, notification center, music and video
> player, voice control and much more – for its own apps … It put TouchWiz
> on its smart TVs, another market it dominates, and began building its own
> Android rival – Tizen.[16]

Google responded to this threat to its Android monopoly by buying Motorola Mobility in 2011, which included the acquisition of twenty thousand patents, an R & D lab and a phone-handset production business. Kelly observed: 'Should Google use Motorola to ramp up its own major handset business the market would be theirs. The phones would have stock Android and no one, not even Samsung, could afford to subsidise their cost as Google can [by] leveraging its mammoth advertising revenue.'[17] Thus Google, in response to Samsung's threat to its monopoly on mobile-phone operating systems, responded by threatening Samsung's own monopoly in building mobile-phone handsets.

> On 27 January 2014 Google and Samsung signed a wide-ranging global patent deal which will last a decade. Buried within it was an agreement that Samsung would tone down TouchWiz, refocus on core Android apps over its own customisations and cancel more radical customisations such as its 'Magazine UX' interface. Two days later Google announced the sale of Motorola Mobility to Lenovo.[18]

As Kelly notes above, 'no one, not even Samsung, could afford to subsidise their cost as Google can [by] leveraging its mammoth advertising revenue'. That is, Google's profits are so high – owing to its degree of monopoly in online advertising it had huge resources available to invest in production and cross subsidisation of prices – that Samsung's prospects of competing with it in handset production were dubious. Yet Google's share of the worldwide digital ad market – 41.3 per cent in 2012 – was lower than Samsung's share of phone production.[19] Why then was Samsung and not Google compelled to back down? The answer is because handset manufacture is not such a high-end labour process as development of operating systems or control of the advertising market. This is why Apple, which does both, outsources large parts of its phone manufacturing but keeps higher-end processes in-house. Hence Google's threat to encroach into a relatively lower sphere from a higher profit base was far more credible than Samsung's excursions in the opposite direction.

The monetary cost, or potential cost, to each company is the outward expression of the real underlying issue – the amount of labour time necessary in each case. The labour processes in this example involve skilled labour. Marx argues skilled labour can be reduced in the final calculation of value to simple average labour.[20] Thus Google's higher-end labour rather than Samsung's counts on the market as a greater quantity, of simple average labour – the common denominator of value.

The extension of the operation of the law of value (or our understanding of it) to encompass the interaction between distinct branches of production and the transfer of surplus value between them is consistent with the actual operation of capitalist competition in monopoly conditions. Monopoly capital does not operate in just one sphere. It has the resources to jump quickly from one to another if the opportunity or compulsion arises. In this way, the greater social scope of modern capitalist productive forces extends Marx's law to more thoroughly regulate and compare all labour processes across the entire spectrum of capitalist commodity production.[21]

This does not mean the degree of monopolistic price markup is *exactly* proportionate to the degree of monopolistic technical superiority. On the contrary, it is in the nature of monopoly in general that a second helping be added on top of that which is 'deserved'. Deserved means that portion which is caused by the superior labour productivity itself, as opposed to whatever else can be leveraged and stolen as a result of the productive superiority.

The second helping is possible due to incumbency. By controlling a large portion of a given market, possessing a large magnitude of capital, a brand and established supplier relationships and customers, established monopolies possess substantial resources to destroy any new entrants. This second helping therefore is purely parasitic. Yet highest labour productivity remains the material basis that determines which individual capitals and national capitals are able to secure this monopolistic position and thus secure both forms of surplus profit.

Even the size of the second helping – the parasitic reward for a monopolistic position – is also generally proportionate to the degree of labour superiority. A weak and relatively insecure monopoly (i.e. one that possesses only a small or uncertain labour superiority) can hardly command the same long-term premium as a firm with overwhelming technical superiority. The size of the premium 'must be defensible in the medium term', as Shaikh aptly puts it.[22] In most of the important branches this means defensible by greater labour productivity and, what amounts to the same thing, labour superiority in the highest labour processes.

For this reason we can say that monopoly capital is parasitic. It may or may not be the case that *most* of its surplus profit is usurped parasitically. The present book makes no measurement. We can say it is not the pure parasitism of Hobson and Schulze-Gaevernitz's description. Monopoly capital and the imperialist states would be unable to sustain its parasitism if it did not also dominate the labour process. This is the key to imperialism's longevity. In monopoly capitalism, productivity begets parasitism.

The example given above was of struggle between two monopoly corporations of different rank. Yet the overall and long–term result of competition carried out in monopoly conditions is the consolidation of two groups – the winners and losers of the fight to control the highest economic spheres: monopoly and non-monopoly capital. As said, this primary division results in the development of not one but two average rates of profit – at least for the largest corporations (see Chapter 11) – and on this basis, not one but two types of nations.

We started the book by describing perhaps the most important empirical fact of capitalist imperialism – the global polarisation between rich and poor societies. It was asserted that this divide can be explained theoretically by showing it is caused by the parallel polarisation between monopoly and non-monopoly capital. Via an extensive critique of contemporary literature and Lenin's classical theory, it has been shown what such an explanation looks like theoretically. It is now finally possible to begin to apply it to the neoliberal period, to see how closely it corresponds to the realities of the modern economy and what insights it can provide. This is the real test of what the book has said so far.

Notes

1 Marx, *Capital*, vol. 3, chap. 50.
2 Dobbs, 'Centenary of Lenin's Theory'.
3 Sweezy, *The Theory of Capitalist Development*, pp. 270, 55.
4 Sweezy, *The Theory of Capitalist Development*, p. 53.
5 Amin, *Unequal Development*.
6 Smith, *Imperialism in the Twenty-First Century*, p. 205.
7 Smith, *Imperialism in the Twenty-First Century*, p. 217.
8 Smith, *Imperialism in the Twenty-First Century*, p. 222.
9 Smith, 'Imperialism in the Twenty-First Century'; Smith, *Imperialism in the Twenty-First Century*, p. 230.
10 Shaikh, 'The Laws of International Exchange', in Nell, *Growth, Profits and Property*, pp. 208–9.
11 Marx, *Capital*, vol. 1, chap. 15.
12 Mandel, *Late Capitalism*, p. 70.
13 Marx, *Capital*, vol. 3, chap. 10.
14 G. Gereffi, J. Humphrey and T. Sturgeon, 'The Governance of Global Value Chains', *Review of International Political Economy*, 12:1 (2005), 81.
15 Marx, *Capital*, vol. 1, chap. 10.
16 G. Kelly, 'How Google Used Motorola to Smack Down Samsung – Twice', *Forbes* (2014), 10 February.
17 Kelly, 'How Google Used Motorola'.
18 Kelly, 'How Google Used Motorola'. Though Google kept around fifteen thousand to seventeen thousand Motorola patents.
19 *eMarketer*, 'US Digital Ad Spending to Top $37 Billion in 2012 as Market Consolidates' (2012), 20 September.
20 'In every process of creating value, the reduction of skilled labour to average social labour, e.g., one day of skilled to six days of unskilled labour, is unavoidable'. Marx, *Capital*, vol. 1, chap. 7.

21 According to Itoh, the latter half of the items planned in Marx's lifework – state, foreign trade and world market – are all introduced in the concrete analysis in Lenin's imperialism. See Itoh, 'Unequal Exchange Reconsidered', p. 5.

22 Shaikh, *Capitalism*, pp. 15, 272; Mandel, *Late Capitalism*, p. 95. Chamberlin had earlier observed that 'both monopolistic and competitive forces combine in the determination of most prices'. See E. H. Chamberlin, *The Theory of Monopolistic Competition: A Reorientation of the Theory of Value* [1933] (Cambridge, MA, Harvard University Press, 1969) p. xi.

Part IV

Monopoly and non-monopoly capital:
the economic core of imperialism

9

Neoliberal polarisation of capital

> Force, extortion or robbery may bring a high return, and they are important
> features of imperialism. But they are not the modus operandi of an economic
> system any more than piracy can be seen as a mode of production (Norfield,
> 2016).

Far from signifying 'free trade' or removal of all international barriers,
the neoliberal period was characterised by only *relative* trade freedom and
open capital markets compared with other periods of monopoly capitalism.
Nevertheless, the policy reveals, among other things, the high degree of economic power enjoyed by the imperialist states collectively and the domination of US imperialism in particular. Economic domination replaces the
need for imperialist states to erect as many or as rigid non-economic protections to ensure the dominance of its companies. For example, imperialist
exploitation of *politically independent* underdeveloped states represents a
more advanced form of imperialism than its predecessor – colonialism – just
as 'free' wage labour represents a more advanced form of labour exploitation than capitalist slavery.

As Lorimer points out, US imperialism has long 'eschewed' formal empire:

> This policy was first articulated by Secretary of State John Hay in his 'Open
> Door Notes', circulated in 1898, which sought to prevent European colonial
> expansion in China and preserve open access for all the imperialist powers to
> the Chinese market. This open door, as Woodrow Wilson aptly described it,
> was 'not the open door to the rights of China, but the open door to the goods
> of America'. As a political strategy, the open door policy represented the nat-
> ural policy of a new great economic power, which recognised that open com-
> petition, in foreign as well as domestic markets, was the most efficient way of
> ensuring domination for the strongest.[1]

The United States was not able to impose an open door policy internationally in 1898. Even after its victory in the Second World War and emergence
as the world superpower, this preferred policy was still held back by the
concurrent victory of the Soviet Red Army, the Chinese revolution and a
series of Third World anti-imperialist rebellions.[2] However, the neoliberal
period – especially the years between the collapse of the Soviet Union in

1991 and the great recession in 2008 – appears as a coming of age of the US open-door policy.

The most essential economic basis of imperialism in the neoliberal period is imperialist monopoly over the labour process. Several characteristic features of monopoly occur in connection with this: (1) increasing technical specialisation results in a hierarchical and polarised world division of labour, (2) intensifying impetus for continuous R & D, (3) a tendential shift in competition from the sphere of production towards the sphere of reproduction of the most advanced forms of labour, (4) an increasingly central role for the capitalist state and the tendency for this role to shift towards supporting the production process, (5) division of capital into monopoly and non-monopoly and (6) division of the world into monopoly and non-monopoly capitalist countries and states on this basis.

As *The Economist* noted in 2014, 'years of trade liberalisation culminated in the establishment of the World Trade Organisation in 1995, with China acceding to it in 2001'.[3] At the time Schwartz observed that the United States 'shows a strong preference for letting markets dictate the distribution of production, since the natural working of the market will distribute most new high-value-added production to existing areas of high-value-added production'.[4] The overall tendency in the neoliberal period was to protect only economically or politically sensitive labour processes, while many other processes were offshored or abandoned. The trend towards greater outsourcing of routine labour processes to independent contractors also implies a further expansion of the reach of the market as a regulating mechanism for the distribution of value, namely its extension to transactions that take place within production processes. This enables a greater degree of value transfer on the market to those capitals that dominate it.

Neoliberal monopoly-dominated 'free trade' represented a more advanced form of domination and surplus-value extraction than direct ownership of relatively undifferentiated assets protected by high-tariff walls. Steinfeld identified that contemporary advances in information technology, digitisation and its capacity for massive data storage and retrieval meant that 'codified' labour 'processes can be split into discrete steps – modules, in effect – and standards to ensure their connectivity can be established'.[5] He notes that 'modularization, in turn, has permitted activities that once had to be co-located geographically and managed organizationally within the confines of a single firm to be spread out across great geographic and organizational expanses'.[6]

Indisputably, contemporary technology, and not just information and communication technology, does permit geographical separation of ever more sophisticated labour processes. As *The Economist* outlines,

Technological improvements made possible longer and more complex supply chains. By the 1990s container shipping had made transporting goods around the world easier and cheaper than ever before, and the new ports needed to add trade capacity could be built quickly and easily ... the development of computer-based design technologies ... allowed precise details of components to be easily sent from place to place, and to be changed on the fly.[7]

These advances allowed MNCs specialising in only highest labour processes to take advantage of and profit handsomely from the abundant cheap labour that entered the world labour supply during the 1980s, 1990s and 2000s, in particular from China and resulting, as seen in Chapter 1, in increased income in imperialist societies since 1980.

Internationalisation is a typical feature of capitalism in general. Internationalisation of production processes (as opposed to internationalisation of trade or finance, which earlier became widespread) was widely acknowledged by researchers in the 1970s. Mandel said the post-war period had brought, 'for the first time in man's history, a genuine world-wide division of labour, a real universal world market, which intimately bound together all the countries in the world'.[8] Earlier, for certain commodities such as oil, internationalisation was acknowledged by Lenin and other classical writers.[9] What seems unique in the neoliberal period is only the *degree* of separation and international distribution of relatively specific aspects of the overall labour processes and the degree of specialisation this permits, even within a single industry or single commodity – the 'fine slicing' of production as it is sometimes called in heterodox literature.

A major incentive for this particularly 'fine' division of production, as said, was to take advantage of the large differences in the cost of labour power and increase in supply of cheap Third World labour in the period. The increase in cheap Third World labour increased the profitability of firms able to incorporate that labour into production processes they control in a monopolistic manner.

It is the monopolistic unequal exchange brought about on this basis that simply explains the apparent paradox that firms can raise profits by downsizing their operations.

Polarisation and hierarchical specialisation among capitals

'Globalisation' of production processes is hardly new. As Lenin observed,

Raw materials are transported in a systematic and organised manner to the most suitable places of production, sometimes situated hundreds or thousands of miles from each other; when a single centre directs all the consecutive stages of processing the material right up to the manufacture of numerous varieties of finished articles; when these products are distributed according to a single plan among tens and hundreds of millions of consumers (the marketing of oil in America and Germany by the American oil trust) – then it becomes evident that we have socialisation of production.[10]

Yet, in Lenin's time, individual firms or trusts often possessed a vertical monopoly where they owned and themselves carried out different stages of the labour process in a single industry. While this remains common, modern writers show that in the neoliberal period, many of the most profitable firms specialised in particular labour processes within an overall division of labour in which independent firms carry out separate stages of working up raw material to its final form.[11]

The principal method of analysis developed by heterodox writers to study this new form of the international division of labour is the 'global commodity chain' (GCC), or later 'global value chain' (GVC) – a concept originally developed by writers associated with world-systems theory, a discourse that evolved from dependency theory. Work in this framework aims to study how commodities are produced in complex global production networks. Thus, the literature documents the trend towards outsourcing and offshoring by many large MNCs and the effects on income distribution.

From the mid-1980s, Hopkins and Wallerstein sought to explain 'the real division, and thus integration, of labour in complex production processes' internationally and to understand exploitation in that context.[12] Gereffi and Korzeniewicz observed that the 'world system', as originally conceived in world-systems analysis, consisted of an 'unequal distribution of rewards among the various economic activities in the single overarching division of labour'.[13]

Various heterodox literature shows that production processes have been vigorously divided into two opposite labour types – what we might call 'ordinary'[14] and 'sophisticated' labour. These categories differ from Marx's simple and complex labour. The latter also corresponds to skilled and unskilled. The categories 'ordinary' and 'sophisticated' labour are different because skilled labour can be both ordinary skilled labour – which might exist in relatively abundant quantities in many regions of the Third World – or else sophisticated skilled labour, which is rarer.[15] In later literature ordinary labour is also described as 'standardised',[16] 'routine'[17] and 'commodity like'.[18] Most commonly the production processes associated with such labour are referred to as 'bulk production' and the corresponding products as 'undifferentiated'. Regardless of the terminology, the phenomenon is widely noted in heterodox and mainstream work.

The two poles of the labour specialisation stand in contrast to each other technically and, flowing from this, in terms of the income they can generate.

Simple labour processes are more easily replicable, while sophisticated labour, by definition, is far less so.

As Steinfeld puts it, some firms carry out

> activities for which knowledge is embedded and sustainable competitive advantage [i.e. monopoly] is possible, while other firms will not, instead relegated to standardized activities for which competition is intense, churning significant, and returns decidedly low. Therefore, across a range of enterprises, we may witness extensive participation in supply chains, but some types of participation can be characterized as deep and integral, while others may be quite commodified and shallow.

> Whether for aerospace or apparel, we can conceive of some activities within their respective industry supply chains that are standardized and commodified, and other activities that are highly proprietary.[19]

Industrial sectors that previously existed as a more or less single whole organised by one or more monopoly firms through vertical integration have subsequently been broken up and reorganised – in ownership terms – along lines determined by the degree of complexity of each production process.[20]

The process of specialisation had reached such a high stage by 2013, according to UNCTAD, that MNCs were able to 'fine-slice their international production networks, locating each value adding activity in its lowest-cost location on a regional or global basis'.[21]

To cite the most famous example, Apple, based in California, is a non-manufacturing company often ranked as the most profitable MNC in the world. It outsources direct production for the most part to Foxconn, a giant Taiwan-based contract manufacturer later renamed Hon Hai. To quote just one example of research on an Apple product, Milberg and Winkler show that in 2010, Apple imported completed iPhones for $179 each from Foxconn in China and sold them for $600 on the US retail market. Total iPhone exports from China to the United States in 2009 were $2 billion, while income received by Chinese labour and capital from that total was just $73.3 million, or 3.6 per cent.[22]

Looking at the respective profitability of the two companies, by 2018 Hon Hai earned $4.3 billion profit on assets of $110 billion (3.9 per cent return on assets – RoA). Apple's $59.3 billion profit that year was made from $366 billion in assets – 16.3 per cent RoA – over four times higher. Hon Hai employed some 668 thousand workers in 2018, giving it $6,413 profit per worker employed. Apple employed 132,000 workers and earned the $451,000 in profit per worker – seventy times higher. In each case we are talking about company profit per worker. The polarised income levels of Hon Hai and Apple's workers and directors themselves represent another huge inequality (Table 9.1).

Table 9.1 Foxconn's and Apple's Return on Assets and labour, 2018

Hon Hai Precision Industries/Foxconn				
Profits (USD millions)	*Assets (USD millions)*	*Workers*	*RoA*	*Profit per worker*
$4,282	$110,013	667,680	3.9%	$6,413
Apple				
Profits	*Assets*	*Workers*	*RoA*	*Profit per worker*
$59,531	$365,725	132,000	16.3%	$451,000

Source: Fortune (2018).

The 'fine slicing' of industrial sectors caused a rapid growth in trade of intermediate goods and services (i.e. those not sold to the final consumer). In 2012 this reached around 60 per cent of global trade.[23] As such, it has become increasingly problematic to categorise entire industries or products as high, medium or low technology.[24] Virtually all industries and products require both highly sophisticated and ordinary labour processes. That computers, for example, are labelled 'made in China' hardly signifies China's achievement of high-technology production if each machine's most complex components were imported.[25]

The extreme case of this labour division occurs where companies – such as Gap, Nike, Calvin Klein, Mattel, Apple, Dell, Toshiba, Cisco Systems and Xilinx – do not manufacture at all but outsource their production. This is a striking illustration that competition occurs not only in the sphere of actual production. In other cases, the specialisation is only partial. Technologically advanced companies do not always outsource less advanced aspects of their production. These may be kept in-house to defend 'intellectual property' or for practical reasons like simplification of logistics and management, speed to market or control of overall operations.[26]

Within low-end industries like clothing and textiles, the same technical polarisation of labour processes occurs. MNC-controlled clothing production today is usually outsourced to independent producers. However, MNCs monopolise development and production of new synthetics, dyes and production equipment together with fashion design. Cutting, sewing and other processes intense in low-end or ordinary labour are then outsourced, before finished items are returned to the MNCs, which handle logistics, marketing and sales and act as the overall 'systems integrator firm' (i.e. organiser of the overall process).[27]

The important example of the automotive industry demonstrates how this polarisation works. The leading global automakers are all still imperialist-based MNCs. Most aspects of the production of autos today represent increasingly commonplace technology and therefore ordinary labour – at least in the production phase. High prices for vehicles are possible where firms add advanced electronic equipment, software and marketing. This is reflected in the often wide variety of sales prices for a single model, depending on what add-ons are included – a phenomenon that will likely increase as self-driving cars are rolled out commercially. The process of car production itself is also divided along technical lines. As Sturgeon et al. explain: 'The heavy engineering work of vehicle development, where conceptual designs are translated into the parts and subsystems that can be assembled into a drivable vehicle, remain centralised in or near the design clusters that have arisen near the headquarters of lead firms.'[28] All the important automotive design centres in the world are located in imperialist states. Detroit boasts General Motors (GM), Ford, Chrysler, Toyota and Nissan. Cologne in Germany is home to Ford Europe. Also in Germany, Wolfsburg hosts Volkswagen, and Stuttgart, Daimler-Benz. GM's European division is in Russelsheim. Renault designs in Paris, while Nissan and Honda maintain design centres in Tokyo, and Toyota is in Nagoya, Japan.[29]

While these major firms are fairly well spread across major imperialist societies, there has also been a convergence on Detroit. European and Japanese auto giants, Sturgeon et al. note, all established a larger presence there:

> The Detroit, Michigan area has been a centre of vehicle design and engineering for nearly 100 years, the cluster boasts specialized labor markets and a host of institutions to support the field of automotive engineering. As a result, the regional headquarters of foreign automakers and global suppliers – typically the site of regional sales, program management, design and engineering – have gravitated to the Detroit area.[30]

'Monopolist parts suppliers' like Yazaki (Japan), Bosch (Germany), Autoliv (Sweden) followed. Thirty-four of the fifty largest suppliers were in Detroit by 2005.[31]

Ford, Schwartz writes, 'launches models in the US, then once all the bugs have been ironed out (the completion of which becomes solidified in improved/standardised machines and production techniques) then the same model (by this time no longer representing an advanced technology) can be shifted to Mexico'.[32] In imperialist countries like Australia, where large-scale domestic auto manufacture ceased due to the small size of the domestic market, vehicle design work continues, and more advanced suppliers from the now defunct vehicle assembly industry seek an international market for their high-end products.[33]

There are also forms of labour specialisation that are not derived from the separation of high- from low-labour tasks. Examples include the City of London's specialisation in banking services, which differs from Toulouse (home to Airbus) or Wolfsburg (Volkswagen), Galicia (Zara) and so on. Obviously firms also have a division of labour between them. Yet this largely non-hierarchical (or only incrementally hierarchical but not polarised) division of labour between firms and centres typically occurs among the various monopoly capitals or, separately, among non-monopoly capitals. The division of labour between monopoly and non-monopoly capital is also cooperative and complementary – that is a fact of any division of labour by definition. But its distinguishing characteristic is that it is hierarchical and polarised. The power relations involved are highly uneven owing to the different capitals carrying out different types of labour processes.

It should follow that the largest monopoly firms – those obtaining surplus profits – would be the same firms that sit at the top of this labour division. That is the case (see Chapter 11). Apple and Foxconn are far from unique in this respect. Milberg and Winkler note that

> there continues to be a high degree of markup pricing power and concentration of industry for global lead firms. On the other side, there is evidence of persistently high levels of dispersion as more developing countries entered lower- and medium-tech industries in manufacturing and services throughout the 1990s and continued ... through [the] mid-2000s. The result is an asymmetry of market structures within GVCs, with oligopolistic lead firms at the top, and competitive markets among the lower-tier suppliers.[34]

For UNCTAD,

> In general, the economic gains from GVCs are not distributed equally along the chain. The ability of local firms and workers to capture value depends to a significant extent on power relationships in the chain. TNCs [transnational corporations] with a multitude of potential supply sources will be in a strong position to dictate contractual terms with suppliers.[35]

> [M/TNCs] tend to control higher-value-added activities (from innovation and technological activities to branding and new product development), while other firms (often operating under contractual arrangements in developing countries) engaged in *routine* assembly tasks or services ... may earn less, have fewer opportunities to grow and be more vulnerable to business cycles.[36]

Milberg and Winkler found that even 'very large' contract manufacturers in China have 'surprisingly' little power.[37]

Against this outline of the labour process as the principal arena of monopoly, it may be countered that a valuable brand can bring above-average profits to a capital that does not possess the technical sophistication to deserve them. This is clearly true. Yet even in this case, an undeserved brand reputation may be a legacy of past labour quality associated with that brand. If an undeserved reputation is the only source of a firm's above-average profits, it is unlikely to be able to sustain them in the longer term for the most important commodities. It can sustain them only if it is able to invest these surplus profits in a way that generates some other form of monopolistic advantage.

Alternatively, an undeserving company branding their products 'made in the United States', 'made in Germany', etc. may sell them above their value due to the reputation of US or German labour. In this case, the price markup still relates to labour quality – if not that of the branding firm itself, it comes from that of other German or US monopoly capital, either contemporaneously or historically. In this case the individual firm benefits parasitically simply by virtue of being a member of the imperialist club – a benefit not available to Third World producers.

In other cases, sales monopolies may result from a yet more sophisticated form of human labour – psychological manipulation of other human beings or appropriation of culture through marketing. A complex logistics and procurement operations (i.e. advanced labour processes of a particular type), as well as scale provide a monopoly – as in the case of Walmart.

Alternatively, monopolistic price markups may be undeserved. Still, underserved monopoly – that which cannot be defended by advanced labour technique – is not sustainable for a long period in the most important spheres of production. While very real, the degree of attention given to these non-labour forms of monopoly, such as that of oil or other natural resources, has obscured the principal form of capitalist monopoly in our period – the labour process.

In practice, different types of monopoly are combined within given economies, industries and firms. For example, Walmart's sales monopoly cannot be explained just by reference to the magnitude of its capital and monopoly on land for its stores. Neither of these things could have been achieved to the extent they have without its sophisticated logistical, procurement and financial operations – that is, its use of advanced labour and technology to take advantage of commodities produced using cheap labour abroad and realise a surplus profit on that basis. Walmart's actual operations (i.e. its labour process) explain why it and not another firm was able to secure this monopolistic position – even if its chain of stores (i.e. monopolistic ownership of land) is also a large part of its overall monopolistic position. Other 'sales' monopolies result even more directly from labour superiority, such as that of Apple.

The widespread use of cheap labour by the MNCs to increase profits of individual firms in the neoliberal period represents not simply the use of that labour in and of itself but also the MNCs' ability to *incorporate* cheap labour into an overall labour process for which they possess monopolistic control. Incorporation of cheap labour can achieve a sustainable surplus profit only when some aspect of the process in which it is incorporated has not yet become generalised. For example, the use of cheap labour to produce a standard commodity, say T-shirts, as the Bangladeshi contract manufacturers know, does not result in a monopoly profit for those employers, whereas cheap labour's incorporation into an iPhone does. This is because the phone embodies both types of labour and it is controlled by the firm that possesses the highest type.

In between the natural origin of commodities as raw materials and their final sale lie production and the labour process itself. In general, Marxists might be expected to emphasise this sphere as the most durable source of monopolistic advantage due to the centrality of the labour process in Marxist theory. The neoliberal period perfected and demonstrated the importance of this form of monopoly over all others and hence demonstrated the importance of Marx's insight.

Notes

1 D. Lorimer, *Imperialism in the 21st Century: War, Neo-liberalism and Globalisation* (Sydney, Resistance, 2002), p. 9; S. Starrs, 'China's Rise Is Designed in America, Assembled in China', *China's World*, 2:2 (2015), 19.

2 Lorimer, *Imperialism in the 21st Century*, pp. 5–6.

3 *The Economist*, 'The Headwinds Return' (2014), 13 September.

4 H. Schwartz, *States Versus Markets: The Emergence of a Global Economy* (Basingstoke, Palgrave Macmillan, 2000), p. 314.

5 E. Steinfeld, 'China's Shallow Integration: Networked Production and the New Challenges for Late Industrialization', *World Development*, 32:11 (2004), 1972.

6 Steinfeld, 'China's Shallow Integration', p. 1972.

7 *The Economist*, 'The Headwinds Return'.

8 E. Mandel, *Marxist Economic Theory* (New York, Merlin, 1968), p. 463; C. Palloix, 'Self Expansion of Capital on a World Scale', *Review of Radical Political Economics*, 9:2 (1977), 11. For an overview of the 1970s 'internationalisation of capital' discussion, see Barone, *Marxist Thought on Imperialism*, p. 182.

9 Lenin, *Imperialism*, chap. 10.

10 Lenin, *Imperialism*, chap. 10.

11 G. Starosta, 'Global Commodity Chains and the Marxian Law of Value', *Antipode*, 42:2 (2010), 439.

12 T. Hopkins and I. Wallerstein, 'Commodity Chains in the World-Economy Prior to 1800', *Review*, 10:1 (1986), 160.

13 G. Gereffi and M. Korzeniewicz, 'Commodity Chains and Footwear Exports in the Semiperiphery', in W. Martin (ed.), *Semiperipheral States in the*

World-Economy (New York, Greenwood, 1990), p. 47; E. Rabach and E. M. Kim, 'Where Is the Chain in Commodity Chains? The Service Sector Nexus', in G. Gereffi and M. Korzeniewicz (eds), *Commodity Chains and Global Capitalism* (Westport CT, Praeger, 1994), p. 127; D. Clelland, 'The Core of the Apple: Dark Value and Degrees of Monopoly in Global Commodity Chains', *American Sociological Association*, 20:1 (2014), 83.

14 Amin, *Unequal Development*, p. 211.
15 Marx, *Capital*, vol. 1, chap. 7.
16 Steinfeld, 'China's Shallow Integration', p. 1972.
17 UNCTAD, *World Investment Report 2013* (New York and Geneva, UNCTAD, 2013), p. 148.
18 Schwartz, *States Versus Markets*, p. 258.
19 Steinfeld, 'China's Shallow Integration', p. 1972.
20 Steinfeld, 'China's Shallow Integration', p. 1983; G. Gereffi and M. Korzeniewicz, 'Introduction', in Gereffi and Korzeniewicz, *Commodity Chains and Global Capitalism*, p. 12; Gereffi et al., 'The Governance of Global Value Chains', p. 79; T. Sturgeon, 'From Commodity Chains to Value Chains: Interdisciplinary Theory Building in an Age of Globalization', *Industry Studies Association Working Paper Series No. 2008-02* (2008), 8; W. Milberg, 'Shifting Sources and Uses of Profits: Sustaining US Financialization with Global Value Chains', *Economy and Society*, 37:3 (2008), 434; W. Milberg and D. Winkler, *Outsourcing Economics: Global Value Chains in Capitalist Development* (New York, Cambridge University Press, 2013), p. 12. Milberg and Winkler also highlight R & D in this connection (p. 33); contra Harvey, Schwartz says that 'labour and firm-specific non-transferable skills' have become the specialisation of leading firms. See Schwartz, *Subprime Nation*, p. 155.
21 UNCTAD, *World Investment Report 2013*, pp. 156, 141.
22 Milberg and Winkler, *Outsourcing Economics*, pp. 36–41.
23 UNCTAD, *World Investment Report 2013*, p. 122.
24 Gereffi and Korzeniewicz, *Commodity Chains and Global Capitalism*, p. 12.
25 Gowan refers to this as 'production-for-sales activity'. See Gowan, 'Industrial Development and Conflict', in Anievas, *Marxism and World Politics*, pp. 139–40.
26 B. Potter, 'Skilled Manufacturing Labour Has Edge over US', *Australian Financial Review* (2016), 14 November.
27 P. Nolan and J. Zhang, 'Global Competition After the Financial Crisis', *New Left Review* (2010), 98; P. Nolan, *Is China Buying the World?* (Cambridge, UK, Polity, 2012), pp. 17, 21; Steinfeld, 'China's Shallow Integration', p. 1972; G. Gereffi, 'Global Value Chains in a Post-Washington Consensus World', *Review of International Political Economy*, 21:1 (2014), 6; Schwartz, *States Versus Markets*, p. 286.
28 T. Sturgeon, J. V. Biesebroeck and G. Gereffi, 'Value Chains, Networks and Clusters: Reframing the Global Automotive Industry', *Economic Geography*, 8 (2008), 303.

29 Sturgeon et al., 'Value Chains, Networks and Clusters', p. 303.

30 Sturgeon et al., 'Value Chains, Networks and Clusters', p. 315.

31 Sturgeon et al., 'Value Chains, Networks and Clusters', p. 316. Marx had earlier argued that 'the inventions of Vaucanson, Arkwright, Watt, and others, were, however, practicable, only because those inventors found, ready to hand, a considerable number of skilled mechanical workmen, placed at their disposal by the manufacturing period'. Marx, *Capital*, vol. 1, chap. 15.

32 Schwartz, *States Versus Markets*, p. 276; R. Vernon, 'International Investment and Trade in the Product Cycle', *Quarterly Journal of Economics*, 80 (1966), 190–207.

33 J. Dowling, 'Ford GT Supercar Gets Hi-Tech Wheels Made by Geelong Company Carbon Revolution', *news.com.au* (2016), 16 May; B. Park, 'Australia Takes Lead on Lightweight Car Technology', *Wheels Magazine* (2017), 21 November; Potter, 'Skilled Manufacturing Labour Has Edge'.

34 Milberg and Winkler, *Outsourcing Economics*, p. 123; Gereffi and Korzeniewicz, 'Commodity Chains and Footwear Exports', in Martin, *Semiperipheral States*, p. 47.

35 UNCTAD, *World Investment Report 2013*, p. 184.

36 UNCTAD, *World Investment Report 2013*, p. 148.

37 Milberg and Winkler, *Outsourcing Economics*, p. 281; J. Heintz, 'Low-Wage Manufacturing and Global Commodity Chains: A Model in the Unequal Exchange Tradition', *Cambridge Journal of Economics*, 30:4 (2006), 516.

10

Polarised specialisation of nations

Polarisation of labour processes and profit rates between monopoly and non-monopoly firms corresponds to the division between First and Third World societies. As Schwartz writes,

> A clear qualitative difference divides the industrial activity occurring in the former agricultural periphery from that occurring in the mature industrial economies. Most manufacturing in the old agricultural periphery involves the production of commodity-like [i.e. standardised] manufactures, ranging from undifferentiated garments to almost undifferentiated cars.[1]

Similarly, Steinfeld observes that

> Chinese specialization in manufacturing *assembly* has facilitated not only US but also Western European and Japanese specialization in something much more difficult to replicate: knowledge creation and invention.[2]

Further, he argues that

> the incumbents – global lead firms – are hardly stationary, and in many cases have completely transformed themselves. Chinese firms such as Legend, Haier, Huawei, and Bird may be rising on the basis of their low-cost manufacturing expertise. At the same time, most lead firms – whether IBM, Electrolux, Cisco, Motorola, Dell, or many others – are moving away from manufacturing entirely, [instead focusing on] overall product definition, design, marketing, and supply chain management.[3]

Upward specialisation occurred in the United States. As Schwartz points out: 'large investments in production of durable goods' in the United States from 1991 to 2005 outweighed loss of investment in non-durables: 'Leather goods, textiles and clothing, and foods and beverages that combined account for just 10 percent of manufacturing gross fixed capital formation, saw absolute declines. On the other hand, machinery and equipment, transportation equipment, and electrical and optical equipment, combining to make up 40 percent, saw relative increases.'[4] US 'long-term extrusion of obsolete means of production' from the 1980s, Brenner argues, kick-started manufacturing productivity growth.[5] The same occurred in Japan. Brenner shows that from 1975 to 1979, the yen rose 7.6 per cent per annum (p.a.) against the dollar, making Japanese exports more expensive. Japanese manufacturers responded with enormous investment in technology-intensive production: general machinery, electrical machinery, transport equipment and precision instruments, while leaving behind heavy chemical, petroleum and metal industries as well as labour-intensive textiles and food.[6] From the time of the plaza accord, Japanese capital sought 'to focus domestic production in Japan ever more exclusively on the highest tech lines by relying on the country's highly skilled but expensive labour force, while sloughing off less advanced production to East Asia'.[7] In arguing why, in their view, the conditions of IMF emergency loans in the East Asian region from 1998 were 'not really about securing special privileges for US capital' but keeping the region's door open to 'capital in general', Panitch and Gindin thought

> US corporations which had shifted their interest to more science-based and knowledge-intensive production were not particularly interested in taking over low-tech Asian firms, even at bargain basement prices. US corporations that needed low-cost inputs for their high-tech production could obtain these by farming the work out to Asian firms without having to make the investment and take the risks involved in formally taking them over.[8]

On the other hand, Third World 'firms become tied into relationships that prevent functional upgrading'.[9] UNCTAD found that 'participating in international production chains often leaves the host country "locked into its current structure of comparative advantage ... thereby delaying the exploitation of potential comparative advantage in higher-tech stages of production".[10] This occurs especially when firms depend on powerful buyers for large orders.[11] To take the extreme example, in the wake of Rana Plaza collapse in Dhaka, Bangladesh, a UK parliamentary enquiry found that 'Bangladesh's comparative advantage, its sole asset value, is cheap labour and its correspondingly low unit costs'.[12]

Citing a World Bank survey of 1,500 enterprises in five cities, Steinfeld observed in 2004 that 'Chinese firms are integrating extensively with the global economy, but they remain concentrated in primarily low-end commodity manufacturing'.[13] The resultant weak market power meant, Steinfeld argued, 'much of Chinese industry today consists of small-scale firms competing intensely on the basis of discounting'.[14]

In 2020 China is the world's largest producer of electronic products. The country accounts for nearly a third of global demand for integrated circuits (semiconductors), the key, often high-end, component of these products. However, as Dieter points out, '[Chinese capital's] ability to design and produce this critical input remains seriously constrained. Despite decades and many billions of dollars of state-led investment, China's domestic production of semiconductors covers less than 13% of the country's [*domestic*] demand.'[15] Richard Herd, head of the China division of the Organisation for Economic Co-Operation and Development (OECD) thinks 'China is not a threat to Japan's core industries'. Chinese and Japanese exports 'are not competing, they are complementary'.[16] The statement is true with regard to Japan's 'core' industries (i.e. technology-intensive production). Competition from Chinese or other Third World capital is certainly felt by sections of First World capital. But, in Schwartz's words, this is 'along the lines of comparative advantage';[17] peripheral countries 'are selling raw materials, intermediate goods' that are partial inputs in leading sectors or else selling 'finished goods from other, non-leading sectors'[18] – in other words, Third World capital *is* competitive with imperialist monopoly, but only in the lowest areas.

For this reason firms continuing to use expensive First World labour for labour processes that could be done effectively by cheap Third World labour are, in effect, paying too much for labour and, to the extent this occurs, become less profitable. Continued justifiable use (from the perspective of profitability) of expensive First World labour can occur only to the extent this labour is performing tasks above that possible for ordinary labour, or if it plays a necessary ancillary role to labour that is doing high-level tasks (whether or not that occurs in the same firm). Thus First World capital that is unable to upgrade its processes technically, if it is trade exposed, may be bankrupted by Third World competition.

At the same time, imperialist upgrading and specialisation in high-tech production has been assisted by the cheap inputs from expanding capitalist production in Third World economies. This has helped cheapen the value of labour power in the imperialist centres and also provides all sorts of cheap components and services – factors that helped increase profits thus helping to finance imperialist societies' technological upgrading.[19] Hence the tendency in all imperialist societies – not only the United States and Japan – in the neoliberal period to specialise in advanced labour processes is a result not only of lead-firm initiative, but also the competitive pressure of non-monopoly capital.

When IBM sold its personal computer business to the Chinese company Lenovo in 2005, it was not a case of IBM retreating in the face of indefatigable Chinese competition – except perhaps in the lowest-value aspects of the computing industry. Worldwide PC shipments have been in decline since 2011. Lenovo, while holding its leading market share, successfully defended a turf that was both shrinking and becoming lower value. IBM, no longer among the most profitable US tech giants, made US$9.4 billion in profit in financial year 2018–19 (6.2 per cent RoA), compared to Lenovo's profit that year of less than US$1 billion profit (2.1 per cent RoA).[20]

An alternative example is Huawei, which is one of the few, or perhaps the only Chinese company able to transform itself into a true multinational and technology company with (for now) a high rate of profitability. The company's RoA for financial year 2016–17 – 8.7 per cent – was the highest of all large Chinese companies and higher than the average for large imperialist-based companies. For financial year 2018–19 the company's US$9.1 billion profit earned a RoA of 7.4 per cent. Huawei's achievement was due to spending a high proportion of revenue on R & D), just as imperialist-based MNCs do.

According to company material, 'In 2015, approximately 79,000 employees were engaged in R & D, comprising 45% of our total workforce'.[21] However, Huawei's strategy has not been to develop world-beating R & D in China. Rather, it has funded R & D centres in China, the United States, Germany, Japan, the United Kingdom, Russia, Israel, Turkey, Canada, India, Belgium, Finland, France, Brazil and other states.[22] This is consistent with a strategy whereby companies maintain a global network of R & D facilities and a hierarchical division of labour between them, much as in production.

The polarisation of profits between monopoly and non-monopoly capital and the fact that monopoly capital is principally located in the imperialist economies are what explains the stark geographical polarisation in world-wide incomes shown in Chapter 1. The *increase* in international income polarisation pertains to the *increasing* technical polarisation that underlies the hierarchical international division of labour described above. This is also shown in statistics on international terms of trade, as these measure the prices that different countries' capitalist classes can get on the world market for the commodities they produce.

Third World terms of trade losses

Before the turn of the century, UNCTAD had already observed that 'terms-of-trade losses are no longer confined to commodity exporters' (i.e. raw materials exporters) and that many developing country manufactured exports were already suffering terms of trade losses also.[23] 'The prices of manufactured goods exported by developing countries fell relative to those exported by the European Union by some 2.2 per cent per annum from 1979 to 1994'.[24] For the period 2000–11, UNCTAD says, net barter terms of trade (NBTT) for countries it classifies as 'exporters of manufactures'[25] were the worst performing of any countries. Agricultural exporters improved their NBTT marginally. Mining, minerals and oil exporting countries improved 60–100 per cent, while manufacturing exporters' NBTT declined 25 per cent.[26]

In 2016, UNCTAD showed that 'developing countries' as a whole experienced a decline in NBTT of 0.6 per cent *annually* between 1980 and 2014. Developing countries classified as 'exporters of manufactures' suffered annual declines of some 1.1 per cent. Asian developing countries' (excluding West Asian commodity exporters) NBTT declined annually by 1.3 per cent. Asian 'exporters of manufactures' suffered an eye-popping 1.5 per cent *annual* decline in NBTT over thirty-four years of export-led economic expansion![27]

According to World Bank data, China's NBTT with the United States fell from an index of 117 to 94 between 1980 and 2016. Between 2000 and 2016 (the years data is given) it fell against the United States, Japan and Germany.[28] The 2016 UNCTAD report finds this result 'somewhat surprising, as the performance of the Asian region in exports of manufactures might be expected to stand out in terms of NBTT growth, if indeed exporting manufactures is supposed to be associated with export values converging towards those of developed countries'.[29] In these terms of trade figures we have the most general empirical expression of the meaning of the neoliberal expansion. What the data shows is that in the neoliberal period, only *monopolistic* control of production enables a given capital to demand a higher price for its labour product and thus earn a high rate of profit. Rapid expansion of non-monopoly production is fully possible, but has to be understood as a distinct phenomenon. As Schwartz observed, in relation to Chinese firms, they 'are perhaps profitable, but US firms that control their domestic and foreign commodity chains are even more profitable'.[30]

Marx appears to have foreseen something similar to this dynamic when he wrote:

> From the possibility that profit may be less than surplus value, hence that capital [may] exchange profitably without realizing itself in the strict sense, it follows that not only individual capitalists, but also nations may continually exchange with one another, may even continually repeat the exchange on an ever-expanding scale, without for that reason necessarily gaining in equal degrees. One of the nations may continually appropriate for itself a part of the surplus labour of the other, giving back nothing for it in the exchange, except that the measure here [is] not as in the exchange between capitalist and worker.[31]

Notes

1 Schwartz, *States Versus Markets*, p. 258. A complementary explanation is in A. Freeman, 'The Poverty of Statistics', *Third World Quarterly*, 30:8 (2009), 1437.
2 E. Steinfeld, *Playing Our Game: Why China's Rise Doesn't Threaten the West* (New York, Oxford University Press, 2010), p. 18 (emphasis added).

3 Steinfeld, 'China's Shallow Integration', p. 1983 (emphasis added).
4 Schwartz, *Subprime Nation*, p. 123.
5 Brenner, *The Boom and the Bubble*, p. 77.
6 Brenner, *The Boom and the Bubble*, p. 104.
7 Brenner, *The Boom and the Bubble*, p. 116.
8 Panitch and Gindin, *The Making of Global Capitalism*, p. 280.
9 UNCTAD, *World Investment Report 2013*, p. 169.
10 UNCTAD, *Trade and Development Report 2002*, cited in M. Hart-Landsberg and P. Burkett, 'China and the Dynamics of Transnational Accumulation: Causes and Consequences of Global Restructuring', *Historical Materialism*, 14:3 (2006), 18.
11 UNCTAD, *World Investment Report 2013*, p. 169; N. Tokatli, 'Toward a Better Understanding of the Apparel Industry: A Critique of the Upgrading Literature', *Journal of Economic Geography*, 13:6 (2012), 2.
12 All Party Parliamentary Group on Bangladesh [UK], *After Rana Plaza: A Report into the Readymade Garment Industry in Bangladesh 2013*, Parliamentary Liaison Office, cited in Smith, *Imperialism in the Twenty-First Century*, p. 14.
13 Steinfeld, 'China's Shallow Integration', p. 1971.
14 Steinfeld, 'China's Shallow Integration', p. 1974; E. Steinfeld, 'Chinese Enterprise Development and the Challenge of Global Integration', *MIT Special Working Paper Series No. 02-001* (2002), p. 3.
15 E. Dieter, 'China's Bold Strategy for Semiconductors – Zero-Sum Game or Catalyst for Cooperation?' *East-West Center Working Papers IEGS No. 9* (2016), 1.
16 Quoted in M. Nakamoto, 'Asia: Displacement Activity', *Financial Times* (2010), 23, August, cited in Smith, *Imperialism in the Twenty-First Century*, p. 84.
17 Schwartz, *States Versus Markets*, p. 101.
18 Schwartz, *States Versus Markets*, p. 74; H. A. Zavareei, 'Industry and Trade in Some Developing Countries: A Comparative Study' [book review], *Science and Society*, 39:4 (1975), 496.
19 Panitch and Gindin, *The Making of Global Capitalism*, p. 192.
20 *Fortune*, 'Global 500', fortune.com (2018). These figures are consistent with previous years, though Lenovo's RoA has fallen since 2015. See also O. Cattaneo, G. Gereffi and C. Staritz (eds), *Global Value Chains in a Post-Crisis World: A Development Perspective* (Washington, DC, World Bank, 2010), p. 18.
21 Huawei, 'Research and Development' [corporate publicity material] (2018), www.huawei.com/uk/corporate-information/research-development.
22 W. Sekiguchi, 'Huawei to Set Up R & D Base in Tokyo', *Nikkei Asian Review* (2016), 26 November.
23 UNCTAD, *Trade and Investment Report 1999*, cited in Smith, *Imperialism in the Twenty-First Century*, p. 93.
24 UNCTAD, *Trade and Investment Report 1999*, p. vi, cited in J. Smith, *Imperialism and the Globalisation of Production* (PhD thesis) (Sheffield, University of Sheffield, 2010), p. 228.
25 Countries where 50 per cent or more of exports are manufactured.

26 UNCTAD, *Trade and Development Report 2016*, p. 130; Smith, *Imperialism in the Twenty-First Century*, p. 97.

27 UNCTAD, *Trade and Development Report 2016*, p. 130.

28 World Bank, 'Databank' (2018), databank.worldbank.org. Milberg calculates that manufacturers within 'highly developed value chains' (e.g. clothing, textiles, footwear, furniture and toys) suffered a price decline between 1986 and 2006 of 40 per cent relative to their retail price. See Milberg, 'Shifting Sources and Uses of Profits', p. 433.

29 UNCTAD, *Trade and Development Report 2016*, p. 130; Milberg and Winkler, *Outsourcing Economics*, p. 240; Gereffi, 'Global Value Chains', p. 12; Cattaneo, Gereffi and Staritz, *Global Value Chains in a Post-Crisis World*, p. 18; Heintz, 'Low-Wage Manufacturing', p. 516.

30 Schwartz, *Subprime Nation*, p. 10.

31 K. Marx, *Grundrisse: Foundations of the Critique of Political Economy* [1857–61] (Penguin, 1973), chap. 17.

11

Non-monopoly Third World capital

Amin observed that 'all through the nineteenth century, technical progress was translated into reductions in prices'.[1] At that time, technical advance could deliver a temporary extra profit to a firm that introduced it. Due to the still small size and low level of development of capitalist production, firms' ability either to prolong the period of above-average profit or to produce a stream of technical advances and hence a succession of surplus profits was not yet generalised. This changed at the dawn of the imperialist period: 'about 1880 … the appearance of monopolies … caused the economic system to resist the downward movement of prices … after 1880–90 we find a steady rise in prices, and a faster rise in incomes [in the core capitalist countries]'.[2] However, it was not 'the economic system' that resisted downward movement of prices. Rather, the new monopolies themselves resisted downward pressure on the prices of the commodities they produced.

For non-monopoly capital, downward pressure on the prices of *their* produce remained, and still remains. That pressure, which reflects their non-monopoly position, not only remains but is also intensified by their subjugation to monopoly capital, which systematically seeks not only to raise the prices of commodities it owns but also reduce those of the commodities it buys. For this reason, technical progress among non-monopoly Third World capital today results in intense downward pressure on their sale prices. This is what underlies the steep fall in terms of trade for Third World manufacturers already shown. As UNCTAD puts it, 'productivity gains are transferred abroad via lower prices'.[3] That is, the increased surplus value derived from increased productivity is transferred to MNCs and imperialist societies via monopolistic price setting. This is the case even though individual innovating Third World firms can sometimes obtain a temporary, though typically thin, surplus profit.

Undifferentiated production

As already outlined, where a given industry or process is less conducive to technical upgrading or is intensive in ordinary labour (skilled or unskilled), it is more likely to be either abandoned by imperialist state-based monopolies or lost in competition to Third World producers, due to the latter's greater access to cheap labour and willingness to invest in low-profit production processes. Third World capital can sometimes win in competition with imperialist capital for the production of such commodities because, to the extent any given labour processes can be achieved by ordinary labour, which is cheap and abundant in the Third World, the price of that Third World labour tends to determine the world market price of the commodities thus produced. This means that capitalists paying a high price for labour that is doing the same thing is overpaying – according to the market. The market price of the expended labour contained in the ordinary commodity oscillates around the average cost of the reproduction of that type of labour power.

Assume that standard car mirrors can be produced at an average level of efficiency by many reasonably competent firms across all the most developed Third World states. In that case, a standard mirror maker raising prices above that needed to get an average rate of non-monopoly profit, all else being equal, will lose market share to its competitors. This scenario applies to low-end undifferentiated producers in general. If, by contrast, a car's high-end transmission system or automatic driving system requires specialist skills and equipment to produce, then firms involved in the latter can raise prices for their inputs to levels sufficient to obtain a monopoly profit. For this reason, that firm will command a greater portion of the total money obtained with the car's final sale than the portion their labour hours contributed to the car's production.

Inability to raise prices much for standard commodities is why, no matter which technologies non-monopoly capitals are able to reverse engineer or otherwise imitate, these cannot be the basis for a sustained surplus profit if the new production process developed (and this is what must happen) is adapted to non-monopoly production conditions. When a process is simplified in a manner that makes it possible for one non-monopoly to achieve it, by definition it becomes relatively simple for other capitals with a similar level of development also to achieve it.

If any innovation of a new technique replaces undifferentiated low-cost Third World labour and displaces only lowest-level capital, the extra surplus profit obtained on that basis will tend to be correspondingly low because the new technology must compete on the basis of price against a vast supply of cheap and desperate capital and labour. Hence to obtain a large surplus profit on this basis usually requires the wide-scale replacement of such labour (i.e. it requires revolutionising of productive technique, generally involving its greater mechanisation or robotisation). That type of innovation is the almost exclusive domain of the imperialist states.

Under today's conditions of monopoly capitalist competition, in Schrank's words, 'a general theory of industrial upgrading is a contradiction in terms, for readily replicable development strategies are likely to undermine the oligopolistic underpinnings of developmentally nutritious sectors'.[4] To put it more plainly, if something is easy to do, someone has already done it.

Lenin quoted Hermann Levy to make a related point:

> Every new enterprise that wants to keep pace with the gigantic enterprises that have been formed by concentration would here produce such an enormous quantity of surplus goods that it could dispose of them only by being able to sell them profitably as a result of an enormous increase in demand; otherwise, this surplus would force prices down to a level that would be unprofitable both for the new enterprise and for the monopoly combined.[5]

Breaking monopoly, on its own, does not create a new monopoly but a mess that wrecks the monopolistic character of that sphere. It wrecks also the monopolistic character of the capitals that operate only in that sphere.

From the rubble of non-monopoly producers we might expect new monopolies to eventually emerge. This would be the case if the competing non-monopoly producers existed in a vacuum – or if they existed prior to capitalism's monopoly stage of development. But today they exist as non-monopoly producers within an established hierarchy – the polarised world division of labour. The monopoly pole feeds off the non-monopoly sector by appropriating a part of the surplus value it produces. This loss of its surplus value forces it to reproduce anaemically, unable to realise its full self-expansion.

Hence even breaking imperialist monopoly over the production a given sector or process does not break the overall monopolistic position of imperialism – even over the surplus value created in that sector. It only forces imperialism to retreat from direct control of that sector. As such the now non-monopoly sector is converted from a mechanism of value capture into a field for the extraction of value. The 'retreat' therefore will at the same time expand the field of non-monopoly labour processes that the remaining monopoly areas feed off. Potentially, a smaller group of remaining monopolies, drawing from a greater sphere of non-monopoly, can obtain an equal or even a greater share of total surplus value than before. A more familiar (micro) example of this general phenomenon is outsourcing – where a shrunk-down monopolistic core can increase its profits by retreating from a productive process.

For the same reasons, even relatively complex processes cannot be the basis for monopoly once they have become generalised (i.e. mastered by sufficiently large sections of Third World capital). To prosper under conditions of monopoly requires that one be the monopolist. Where that is not the case, any other capital will be subject to the monopolies and robbed by them. This is precisely what did occur in the case of the massive Third World manufacturing expansion that characterises the neoliberal period, as we have seen.

Large non-monopolistic Third World corporations

It has been emphasised that the dominance of monopoly capital in no way lessens competition but raises it to higher levels. This is the case among monopoly capitals and also between monopoly and non-monopoly capital. Another effect of overall monopoly dominance is increased competition among non-monopoly capitals. Steinfeld refers to this as 'small-scale firms competing intensely on the basis of discounting'.[6] This remains the predominant business model for Third World capital. Usurpation by imperialist monopolies of the bulk of surplus value – and hence deprivation of non-monopoly Third World business of funds for investment – works to maintain this situation. So does the integrated hierarchical global labour division.

At the same time, as might be expected, the intense competition between Third World capitals results not in an undifferentiated mass of small producers but in sectoral and national-level winners and losers and hence the tendency towards the concentration and centralisation of even non-monopoly capital. This phenomenon is caused by the same general tendency inherent to capitalist competition that brings about the concentration and centralisation of all capital. It results ultimately in the formation of what we might describe as non-monopolistic monopolies – a highly contradictory and therefore unstable phenomenon.

Large Third World corporations, some of which rival the scale of imperialist MNCs, grew from different social formations and competitive positions to imperialist capital. For that reason, they possess different essential characteristics, even while sharing certain features. There are two basic forms of large non-monopolistic corporations: companies that establish a globally dominant position in one or another aspect of the low-end of the labour process, and those that possess a monopolistic position nationally – typically a national electricity or oil monopoly.

National monopolies are both monopolistic and non-monopolistic at the same time. They are monopolistic domestically but not internationally. On the other hand, global low-end monopolies exhibit the same characteristic of being both monopolistic and non-monopolistic simultaneously. They monopolistically dominate certain *ordinary* labour processes, yet the position of that labour is non-monopolistic within the worldwide labour division. Cattaneo et al. observe that in electronics, 'even the world's major contract manufacturers have been trapped in low value-added segments of the value chain'.[7] The national monopoly is the most stable and common of these two forms because neither imperialist monopoly (which holds it down) nor the Third World nation state and national economy (which holds it up) can be abolished.

Some Third World national monopolies, if their position is particularly preponderant in relation to domestic competitors, such as Chinese online retailers Alibaba and Tencent, or certain banks, resource, telecommunications and other companies, can secure profit rates comparable to large imperialist country-based MNCs (though usually well below the *most* profitable MNCs). These profits are generally lower than leading MNCs simply because the global ranking of the Third World countries they are part of is so low that the total income allocated to those nations is low. Therefore the size of the national 'pot' of income these companies can draw from is smaller.

Low profit rates for low-tech Third World labour

Third World corporations that monopolise the lowest parts of the world division of labour have a less stable position. There are very few of this type of corporation among the *Forbes* 'Global 2000' list. These corporations are subject both to the constant revolutionising of the labour process that bears down on them and to catching up by other non-monopoly capital that pushes up against them. In addition, they also have to manage these constant pressures with relatively few financial resources because of their low profitability.

Meanwhile, the financial resources demanded of them are often enormous. Because of their meagre or absent technical advantages, their monopolistic position often relies on low margins and large scale. This is especially so in China, where important examples include Lenovo, Haier and Huawei's handset businesses. Their success, to the extent that it occurs against plausible Third World rivals, must be in the production of low-margin commodities because price cutting becomes a necessary part of warding off competitors.

It may be feasible for Third World producers to achieve world's *best* productivity for specific low-end labour processes. Yet if that process is relatively easy to achieve by other Third World producers (albeit at a slightly lower level of productivity than world's best), the top firm cannot set prices far above that of the other Third World capitals. Moreover, the older and more well known any given technology becomes, the more difficult it is (short of its complete revolutionising) to increase labour productivity radically, as opposed to marginally. Such marginal innovative improvements are usually not as difficult to replicate.

Their success in non-monopolistic low tech reduces their own value because it paves the path for others. Their success at developing higher technique, if this is ever possible, will bring the attention of a still more formidable competitor, which specialises in competing precisely in this type of production and has far greater resources to do so – imperialist monopoly capital.

Third World global monopolists of low-value processes directly compete principally against other Third World capital or else against lower-value, marginal or declining segments of First World capital. For this reason the overall portion of the world surplus value that is allocated to their entire sector will be low because – just as for Third World nations – the sector is technically subordinate to higher-tech labour processes. This is the same as saying that, to the extent that a monopolistic position of a Third World firm exists only in relation to non-monopolistic capital (or among it), it can appropriate extra surplus value from only that capital. Therefore, the average rate of profit that a non-monopolistic monopoly seeks to beat starts very low, does not rise easily and always risks being undercut. The limits of its potential price setting are defined by the portion of world surplus value that sector can capture.

As with true monopoly capital, large Third World corporations never express their essential characteristic – the technical level of their labour power – in a pure form. All capital, in practice, attempts to leverage any and every type of monopolistic advantage it can. Large Third World corporations' control of land and natural resources, local political or cultural connections and access to finance, markets and contracts are combined with cheap or cheap and skilled labour, and leveraged to extend an individual company's overall position.

Marini observed a similar phenomenon to this in 1977, which he called 'sub-imperialism' and described as 'the form that dependent capitalism takes when it reaches the monopoly and finance capitalism stage'.[8] For Marini, in a still 'dependent and subordinate manner', Brazil 'would enter the capital-exporting stage as well as in the pillage of external energy sources such as petroleum, iron and natural gas'.[9] Today Brazil as well as Bolivia and other bottom Third World states all export capital because all large capital must assume certain modern financial forms. However, we can see other newer ways that, in a still 'dependent and subordinate manner', not only Brazilian but also Chinese and other non-monopoly capital takes on certain monopoly forms.

Marini's term 'sub-imperialism' has more recently come to be understood not as Marini used it but according to the prevalent contemporary view. It is assumed to indicate that leading Third World societies are beginning to achieve a form of imperialism *of the same type* as the imperialist powers (or of a type that will challenge their dominance) albeit embryonically. However, three decades after Marini made the above observations, even the largest Third World companies remain non-monopolistic in relation to imperialist capital as shown by their low rates of profit.

Non-monopolistic monopolies sit at the top of the Third World. These capitals, where possible, adopt the efficiencies of modern production and business techniques. The trend was also noted by Gereffi, who observed an increasing predominance of top manufacturing suppliers, particularly those located in the larger Third World states like China, India, Brazil, Turkey and Mexico, as opposed to smaller suppliers, within global production networks.[10] According to Nolan and Zhang, 'in the process of consolidating their lead', imperialist country-domiciled MNCs 'exert intense pressure upon their suppliers, further increasing concentration as components' firms struggle to meet their requirements'.[11] In this case Nolan and Zhang refer to top suppliers that are themselves mostly also imperialist country-based MNCs. But the same competitive pressures are also felt by lower-ranking suppliers.

The increasing tendency towards concentration of even non-monopoly capital expresses the increasing general tendency for modern means of production to reach such a scale that their necessary field of operation is enormous, often global, and hence competition also becomes increasingly global in character, regardless of which aspect of the world labour division is undertaken. The global character of production is in contradiction to the national-level formation of states and hence of national organisation of economies. It is this contradiction that gives rise to the imperialist system itself,[12] which also gives rise to the contradictory formation of Third World non-monopolistic monopolies.

The continued existence of the nation state and national economies and the contradiction of national political units to the global character of the social labour process gives rise to not one but two basic types of businesses that are not fully global and still nationally rooted. As well as Third World 'non-monopolistic monopolies' as I have described them, which are rooted in Third World societies, there are also the MNCs – which are overwhelming based in the imperialist states. Non-monopolistic Third World monopolies and imperialist MNCs therefore appear as the two most advanced forms of the two sides of the global labour polarisation. In this way, Third World corporations, even Third World MNCs where they exist, cannot be understood as the same thing as imperialist MNCs but as their necessary counterpart.

Their superficial similarities arise from the generalised advance of capitalist forces and relations of production and hence the generalised adoption

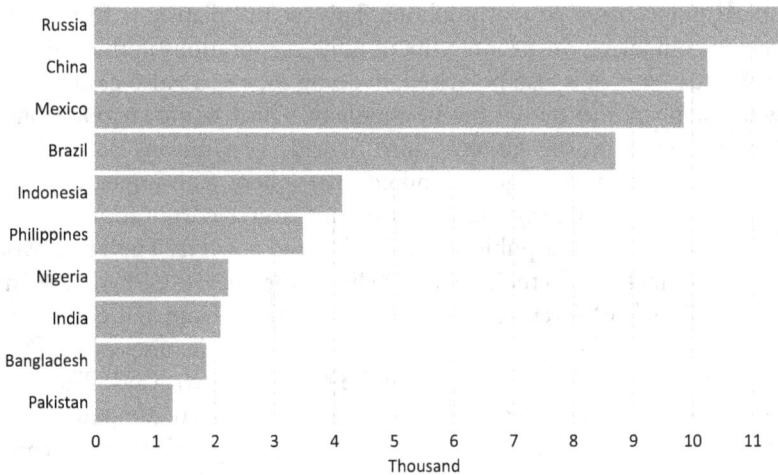

Figure 11.1 Ten largest Third World states, GDP per capita,
USD, 2016.

of certain modern business practices and processes. Yet, arising from completely different and polarised social formations (First and Third World
nations), these two types of corporations are essentially characterised by an
opposite social character.

In Chapter 1 it was observed that the major, more developed Third World
States including China, Mexico, Turkey and Brazil as well as Russia, which
are together home to more than a quarter of world population, are tending
to converge around a similar per capita income level between US$8,000
and $8,750 (in 2016). They form the core of an upper band of Third World
countries. It was also noted that the Third World as a whole seems to be
polarising between these states on the one hand and the bulk of the Third
World – 43 per cent of world population – on the other, which has a much
lower development and income level. This tendency towards polarisation
within the Third World can be seen in Figure 11.1, which represents the ten
largest Third World countries, or 54 per cent of world population.[13] This is
consistent with a pattern of winners and losers within non-monopoly capitalist competition as described.

Low profitability of Third World corporations

The most powerful polarisation, however, is between the two principal poles,
the First and Third Worlds, as shown. As outlined, national income polarisation corresponds to the polarisation of capital and the corresponding

technical polarisation of world labour. This overall picture is further rein-
forced by comparing the profitability of large corporations in the Third and
First Worlds – which is also polarised. In doing so, we can also gain a clearer
view of the phenomenon of non-monopolistic Third World corporations.

We can examine the largest Third World corporations according to
their published financial figures, and compare these with imperialist state-
domiciled MNCs, by examining lists of the largest corporations globally
produced by US business publications *Forbes* and *Fortune*. The Third World
corporations included in their respective lists – the *Forbes* 'Global 2000' and
Fortune 'Global 500' represent the largest winners from the competition
among Third World corporations: the non-monopolistic monopolies.[14]

The polarisation in profitability will be shown in two ways. The first is
by comparing the rate of RoA of the largest non-financial companies – that
is, how much profit companies make as a percentage of the total capital
invested. The second is by looking at each of the eighty-two sectors into
which *Forbes* divides its 'Global 2000' list. By doing this, it is possible to
see clearly the differences in profitability between comparable corporations
within each sector and also to better map the character of the technical
dominance of imperialist monopoly.[15]

Forbes.com publishes data on the largest two thousand public companies
globally. This excludes Huawei and a handful of large US companies such
as Cargill and Koch Industries, which are private – but still provides a useful
overview. According to *Forbes*'s ranking system (which considers volume of
sales, profits, assets and market value), Chinese companies make up five of
the top twenty companies – positions one, three, four, seven and eight. The
other fifteen positions in the top twenty are made up of companies from the
United States (eleven companies), plus Holland, South Korea, Japan and
Germany. The apparent dominance of Chinese corporations on the list –
like other indications of China's size – is frequently understood as powerful
evidence of China's rise.

However, as soon as we ask the *Forbes* website to order the companies
according to market value, we get a completely different list. Market value
expresses what capitalists think companies are worth and hence the profits
one could expect to earn by owning shares. By market value, the top six
positions are all US companies, as are fourteen of the top twenty. China's
share of the top twenty drops from five to three, while the remaining three
positions are filled by Switzerland, South Korea and Holland.

Looking at the top fifty companies by market value, we get a similar picture. Forty-two companies are from the First World countries: United States
(32), Switzerland (3), Hong Kong, Japan, Belgium, United Kingdom, South
Korea, Taiwan and Holland (one each). Only eight companies come from

the Third World – all from China. When we look at the top one hundred companies by market value, the same picture reappears.[16]

There is a striking contrast between China's apparent domination on *Forbes*'s measure, which emphasises size, and its relative absence on the market value measure, which emphasises profits. However, market value still measures *gross* profits and hence includes large companies with relatively low profit *rates*. If we want to understand the reason for the discrepancy between the two measures we need to look at companies' profit rates.

Forbes also gives figures for the RoA of each company. While far from the only measure of company profitability, RoA gives a general picture of the wide gap in profit rates separating almost all large Third World capital from large First World capital. Taking *Forbes*'s largest ten First World and Third World non-financial companies (according to *Forbes*'s rank), First World RoA is almost *double* that of the Third World firms. If Third World capital was catching up, it would need to achieve a higher return on its investments than its much larger competitors, not a far lower return. Notably, the largest companies, particularly from the Third World are financial firms, especially banks, but these cannot be meaningfully measured by RoA (Table 11.1).

Table 11.1 Largest non-financial public corporations, RoA (USD billions), 2019

First World corporations

Forbes rank	Company	Country	Assets	Profits	RoA (%)
#6	Apple	United States	374	59.4	15.9
#9	Royal Dutch Shell	Netherlands	399	23.3	5.8
#11	ExxonMobil	United States	279	20.8	7.5
#12	AT&T	United States	532	19.4	3.7
#13	Samsung Electronics	South Korea	304	39.9	13.1
#15	Toyota Motor	Japan	466	17.2	3.7
#16	Microsoft	United States	259	33.5	12.9
#17	Alphabet	United States	233	30.7	13.2
#18	Volkswagen	Germany	554	14	2.5
#19	Chevron	United States	254	14.8	5.8
		Total	3654	273	7.5

(*continued*)

Table 11.1 (Cont.)

Third World corporations

Forbes rank	Company	Country	Assets	Profits	RoA (%)
#22	PetroChina	China	354	8	2.3
#35	Sinopec	China	233	9.5	4.1
#40	Gazprom	Russia	306	18.9	6.2
#50	Petrobras	Brazil	222	7.1	3.2
#52	Rosneft	Russia	191	8.7	4.6
#59	Alibaba	China	134	10.3	7.7
#71	Reliance Industries	India	125	5.6	4.5
#74	Tencent Holdings	China	105	11.9	11.3
#80	China State Construction Engineering	China	271	5.8	2.1
#94	Evergrande Group	China	274	5.8	2.1
		Total	2215	91.6	4.1

Source: Forbes (2019).

This is no statistical fluke. If we take a different year – this time 2017 – and use *Fortune*, not *Forbes*, we get the same result. I selected all of the Third World corporations listed within the top one hundred positions of the *Fortune* 'Global 500' list. *Fortune* includes both publicly traded companies (i.e. those listed on stock markets) and 'private' companies that are not, and ranks them according to total revenues. There were fifteen Third World non-financial companies on *Fortune's* 2017 list. So I take these and compare them with the fifteen largest imperialist-based non-financial MNCs and calculate RoA for each group (Table 11.2).

Imperialist country-domiciled corporations have an average RoA of 4.8 per cent compared to just 2.7 per cent for Third World corporations – again, RoA is almost twice as high in the First World. If we compare RoA for the most important of these firms – those ranked within the top twenty by revenues – imperialist firms are *four times* as profitable (3.7 vs 0.9 per cent). There are only four Third World non-financial companies ranked in the global top forty, all are Chinese, and these have an average RoA of less than 1 per cent. In the top one hundred, there are only four Third World companies that achieve a RoA equal to or above the First World average: SAIC Motor (5.7 per cent), Gazprom (5.1 per cent), Huawei (8.7 per cent) and Pacific Construction Group (6.6 per cent). Gazprom is Russian, while the rest are Chinese. All are relatively small, ranked at numbers forty-one, sixty-three, eighty-three and eighty-nine respectively.

Table 11.2 Fifteen largest non-financial corporations by revenue, RoA, 2017

15 largest imperialist-based corporations	RoA (%)	15 largest Third World corporations	RoA (%)
Walmart	6.9	State Grid	2
Toyota	3.9	Sinopec	0.4
Volkswagen	1.4	China National Petroleum	0.3
Shell	1.1	China State Construction Engineering	1.2
Berkshire Hathaway	3.9	SAIC Motor	5.7
Apple	14.2	China Mobile	3.9
Exxon-Mobile	2.4	China Railway Engineering	0.8
McKesson	8.3	China Railway Construction	1.1
BP	0	Gazprom	5.1
United Health Group	5.7	Dongfeng Motor	2.4
CVS Health	5.6	Petrobras	–2
Samsung	8.9	Huawei	8.7
Glencore	1.1	China Resources National	1.6
Daimler	3.7	Pacific Construction Group	6.6
General Motors	4.3	China Southern Power Grid	2.3
Average RoA	4.76%	Average RoA	2.67%

Source: Fortune (2017).

Based on these samples, it appears no generalised corporate 'catch-up' is occurring. A company winning in capitalist competition should have a higher rate of profit. Yet the largest Third World capital achieves a RoA just over half as high, and even lower for the biggest firms. China's non-financial state firms seem to be in worse shape, with RoA of 0.53 per cent in the first half of 2019.[17]

It seems to be the case, as Mandel suggested, that 'two average rates of profit come into existence side by side, one in the monopolized and the other in the non-monopolized sector'.[18] However, while Mandel tended to expect both to occur inside the imperialist states, the spread of capitalist commodity production in the neoliberal period has increasingly meant the two sectors are divided between the First and Third Worlds.

First World and Third World dominance by sector

The *Forbes* Global 2000 list also gives us an indication of the degree of participation of different national capitals in the eighty-two economic sectors *Forbes* uses to categorise them. The Third World has 85 per cent of world population but just 21 per cent of listed companies (414 of 2,000). The overwhelming majority of these Third World firms are domestically oriented financial, oil or utilities companies.[19] These companies' size, and hence inclusion on the list, generally reflects the size of their domestic markets and the degree of their domestic monopoly. Beyond this, in the larger Third World countries we find listed some construction, chemicals or manufacturing companies, again predominantly for the local market, such as India's Tata Motor (which dominates the domestic market[20]) or China's Dongfeng Motor.

In addition, there are a small number of internationally competitive companies, each expressing the various competitive attributes of the largest Third World states. From Mexico, there are two beverage companies and an international telecom, from India software and IT services, from Brazil mining and meat packing, from Russia gas, metals and defence, and from China manufacturing companies in home appliances and consumer electronics.

In almost all such cases, the sector as a whole remains dominated by numerous First World firms that are equally or more profitable. For example, in 'heavy equipment' production, the largest firm, CRRC, is Chinese, and six of the total twenty-two firms are from the Third World. Yet eight of the top nine makers are from imperialist states. The combined $2.3 billion profit for all six Third World companies (including CRRC) was just one-third of the $7 billion profits for the top six imperialist-domiciled companies.

The only large sector statistically dominated by Third World companies was 'regional banks', which appears to indicate domestic, not international monopoly. The only sector dominated by Third World capital that *is* the site of significant international competition is 'home appliances'. This may give consumers the impression that China is 'catching up', yet the entire sector had comparatively tiny profits. To give a picture of the degree of First World domination and in what sectors it is strongest and weakest, *Forbes*'s eighty-two sectors have been divided into five categories according to the actual state of competition (Table 11.3). These are: (1) no Third World firms in the sector at all, (2) overwhelming imperialist dominance with negligible Third World presence, (3) decisive imperialist dominance but with significant Third World presence, (4) neither First World nor Third World dominance and (5) Third World dominance. There are no sectors with negligible or no imperialist presence.

Twenty-four sectors with no Third World corporations at all

Some of these sectors are small, yet others are highly important. In semiconductors, for example, there are twenty-seven companies, many of which are highly profitable. The top three companies alone made a combined profit of $40 billion in 2017. In medical equipment supplies, there are eighteen companies, and the top three made $22.2 billion. In discount stores, the top three made a further $18.7 billion.

Forty sectors with overwhelming imperialist dominance

By 'overwhelming' it is meant that there is some Third World presence but of only minor importance. For example, in 'airlines' there are twenty-four companies, and eighteen are domiciled in imperialist states, including the top six. Each of the top six made close to, or more than, the profit of all six Third World airlines combined. The top company – Delta Air, from the United States – made close to twice the profit of the six Third World companies. In 'apparel and footwear', there are thirteen companies; only one is not from an imperialist state – Shenzhou International, from China. Shenzhou's profit was around one-ninth of Nike's. Considering China is by far the world's largest exporter of footwear and clothing, this particular result is significant.

In 'auto and truck manufacturers', there are thirty-one companies, eleven of them from the Third World. However, the top nine companies and fifteen of the top seventeen are all from imperialist states. China's eight companies had a combined profit less than Toyota's. The above examples of airlines, apparel and footwear and auto and truck manufacturers are hardly trivial. Yet this is only a selection of those starting with the letter 'a'. There are another forty examples of sectors beginning with the other letters.[21]

Ten sectors of imperialist dominance but significant Third World presence

If we look at the ten sectors of imperialist dominance that also have a significant Third World presence, most Third world companies are primarily domestic in their operations. These are largely: 'electric utilities', 'telecommunications services', 'real estate', 'diversified insurance' and 'other transportation' – the latter being mostly airports and seaports.

In electric utilities, the top five companies and nine of the top ten are all imperialist, though almost one-third of the eighty-eight companies in total are Third World, including ten from China. In telecommunications services, nine of the top ten companies are imperialist; however, the biggest company is Chinese state-owned China Mobile, listed in Hong Kong. The top five Third World companies' profit was $25.2 billion, while that of the top imperialist companies was $46.9 billion.

Perhaps the most important trend is that 'diversified mining and metals', 'specialised chemicals', 'oil and gas operations' and 'oil services and equipment' all have significant Third World presence and also relatively similar levels of profitability between First World and Third World firms. In diversified mining and metals, for example, fifteen of thirty-eight firms are from the Third World. While the twenty-four First World firms were more profitable, the difference was only marginal. Similarly, in specialised chemicals, there were twenty-four First World companies to ten Third World. The profits of the top five of these First World companies were $8.5 billion, compared to $5.4 billion for the top five Third World companies. There is a similar statistical trend in both oil and gas operations and oil services and equipment. However, in both cases, the figures for Third World refer almost exclusively to profitable Russian companies. As such, it is difficult to view this as a rise of Third World profitability in a similar sense to the ex-colonial countries.

Five sectors of no dominance

In the smaller undiversified metals sector, Third World presence goes even further. In 'iron and steel', there is almost the same number of imperialist as Third World companies, yet Third World-based companies make up six of the top ten companies, including the top two. The top five Third World firms made $13.6 billion in profits, while the top five First World firms made only $6.8 billion. In 'aluminium', five of the nine companies are Third World based. The only firm to make a profit over $1 billion was the Russian firm, Rusal, indicating just how low profit this sector was in 2017.

The more profitable sectors of 'no dominance', in contrast to the raw materials sectors above, are characterised by domestic monopoly. In 'major banks', for example, giant Chinese banks with the highest profits are all domestic. None of these are international banks that compete with the US and European banks in global operations. Similarly, 'construction services' and 'diversified utilities' are characterised, principally, by domestic monopoly. 'Diversified utilities' is in fact a small sub-branch of 'utilities'. With only twelve companies, it is tiny compared to the imperialist-dominated 'electrical utilities', which has 116 companies listed. Construction services is certainly a big sector, especially in China. However, what the large number of Chinese corporations in this sector reveals is largely the huge domestic construction activity in that country.

Three sectors of Third World dominance

Easily the most profitable sector of Third World dominance is 'regional banks', which we discover are bigger and more numerous (133 versus 123) in the Third World than in the imperialist states. No doubt this is partly because the Third World, with 85 per cent of world population, has many regions. This is certainly a big and lucrative sector. The top five banks (Chinese, Brazilian and Russian) made a combined profit of $56.3 billion. Yet, again, this does not indicate a competitive victory against imperialist capital but a domestic monopolistic position.

Another of the sectors – 'educational and training services' – is not really a sector at all. The sole company listed is Kroton Educacional from Brazil, with a profit of only half a billion dollars. While Kroton's lonely 'success' may represent a high degree of domestic monopoly, it seems clear this is a statistical anomaly reflecting that large US and other imperialist universities are not publicly traded and hence not listed.

This leaves just one category of true Third World dominance where there is international competition – 'household appliances'. There are just six firms in the sector. The three Third World firms (all Chinese) made double the profit of the three imperialist firms. However, the total profit for the entire sector was just $7.3 billion – that is, less than half the profits of, for example, Johnson and Johnson or Gilead Sciences (Table 11.3).

Capitalist expansion in the neoliberal period resulted in few Third World companies rising to the apex of the global economy. If it were justified to count Russia separately, owing to its exceptional history and development, the numbers are even starker. The small number of exceptional sectors in which Third World competition has either displaced imperialist dominance or threatened to do so are either small, relatively unprofitable sectors or are made so by the presence of Third World capital. That is, by breaking imperialist monopoly in these sectors, Third World capital also breaks monopoly as such, including for itself. This pattern conforms entirely to the thesis presented in this chapter that what has developed in the Third World is non-monopolistic capitalism.

Nothing is new in this. Just as clothing manufacture long ceased to be the domain of the imperialist world, we should not be surprised if low-end steel and aluminium production, or the mass production of domestic washing machines, refrigerators, air-conditioners or basic automobile assembly are in the future transferred more fully to the Third World (assuming these are not further mechanised). It is hardly conceivable that this not be the case for certain lines of production. If low-end steel and aluminium is further mechanised, preventing Third World dominance of that sector, then Third World dominance could be expected in a different sector – conceivably in bulk production of automobiles.

The Third World's 'dominance' of clothing manufacture has evidently not led to the rise of Third World clothing monopolies. As noted, the sector footwear and apparel is most thoroughly dominated by imperialist capital.[22] Similarly, to the extent household appliances, aluminium or other sectors

Table 11.3 Eighty-three economic sectors: imperialist and Third World dominance

No Third World corporations listed at all	24 sectors	Advertising, air courier, business products and supplies, computer and electronics retail, computer storage devices, containers and packaging, diversified media, discount stores, environmental and waste, forest products, furniture and fixtures, health care services, home improvement retail, insurance brokers, managed health care, medical equipment supplies, paper and paper products, precision health care equipment, printing and publishing, restaurants, security systems, semiconductors, thrifts and mortgage finance and trucking
Overwhelming imperialist dominance with only minor Third World presence	40 sectors	Aerospace or defence, airlines, apparel and footwear, auto and truck manufacturers, auto and truck parts, beverages, biotech, broadcasting and cable, casinos and gambling, communications equipment, computer hardware, computer services, conglomerates, construction materials, business and personal services, consumer electronics, department stores, diversified chemicals, drug retail, electrical equipment, electronics, food processing, food retail, hotels and motels, household/personal care, internet and catalogue retail, natural gas utilities, other industrial equipment, pharmaceuticals, railroads, recreational products, rental and leasing, software and programming, speciality stores, tobacco, trading companies, consumer financial services, investment services, property and casualty insurance, life and health insurance
Imperialist dominance with significant Third World presence	10 sectors	Electric utilities, telecommunications services, real estate, diversified mining and metals, specialised chemicals, heavy equipment, oil and gas operations, oil services and equipment, other transportation, diversified insurance
No dominance	5 sectors	Construction services, diversified utilities, iron and steel, aluminium, major banks
Third World dominance	3 sectors	Educational and training services, household appliances, regional banks

Source: Forbes (2017).

(with the exception of natural resource monopolies) are taken over by Third World capital, these too will cease to generate large profits. It appears such a trend may have already started, judging by the low profits in household appliances and aluminium, and perhaps low-end steel. This is distinct from high-end steel production, which remains concentrated in Japan.[23]

The highest type of Third World capital – non-monopolistic monopoly – plays a double role. On the one hand, due to its domestic monopolistic position, it is a usurper of surplus value from all manner of petty producers that exist underneath it. In this role it acts as an apex predator fattening itself on much of the value produced by all manner of producers within Third World societies. Also, due to its large workforce and through its own prowess at ordinary labour processes, it directly generates a large magnitude of surplus value. Thus in relation to its home country it acts as both producer and usurper of value – the productive parasite characteristic of modern monopoly in general.

However, being also subordinate to imperialist monopoly capital it is itself subject to having this value plundered. Thus, as both producer and as conveyer belt, the highest non-monopoly capital becomes a convenient, centralised and highly lucrative source for large-scale value transfers that bolster imperialist profits. Non-monopoly capital is the economic tributary of the highest order.

Notes

1 Amin, *Unequal Development*, p. 170.
2 Amin, *Unequal Development*, p. 170; H. Singer, 'The Distribution of Gains Between Investing and Borrowing Countries' (1950), cited in J. L. Love, 'Raul Prebisch and the Origins of the Doctrine of Unequal Exchange', *Latin American Research Review*, 15:3 (1980).
3 UNCTAD, *Trade and Development Report 2016*, p. xi.
4 A. Schrank, 'Ready-to-Wear Development? Foreign Investment, Technology Transfer and Learning by Watching in the Apparel Trade', *Social Forces*, 83:1 (2004), 125, cited in Tokatli, 'Toward a Better Understanding of the Apparel Industry', p. 5.
5 H. Levy, *Monopole, Kartelle und Trusts* (1909), cited in Lenin, *Imperialism*, chap. 1.
6 Steinfeld, 'Chinese Enterprise Development'.
7 Cattaneo et al., *Global Value Chains in a Post-Crisis World*, p. 18; Nolan and Zhang, 'Global Competition After the Financial Crisis', p. 97.
8 R. M. Marini, 'La Acumulacion Capitalista Mundial y el Sub-Imperialismo', *Ediciones Era*, 12 (1977), cited in M. Luce, 'Sub-imperialism, The Highest Stage of Dependent Capitalism', in P. Bond and A. Garcia (eds), *BRICS: An Anti-Capitalist Critique* (Chicago, Haymarket, 2015), p. 31.

9 Marini, 'Sub-Imperialismo', p. 31.
10 Gereffi, 'Global Value Chains', p. 7.
11 Nolan and Zhang, 'Global Competition after the Financial Crisis', p. 98; Gereffi, 'Global Value Chains', p. 6; Schwartz, *States Versus Markets*, p. 286.
12 Bukharin, *Imperialism and World Economy*, p. 17.
13 Polarisation is also true for most other major Third World countries not listed. An exception is lowest-income Latin American countries, which sit between the two poles.
14 *Fortune* magazine selects and ranks companies by their aggregate revenue – a measure that emphasises sales, not profits. *Forbes* ranks firms using a 'composite score from equally weighted measures of revenue, [aggregate] profits, [aggregate] assets and market value'. Thus *Forbes* takes aggregate profit and market expectations of profits into account. This may be one reason Chinese companies make up only 10 per cent of the 'Global 2000' list but 22 per cent of the 'Global 500'.
15 For simplicity, the corporations have been classified into two lists – First World and Third World – with any 'Second World' corporations included in Third World totals.
16 Of the companies ranked 51–100, 42 are from the rich countries: United States (22), United Kingdom (4), France (3), plus Holland, Germany, Canada and Ireland (2 each) and Australia, Hong Kong, Denmark, Japan and Spain one each. The remaining eight companies are from China (4), India (2) and one each from South Africa and Saudi Arabia.
17 F. Tang, 'China Ignoring US Demand for Trade War Reform by Reinforcing State-Directed Economic Model', *South China Morning Post* (2019), 13 July.
18 Mandel, *Late Capitalism*, p. 95.
19 For example, there are oil and electricity monopolies and a bank from Argentina; an oil company, an electricity company and four banks or financial service providers from Colombia; one bank from each of Egypt and Pakistan; two banks from Peru; banks, holding companies and an electricity company from the Philippines; two oil companies, a bank, an insurance company and electric utility from Poland and so on.
20 India Infoline, 'Tata Motors Domestic Sales Up 58% in Nov.' (2017), 1 December, www.indiainfoline.com/article/capital-market-hot-pursuit/tata-motors-picks-momentum-on-strong-sales-in-nov-117120400024_1.html.
21 For a more detailed breakdown see King, *Lenin's Theory of Imperialism Today*, appendix 3.
22 See Starrs, 'Designed in America', p. 17.
23 Japan News/Yomiuri, 'Japanese Steelmakers Prioritize High-Grade Production in Glut', *Guam Post Daily* (2017), 31 January.

12

Neoliberal globalisation in historical context

In highlighting 'modularisation' as the basis for the new extent of special-isation in the labour division, Steinfeld was not referring to a new phenom-enon. A 'module', according to the *Oxford Dictionary*, is a standardised part or independent unit. While that particular word may be new in this context, the phenomenon of 'modularisation' of labour existed long before the neoliberal period.

Isolation, simplification and standardisation of aspects of labour pro-cesses appeared as an inherent trend of capitalist development identified by Marx 150 years ago in *Capital*. 'Modularisation' – if we are to use the modern word – was necessary to overthrow pre-capitalist artisan producers and replace them with a proletariat.[1] Such a dynamic was established even before machine production, during capitalism's early manufacturing stage.[2] As Braverman put it: 'In the first form of the [capitalist] division of labour [i.e. in the manufacturing stage] the capitalist disassembles the craft and returns it to the workers piecemeal.'[3]

In the subsequent stage – early industrial capitalism – the primitive machines could replace certain simple, repetitive human labour. The same separation, isolation and simplification of specific processes that paved the way for manufacture was also a prerequisite for machine production. Obviously it would be impossible to design and build a machine to replace human labour in the production process had the particular processes not already been classified, defined or 'codified' and simplified (even if the actual definition and recording of this codification remained rudimentary and informal by today's standards).

Both historically and technically, for workers to be replaced by a machine, they must first be transformed, for a time, into a machine in the sense of performing machine-like tasks. This continues until these have become so routine and standard, or machine technology has advanced to such a point, that an actual machine can displace them. This is important in understand-ing the specific dynamics of imperialism today.

In his study of China at the beginning of the present century, Steinfeld usefully highlights not only codified, modular processes (which he says characterised Chinese firms) but also their opposite – 'other activities that are highly proprietary, as yet utterly uncodifiable, and highly lucrative', in which 'knowledge is embedded and sustainable competitive advantage is possible'.[4] The latter, he points out, is characteristic of global 'lead firms'. While not presented as such in Steinfeld's work, this opposite pole too represents an inherent trend in the development of the human division of labour.

In capitalist society – whether we are talking about pre-industrial manufacture, machine production or the contemporary polarised global division of labour (which is also based around machine production) – the creation at one pole of simple modular tasks (whether carried out by humans or machines) requires, at the other pole, the design, development, control, maintenance and management of these same processes. Hence, the parallel development of highly skilled labour and sophisticated production processes inevitably accompanies simple labour and bulk production. Braverman called this 'the general law of the capitalist division of labor'.[5]

The international character of labour polarisation was observed by Hymer in 1972, when he said international trade is between 'higher and lower functions: one party does the thinking, planning, organizing: the other does the work'.[6] Or as Marx pointed out a hundred years before that: 'A new and international division of labour, a division suited to the requirements of the chief centres of modern industry springs up, and converts one part of the globe into a chiefly agricultural field of production, for supplying the other part which remains a chiefly industrial field.'[7] Obviously the technical composition of this labour division has changed since Marx wrote, though the basic social relationship he describes is little different: higher versus lower labour.

Cheap labour is human, not robotic, and therefore has the advantage to the capitalist of being able to carry out a whole range of production tasks that cannot yet be mechanised, or for which the scale of investment required for mechanisation is too expensive, impractical or risky. This cost advantage of cheap labour over machines in certain spheres is accentuated by the general context of widespread excess productive capacity that has tended to exist in a range of industries since the mid-1970s. Large-scale machine production inevitably tends to produce a mass of undifferentiated 'bulk' commodities. Labour, by contrast, is highly flexible (especially when employed casually, contractually, etc.) and capable of responding more rapidly and easily to changes in market demand or to the types of boutique production employed by some contemporary MNCs such as Zara and other companies that superficially 'upgrade' models, sometimes each year.

Overall, therefore, we can identify two poles in the production process that are continuously reproduced by its advances. On the one side, we have ordinary bulk processes and, on the other, sophisticated labour. The bulk production pole may be human or machine while sophisticated labour can only be human. Therefore prices for the bulk production carried out by non-monopoly capital are forced down not only by the intense competition between non-monopoly capitals – a factor that Smith and GVC writers rightly highlight – but also due to the threat of competition from machines.

We considered in chapter 8 that the markup price available to monopoly capital is determined by the theoretical cost to its competitors of producing its product(s). Now we can see also that the markdown forced on to non-monopoly capital is also equal to at least the actual or theoretical cost of producing those same commodities under monopoly conditions (i.e. of mechanising them or producing them in a new advanced manner).

Within that general context it becomes apparent that the key to understanding the neoliberal hyper-globalisation is not advances in productive technique or communications, but the context in which these occurred. The key seems to be the abolition of socialised property in the former socialist societies and the resulting 'doubling' of global labour supply available to world capitalism.[8] This underlay the peculiar rapidity of globalisation in the period and the extreme form of it (i.e. the extreme degree of the tendency towards 'fine-slicing' labour tasks). The degree of differences in the cost of labour power was its motive force, and the sheer size of this gap, abundance of cheap labour and the degree of the technical gap between non-monopoly and monopoly capital was the source of the relative bonanza of imperialist profitability in the period.

In the neoliberal period the development and adoption of those productive technologies complementary to the employment of this human army (as opposed to its replacement) – were prioritised. Information technology, communications and other technical prerequisites to its incorporation into the global division of labour had to be prioritised compared with the development and adoption of other technologies which displace or directly compete with such a gigantic and cheap human resource – namely automation. Marx had already observed the possibility for low wages to retard mechanisation and vice versa.[9] It seems this is what actually occurred on a wide scale in the neoliberal period.

The future of globalisation

Imperialism's second 'belle époque'[10] may have been capitalism's reward for its defeat of Eastern bloc socialism, however that dividend appears to have come to an end as a fast-expanding source of differential profit. It is therefore incorrect to conclude, as Smith has done, that an ever-increasing pursuit of cheap labour has become the *principal* characteristic, of modern imperialism. It is true, as argued, that competition for the exploitation of differential labour costs, and hence super-exploitation, was the characteristic feature of imperialism's neoliberal period. It is also *one* inherent general characteristic of modern imperialism. However, individual capitals, as said, can reduce their labour cost not only by finding cheaper humans, but by replacing them with machines.

In the case of full mechanisation of a given labour task, one of the poles in the labour process – ordinary labour – is abolished, leaving only (or, in practice, mostly) advanced labour and robots. In this case, the advantage of geographical separation of production processes in order to take advantage of cheap Third World labour is also abolished.

Capitalism attempts to do both. The hunt for cheap labour always ultimately comes up against definite limitations beyond which the rate of exploitation cannot easily be pushed. As Marx said, 'So soon as this point is at last reached – and it takes many years – the hour has struck for the introduction of machinery, and for the thenceforth rapid conversion of the scattered domestic industries and also of manufactures into factory industries.'[11] With further advances in technology (or with preferential development of technologies that bring about mechanisation as opposed to development of those that bring advances in communications which facilitates organisation of labour arbitrage) many simple labour processes could be more thoroughly automated or semi-automated – creating a tendency for production processes to return to the imperialist states.

Looking at actual developments over the past few years, there is some evidence that trend is already under way. Certainly, important sections of the US ruling class are campaigning for 'reshoring' US industries. According to the chief executive officer of GE, 'The days of outsourcing are declining'; 'chasing the lowest labour costs is yesterday's model'.[12]

The US-based Reshoring Initiative claims:

> In 2014 and 2015 parity was reached between offshoring and returning jobs, indicating that the net bleeding of manufacturing jobs to offshore had stopped. As of 2016, for the first time, probably since the 1970s, there was a net positive gain in U.S. jobs. The U.S. has gone from losing about 220,000 manufacturing jobs per year at the beginning of the last decade, to adding 30,000 jobs in 2016.[13]

According to the same source, 2017 saw greater acceleration of reshored jobs. The Reshoring Initiative, or indeed Donald Trump, for political reasons emphasised manufacturing jobs. However, the number of jobs created is hardly the relevant figure if we wish to measure the movement of production processes that are increasingly automated or mechanised.[14] Thus, assuming the figures are correct, even the 2014–15 parity between offshored job losses and reshored job gains would indicate a substantial production shift to the US economy.

Besides 'reshoring' of formerly offshore production, perhaps a more important trend is simply where new productive investment is located. According to the Boston Consulting Group's 2015 survey of 'manufacturing executives at companies with at least $1 billion in annual revenues', 31 per cent indicated they 'are most likely to add production capacity in the US within five years for goods sold in the US', while 20 per cent said they are 'most likely to add capacity in China'.[15] The US economy now commands an increasing share of inbound FDI.[16]

UNCTAD suggests the days of what it now calls 'hyper-globalisation' may be numbered:

> There are already signs that industrial robots are increasing the tendency towards concentration of manufacturing activities in a small group of countries [while] developing countries' employment and income opportunities in these sectors may be adversely affected by the reshoring of manufacturing activities and jobs back to developed countries.[17]

> After the global financial crisis, and especially after 2010, the growth momentum of international production stalled. This was first reflected in trade: worldwide exports of goods and services, which had grown at more than double the rate of GDP for decades, slowed down significantly relative to economic growth.[18]

> Labour cost arbitrage has been one of the major forces, if not the major force, shaping modern patterns of international production and GVCs. The increasing availability of cheaper industrial robots has the potential to revert this trend. It will reduce, potentially dramatically, the competitive advantage of low-cost manufacturing hubs in developing countries.[19]

The COVID-19 pandemic is seen to have rapidly accelerated conflict between the United States and China and pushed all the imperialist countries to reduce their exposure to disruption by reducing the length of their supply chains and reshoring some production. Where this has occurred, it is in continuation of the existing trend.

Still, the extent of this should not be exaggerated. The pandemic has not created or brought to maturity major new production techniques in many industries. These continue to come on board relatively slowly as overall rates of investment are subdued. Where automated processes are not mature enough, these can only replace Third World labour at great cost. The pandemic has not abolished the limited advantages that Third World non-monopoly producers possess in certain areas. So far it has only been in a small number of strategic sectors – especially health care – where imperialist states are subsidising or compelling companies to bring their supply chains closer to home.

The recent trends tend to verify, as Mandel argued, that the differential price of labour appears as just one – albeit highly important – factor that MNCs attempt to exploit to raise their profits. Others include differential labour productivity, differential cost of materials, capital, tax and regulations as well as distance from suppliers, developers and markets. Mandel emphasised that no single factor can explain the trajectory of capitalist development, but only a historically specific analysis of their combination at different times can explain the various periods of imperialism's development.[20]

The extent, speed and precise nature of any future production shift to the imperialist states is far from clear. However, from a purely technical perspective, it is possible to imagine a return to a situation more similar to the post-war period (until the mid-1970s), characterised by relatively rapid expansion of the imperialist states' own economies. Differential profit (and hence most rapid growth) in that period was based on the widespread introduction of semi-automated technology (the 'Third Industrial Revolution'[21]). The technical component of any renewal of this dynamic would be automation of wider sections of energy (renewables), transport and industry. The latter is referred to variously as the Fourth Industrial Revolution, New Industrial Revolution or Industry 4.0. It involves robotisation or greater automation of industry using advanced automation robotics, machine-to-machine communication, artificial intelligence, sensor technology and data analytics among other technologies.

On the other hand, technical progress *also* continues, and will continue, in the direction of further simplification and standardisation of yet more existing *labour* processes that cannot yet be mechanised or automated. Complementary to this movement is improvements in technologies that facilitate their exploitation as labour – that is, improvements in digital communications and logistics – and these are hardly standing still either. This may also make possible new waves, mini-waves, currents or countercurrents of 'offshoring' in hitherto little affected areas, thus counterbalancing the tendency to concentrate increasingly mechanised production in the imperialist states.

We now have post-war examples, occurring back to back, of *relative* neglect of the Third World development, followed by its hyper-development, in a lopsided manner (i.e. the development of underdevelopment, to use Gunder Frank's apt phrase). This suggests neither extreme form is typical. What represents the continuity between these and all the different periods of capitalist imperialism – its true typical feature – is imperialist dominance over the labour process and imperialist monopoly on that basis. Hence, we cannot know the future extent or forms of globalisation just from looking at developments in technology.

What does seem possible to anticipate is that, just as in the neoliberal period, the price and availability of labour power (in the Third and First Worlds) as well as levels of political consciousness and organisation among workers, are likely to be important to the decisions made by the capitalist owners about what forms of production to prioritise and where.

There is one sense though in which neoliberalism may come to look like imperialism's apogee. As Marx showed, human labour creates exchange value while machines do not. Thus, while it is possible to foresee a scenario in which imperialism maintains its domination of the global labour process on a new technical basis via monopolistic control of increasingly mechanised production, it is less easy to see how, if this is achieved by widespread displacement of labour, it could result in such a profitable and politically stable system, or with such widespread cooperation from Third World capital and acquiescence of labour, as occurred in the neoliberal period.

Notes

1 Marx, *Capital*, vol. 1, chap. 14.

2 Marx, *Capital*, vol. 1, chaps 14–15.

3 Braverman, *Labor and Monopoly Capital*, p. 170.

4 Steinfeld, 'China's Shallow Integration', pp. 1972–3.

5 Braverman, *Labor and Monopoly Capital*, pp. 57–8.

6 S. Hymer, 'Robinson Crusoe and the Secret of Primitive Accumulation', in Nell, *Growth, Profits and Property*, p. 30.

7 Marx, *Capital*, vol. 1, chap. 15.

8 R. Freeman, *The Great Doubling: The Challenge of the New Global Labor Market*, [unpublished manuscript] (Berkeley, University of California Press, 2006).

9 'This industrial revolution which takes place spontaneously, is artificially helped on by the extension of the Factory Acts to all industries in which women, young persons and children are employed.' See Marx, *Capital*, vol. 1, chap. 15.

10 S. Amin, 'Globalization and Capitalism's Second Belle Epoque', *Radical Philosophy Review*, 5:1–2 (2002), 86–95.

11 Marx, *Capital*, vol. 1, chap. 15.

12 Quoted in G. Tett, 'Executives Take a Quiet Turn Away From Globalisation', *Financial Times* (2017), 2 June.

13 Reshoring Initiative, *Reshoring Initiative 2016 Data Report: The Tide Has Turned* (2017), 9 May, http://reshorenow.org/content/pdf/Reshoring_Initiative_2016_Data_Report.pdf.

14 UNCTAD, *Trade and Development Report 2017*, p. 50; UNCTAD, *World Investment Report 2013*, pp. 26–9.

15 Boston Consulting Group, 'Reshoring of Manufacturing to the US Gains Momentum' (2015), 10 December, www.bcg.com/publications/2015/reshoring-of-manufacturing-to-the-us-gains-momentum; H. L. Sirkin, M. Zinser, D. Hohner and J. Rose, 'U.S. Manufacturing Nears the Tipping Point: Which Industries, Why, and How Much?' *BCG* (2012), 22 March, www.bcg.com/publications/2012/manufacturing-supply-chain-management-us-manufacturing-nears-the-tipping-point.

16 From 2011 to 2016, World FDI flows increased less than 10 per cent, while US inbound FDI increased 70 per cent, taking the US share of global inbound FDI from 14 per cent to 22 per cent. See UNCTAD, *World Investment Report 2017*, p. 222.

17 UNCTAD, *Trade and Development Report*, 2017, pp. ix–xi, 50.

18 UNCTAD, *Trade and Development Report 2020: From Global Pandemic to Prosperity for All: Avoiding Another Lost Decade* (New York and Geneva, 2020), p. 124.

19 UNCTAD, *Trade and Development Report 2020*, p. 143.

20 Mandel, *Late Capitalism*, pp. 78–80.

21 Mandel, *Marxist Economic Theory*, pp. 605–8; Mandel, *Late Capitalism*, pp. 184–222.

13

The industrialisation of everything

Historically, industrialisation has been seen as a virtual definition of development in both bourgeois and Marxist literature. Marx, for example, once commented: 'The country that is more developed industrially only shows, to the less developed, the image of its own future.'[1] Thus the idea that the Third World is industrialising tends to be synonymous with the idea of Third World catch-up. New factories set up in Asia and elsewhere are commonly thought to represent 'industrialisation' though usually in some undefined sense. However, the spread of monopoly competition to all spheres of social life fundamentally changes the definition and meaning of industrialisation in the modern world.

During the neoliberal period, China and other Third World states rapidly expanded the local presence of certain industries and aspects of industries that had historically been central to imperialist monopoly – such as coal, steel and autos. Third World industry is nothing new. However, China's emergence as the largest producer of each of those industries and many others represented a much larger scale of the phenomenon than previously. China's quantitative superiority in many industries was itself seen to represent its qualitative or overall industrial superiority, or rapid development towards that.

Harvey thought that in the United States, 'the 1980s, after all, gave us deindustrialisation through automation'[2] – a contradiction in terms. He even saw Indonesia as having undergone 'rapid capitalist industrialisation' in the 1980s and 1990s and Bangladesh as industrialising today.[3] Prashad contrasts the supposed 'deindustrialization of America' to China, which he believes 'turned to a form of labor-intensive industrialization'[4] – also a contradiction in terms. Similarly, Foster perceives 'industrialization in the low wage periphery'.[5] Brenner believes 'the huge expansion of the non-manufacturing sector' in the United States, which he asserts has stagnant labour productivity, 'can usefully be called "deindustrialization", with all its negative connotations'.[6] Smith and Selwyn, contra Marx, simply conflate manufacturing with industrial production.[7] As we saw, Harman, following Warren, conflates GDP growth (i.e. growth of capitalist commodity production in general) with *industrial* production[8] and 'industrial development' with 'development of capitalism'.[9]

Some world-systems writers make similar formulations, but at least point out the contradiction. Arrighi et al. claim there has been 'widespread convergence in the degree of industrialization between former First and Third World countries over the past four decades'.[10] Aware that no convergence in income has occurred, these authors refute what they call the 'false identification of "industrialization" with "development" and "industrialized" with "wealthy"'.[11] Gereffi finds that 'export-oriented industrialization ... has opened up a radical new development path. Today, nations seek to industrialize by simply joining a supply chain to *assemble* final goods'.[12] Yet he also notes that 'it may also be less meaningful [if] countries are only engaged in the simplest forms of EOI [export-oriented industrialisation], such as assembling imported parts for overseas markets in export-processing zones'.[13]

The supposed deindustrialisation of the United States during the neoliberal period is an indefensible assertion. Panitch and Gindin show this clearly, at least up until the turn of the century:

> The number of workers employed in durable manufacturing industries like auto and steel actually increased by 8.7% in the Great Lakes region 1983–99, but this paled in comparison to the 27% increase in the south-east ... Shored up by high-tech sectors, during 1983–99 US manufacturing output grew faster ... than overall GDP ... Manufacturing productivity grew faster in these years (3.3% p.a.) than it had in the 1950s and 1960s (average 2.4% p.a.) ... Overall, manufacturing volume grew 90% in this period, while employment in the sector was almost stagnant.[14]

What these figures demonstrate is that, while relatively labour-intensive *manufacturing* employment shrank, employment actually grew in higher-productivity sectors where much, or more, of the basic labour had been mechanised. This is why output almost doubled on a stagnant employment base. So, unless we define industrialisation as the production of goods using abundant manual labour and not, with Marx, as the replacement of manual labour by machines, then clearly the United States had not deindustrialised by 2000.

US 'manufacturing employment' (the statistical category used by the US Department of Labor) did fall sharply from the 2001 recession (which coincides with China's accession to the World Trade Organisation) through to the end of the 2008–9 recession. From a peak of 17 million it fell as low as 11.5 million, then recovered to 12.9 million in 2019 before the COVID-19 pandemic again hit employment.[15] While the employment drop is construed by Harvey and others as deindustrialisation, it is actually a continuation, and acceleration of the same trends noted by Panitch and Gindin: mechanisation and US specialisation in mechanised and high-technology industry.

Marx's distinction between manufacturing and industrialisation

The words 'industry' and 'industrialisation' tend to get conflated with 'manufacture' in mainstream economics. Typically no distinction is made between machine production – which is how Marx defines industry – and assembly operations even if these mostly use hand tools. Referring to both simply as 'manufacture', Chenery, defines ' "the rise of industry" as increase in manufacturing plus social overhead facilities'.[16]

For Marx, the distinction between manufacture and industry forms a crucial part of volume 1 of *Capital*, which he elaborates in chapters 13 through 15. Marx views manufacturing as the technically lower, more backward historical precursor to industrial production.[17] Critical of the mainstream conflation of the two that was also occurring in his time, Marx observed, 'mathematicians and mechanicians, and in this they are followed by a few English economists, call a tool a simple machine, and a machine a complex tool'. However, 'from the economic standpoint this explanation is worth nothing, because the historical element is wanting'.[18]

Labour-intensive Third World assembly operations (as distinct from Third World industry, which also exists but must be treated separately) have an almost opposite technical character to that of machine industry, as Marx defined it, and are far more similar to the pre-industrial manufacture and domestic industry that Marx describes as existing alongside the factory system (and still exists today).

Marx distinguishes 'a real machinery system' from a system of 'independent machines' such as 'a sewing factory of a number of sewing-machines all in the same building'.[19] 'The machine, which is the starting-point of the industrial revolution, supersedes the workman, who handles a single tool, by a mechanism operating with a number of similar tools.'[20]

The key feature of the revolutionary character of the machine is that 'the number of tools that a machine can bring into play simultaneously is from the outset independent of the organic limitations that confine the tools of the handicraftsmen' (i.e. the organic limitations of the human body).[21] Hence the productivity of labour is also liberated from the limitations of human strength, size, endurance, number of limbs, etc. This is inseparably tied with the liberation of the human from such work and forms the truly revolutionary aspect of the Industrial Revolution.

The most advanced form of industry for Marx was an integrated system of machines:

> As soon as tools had been converted from being manual implements of man into implements of a mechanical apparatus, of a machine, the motive mechanism also acquired an independent form, entirely emancipated from the restraints

of human strength. Thereupon the individual machine, that we have hitherto been considering, sinks into a mere factor in production by machinery.[22]

This is industrialisation proper:

> An organised system of machines, to which motion is communicated by the transmitting mechanism from a central automaton, is the most developed form of production by machinery. Here we have, in the place of the isolated machine, a mechanical monster whose body fills whole factories, and whose demon power, at first veiled under the slow and measured motions of his giant limbs, at length breaks out into the fast and furious whirl of his countless working organs.[23]

Contrast this to the labour-intensive factory production exported to the Third World such as garment sewing and basic assembly. The tendency to export *labour-intensive* operations already presupposes the opposite of the production processes Marx considered most advanced. The typical large Chinese manufacturing operation will consist of hundreds or thousands of desks or workstations, where individual humans sit or stand and mobilise an individual hand-operated tool such as a sewing machine or screwdriver. They do so with all the organic limitations to increases in productivity that characterise all such human labour. In the most basic Marxist sense, cheap labour factories in the Third World are not industry but manufacture. In the cases where the needle, screwdriver, etc. can be taken from a human hand and fitted into a machine, the seats and desks will also be taken away, along with their human occupants, and the factory will cease to be the type that is found predominantly outside of the imperialist states. The reason for its location in a cheap labour country will have been abolished.

As suggested, Marx viewed manufacture as the historical precursor to industrialisation. However, to imagine the same historical sequence – a generalised phenomenon of manufacture growing into industry – repeating today under conditions of modern monopoly would be absurd. Leave aside the problems of competition with incumbent monopoly producers in higher-labour processes and foreign ownership of many Third World factories: today's globalised hierarchical specialisation means that the social characteristics of Third World manufacturing are not identical to classical manufacture even in the most general sense.

Describing the pre-industrial manufacturing system, Marx commented:

> The collective labourer, formed by the combination of a number of detail labourers, is the machinery specially characteristic of the manufacturing period. [This] is made up of numerous individual specialized workers ... the combination of various kinds of labour. [That is, a labour division among] handicraft skill is the foundation of manufacture.[24]

Yet modern labour-intensive factories might specialise in only one type of labour and are not founded on handicraft skill. A sewing factory today is not predominantly characterised by a specialised division of labour but a large number of workers carrying out similar or the same labour in the one location. Other assembly operations, typically in consumer electronics, may involve a detailed labour division. However, these consist of only part of the entire labour process – that part most intensive in low-skill labour – while higher-labour types are part of a separate capital, which confronts it as master and usurper of value.

There are several senses in which modern cheap labour factories might be considered most similar, not to pre-industrial manufacture, but to what Marx calls 'modern domestic industry ... in which capital conducts its exploitation in the background of modern mechanical industry ... [where labour processes] are not yet carried on by the aid of machinery, and that as yet do not compete with branches carried on in factories or in manufactories'.[25] Taking the example of lace finishing, Marx says,

> The workroom is in a private house. The mistresses take orders from manufacturers, or from warehousemen, and employ as many women, girls, and young children as the size of their rooms and the fluctuating demand of the business will allow. The raw material is supplied by mechanical industry, the mass of cheap human material (*taillable à merci et miséricorde*) is composed of the individuals 'liberated' by mechanical industry and improved agriculture. The manufactures of this class owed their origin chiefly to the capitalist's need of having at hand an army ready equipped to meet any increase of demand.[26]

The modern manufacturers of Marx's time, he continues,

> nevertheless, allowed the scattered handicrafts and domestic industries to continue to exist as a broad foundation. The great production of surplus-value in these branches of labour, and the progressive cheapening of their articles, were and are chiefly due to the minimum wages paid, no more than requisite for a miserable vegetation, and to the extension of working-time up to the maximum endurable by the human organism. It was in fact by the cheapness of the human sweat and the human blood, which were converted into commodities, that the markets were constantly being extended, and continue daily to be extended.[27]

Today's Third World sweatshops are not typically in private houses. But even large-scale manufacturing or assembly operations might play a similar role in relation to First World industry.

In Marx's definition, industrialisation principally referred to the scientific harnessing of physical processes (chemical reactions) to propel instruments of production wielded by an integrated system of machinery – machine production. This perhaps remains the basic definition of industrialisation, as the elementary needs of human consumption will always remain physical and hence mechanisation must also be physical at its base.

However, as the processes of production, distribution and reproduction become more complex and automated, the element of social organisation, social control and social science assumes an ever more important role as a collective *mechanism* of control over production processes. Hence social formations, social mechanisms and social science assume an ever-larger portion of necessary labour time and an ever-growing importance.

It can be seen from volume 1 of *Capital* that Marx viewed the application of science to production – not its application exclusively to physical production processes – as the essential definition of industrialisation. This was true even though machine industry, which had then still colonised only certain branches of production proper, provided the most advanced example of his time. Marx said, 'The principle, carried out in the factory system, of analysing the process of production into its constituent phases, and of solving the problems thus proposed by the application of mechanics, of chemistry, and of the whole range of the natural sciences, becomes the determining principle everywhere.'[28] One example is Marx's prediction of the coming industrialisation of agriculture. Marx also said that 'division of labour seizes upon, not only the economic, but every other sphere of society'.[29] As quoted above, when referring to the manufacturing period, for example, Marx said that 'the collective labourer, formed by the combination of a number of detail labourers, is the *machinery* specially characteristic of the manufacturing period'.[30] Thus, in this case the 'machine' is a mechanism whose parts are human beings.

Mandel argued that in 'late capitalism' this application of science had already begun to spread beyond the production process proper:

> Far from representing a 'post-industrial society', late capitalism thus constitutes generalized universal industrialization for the first time in history. Mechanization, standardization, over-specialization and parcellization of labour, which in the past determined only the realm of commodity production in actual industry, now penetrate into all sectors of social life. It is a characteristic of late capitalism that agriculture is step by step becoming just as industrialized as industry, the sphere of circulation just as much as the sphere of production, and recreation just as much as the organization of work. The industrialization of the sphere of reproduction constitutes the apex of this development.[31]

For this reason we can say the whole of advanced countries like Japan, the United Kingdom and United States are 'industrialised', not just the areas where large-scale factory production is or was carried out.

Conscious scientific management of production (Taylorism) dates back to the dawn of imperialism. Its application was initially in the production process itself. Today we can see the growing trend towards standardisation, rationalisation and control of intellectual labour. This amounts to the proletarianisation of professional labour and represents one pole of the contemporary development of intellectual labour.

The efficient overall organisation, management and control of a supply chain consisting of hundreds of companies, located in different countries and dealing in multiple products, of course requires the application of scientific principles by skilled labour. The conceptualisation, design, R & D and overall management of the process of bringing new products to market represent another such application. The term in contemporary literature for companies able to achieve this fusion is 'systems integrator firms'.[32]

As Lenin already pointed out, systematic organisation of financial research constituted a special branch of skilled labour in aid of monopoly capital even before the First World War. None of these complex, skilled labour processes involve the immediate process of production. If the 'components' being engineered are humans, not materials, this makes their management hardly less complex, difficult or demanding of scientific methodology than that of production proper.[33] These are new forms of industrialisation.

The appearance of the lowest types of physical means of production in the Third World can hardly be taken to signify a form of industrialisation that challenges or surpasses the industrialisation of imperialist societies. Well before the disaggregation of the neoliberal period, Baumol grouped

> economic activities ... into two types: technologically progressive activities in which innovations, capital accumulation, and economies of large scale all make for a cumulative rise in output per man hour and activities which, by their very nature, permit only sporadic increases in productivity ... the place of any particular activity in this classification is ... a manifestation of the activity's technological structure, which determines quite definitely whether the productivity of its labor inputs will grow slowly or rapidly ... The basic source of differentiation resides in the role played by labor in the activity. In some cases labor is primarily an instrument an incidental requisite for the attainment of the final product [i.e. by way of machine production], while in other fields of endeavour, for all practical purposes the labor is itself the end product.[34]

For Harvey,

> to the degree that intelligence is increasingly incorporated into machines, so the unity between mental and manual aspects of labouring is broken. Workers are deprived of mental challenges or creative possibilities. They become mere machine operators, appendages of the machines rather than masters of their fates and fortunes.[35]

This may be based on Marx's comment:

> The separation of the intellectual powers of production from the manual labour, and the conversion of those powers into the might of capital over labour, is, as we have already shown, finally completed by modern industry erected on the foundation of machinery. The special skill of each individual insignificant factory operative vanishes as an infinitesimal quantity before the science, the gigantic physical forces, and the mass of labour that are embodied in the factory mechanism and, together with that mechanism, constitute the power of the 'master'.[36]

However, notably for Marx, the 'intellectual powers of production' are separated not from workers in general but only from 'manual labour'. Marx also observed the other side of this equation: 'An exception to this law holds good whenever the decomposition of the labour-process begets new and comprehensive functions, that either had no place at all, or only a very modest one, in handicrafts.'[37] The modern mass of this latter type of labour appears both in the form of highly skilled proletarians and professionals. This sophisticated labour is the special product of the revolutionising of the means of production and is also the conscious agent revolutionising the means of production. It is constantly reproduced in the rich countries both as an organic product of the advance of the labour process itself and by the conscious intervention of the imperialist state which makes that possible. It is of special value to the imperialist bourgeoisie because it is the most important *monopolisable commodity* of all (see Chapter 15). Like all valuable commodities, imperialism treats this one – us – with an especially high regard, though not usually with tenderness.

Notes

1 Marx, *Capital*, vol. 1, preface to the first German edition [1867].
2 Harvey, *Seventeen Contradictions*, p. xii.
3 Harvey, *The New Imperialism*, p. 164; Harvey, *Seventeen Contradictions*, p. 123.
4 Prashad, *Poorer Nations*. This occurs, according to Prashad, because 'leaders would collude to allow deindustrialization, and the consonant increased power for finance over industry' (p. 41).
5 Foster, 'The Age of Monopoly-Finance Capital'.
6 Brenner, *The Boom and the Bubble*, p. 79.
7 Smith, *Imperialism in the Twenty-First Century*, p. 102; B. Selwyn, 'Trotsky, Gerschenkron and the Political Economy of Late Capitalist Development', *Economy and Society*, 40:3 (2011), 434.
8 Harman, 'China's Economy and Europe's Crisis'.

9 Harman, 'Analysing Imperialism'.

10 G. Arrighi, B. J. Silver, and D. B. Brewer, 'Industrial Convergence, Globalization, and the Persistence of the North–South Divide', *Studies in Comparative International Development*, 38:1 (2003), 3.

11 Arrighi et al., 'Industrial Convergence', p. 3.

12 Gereffi, 'Global Value Chains', p. 18.

13 Gereffi, 'Global Value Chains', p. 18.

14 Panitch and Gindin, *The Making of Global Capitalism*, pp. 187, 191.

15 U.S. Bureau of Labor Statistics, 'All Employees, Manufacturing [MANEMP]', *FRED: Economic Data* (2020), fred.stlouisfed.org/series/MANEMP.

16 H. B. Chenery, 'Growth and Transformation', in H. B. Chenery, S. Robinson and M. Syrquin (eds), *Industrialization and Growth: A Comparative Study* (New York, World Bank and Oxford University Press, 1986), p. 36; G. Gereffi, 'Development Models and Industrial Upgrading in China and Mexico', *European Sociological Review*, 25:1 (2009), 48.

17 Marx, *Capital*, vol. 1, chaps 14–15.

18 Marx, *Capital*, vol. 1, chap. 15.

19 Marx, *Capital*, vol. 1, chap. 15.

20 Marx, *Capital*, vol. 1, chap. 15.

21 Marx, *Capital*, vol. 1, chap. 15.

22 Marx, *Capital*, vol. 1, chap. 15.

23 Marx, *Capital*, vol. 1, chap. 15.

24 Marx, *Capital*, vol. 1, chap. 14.

25 Marx, *Capital*, vol. 1, chap. 15.

26 Marx, *Capital*, vol. 1, chap. 15.

27 Marx, *Capital*, vol. 1, chap. 15.

28 Marx, *Capital*, vol. 1, chap. 15.

29 Marx, *Capital*, vol. 1, chap. 14.

30 Marx, *Capital*, vol. 1, chap. 14.

31 Mandel, *Late Capitalism*, p. 387.

32 Nolan, *Is China Buying the World?* p. 16.

33 According to Rabach and Kim, 'the technical, financial, marketing and economic know-how that comprise high-end services have replaced embodied technology (the industrial means of production) as a firm's primary competitive advantage'. See Rabach and Kim, 'Where Is the Chain in Commodity Chains?' in Gereffi and Korzeniewicz, *Commodity Chains and Global Capitalism*, pp. 137–8.

34 W. J. Baumol, 'Macroeconomics of Unbalanced Growth: The Anatomy of Urban Crisis', *American Economic Review*, 57:3 (1967), 415–16.

35 Harvey, *Seventeen Contradictions*, p. 180.

36 Marx, *Capital*, vol. 1, chap. 15.

37 Marx, *Capital*, vol. 1, chap. 14.

14

Growing state dominance

One of the typical features of contemporary imperialism is the growing and indispensable importance of state support, particularly for big capital. Boron argues that 'virtually all of the world's largest corporations have experienced decisive support from government policies and trade barriers to make them viable'.[1] However, much contemporary writing tends to overlook state support given in the production process itself, instead emphasising fiscal and financial support,[2] state repression and military, legal and regulatory functions.

For example, Gowan points out that the huge scale of modern advanced plants requires such a scale of cheap credit that states must be 'deeply implicated in creating the conditions for the supply of such credit'.[3] Where Marxist work mentions state involvement in the creation of conditions of production, this often refers to the most elementary conditions such as construction of public roads and other communications infrastructure, as well as state organisation of the reproduction of labour power in general, such as universal schooling or provision of higher education in general.[4]

Norfield says, 'What in economic terms distinguishes an imperialist state is its ability to exert power in the world economy *on behalf* of its "national" capitalist companies.'[5] Such a definition tends to omit the role of imperialist states in providing a particularly high level of support to its companies' production or labour processes – which often occur domestically – so that the companies themselves, in general, do not require their state to exert power in the world economy on their behalf beyond establishment of a basic legal, regulatory, financial and political framework.

All these functions are important. The problem is that the state is separated from labour in the literature. Or else a developed explanation of its role in developing highest labour processes is lacking. This is symptomatic of the broader neglect of the labour process, as outlined. It is a major factor underpinning many Marxists' view that advanced production is migrating to the Third World. Mandel attempted an overview that does include the labour process:

> An inherent trend under late capitalism ... [is] for the state to incorporate an ever greater number of productive and reproductive sectors into the 'general

conditions of production' which it finances ... Without [state] socialization of costs, [many] sectors would no longer be even remotely capable of answering the needs of the capitalist labour process ... Direct examples of this tendency are the increasing use of state budgets to cover research and development costs, and of state expenditure to finance or subsidize nuclear power stations, jet aircraft and large industrial projects of every sort.[6]

For Chomsky, 'the dynamism of the modern economy comes mostly out of the state sector, not the private sector ... In fact, it's very hard to find anything in the economy that doesn't rely critically on the state sector.'[7] A clear contemporary example of this kind of financial assistance is given in the case of the so-called public–private partnership. However, state assistance to private monopoly capital is not only financial. The state plays an indispensable leadership role in both the reproduction of labour power and the revolutionising of the means of production. This makes it the principal organisation in developing both of the key factors that determine the MNCs' monopoly of highest labour productivity.

Imperialist states, and especially the United States, are the driving force of technological change under capitalist imperialism. The US Department of Defense (DoD) and Department of Energy (DoE) in particular have been responsible for revolutionising the production process. Lorimer noted,

> It was massive government deficit spending on technical improvements on war goods, on armaments, during World War II and during the Cold War, that created practically all of the technological innovations of the second half of the 20th century. From radar (microwave transmitters and receivers) and electronic computing machines in the early 1940s to carbon fibre in the 1960s – all of the major technological innovations of the last 50 years were created and developed initially for waging war or preparing to wage war by researchers working for the military departments of imperialist states.[8]

In the case of the development of semiconductors – crucial, for example, in the explosive growth of the consumer electronics market – Gowan points out that the United States funded 40–45 per cent of R & D from 1958 to 1970. One in four semiconductors produced in the United States was for defence agencies.[9] Taking the example of digital signal processing (DSP) chips – a type of semiconductor – Schwartz argues that the DoD programme in 1979–87 generated several generations of chips, along with manufacturing technologies for progressively denser integrated circuits. Originally developed for *Star Wars*, these became the key motor for wireless communication technologies.[10]

Chomsky says,

> Almost every aspect of what's called the 'New Economy' is developed and designed at public cost and public risk: computers, electronics generally,

telecommunications, the internet, lasers ... Radio was designed by the US Navy. Modern mass production was developed in armouries ... a century ago, the major problems of electrical and mechanical engineering had to do with how to place a huge gun on a moving platform, namely a ship, designing it to be able to hit a moving object, another ship – so naval gunnery. That was the most advanced problem [at the time].[11]

It was addressed, Chomsky says, by massive research efforts funded by the German and British states. He argues that 'out of associated innovations comes the automotive industry'.[12]

According to Block et al., federally funded R & D in the United States may be becoming *increasingly* dominant today compared with private industry:

University-based science efforts are now linked to industry [while] government agencies are playing an increasingly central role in managing and facilitating the process of technological development ... the majority of [research] awards are now won by either federal laboratories, universities [or their] supported spin-offs ... most of the winning innovations originate in the Department of Energy laboratories that were initially created to develop atomic weapons in the early years of the Cold War.[13]

At the same time, these incursions of the state sector into production or its prerequisites clash with the need for continuous accumulation of private capital by 'crowding it out'. Thus, a further (and contradictory) state role is to create additional opportunities on an unprecedented scale for profitable investment of excess capital where 'profitable' means made profitable by the state guarantee or subsidy. In this way the unprofitable (and expanding) state sphere involved in creating the 'general conditions of production' is itself simultaneously opened up as a new frontier of subsidised 'private' business.[14] Lucrative state contracts proliferate on everything from military equipment to garbage collection, where the state funds and organises for the needs of capital in general but then hands this process back to private capital as contractor or regulated private owner.

The Third World state

Third World state support is also crucial for the largest Third World capitalist firms, and this is particularly so in the most developed Third World countries, which possess a larger magnitude and complexity of capital relative to less advanced regions. The role demanded of Third World states, in order to assist their capitalist groups to function, even as non-monopolistic firms, is no less crucial. Chinese or Brazilian capital could not function at the level it does without state support. Yet there is a difference in quality between Third World and imperialist capital. Hence also there is a qualitative difference between the type and degree of state support required by each to function.

As Chibber points out, the state role in pre-imperialist late development was relatively simple, but by the twentieth century, states needed to control private investment and make direct state investment.[15] Schwartz notes that 'even Ricardian comparative advantage development strategy requires state mobilisation of capital for social overhead capital (such as the provision of the transportation networks needed to get products to the market)'.[16] However, the competitive requirements for the reproduction of monopoly capital are qualitatively different. These can hardly be met by a relatively weak, under-resourced state, as predominantly exists in the Third World. The capacity of imperialist states in relation to Third World states stands as monopoly private capital does in relation to non-monopolies. Not only are imperialist states blessed with the substantial resource advantages owing to their own incumbency as the beneficiaries of prior accumulation, they are also continuously energised by fresh flows of large revenues owing to their association with the largest and most profitable companies in the world.

The ideal Third World state, from the point of view of imperialist monopoly, aims not to organise and subsidise the development of new competitors – but to actively facilitate the penetration of FDI and to promote complementary forms of economic development within its territory (i.e. that which uses its competitive advantages, principally cheap labour). This is what is meant by the aid and multilateral agencies' and imperialist ideologues' promotion of institutional 'capacity building' for Third World development.

Owing to its meagre financial resources, limited established infrastructure and the relative underdevelopment of the bulk of its own personnel, for the most part the Third World state is only able to provide relatively meagre financial subsidies, relatively basic business services and support only relatively minor, locally oriented or undifferentiated R & D. This means it can assist in the reproduction of only ordinary labour power and labour processes. In short, even the most developed Third World state, regardless of the desires of local capital, is able to support only the reproduction of non-monopoly capital. The gulf between it and the imperialist state is manifested in countless concrete ways. Perhaps among the most important is the technical inability to collect tax in many Third World states, in all but the most rudimentary methods, such as import and export duties.

The inability of Third World states to support the initial development or reproduction of globally monopolistic labour power explains why imperialist country-based monopolies do not simply move to the Third World, even when Third World countries have become their largest markets or production sites. As Schwartz points out, 'Despite this dispersion of production activities and sales globally, most TNCs remained firmly rooted in their home economies, whose particular institutional structures, including finance and labour markets, had constituted the initial competitive advantages that allowed the firm to become a transnational in the first place.'[17] The view that the nation state is beholden to MNCs confuses the relationship of MNCs to Third World states with their relationship to First World states. Such views are hardly new. In 1974, Goldstein suggested that large corporations 'can threaten, if they so choose, the sovereignty and the viability of the nation state'.[18] Half a century later, there are no cases of this in relation to imperialist states.

On the contrary, as Lorimer notes,

> The qualitatively greater role that the capitalist state plays in the economic life of the imperialist countries [compared with previous epochs] is a reflection of the inability of imperialist capitalism to spontaneously reproduce itself by simply relying on the laws of the capitalist market – a reflection of the fact that, as Lenin pointed out, imperialist capitalism is the epoch of decaying capitalism, capitalism which has reached the stage where it has to be propped up by the use of mechanisms that run counter to its own spontaneous laws of motion.[19]

Notes

1 Boron, *Empire and Imperialism*, p. 46.
2 P. Bose, '"New" Imperialism? On Globalisation and Nation-States', *Historical Materialism*, 15:3 (2007), 100.
3 Gowan, 'Industrial Development and Conflict', in Anievas, *Marxism and World Politics*, p. 130.
4 R. Barrigos, 'The Neoliberal Transformation of Higher Education', *Marxist Left Review*, 6 (2013), 80.
5 Norfield, *The City*, p. 126.
6 Mandel, *Late Capitalism*, p. 484.
7 N. Chomsky, 'State and Corp' [interview], *Znet, Germany* (2005), 18 May.
8 D. Lorimer, 'Imperialism at the Beginning of the 21st Century', in P. Chandra, A. Ghosh and R. Kumar, *The Politics of Imperialism and Counterstrategies* (Delhi, Aakar, 2004), p. 64; Lorimer, *Imperialism in the 21st Century*, p. 32.
9 Gowan, 'Industrial Development and Conflict', p. 135.
10 Schwartz, *States Versus Markets*, p. 296.
11 Chomsky, 'State and Corp'.
12 Chomsky, 'State and Corp'.

13 F. Block and M. R. Keller, 'Where Do Innovations Come From? Transformations in the US Economy, 1970–2006', *Socio-Economic Review*, 7:3 (2009), 470, 472.

14 Mandel, *Late Capitalism*, pp. 484–5.

15 V. Chibber, *Locked in Place: State-Building and Late Industrialization in India* (Princeton, NJ, Princeton University Press, 2003).

16 Schwartz, *States Versus Markets*, p. 60.

17 Schwartz, *States Versus Markets*, p. 237. See also H. M. Schwartz, 'Dependency or Institutions? Economic Geography, Causal Mechanisms, and Logic in the Understanding of Development', *Studies in Comparative International Development*, 42:1 (2007), 129.

18 W. Goldstein, 'The Multi-National Corporation: A Challenge to Contemporary Socialism', *Socialist Register*, 11 (1974), 279.

19 Lorimer, *Imperialism in the 21st Century*, p. 15.

15

Stranglehold: the reproduction of highest labour power

The rapid pace of technical change means that technical superiority in any *one* labour process or series of labour processes is an inadequate basis for long-term domination because, over time, each of these become more commonplace and cease to be advanced in relation to competing producers. They will thereby lose their monopolistic character. Reproduction of dominance by any given section of capital therefore requires it to be involved with constant innovation of new technology. In monopoly conditions, as Lenin highlighted, this occurs through the systematic organisation of R & D (i.e. application of science to discovery and refinement of new labour technique).

What we can add today – and this was added by Mandel in 1972 – is that the complexity and scale of the production process has reached such a high degree that meeting its needs and developing it further requires such a scale of resources that it can only be advanced under the leadership of one institution: the highest and most powerful institution of capitalist imperialism, the imperialist state. Hence the state's role in scientific R & D has become key to ensuring the competitiveness, or dominance, of the capitalist groups associated with it against competing blocks of capital.

Surveying the effects of the post-war shift to semi-automated production (the 'third technological revolution'), Mandel observed an increasing 'compulsion to accelerate technological innovation' coupled with 'a steep increase in the cost of "research and development" … [and] a shorter lifespan of fixed capital, especially machines'.[1] Following Lenin, Mandel's work highlights the growing number and importance of industrial research laboratories.[2] He says that, overall, 'the continuous and systematic hunt for technological innovations and the corresponding surplus-profits becomes the standard hallmark of late capitalist enterprises and especially the late capitalist large corporations'.[3]

There is a large body of contemporary mainstream opinion in broad agreement on the importance of R & D and the need to improve labour productivity. As Krugman once commented: 'Productivity isn't everything, but in the long run it is almost everything.'[4] Block and Keller also draw the conclusion that 'innovation capacity is centrally important as nations seek to gain advantage in the world economy'.[5] Every imperialist government

and almost all large firms in the current period view 'innovation' as of para-
mount importance. To the extent that there is any debate, this tends to
revolve around the *degree* to which the state should directly fund research
and the education system or what aspects of these should be prioritised.

Mandel's most important insight may be his observation that competition for domination of the labour process has tended to shift the field of
competitive action from exclusive concern with the development of labour
technique in production, to now also include competition to develop the
necessary conditions of production, to promote R & D and also for the
reproduction of highest labour power.

Mandel says:

> The real consequences of the reduced turnover-time of fixed capital, of the
> accelerated obsolescence of machinery and of the corresponding increase in
> the importance of intellectual labour in the capitalist mode of production is a
> shift in the emphasis of the activity of the major owners of capital. In the age
> of freely competitive capitalism, this emphasis lay principally in the immediate
> sphere of production, and in the age of classical imperialism in the sphere of
> accumulation (the dominance of financial capital); today, in the age of late
> capitalism, it lies in the sphere of *reproduction*.[6]

Thus, for Mandel, effective reproduction of labour power increasingly
becomes the principal competitive arena determining corporations'
and national economies' long-term ability to achieve surplus profits.
Reproduction here refers to social reproduction, that is, the reproduction,
through society's established means of production and corresponding division of labour, of the next generation of that society's labour force.

Continuous development of more advanced means of production is inconceivable without the continuous development of more advanced skilled, scientific and technical labour. First, a sufficiently deep and varied supply of
this skilled labour is needed to carry out complex production tasks. Second,
new production processes can only be developed by such intellectual labour.
Reproduction of monopoly therefore, if it is taken to mean development of
new forms of technical dominance in the labour process, cannot be achieved
without a corresponding domination over the reproduction of the highest
types of labour power (including professional labour).

There is acknowledgement in heterodox literature of the need for
increased education funding in order to raise the level of labour productivity
in Third World societies. However, the question is usually understood in the
limited sense of formal education alone.[7] But the highest-level labour power
is determined by human social capacity more generally, or, as Mandel puts
it, by 'the total accumulated result of the scientific and technical development of the whole society and humanity'.[8]

The competition between states (and total national capitals) therefore becomes competition for the *general* social-cultural, scientific and technological development of the societies concerned (insofar as this is possible within the bounds of capitalist commodity production). Culture here refers not to the commonly understood use of the term that can refer to the peculiarities or differences between various national or regional groups, such as language, food, behavioural norms, etc. Rather it refers to the totality of human social development in all spheres, such as production, science and – especially – the degree of development of the means of production.[9] Monopolisation becomes the monopolisation of human culture and science, of the total accumulated achievements of humanity, especially of its highest aspects.

It is the whole of active society, not just teachers and professors, that pass to each subsequent generation, via the entire activity of that society, its already achieved level of social development. Hence it is the level of social development of society as a whole – its cultural level – that stands as the basic prerequisite for reproduction of the social capacity for advanced labour and scientific development. At the same time, already existing technically high-level labour processes are the backbone of the existing social-cultural level and the necessary mechanism for its transmission. In this context, the greater funding of schools or universities, for example, in societies like India and China, cannot solve the problem of imperialism's overarching monopoly over the development of advanced labour power – even if it does have a positive social impact.

Both the development of advanced productive technology and the creation of the capacity for such development tend to become transformed into the broadest question: that of *general* social development (albeit, in this case, confined to capitalist forms). This is what Mandel referred to when he described the extension of the sphere of capitalist competition to the sphere of reproduction of labour power as the 'apex' of this struggle.

A competitive struggle for the most effective reproduction of advanced labour power therefore consists of the competitive struggle for the most effective self-development of the imperialist societies. On the other hand, Third World societies that have experienced colonial subjugation and continue to experience modern forms of imperialist exploitation and oppression are excluded from the benefits of the common human development. This is the case even though the outstanding achievements of all societies are usurped and incorporated into world culture (such as the incorporation of plants developed by indigenous American societies that now make up many of the global staples).

The most fundamental aspect of imperialist monopolisation of human development from a Marxist point of view is monopolisation of advanced means of production, because social reproduction is, for Marx, necessarily mediated by the production process. Yet it is precisely the productive forces that are most subject to monopolisation because it is production that is directly the subject of market competition and hence most subject also to the result of competition – monopoly.

Imperialist monopolisation, usurpation of common human social-cultural achievement on a world scale and its concentration and centralisation of this in the imperialist societies, therefore, parallels the same process of its concentration of the physical means of production or, more recently, of the highest aspects of that. Third World societies subject to historical exclusion cannot quickly or easily raise their national sociocultural level. Nor therefore is it easy for these societies to produce the highest types of labour power on a sufficient scale that their firms, or a large number of them, can conceivably triumph in market competition with the established global MNCs, which draw on the highly developed labour power of the imperialist states.

Monopolistic competition for reproduction of high-end labour

It follows that, where a given society's level of social development is not commensurate with that of the imperialist countries, such a society is forced into a process of social production (and reproduction) on a qualitatively lower level, but in constant interaction with the imperialist societies. It is not only that imperialism has an incumbent advantage in reproduction. The extension of monopoly competition to field of reproduction means that this sphere too is forced into the same patterns of technical hierarchy and polarisation that occur in the sphere of production proper. Thus, if we are to talk of Third World societies moving up the 'value chain' to a position alongside that of imperialism, as opposed to merely switching positions with other poor societies, their reproduction of labour power must do more than make incremental improvements. It must break imperialist 'dominance over the global production of techno-scientific as well as social-scientific intelligentsias',[10] as Ahmad put it, and of scientific knowledge and development more broadly. Otherwise, the incremental improvements can result only in the same types of outcome as incremental non-revolutionary and non-monopolistic improvements in the production process proper. The best that can result from such non-monopolistic improvements is to move up the rankings within the Third World, or to partially cramp the lowest monopolies.

National development, and particularly the development of advanced science, can never be adequately built upon a productive foundation that specialises in the simplest labour processes. The idea that labour can be developed to a qualitatively higher sphere when the actual daily activity of most workers is the most mind-numbing, back-breaking and life-shortening tasks is a fundamentally un-materialist argument. Third World catch-up cannot take place in an evolutionary manner, via a world division of labour that is both complementary to the imperialist societies and hierarchically polarised.

Collective social struggle, on the other hand, represents a most powerful impetus and mechanism for social development[11] and perhaps the only one available to underdeveloped societies given the relative backwardness of their productive forces. Besides marginal cases, catch-up can only occur by breaking the imperialist division of labour and liberating humanity's accumulated social achievements from monopoly control – by breaking, overthrowing, the imperialist system.

In reality 'catch-up' requires a society-wide mobilisation and social struggle consciously aimed at advancing the national culture – a battle that can only be waged through the organisation and mobilisation of Third World people for this purpose. To fully achieve this, such a struggle will have to be in collaboration with the mass of people within the present-day imperialist core. This fundamentally revolutionary task of raising the social-cultural level of Third World societies is not even being attempted (outside of revolutionary societies such as Cuba and Venezuela) and has not been attempted on any large scale since the upsurges of the national liberation movements coming out of the Second World War.

It is unlikely to be attempted and cannot succeed on a wide scale under the leadership of Third World capitalists who, like all capitalist classes, rely on the passivity, not mobilisation, of the masses. Nor can it succeed if attempted by mass movements that remain within the limits that a capitalist development model must impose. With the defeat, wind back, containment and diversion into capitalist development of the Third World national liberation struggles (i.e. since the onset of the neoliberal era), the development of labour power in the Third World has been limited by the parameters allocated to 'developing' countries within the broader imperialist division of labour – basically that of increasingly organised, efficient and disciplined 'coolies', to use Sukarno's apt term.[12]

In periods lacking extraordinary social struggle, the more advanced society tends to reproduce organically a more advanced cultural level because its more advanced means of production call upon a greater number of people to cooperate within a more complex overall social organism. The more advanced means of production stand as the physical embodiment and store of the plundered and monopolised common human social and cultural achievements.

Besides its organic reproduction, higher-level social development in the imperialist societies is also consciously reproduced via state policies aimed at reinforcing social productivity in ways advantageous to capitalist profit – such as mass university systems, schooling and technical training, scientific research institutions and industry-specific technical assistance organisations.

Particular sections of the ruling class may attempt to channel funding disproportionately towards the development of specific capabilities that will be useful to their own segment of capital (i.e. skills and technologies they have the capacity to bring to market and use). That is, debates occur over how much state funding is necessary overall and to which organisations. Yet owing to constant changes in the labour process, the uncertainties of future development, the need to guard against competitors and the nebulous nature of future 'innovation', broad-based state assistance for education and research is a necessary feature of all the imperialist countries and the relatively developed Third World societies.

The importance of labour (and imperialism's monopoly over it) is perhaps epitomised by education itself becoming a major commodity sold by imperialist capital to better-off Third World families. The service is 'exported' to families of foreign students – the latter becoming the value-added commodity. Once value is added at foreign expense, this most valuable of all commodities is often not exported after all but retained within imperialism's borders through skilled-worker and other migration programmes. So dominant is imperialism's labour market that even Third World *professionals* are not guaranteed visas but must compete for the opportunity to provide imperialism with their highly skilled labour.

None of this assumes that the level of social-cultural development in the imperialist societies is high. On the whole it is not, and it is held back by the imperialist system, even if competition does push in the direction of prowess in marketable commodities (and weapons). The point made here is about imperialist countries' level of development *relative* to Third World societies and imperialist competitors.

It is also not the case that the above argument implies Third World workers are less *capable* than workers in the imperialist states. On the contrary, it is pointing out that imperialism prevents this capability from being realised. Cope conflates labour productivity with the capacity of the workers involved when he writes: 'Of course the social-imperialists consider that workers in the plantations, export processing zones and outsourced factories of the Global South are so hopelessly inefficient that their labour only entitles them to consume a much smaller quantity of the commodities that they produce.'[13] Against Marx, Cope suggests 'labour efficiency' should result in decreased capital investment rather than itself result *from* increased investment.[14] For Marx, by contrast, 'The specific development of the social productivity of labour in each particular sphere of production varies in degree, higher or lower, depending on how large a quantity of means of production are set in motion by a definite quantity of labour.'[15] From a Marxist point of view, the key determinant of labour productivity is not the skill level of the worker directly involved in the production process, such as machine operators. Rather, the machines themselves are the expression of labour productivity of the society as a whole. It is the case that Third World labour in certain spheres will be *more* skilled than its imperialist equivalent. Where the lesser development of the productive forces means that the division between manual and intellectual labour is less developed, skilled small producers must take greater responsibility within the overall labour process. In other words, the tendency towards deskilling is less advanced. However, this cannot help to create greater overall productivity unless these skills could be somehow enlisted in developing a more advanced overall labour process. But that can no longer happen through incremental improvements of small-scale production processes – it requires high-level R & D.

Where the global polarisation of labour has already separated low- from high-labour processes, the perfecting or improvement of low processes does not lead towards high-end processes. Indonesian and Vietnamese textile workers, for example, may work with greater speed and intensity than textile workers in Australia or the United States. If they achieve productivity double that of the imperialist states in sewing standard garments, this will not change the subjugated position of that labour within the global division.

The examples of revolutionary Cuba, Venezuela and historically Russia and elsewhere illustrate that a high level of development of labour cannot be created simply by political will. Unlike an individual factory, social capacity cannot be expropriated by a Third World state. It can only be created by sustained dedication to human development – something that has historically proven extremely difficult to achieve if undertaken outside of and in opposition to the existing centres of scientific knowledge – though some far-reaching achievements have been made. Reflecting on this most difficult problem, Ernesto Che Guevara, a medical doctor, likened Third World societies to a human dwarf:

> A dwarf with an enormous head and a swollen chest is 'underdeveloped' inasmuch as his weak legs or short arms do not match the rest of his anatomy. He is the product of an abnormal formation distorting his development. In reality that is what we are – we, politely referred to as 'underdeveloped', in truth are colonial, semicolonial or dependent countries. We are countries whose economies have been distorted by imperialism, which has abnormally developed those branches of industry or agriculture needed to complement its complex economy.[16]

By contrast, the historical examples of post-Second World War reconstruction of Germany and Japan as advanced imperialist powers tends to support the contention that human cultural development is key to the development of the productive forces and of imperialist monopoly. Being members of the small club of imperialist powers since around the turn of century, those societies already possessed highly developed social and physical means of production, despite the fascist political regimes. Even though the war destroyed much physical infrastructure, both achieved post-war development sufficient to ensure they retained their position within the imperialist club. After the war, their highly developed labour was backed by US finance as a bulwark against communist Russia and China.

Bukharin may have anticipated this outcome when he observed that in 'the international division of labour, the difference in the social conditions, are an economic prius which cannot be destroyed, even by the world war'.[17] As Andersson also noted, 'Marxists make a distinction between physical and human productive forces. Of these, human productive forces are the most important.'[18]

Notes

1 Mandel, *Late Capitalism*, p. 197.
2 The number of research laboratories was 'less than 100 at the beginning of the First World War, but by 1920 it had risen to 220'. By 1960 the figure had risen to 5,400 and by 1961 it was 387,000. Mandel, *Late Capitalism*, p. 252.
3 Mandel, *Late Capitalism*, pp. 223–4; Frank also argued 'technology has always been the basis of the metropolitan monopoly' and 'the underdeveloped areas have been unable to establish a complete industrial structure because they have been unable to establish industries possessing at the time the most complex and advanced technology'. See Frank, *Capitalism and Underdevelopment in Latin America*, p. 190.
4 P. Krugman, *The Age of Diminishing Expectations: US Economic Policies in the 1990s* (Cambridge, MA, MIT Press, 1997), p. 11.
5 Block and Keller, 'Where Do Innovations Come From?' p. 462. For Marxist work, see Nolan and Zhang, 'Global Competition After the Financial Crisis', p. 100; S. Starrs, 'American Economic Power Hasn't Declined – It Globalized! Summoning the Data and Taking Globalization Seriously', *International Studies Quarterly*, 57 (2013), 818–19.
6 Mandel, *Late Capitalism*, p. 245 (emphasis added).
7 W. T. Woo and C. Hong, 'Indonesia's Economic Performance in Comparative Perspective: A New Policy Framework for 2049', *Bulletin of Indonesian Economic Studies*, 46:1 (2010), 58. See especially S. Dhanani, *Indonesia: Strategy for Manufacturing Competitiveness*, vol. 2, *Main Report* (Jakarta, United Nations Industrial Development Organization, 2000).

8 Mandel, *Late Capitalism*, pp. 267–8.

9 See V. I. Lenin, *The New Economic Policy and the Tasks of the Political Education Departments: Report to the Second All-Russia Congress of Political Education Departments, October 17, 1921*, vol. 33, *Collected Works* (Moscow, Progress, 1965).

10 Ahmad, 'Imperialism of Our Time', p. 46.

11 Lane, *Unfinished Nation*, p. 291.

12 R. K. Paget (ed. and trans.), *Indonesia Accuses! Sukarno's Defence Oration in the Political Trial of 1930* (New York, Oxford University Press, 1975), p. 40.

13 Cope, *Divided World Divided Class*, p. 25.

14 Cope, *Divided World Divided Class*, p. 306. Cope falsely equates 'white-collar' workers with unproductive labour (p. 306). Marx by contrast, though in this case speaking of merchants, argues: 'If by a division of labour a function, unproductive in itself although a necessary element of reproduction, is transformed from an incidental occupation of many into an exclusive occupation of a few, into their special business, the nature of this function itself is not changed.' See K. Marx, *Capital: A Critique of Political Economy*, vol. 2, *The Process of Circulation of Capital* [1893], ed. F. Engels (Moscow, Progress, 1956), chap. 6.

15 Marx, *Capital*, vol. 3, chap. 9; Marx, *Capital*, vol. 1, chap. 15.

16 E. Guevara, 'Cuba: Historical Exception or Vanguard in the Anticolonial Struggle?' [Speech, 9 April 1961], in E. Guevara and D. Deutschmann, *Che Guevara Reader* (Melbourne and New York, Ocean Press, 2003).

17 Bukharin, *Imperialism and World Economy*, p. 148.

18 J. O. Andersson, *Studies in the Theory of Unequal Exchange Between Nations* (Turku, Åbo Akademi, 1976), p. 28.

Part V

Super-exploitation of China and why
catch-up is not possible

16

China: Third World capitalism par excellence

The imperialist epoch was heralded in 1900, among other military campaigns, with an eight-nation imperialist invasion of China by Austria-Hungary, France, Germany, Italy, Japan, Russia, the United Kingdom and the United States to put down the Boxer Rebellion. The importance of China for world development has long been recognised. For example, Marx commented in the *New York Daily Tribune* in 1853: 'The next uprising of the people of Europe, and their next movement for republican freedom and economy of Government, may depend more probably on what is now passing in the Celestial Empire – the very opposite of Europe – than on any other political cause that now exists.'[1] Both Lenin and Hobson also paid particular attention to China in their analysis of imperialism's future. As we saw, Hobson accurately identified China as 'the greatest potential reservoir of profit the world has ever known'.[2]

Modern growth of Chinese capitalism has acquired an unprecedented economic importance with vast social implications. Its success or failure in bringing social progress is central to assessing the prospects for capitalist development across the Third World. The most powerful of all Third World states, China indicates the broader possibilities – or lack of. The neoliberal period has, it is widely believed, provided the platform from which China can establish labour processes comparable to those of the imperialist states. If this were true, it would be possible for Chinese workers to wrest from imperialist states some of the huge social surplus that they create but are forced to forfeit to imperialism through world trade, investment and other channels.

From IMF-led 'structural adjustment packages' to the establishment of the World Trade Organisation, the largest corporations and imperialist governments got many of the international policy and developmental outcomes they wanted during the neoliberal period. China did not develop outside of this global framework, but in many respects exemplifies the so-called export-oriented industrialisation model touted as the path to Third World development. Its economic history in the period is characterised by cooperation with the operations of important MNCs. As the centre of export processing in East Asia, China is more integrated into world trade than any other large nation.

China formally joined the World Trade Organisation in 2001, 'binding itself', according to Steinfeld, 'to an accession protocol more expansive, in terms of both market access and permissible trade practices, than that faced by any other developing country in history'.[3] A surge of FDI into China followed.

By the late 1990s, the Chinese government was trying to 'revive key state-owned enterprises (SOEs) by exposing them to foreign competition and oversight'. Eventually the same goal was pursued through publicly listing Chinese 'national champion' companies on the New York, London and Hong Kong stock exchanges, implying adherence to 'the regulatory strictures of the stock market on which it is listed'.[4] This meant state firms in that period were often, in practice, more accountable to the US Securities and Exchange Commission than to the Chinese state bureaucracy, which lacked sufficient technical personnel to direct firms at a micro level, in the increasingly sophisticated financial, organisational and legal arrangements of international business.[5]

FDI, foreign capital, foreign contracts, foreign technology and foreign markets have been key drivers of China's expanded commodity production, even as domestic markets also played important roles. In 2010, three-quarters of China's top two hundred exporting companies were foreign-owned.[6] Starrs points out that in the decade after 2005, foreign-owned enterprises and foreign joint ventures combined accounted for over 80 per cent of all Chinese processing and assembly exports.[7] By 2012, UNCTAD reported that 'foreign affiliates [of MNCs] accounted for some 50 per cent of [all] exports and 48 per cent of imports'.[8] China's development was an integral part of the neoliberal project and was fundamentally shaped by that integration.

If this same period has paved the way for China's ascent as an imperialist power, it was presided over by the imperialist states themselves. If the period has raised China on the crest of – as Amsden dubbed it – the 'rise of the rest', it has done so along lines that Schwartz described as typically Ricardian – that is, utilising 'comparative advantage'.[9] The effect on Third World economies of 'Ricardian' development is widely criticised. Reinert, for example, proposes that specialisation according to existing 'factor endowments' leads to 'competitive advantage in being poor and ignorant'.[10] For UNCTAD, 'liberalization without technological learning will result, in the end, in increased marginalization'.[11] It might be true that neoliberal globalisation helped to increase the world rate of profit (or slowed its decline), yet the monopolies were able to capture a disproportionate part of that.

Limited upgrading

Reflecting on rapid GDP growth, Harvey comments that China has 'moved far ahead in the global stakes for competitive pre-eminence in certain lines of production' and 'is quickly moving up to the higher-value-added commodities'.[12] Yet leadership in 'certain lines of production' tells us little about China's relationship to imperialism. Guatemala too might be described as having pre-eminence 'in *certain lines* of production', but this is not the basis for catch-up. Panitch and Gindin cite dubious statistics to make the plainly absurd statement that 'high-tech manufacturing already represented 27 percent of China's manufactured exports, compared to an OECD average of 18 percent'![13]

China's strongest export growth in the neoliberal period was in electronics, computers and telecommunications equipment, which increasingly supplanted lower-value apparel, textiles, footwear and toys. By 2006, electrical machinery and mechanical appliances (e.g. televisions and DVD players) already accounted for half of all exports.[14] In this basic sense, it is true that Chinese production, at least at its top end, has moved away from lowest labour processes, such as sewing garments, towards those of a higher-ranking Third World state.

One problem of actual measurement of the technological level of this production is that in conventional statistics, production of TVs, keyboards and all manner of cheap standard items are erroneously counted as 'high-tech' products. UNCTAD, for example, divides products into technological categories based on a study of manufacturing exports that took place between the 1985 and 1998.[15] Clearly production processes have progressed over the past three decades. Something that may have represented an advanced technology in the 1980s, say a computer monitor or DVD player, is no longer advanced but standard or obsolete.

Second, standard statistical categories take little account of the locations were the various intermediate stages of the labour processes needed to produce any given commodity are performed. Tallying goods like 'computers and peripheral equipment' or iPhones based on the location of their *final assembly* is a manifestly inadequate way of measuring the technological level of the labour from each country that goes into the commodity.[16] China's apparent 'monopoly' on the export of iPhones tells us little about the technical level of its producers.

If such statistics actually indicated technological advance relative to the imperialist economies, it would not only be China but all the *least* developed Third World states that are catching up. The United Nations Industrial Development Organisation (UNIDO) reported in 2013 that the 'share of medium- and high-technology activities in manufactured exports' for the world's 'least developed countries' – the bottom-ranking states such as Chad and Eritrea – was 17 per cent of their total manufacturing exports 2007–11, only 1 per cent shy, apparently, of the figure Panitch and Gindin cite for the OECD.[17]

Starrs observes, 'China has been the world's biggest exporter of electronics since 2004, including computer hardware. Yet its profit share in the electronics sector is just 3 per cent – no match for Taiwan's 25 per cent, let alone the 33 per cent accruing to US companies.'[18] According to Steinfeld in 2010, some 70 per cent of Chinese so-called high-tech exports were in fact largely foreign-owned 'export-processing operations'.[19] It is this type of export-processing operation, which exists not only in China but across many cheap labour countries, that explains the unlikely 'high-tech' statistics.

High- and low-end R & D

The more recent growth of R & D in China indicates a move into high-tech production. However, the argument has similar flaws to those outlined for production itself. The emphasis is on the quantitative growth of R & D in China and other Third World states rather than on qualitative assessment of the *type* of R & D that is being developed in the Third World. Cattaneo et al., for example, point out that 'Fortune 500 companies now have 98 R & D centers in China and 63 in India; IBM employs more people in the developing world than in America; and in 2008, the Chinese telecom giant Huawei applied for more international patents than any other firm in the world'.[20] Certainly, a rise in the quantity of R & D carried out in the major Third World states is a reality, though it remains small-scale compared to imperialist states. However, these statistics indicate two things, neither of which is Third World catch-up. First, the development of almost any modern production process necessitates some sort of investment in R & D. Hence even relatively low-end Third World commodities, if they are in any way new or updated, require some R & D. Second, many global MNCs increasingly run an international R & D operation. What the statistics do not pick up is that global R & D parallels the organisation of the labour process generally – a hierarchy polarised between imperialist and Third World states.

R & D, just like production, is dominated by the globally monopolistic capitalist groupings. Unlike production, the most important work – basic research – is carried out not by private companies but by the imperialist states. However, big private capital also funds and carries out applied research as well as the 'development' necessary to bring existing technologies to market.[21] This forms a central part of their competitive position vis-à-vis other corporations. Increasingly, the largest global companies with a presence in many countries allocate *basic* R & D to cheap labour locations, while concentrating top-tier research in the imperialist economies – typically in their home state.

The difference with production, according to Steinfeld, is that R & D's globalisation is characterised by geographic spread (just as in production), but with far less dispersal of ownership. Rather than *outsourcing* low-end, labour-intensive tasks to cheap labour markets, '[large] technology-focused corporations, who had once operated concentrated, highly centralized R & D operations [in the imperialist states], now appear to be managing highly diversified, highly internationalised research networks they themselves own'.[22] In this way MNCs have been able to dominate the R & D scene in China. Steinfeld reported that graduates from China's top three or four technical universities are 'cherry-picked' by foreign multinationals. In 2006, 37 per cent of all high-tech workers and 41 per cent of engineers worked for foreign firms. Top-level graduates worked for foreign R & D centres by choice.[23]

While Steinfeld considers it less pronounced than in production, there is, in addition, the development of some independent R & D by Chinese and other Third World capital. However, just as in production, this typically involves the development of low-end technologies, usually the simple modification or synthesis of existing technology to suit nationally specific production or market conditions.

The term R & D, Steinfeld reminds us, involves two things: 'research' and 'development'. 'Research' refers to the discovery or invention of new things, whereas the modification of existing technology for the purpose of commercialisation falls under the category of 'development'. In establishing monopoly control, the higher 'R' side takes precedence: 'in general, research on fundamental new-to-the-world technologies – at least on the commercial front – still remains the domain of companies from the world's richest economies. Moreover, this kind of research is often conducted close to corporate headquarters.'[24] Steinfeld considered that China practises some 'D' but little 'R' and gives the example of 'a major global cosmetics company'. Speaking with researchers from the Massachusetts Institute of Technology, company representatives claimed it had a hundred million potential customers in China. Accordingly, China-based R & D has to accompany sales growth because one-third of all its products sold in China are specifically tailored to that market. 'Development' in this case refers to testing and development of slightly different cosmetic varieties suited to Chinese aesthetics using existing technology and technique.[25]

Independent R & D led by Chinese capital typically involves reverse engineering of existing products developed overseas. Motorbike producers in Chongqing famously took Japanese bikes, pulled them apart, copied their basic designs and components and independently modified the original, for simpler and cheaper manufacture.[26] This allowed technologically backward producers to make worse-performing bikes at a competitive price and dominate the domestic low-end market. Their R & D could not develop products to compete with Japanese MNCs in the higher end of the domestic market, or the European brands plus Harley Davidson, which dominate the domestic luxury motorbike market.

For Ge and Fujimoto, the motorcycle industry in China became 'a typical field for examining this problem' of innovation and R & D:

> Although since 1993 China has become the largest production site of motorcycles in the world, almost all the models are developed by foreign companies mainly from Japan. Will [Japanese] history repeat in China? The answer appears to be 'no'. It is paradoxical to observe that after a long span of about two decades of development, even though the top companies have the capacity of one million units and the collective production volume has overtaken Japan to become the No. 1 in the world, the Chinese enterprises still keep on imitating the models from foreign companies.[27]

The R & D in Chongqing might be considered the classical example of non-monopoly development – successful and independent Chinese development of cheap non-monopolistic products helped to create a rapidly expanding market while nevertheless failing to challenge the dominant position of the imperialist-based producers.

Steinfeld saw energy production as a partial exception to this pattern. In energy, foreign MNC-led R & D conducted in China is 'at least in some cases' carrying out fundamental new research. 'In this industry China is a key market defining innovation globally', and the Chinese government insists on the most advanced technologies for all new plants. In practice, this means reliance on French, Russian, Canadian and US corporations, even if the Chinese state has 'an openly stated *ambition* ... to in future learn to develop [energy production] plant more cheaply using Chinese technology'.[28]

If successful, Chinese capital would face the same problems outlined. By cheapening production processes, not in a monopolistic manner, but by their simplification, Chinese engineers in the energy sector would pave the way for other Third World producers to imitate the same techniques. Thus, they are investing resources in the cheapening of production, but not to their own advantage in the monopolistic sense required.

This type of Chinese R & D may provide a service in cheapening electricity prices in China and elsewhere. As such, it may increase capitalist profitability *in general*. But even the most ingenious, large-scale or breath-taking innovation of this type, so long as it fails to achieve a monopolistic position, fails to overcome its own domination by outside monopolies, and hence will lose much of the value created to the monopolistic producers who do retain their price-setting ability.

The success of Chinese capitalist expansion comes from the combination of low wages; huge numbers of reliable, educated workers; efficient organisation and sometimes mechanisation of relatively simple bulk production processes; investment in basic capital equipment and infrastructure; development of cheaper methods to produce already low-cost goods; a large (though mostly poor) domestic market; and leveraging these things, where possible, to create national champions and national economic growth.

Because China's growth in the neoliberal period was characterised by the development of non-monopoly production, while fast, it was still dominated by more advanced capital. China became the most successful practitioner and developer of the non-monopoly labour processes allocated to the periphery within the imperialist-dominated international division of labour. In other words, China's success is as the Third World society par excellence. It moved from one of the poorest Third World states to one of the least poor.

This explanation of China's economic growth has the virtue that it does not seek to deny or downplay the gravity of the economic changes that took place. On the contrary, it emphasises and highlights these changes by seeking to uncover their precise character. The Third World society par excellence can attract to itself a disproportionate share of global investment, contribute a disproportionate share of global labour, suffer a disproportionate unequal exchange of value and was able to develop, on that basis, a capitalist class that was disproportionately prosperous and powerful compared to other Third World capitalist classes. However as non-monopoly capital, its position is always subordinate to imperialist monopoly over the highest labour processes and will remain so.

China's financial tribute to imperialism

The book has outlined how imperialism's monopoly over the labour process allows it to capture value through unequal exchange in world trade. However, this most important mechanism of exploitation remains hidden from standard statistics. What does show up more readily is transfers of value in the form of finance. The true basis of financial exploitation is, as shown, once again based on imperialist control of the labour process. However, because it is transparent, the financial side of imperialism provides another convenient way to demonstrate imperialist dominance over China. It also shows, at least from one angle, what a bonanza for imperialism China's capitalist development has been.

One feature of Chinese development said to demonstrate its encroachment on the imperialist states is its accumulation of large foreign exchange reserves (around US$3.1 trillion in 2020). It is popular to cite China's large reserves alongside US sovereign debt. Often mere mention of this counterposition is presented as strong evidence of China's rise, without any investigation.[29]

In *Imperialism*, Lenin argued that 'the world has become divided into a handful of usurer states and a vast majority of debtor states'.[30] Taking this statement alone, we might assume that China, with the largest foreign exchange reserves in the world and that lends this money, should, on that criterion, be considered a 'usurer state' (i.e. imperialist). However, one does not have to read much further in *Imperialism* to see the differences between then and now. Lenin wrote: 'Consent to grant a loan ... nearly always manages to secure some extra benefit [to the creditor]: a favourable clause in a commercial treaty, a coaling station, a contract to construct a harbour, a fat concession, or an order for guns.'[31] While Chinese credit money may *seek* these types of benefits, there is overwhelming evidence to show that the vast bulk of it is demonstrably unable to achieve that – especially in relation to the most powerful states. In practice, much Chinese money has the opposite character – that of a pool of cheap finance which imperialist capital draws upon and reinvests at better rates of return than the Chinese state can achieve.

This is not a characteristic of the Chinese foreign reserves only. Since the widespread adoption of floating exchange rates in the neoliberal period, and particularly since the financial crisis of the late 1990s, which brought devastating declines in the exchange rates of South Korea, South East Asian nations, Russia and Argentina, all Third World countries are forced to try to maintain large piles of cash and liquid financial securities as insurance against possible currency depreciation or speculative attack. Reserves of underdeveloped countries rose from around 6–8 per cent of GDP in the 1970s to around 30 per cent in 2004, according to Kiely.[32]

Large Chinese foreign reserves are part of this general trend. China's $3.1 trillion represents around 27.6 per cent of its $11 trillion aggregate GDP in 2016. In Indonesia, the ratio was around 12.5 per cent, the Philippines 26.5 per cent and Malaysia 31.9 per cent.[33] While imperialist states like Japan and South Korea with large foreign reserves may be in a position to invest their surpluses more profitably, Third World states like China usually are not.

China's reserves do not appear to give it significant leverage over the United States or allow it to act as the banker to the United States. China holds just 7 per cent of around $16 trillion in total outstanding US Treasuries or 17 per cent of foreign-held Treasuries. If it were to start selling these, it could not blow up the Treasuries market. The likely effect of a Chinese sell-off would be a tendency to push interest rates higher. Yet the underlying tendency at the moment – due to lacklustre growth – is for interest rates to sink lower. It is possible the effect of a China sell-off would hardly even be noticed.

Moreover, as the *Financial Times* reported, 'few see any alternative for China, other than remaining invested in [US] Treasuries. The benchmark 10-year Treasury yield is currently 2.42 per cent, well above the negative yields on equivalent German and Japanese sovereign bonds and still markedly higher than the 1.03 per cent offered on 10-year gilts in the UK.'[34] Reserves to defend a state's currency must be held as readily accessible liquid assets. As Norfield notes, 'in practice this meant that the revenues they earned from their trade surpluses were spent on buying US government securities'.[35] Lawrence Summers estimates the 'striking' cost to developing countries of holding foreign currency reserves is that they are 'earning what is likely to be a zero real return' on this money.[36] This is almost certainly the case for an overwhelming portion of China's reserves 'invested' in US Treasury bonds or other similar low-yield, dollar-denominated financial securities in the US financial markets. Additionally, amassing foreign 'hard currency' reserves exerts downward pressure on Third World currencies' exchange rates, thus reducing their terms of trade.[37]

Once Chinese surplus dollars are parked in US banks, they do not just sit there. They form a pool of cheap finance that US monopoly capital can draw upon and invest. While China may have little choice but zero- or low-return investments, the monopolistic US banks have far better choices available to them through their ties to other US MNCs and vast international operations.

Another imperialist financial privilege exercised against the Third World is that of seigniorage, which benefits not only the United States but all the leading imperialist nations.[38] The benefit comes from the fact that US dollars, Euros and Yen are small pieces of paper (or electronic equivalents) that take, effectively, no labour to produce. When these can be exchanged for real goods composed of real raw materials worked up by real labour, that increases the profitability of the capitals 'printing' the currency. By holding (as opposed to effectively investing) trillions of these papers as foreign currency reserves, or low-yield financial securities on the US capital market, China and other Third World states exchange workers' labour for no direct benefit; for insurance against currency volatility, payable to imperialist states that print the 'hard currencies.'

Another striking example of the financial plunder practised against China and other Third World states is the highly uneven cost of borrowing on the money markets. Most poor countries, even when holding large unproductive currency reserves, are generally forced to pay much higher interest rates on their debt than the imperialist states. The benchmark US ten-year bond yield – that is, the cost to the US government of borrowing money – was 2.55 per cent in January 2018. In the United Kingdom it was 1.29 per cent and Germany 0.54 per cent. In India it was 7.26 per cent, Indonesia 6.2 per cent, Nigeria 12.9 per cent (November 2017), Brazil 10 per cent, Mexico 7.6 per cent and so on. In China it is 4 per cent, meaning that despite holding $3 trillion in reserves, China still pays far more for loans (and it still needs to borrow) than the imperialist states.[39]

Despite the United States borrowing more from overseas than it invests overseas, the rate of return on US investments is relatively high. For this reason, Norfield emphasises, 'the interest costs on US foreign borrowing have been far less than the returns on US foreign investments'.[40] The US net international investment position (NIIP – the net total of all outgoing and incoming foreign investment) for financial year 2015/16 averaged negative $7.5 trillion. That means the US capitalists owned that much less foreign investment in other countries as other countries owned in it. However, US net investment *income* (NII) was *positive* $167 billion – a position basically unchanged for a decade. That is, US imperialism received a $167 billion return on an investment of negative $7.5 trillion! China, by contrast, had a NIIP of positive $1.6 trillion and a net return of negative $80 billion in the same year.[41]

That the Chinese state exchanges the country's hard-sweated trade surplus for 'zero real return' and adopts the absurd position of benevolent funder to US imperialism is one example of clear evidence of the *weak* position of Chinese capital. As we have seen, Chinese capital is, on the whole, locked out of the most profitable activities within the international labour division by the incumbent monopolist MNCs. These financial statistics tend to verify and express that thesis. Chinese capital cannot use its dollar surplus to establish its own high-end MNCs because the lower level of development of Chinese labour productivity makes that impossible. Even zero-gain investments make more business sense than embarking on loss-making direct battles with Google or Qualcomm, which is why, in general, this type of high-end competition has not been attempted.

We have already seen that the neoliberal period has delivered Third World producers declining terms of trade for their increasing share of world labour. We can now see that where a Third World state is able, despite this, to earn a trade surplus, usually through massive labour contribution such as in China, and accumulate money, it will receive mostly lower returns on its investments.

Why the long boom?

Before examining the imperialist attacks on China and China's most recent attempts to upgrade parts of its labour process, it is first necessary to outline how Chinese capitalism, despite its technological subordination, was still able to expand so rapidly in the neoliberal period. It is suggested China was neither able nor aiming to break the monopolistic position of the imperialist states. Rather, the easiest route to accumulation has been to offer up Chinese labour to international capital. Chinese capital could hardly be expected to choose a path of confrontation with the most powerful monopolies when it could more certainly enrich itself through a division of labour with them, even if the exact contours and terms of this division are now contested.

The size and rapid growth of China's labour force are undoubtedly the principal underlying factors in its success. Non-monopoly production is essentially the organisation of ordinary labour power. Therefore, China might be expected to be the most successful non-monopoly state, as its labour is most abundant and, until recently, was among the cheapest. Between 1991 and 2006 China's urban workforce increased by 260 million.[42]

However, labour power, in modern production, must also be well organised. India's population is almost as large as China's. It is younger, growing quickly, has lower wages and will soon surpass China in absolute population size. Yet there is nil possibility – in the near term – of India surpassing China's position as a top, large Third World state, or of even approaching that position. India is far less developed, as revealed by its per capita income, which is around one-fifth of China's. On the other hand, China has caught up to the major top-tier Third World economies, as shown.

It is necessary therefore to explain not only China's inability to compete with imperialism in highest labour processes, but also its ability to move towards the top of the Third World. Gowan sensed China's unique attributes when he argued that 'insofar as China retains a state organized for development it possesses unique potentials to exploit extraordinary scale economies and learning economies and to acquire great state resources for upgrading its production to rise up the international division of labour'.[43]

Legacy of the Chinese revolution

The ascendant capitalist class benefited not only from the size of the labour force but also from its ability to capture and convert into capital the pre-existing social resources, especially the already educated and disciplined workers, industrial establishments and means of communication established during the period of socialised property relations. The degree of development in part expressed the gains of the Chinese revolution. While much

Chinese industry developed in the socialist period was backward compared with imperialist-based industries, it nevertheless represented the pre-existing organisation of labour into modern work units and established division of labour, systems of communication, plant, distribution of goods and so on – most of which could be converted by the embryonic capitalist class into just as many aspects of the capitalist organisation of the economy.

Perhaps the most important of these gifts to capital was the mass of pre-existing, relatively advanced Chinese labour power. According to Prashad, 'the Maoist fruits – namely, the production of a healthy, literate and able population' were China's 'greatest asset'.[44] Salam argues that, among all the nations in the Global South, China had easily the greatest growth in the scientific workforce – rising from just five hundred researchers in 1949 to more than three hundred thousand by 1988.[45] World Bank China analyst Chenery observed in 1982 that 'postwar transformation of production in China was one of the most rapid among large countries', while by the late 1970s, Chinese 'industrialization proceeded much further than is typical for countries of its income level'.[46] Kuey adds that,

> by the time of the economic transition from Mao to Deng in the late 1970s, China's heavy industry, after three decades of self-perpetuating reinvestment in the sector, had already built up and matured to such a stage as to be able to facilitate the new leadership's strategic reorientation … the massive forced-draft industrialization drive under 'maximum austerity' during the 30-year reign of Mao has paid off quite handsomely, considering the marked improvement in the country's overall economic strength and in income and consumption standards of both urban and rural residents over the entire post-Mao era.[47]

These were considerable advantages. It was far faster and cheaper to appropriate existing achievements than to create them.

Overall, we can identify several factors that contributed to China's rapid growth of commodity production. First, the rapid growth of the Chinese and other Third World bourgeoisies in the neoliberal period results from the *general* expansion of the sphere of capitalist commodity production associated with the advancing global labour specialisation and was made possible by the entry of hundreds of millions of new Chinese and other cheap Third World workers into the production of value for the world market with the collapse of communism. This general expansion of value production caused an expansion in both the monopoly and non-monopoly wings of the international bourgeoisie. As was pointed out, it was not principally Chinese income that expanded in the neoliberal period. Imperialist income expanded many times faster per capita and in aggregate – but Chinese income still increased rapidly.

Second, compared with the overall pace of expansion, a more rapid growth rate (in percentage terms) of the lowest income capital is also a generalised phenomenon. As shown at the outset of the book, it was not only China, but also Vietnam, Myanmar and a range of the least developed capitalist states, especially in East Asia, that achieved above-average rates of income growth when this is measured against their previous income.

Third, Chinese expansion also benefited from its special history as capitalistically undeveloped yet – owing to the social gains of the Chinese Revolution – socially relatively advanced compared to other Third World states. That is to say, China's peculiarly rapid GDP growth, which stood well above other formerly lowest-income states, resulted in part from the conversion of non-capitalist development to capitalist values. The latter show up far better in World Bank statistics and can thus appear as miraculous to those who downplay the achievements of the revolutionary period.

The dynamic synergy of these different factors made China a profitable place to do many types of business. The rapid growth created on that basis undoubtedly created a certain momentum of its own.

The Chinese bourgeoisie, and especially its political representatives in the CCP, as is the case for all capitalist states, attempts to use state policy to leverage its advantages to achieve a greater global weight (and income). The CCP had definite advantages in this respect compared to most other Third World states. Because the Chinese masses historically defeated the political power of imperialism and expelled it from the country, this gave the Chinese state greater autonomy and power. An example of the legacy of that historic victory is continuing state ownership control of banks, investment and many of the most powerful corporations. Through the CCP's political command structure, the state is also able to orchestrate a relatively high degree of economic coordination and planning towards national goals identified in the five-year plans and other policy frameworks. Roberts argues this effectively ameliorates or restricts the operation of the law of value in China.[48] Being the largest Third World state also adds many types of leverage.

The characterisation of Chinese growth as a particularly successful variety of Third Word capitalism, and the implication that its growth has not been to the overall detriment of imperialism, also implies that it has, to some extent, been to the detriment of other Third World capitals. As documented, GDP expansion of the most developed Third World countries outside China was significantly slower, even compared to the imperialist states. This suggests that China's growth in part was achieved by concentrating within its borders a larger share of the non-monopoly labour process allocated to the Third World as a whole. For example, Schwartz argues the 1997–98 emerging market crisis was triggered in Asia by China's entry into so-called textiles, toys and trash exports, which had been previously more concentrated in South East Asian economies.[49]

It might be argued that the Chinese rulers today seek to leverage China's unique history and social capacity, plus its location and size, to further improve the country's position within the global division of labour over the next period in a way that, objectively, would subvert imperialism's dominance. That may be what sections of the Chinese leadership *seek* to do. Increasingly the CCP is being forced to try to upgrade some aspects of its labour process as the United States attempts to strangle the country through trade and investment restrictions. However, when we examine China's latest attempts at upgrading (see Chapter 18), it is shown that while the technological level of at least a part of Chinese labour has increased over the most recent decades, it remains utterly unable to break the imperialist stranglehold. Before looking at that in more detail, however, it is necessary to examine what has caused the shift in imperialist policy towards China.

Notes

1   Marx, 'Revolution in China and in Europe'.
2   Hobson, *Imperialism*, p. 386.
3   Steinfeld, 'China's Shallow Integration', p. 1979; Panitch and Gindin, *The Making of Global Capitalism*, p. 293; L. Branstetter and N. Lardy, 'China's Embrace of Globalisation', in L. Brandt and T. G. Rawsky (eds), *China's Great Economic Transformation* (New York, Cambridge University Press, 2008), pp. 633–82.
4   Steinfeld, *Playing Our Game*, pp. 32–3.
5   Steinfeld, *Playing Our Game*, p. 33.
6   Starrs, 'The Chimera of Global Convergence', p. 92.
7   Starrs, 'Designed in America, Assembled in China', p. 15.
8   UNCTAD, *World Investment Report 2013*, p. 136. Norfield notes that one US corporation, Johnson Controls, supplied 44 per cent of car seats to Chinese auto makers in 2012. See Norfield, *The City*, p. 121.
9   A. H. Amsden, *The Rise of 'The Rest': Challenges to the West from Late-Industrializing Economies* (Oxford, Oxford University Press, 2001); Schwartz, *States Versus Markets*, p. 123. Ricardo wrote: 'It is quite as important to the happiness of mankind that our enjoyment should be increased by the better distribution of labour, by each country producing those commodities for which by its situation, its climate, and its other natural or artificial advantages, it is adapted, and by thus exchanging them for the commodities of other countries, as that they should be augmented by a rise in the rate of profits.' See D. Ricardo, 'On the Principles of Political Economy and Taxation' [1817], cited in Schwartz, *States Versus Markets*, p. 123.

10 E. Reinert, *How the Rich Countries Got Rich ... And Why the Poor Countries Stay Poor* (London, Constable and Robinson, 2007), p. 26.

11 UNCTAD, *Least Developed Countries Report 2007*, p. i, cited in Prashad, *Poorer Nations*, p. 282.

12 Harvey, *Seventeen Contradictions*, p. 150; D. Harvey, 'The "New" Imperialism: Accumulation By Dispossession', *Socialist Register*, 40 (2004), 68.

13 Panitch and Gindin, *The Making of Global Capitalism*, p. 297.

14 Steinfeld, 'Chinese Enterprise Development', p. 86.

15 UNCTAD's methodology is based on S. Lall, 'The Technological Structure and Performance of Developing Country Manufactured Exports, 1985–1998', *QEH Working Paper Series*, no. 44 (2000).

16 United Nations Statistical Division, 'Statistics Division' (2018), unstats.un.org.

17 UNIDO, *Industrial Development Report 2013* (Vienna, UNIDO, 2013) p. 213.

18 Starrs, 'The Chimera of Global Convergence', p. 91.

19 Steinfeld, *Playing Our Game*, p. 86.

20 Cattaneo et al., *Global Value Chains in a Post-Crisis World*, p. 18.

21 For the United States, see J. F. Sargent, R. Esworthy, L. A. Harris, J. A. Johnson, J. Monke, D. Morgan and H. F. Upton, *Federal Research and Development Funding: FY2017* (Washington, DC, Congressional Research Service, 2017), p. 5, https://fas.org/sgp/crs/misc/R44516.pdf.

22 Steinfeld, *Playing Our Game*, p. 148; E. Dieter, *A New Geography of Knowledge in the Electronics Industry? Asia's Role in Global Innovation Networks*, East-West Center, Policy Studies No. 54 (Honolulu, HI, East-West Center, 2009), pp. 1, 21–2.

23 Steinfeld, *Playing Our Game*, p. 161.

24 Steinfeld, *Playing Our Game*, p. 164.

25 Steinfeld, *Playing Our Game*, p. 153; Dieter, *A New Geography of Knowledge*, p. 21–2.

26 See D. Ge and T. Fujimoto, 'Quasi-Open Product Architecture and Technological Lock-In: An Exploratory Study on the Chinese Motorcycle Industry', *Annals of Business Administrative Science*, 3 (2004), 15–24.

27 Ge and Fujimoto, 'The Chinese Motorcycle Industry', pp. 15–16.

28 Steinfeld, *Playing Our Game*, pp. 163–7 (emphasis added).

29 Probsting, *The Great Robbery of the South*, p. 265; Callinicos, *Imperialism and Global Political Economy*, p. 8; A. Smith, 'US imperialism's Pivot to Asia', *International Socialist Review*, 88 (2013).

30 Lenin, *Imperialism*, chap. 8.

31 Lenin, *Imperialism*, chap. 4.

32 Kiely, *Rethinking Imperialism*, p. 181.

33 Data Bank, *World Bank, 2018*.

34 J. Politi, S. Wong and A. Edgecliffe-Johnson, 'US Companies Step Up Response to Donald Trump's China Ultimatum', *Financial Times* (2019), 23 May.

35 Norfield, *The City*, p. 11.

36 Cited in Smith, *Imperialism and the Globalisation of Production*, p. 199.

37 C. Somel, 'Surplus Allocation and Development under Global Capitalism', *ERC Working Papers in Economics* 5:5 (2005), 13.

38 Norfield, *The City*, p. 163.

39 Sources: bloomberg.com; asianbondsonline.adb.org; *Reuters* [staff], 'Nigeria's 10-Year Bonds Yield Fall to 11-Month Low on Liquidity' (2015), 17 October; M. Song Loong, 'Greece Takes Rain Check after Savage Equity Sell-Off, *Reuters* (2018), 6 February.

40 Norfield, *The City*, p. 169. The same was true for Britain 2000–11. See Norfield, *The City*, pp. 200, 202.

41 B. Steil and E. Smith, 'China's Exorbitant Detriment, Mirror Image of America's Exorbitant Privilege, Is Costing It Dearly', *Council on Foreign Relations* (2017), 10 January; Bureau of Economic Analysis, *U.S. Net International Investment Position First Quarter 2017, Year 2016, and Annual Update* (US Department of Commerce, 2017), 28 June.

42 Panitch and Gindin, *The Making of Global Capitalism*, p. 298.

43 Gowan, 'Industrial Development and Conflict', in Anievas, *Marxism and World Politics*, p. 142.

44 Prashad, *Poorer Nations*, p. 201.

45 Cited in Prashad, *Poorer Nations*.

46 H. B. Chenery, 'Industrialization and Growth: The Experience of Large Countries', *World Bank Staff Working Paper, SWP539* (1982), 16, 13.

47 Y. Y. Kueh, *China's New Industrialisation Strategy: Was Chairman Mao Really Necessary?* (Cheltenham, Edward Elgar, 2008), pp. 153–4.

48 Roberts, 'Xi Takes Full Control of China's Future'.

49 Schwartz, *States Versus Markets*, p. 94.

17

The new Imperialist cold war against China

To rising China writers, the existence of any economic, political or military conflict between the United States and China seems to prove their view that China is a threat to imperialism. However, imperialism has historically driven extremely hard bargains against even the weakest Third World societies using the most belligerent and violent means. Iraq and Afghanistan never threatened US imperialism even if many reports and much analysis told us they did. The mere presence of conflict tells us nothing about the balance of forces. Workers after all sometimes engage in bitter fights with their bosses both offensively and in defence. That the two sides are engaged in struggle hardly means we should draw an equal sign between them.

The 'trade war', which is an economic attack on China by US imperialism, aims to strengthen imperialist claims to the value brought into the world economy by Chinese labour. This can mean either attempting to increase its parasitism or defend its existing terms. In other words, the battle is over the *degree* of exploitation of China. No Marxist argument can be made that Chinese capital is a net appropriator of value created by US, British or First World workers. The character of the US attacks – and of the conflict as a whole – has to be defined as one of imperialist aggression against China. Sections of US capital evidently believe they can achieve better terms and secure more Chinese surplus value than would otherwise be possible by way of economic war. Though the extent to which that current US aggression is also driven by political imperatives is not yet clear.

As outlined, the success of Chinese capitalism in the neoliberal period has been to move from one of the poorest to one of the most developed Third World societies. Imperialism as the exploiter of the Third World pole of capitalism always exists, to a certain extent, in contradiction and conflict with that pole. This is manifested both in imperialist imposition of economic policy as well as constant imperialist wars in different Third World regions. Perhaps in the economic sphere imperialism's conflict with the Third World is sharpest against the upper echelon of the Third World, given the economic competition with these societies is more direct.

China's development has seen it not only join the ranks of the most developed Third World societies but also to massively expand the overall size of that group. Further, China alone constitutes an absolute majority of this group, thus concentrating considerable power within a single state. It is located in a region not so close to or hegemonically controlled by US imperialism as Mexico or Brazil. Indeed, China borders one of US imperialism's principal historical rivals, Russia, and neighbours another, Japan.

The Chinese state, including its ruling party, as outlined, is the product, albeit ossified, of an anti-imperialist and indeed anti-capitalist revolution. The legacy of the historical defeat Chinese people inflicted upon imperialism is presumably the problem that US ruling-class ideologues perceive when they complain about the lack of democracy – something that never bothered, for example, the United States, United Kingdom and Australia, nor the Paris club of donors, when they gave political and economic support to the military dictatorship that ruled for thirty-three years in Indonesia.

In the new situation of greater development of commodity production in China, US capital today, or sections of it, are looking to reconfigure the terms of its engagement (exploitation) of China to better reflect its new strengths, weaknesses and needs. It is not that China's development presents major US capitalists with competitors capable of defeating them. Rather, they face competitors able to squeeze *certain* aspects of their overall dominance and reduce their profits in lower-end and marginal operations. At the same time, US and broader imperialist monopoly over the high-technology core of the global division of labour has not been eroded. As the production process in general continues to become an ever more high-tech operation, it may be the case that imperialism's monopoly not only holds but is strengthening. Some concrete examples are given in the following chapter.

That the Chinese competition on US capital is overwhelmingly limited to labour processes that, in the imperialist states, are not high-tech areas, was shown by Trump and Biden's bleating about China 'stealing' US 'intellectual property' and demands that the Chinese state enforce intellectual property laws. If China were really developing its own world-beating technologies, the US state would not be demanding strict adherence to intellectual property laws; it would be saying little while quietly trying to copy Chinese innovation.

What US capital seeks is not legal protection aimed at artificially (politically) forestalling the collapse of its tottering economic dominance – although that is likely the case for marginal, individual capitals or sectors. Rather, the dominant sections of US capital seek legal protections that will *increase* the projection of their technological dominance. Greater legal protection extends the period of time that above-average profits can be secured for a given new labour process or product by hindering competitors adopting it, even after this has become technically feasible. Even the complete removal of legal protections would not end the ability of US capitalists to make above-average profits on the basis of technological innovation because US capital is more technically advanced.

Another US aim in the trade war is winding back Chinese state subsidies for large SOEs (many of which also have a large degree of private ownership). The policy is a reaction to another advantage China does possess compared to other Third World societies. As the largest Third World state, subsidies of otherwise uneconomic or marginal producers are a key method for Chinese capital to compete globally despite relative technical backwardness. In doing so it undermines the profitability of competitors by undercutting them on price and taking market share. If Chinese capital was more advanced than the imperialist-based capitalist groups, massive direct subsidies of this type would not be necessary.

State handouts to capitalist producers uses resources that could otherwise have been consumed by workers. When these subsidies are then passed on to buyers in the form of cheap subsidised products, it becomes just another form of competition by cheap labour. In this case, the social wage is reduced, rather than direct wages. Subsidies to capital essentially allows China's cheap labour advantage to be moved from traditional lowest-tech labour-intensive products like textiles and footwear to more sophisticated forms of manufacturing and other production.

Such state support also becomes a handout to imperialism and subsidises the profitability of imperialist economies. This is because subsidising and thereby cheapening products that are then consumed in the imperialist societies reduces costs in those societies. It reduces costs to the businesses that purchase such products directly. Alternatively, where First World workers consume cheap subsidised products, this allows capital to minimise workers' wage rises. Policies that force down the Chinese currency – sometimes a policy of Beijing – has the same effect.

Most observers assume that the increase in conflict between the United States and China flows from China's increased strength and growing US weakness. This new reality, so the argument goes, is leading to a conflict that will somehow recalibrate the relationship and a strengthened China should ultimately emerge. In this view the United States is using its incumbent institutional, legal, political, financial or military advantages to try to arrest or slow the progress of China's supposed underlying economic and productive advantage.

But such an understanding does not match the facts of how the trade war is being fought. The 'trade war' is a conflict being fought on the *economic* front. It was initiated by Trump and the United States has been the aggressor throughout. If it really were the case that declining US economic strength was being fought using US non-economic advantages, then it would make no sense for Trump and his advisors to launch a series of sanctions that restrict Chinese access to US productive technology. If Chinese technology were more advanced, we might expect the sanctions to fail. But as we will see in the next chapter, the economic attacks are the very core of the US policy – and they are not failing.

It is the case, as everybody can see, that China has gained strength in certain spheres and the United States and its imperialist allies seek to contain that. But to understand the current conflict it is necessary to see that the imperialist economies also have a strengthened economic grip in their principal domain. It is this grip over the high-end of the labour process – in particular over microchips – that the United States is now wielding against China in the 'trade war'. As we will see, China has no counter-attack that is based in productive or technological supremacy – even in a limited area. Rather, it is forced to scramble to substitute US technology that is now restricted. Before examining the core economic battle in detail, it is necessary to briefly examine two areas said to demonstrate Chinese imperialism, or its imperial 'ambitions' – the Belt and Road Initiative and its military modernisation programme.

The Belt and Road Initiative

We saw in the previous chapter that China's financial weakness provided a significant injection of surplus value into the imperialist economies. According to Huang and Wang, 67 per cent of China's total international assets during the period 2004–10 were held as international reserves, while 6 per cent was invested as FDI and 10 per cent portfolio investment.[1] The high proportion held in cash is the proximal cause of the low or zero rate of return on this money as outlined.

Part of China's initial response to this problem was to establish a sovereign wealth fund, the China Investment Corporation (CIC) in 2007. Investing money in the CIC was distinct from a strategy instead based on investing that money in the development of the domestic economy. The fund sought to convert a part of China's foreign exchange surplus (earned through its trade surplus) into a portfolio of overseas financial assets to deliver income to the state. The strategy is perhaps economically conservative compared to expectations of Marxist China boosters as it aims to gain ownership of *foreign* production – rather than investing available funds in the development of Chinese production to compete with or displace imperialist dominance. Yet the CIC too made a whole series of marginal and loss-making investments and overall performed little better than cash in its first ten years.[2] It was part of a broader pattern of Chinese purchase of unprofitable or barely profitable overseas assets.[3] These problems partly explain why the CCP pushed ahead in 2013 with its ambitious – but also often uneconomic – Belt and Road Initiative (BRI).

The BRI is perhaps the most notorious example of China's supposedly nefarious global economic expansion plans. It has seen China accused of preying on helpless poor countries and is widely treated in the imperialist press as a strategic plan to consolidate China as the world superpower. What is less clearly argued is, how exactly does such an eclectic policy fit into any sort of plan? As of 2018 the BRI was being used to brand Chinese involvement in anything from fashion shows, art exhibitions and marathons to domestic flights and dentistry.[4] According to statistical analysis that year, investments were just as likely to go outside the designated BRI investment corridors as inside them.[5]

Only a fraction of the projects designated as part of the BRI have any clear strategic economic value. The major example that does – investments in energy infrastructure in Pakistan – clearly has a defensive character. Greater Chinese energy security is a geopolitical defensive necessity to deny US imperialism an easy and decisive stranglehold on the country.

A major aspect of the attacks on China over the BRI revolve around the accusation that it lends poorer countries more than they can afford to repay in order to entrap and force them to hand over strategic assets – so-called debt-trap diplomacy. The case of the Sri Lankan Port of Hambantota is repeated in probably thousands of mass media articles.[6] According to the popular narrative, China financed the port expansion in such a way that Sri Lanka would be unable to repay the loan, allowing China to swoop in and take over the port for use by the People's Liberation Navy. But this narrative has now been debunked by researchers Jones and Hameiri. The project was not proposed by China but conceived by the Mahinda Rajapaksa regime in Sri Lanka in 2006, well before the BRI was launched. The port upgrade was designed for use by the Sri Lankan Navy, which still controls the facility to this day. Jones writes: 'By 2016, Sri Lanka was in a serious debt crisis – caused not by Chinese lending, which accounts for only 6 percent of Colombo's external debt – but rather reckless borrowing on dollar-denominated international markets amid U.S. quantitative easing.'[7] No Chinese naval vessels have called at the port – though ships from the United States, Japan and India have. More generally, Jones and Hameiri show the real character of the BRI is neither a master plan (nefarious or otherwise) nor a debt trap, but principally an attempt to find profitable projects for Chinese firms in the context of chronic domestic excess capacity. Responding to the rapid deterioration in Third World finances in 2020 due to the COVID-19 pandemic, China has been party to G20 arrangements to postponement repayments for the poorest African debtor states. The imperialist dominated G20 has so far refused to do more than mere postponement.

Further, the Export–Import Bank of China has announced plans to completely forgive the interest-free concessional loans to African countries that are on its books.

Jones and Hameiri's narrative better explains the strategic incoherence of the various projects labelled BRI.[8] The difficulties any debtors have in paying back loans is not a boon for Chinese empire but just a plain old bad debt. That is to say, yet more cases of Chinese foreign investment making losses or obtaining only minimal returns. The researchers argue it is recipient 'country governments and their associated political and economic interests', not China, that 'determine the nature of BRI projects on their territory'.[9]

Another popular narrative, suggesting Chinese imperialism, is that its foreign investment in Africa is displacing that of the rich countries. In the most absurd version of this story, the rich country interests in Africa are benevolent while Chinese are exploitative. But, as Chen et al. point out, the notion that Chinese investment in Africa is very large is a serious exaggeration: 'The European Union countries, led by France and the United Kingdom, are the overwhelmingly largest investors in Africa. The U.S. is also significant, and even South Africa invests more on the continent than China does.'[10] The authors quote various sources that put the Chinese proportion of new investment in Africa as between 3 per cent and 4.4 per cent of the total. In 2019, According to UNCTAD, Chinese cumulative FDI ranked fifth in 2019 behind the Netherlands, France, the United Kingdom and the United States.[11]

The largest destination for Chinese outbound direct investment during 2005 to 2018 was not Africa (or Latin America), nor any signatories to the BRI, but the United States. New Chinese FDI in the United States in 2018 was $5.4 billion. That is around 42 per cent of the figure for US investment in China and just 1.8 per cent of all inward FDI to the United States.[12]

A military power?

China is also accused – principally by successive US governments – of military aggression especially in the South China Sea. The hypocrisy is clear, given the long history of imperialist military aggression against China and a whole series of Third World countries that, like China, were considered insufficiently compliant with imperialist dictates. There can be no serious question of China challenging US military supremacy. Chinese military modernisation can only challenge the *degree* that the United States can impose its will in East Asia.

To give a sense of the massive imbalance we can compare the number of overseas military bases held by China and other countries. China has one – in Djibouti, which also hosts US, French, Italian and Japanese military bases. The United States in 2015 had around eight hundred bases in seventy countries (including China's neighbours). Britain France and Russia have around thirty combined.[13] If having a single overseas base is imperialist then India is imperialist too with its Farkhor Air Base in Tajikistan and various other overseas military instillations. India has current projects to upgrade the airstrips in the Andaman and Nicobar Islands for Indian Air Force use. However, being an ally of the United States, Indian militarism – unlike Chinese – is largely unknown outside of its region. Possession of domestic and regional military assets in China, India and other Third World countries can only curtail the degree to which the United States and its imperialist allies can assert power against them.

Perhaps the clearest expression of the balance of forces is the case of Taiwan. A country of 24 million people, Taiwan is a US ally that split from the People's Republic of China (PRC) after the communist victory in 1949. It has been Chinese policy for seventy years that the island forms an integral part of the PRC. Now, it is a concentrated hub of high-tech production, including of semiconductors. If the PRC could control that, it would help ameliorate the crippling US sanctions regime. Despite lying just 160 kilometres from the mainland province of Fujian, the PRC has never *attempted* military action to reincorporate it.

A high-level military alliance and technical cooperation with the United States has made Taiwan's Republic of China Air Force and its land-based missile systems a formidable enemy. These threaten the lower-tech People's Liberation Navy and People's Liberation Air Force with massive losses if an invasion were ever attempted. Under the US umbrella, Taiwan (together with South Korea) has become, as shown, one of the rich, imperialist countries. It may also serve as the outstanding example of what appears to be a key rule of militarism in the contemporary imperialist world: poor countries do not invade rich countries. No country does. Since the 1940s rich countries have not been invaded *even by other rich countries*. Imperialist countries do invade. This happens exclusively in the Third World. The supposed Chinese 'threat' is really a cover for imperialist aggression and imperialist build-up. China is already surrounded. Further, imperialist build-up can only increase the possibilities for imperialist penetration and sabotage.

None of this means that all Chinese foreign policies are justified. Aggression against Vietnam, for example, has been ongoing for decades. More broadly, in the South China Sea, many of China's territorial claims amount to demanding sea borders with poor and poorer neighbours that would effectively grant China mining and fishing rights in areas that are closer to the neighbours than to China. It is easy to see why China might pursue these policies. The South China Sea is a strategic waterway through which much of China's, and the world's, trade passes. For this reason, it is a legitimate strategic interest of China's. Allowing US military control of it – and it is currently surrounded by US military bases – would yield to US imperialism another way to strangle China.

When states like the Philippines and Taiwan have military cooperation agreements with the United States, from a Chinese strategic perspective, allowing them territorial rights in the South China Sea amounts to allowing US access. Even so, it is possible to imagine this could be addressed very differently to Beijing's current approach. Rather than belligerence seen to be directed against its neighbours, China could appeal to regional cooperation. When faced with reactionary governments that refuse this, it would be possible to appeal to the anti-imperialist sentiments of ordinary people in its neighbouring countries against US and imperialist presence in the region. A more effective front against imperialism might be formed at the same time as sowing the seeds of regional development cooperation and raising anti-imperialist consciousness.

In clashes between China and the US–Australian–Japanese imperialist alliance for control of the South China Sea, China's military activities have a defensive character. That flows both from the aggressive military posture of imperialism against China and from the fact that China is a Third World country exploited by imperialism. Therefore, any strengthening of its position can help to reduce its exploitation by imperialism while a weakening will entrench that. That remains the case even if these defensive interests – as well as the cause of anti-imperialism more broadly – could be better served if Beijing were to pursue a policy of internationalism and solidarity, rather than its present course.

Notes

1 Y. Huang and B. Wang, 'From the Asian Miracle to an Asian Century? Economic Transformation in the 2000s and Prospects for the 2010s', *The Australian Economy in the 2000s* [conference proceedings] (Sydney, Reserve Bank of Australia), 2011, p. 15.

2 F. Tang, 'Ten Years On, Where to Now for China's Sovereign Wealth Fund?' *South China Morning Post* (2017), 27 August.

3 See H. Hung, 'America's Head Servant? The PRC's Dilemma in the Global Crisis', *New Left Review*, 60 (2009), 18; J. Kynge, T. Mitchell and A. Massoudi, 'M&A: China's World of Debt', *Financial Times* (2016), 12 February; Q. Webb, 'Broken Record', *Reuters* (2016), 17 February.

4 J. Hillman, *China's Belt and Road Is Full of Holes* (Washington, DC, Center for Strategic and International Studies, 2018).

5 Hillman, *China's Belt and Road Is Full of Holes*.

6 See, for example, M. Abi-Habib, 'How China Got Sri Lanka to Cough Up a Port', *New York Times* (2018), 25 June.

7 L. Jones, 'China's Belt and Road Initiative Is a Mess, Not a Master Plan', *Foreign Policy* (2020), 9 October.

8 L. Jones and S. Hameiri, 'Debunking the Myth of "Debt-Trap Diplomacy": How Recipient Countries Shape China's Belt and Road Initiative', *Chatham House* (2020) 19 August.

9 Jones and Hameiri, 'Debunking the Myth'.

10 W. Chen, D. Dollar and H. Tang, 'China's Direct Investment in Africa: Reality Versus Myth', *Brookings* (2015), 3 September.

11 UNCTAD, *World Investment Report 2020*, p. 28.

12 A. B. Schwarzenberg, 'U.S.–China Investment Ties: Overview and Issues for Congress', *Congressional Research Service* (2019), updated 28 August; D. Scissors, 'Chinese Investments in the United States', *AEI* (2020), aei.org/china-tracker-home.

13 D. Vine, 'Where in the World Is the U.S. Military?' *Politico* (2015) July–August.

18

Trade war and China's latest attempts at upgrading

The policy framework that, for the last five years, has sought to upgrade China's domestic production processes is *Made in China 2025* (MIC-2025). It specifies no less than ten industries for upgrading, including information technology, numerical control tools and robotics, aerospace equipment, ocean engineering equipment and high-tech ships, railway equipment, energy-saving and new-energy vehicles, power equipment, new materials, medicine and medical devices and agricultural machinery. The breadth of this policy is interpreted, by those who view China as a new imperial power, as indicating vast Chinese potential. Yet given the widespread problems in most or all of these sectors, the same breadth might be better understood as a lack of focus and lack of any standout opportunities in even a small number of sectors. Those most impressed with MIC-2025, or at least the idea of it, are usually least familiar with China's various similar past attempts at technical upgrading, or with the policy document itself.

The authors of MIC-2025 appear to hold fewer illusions that China can compete with the imperialist states:

> Chinese manufacturing is large but not yet strong. The capability for independent innovation is weak and external dependence for key technologies and advanced equipment is high. Enterprise-led manufacturing innovation systems have yet to be perfected. Product quality is not high and China has few world-famous brands. Resource and energy efficiency remains low, while environmental pollution is severe. The industrial structure and industry services remain immature. The manufacturing digitalization level is low and digital technologies have not been widely integrated into industry. The overall internationalization level is low and enterprises' capacity to compete globally is deficient.[1]

The overriding motivation for the policy seems to be defensive:

> At the same time, global industrial competition is undergoing a significant adjustment that presents China with great challenges. After the global financial crisis, developed countries implemented 'manufacturing renaissance' strategies in order to regain advantages in manufacturing, and to promote new global trading and investment patterns. Meanwhile, developing countries are

seeking to expand their share of global industrial labor and are investing in industrial capital to develop their export markets. Manufacturing in China is facing severe challenges from this 'two-way squeeze' between developed and developing countries.[2]

Widely touted as a sinister plan to take over the world, in reality MIC-2025 does not even project that. If all goes according to plan, only '[b]y 2035, Chinese manufacturing will reach an *intermediate* level among world manufacturing powers'. Even by 2049 MIC-2025 does not project to dominate industry or high technology, but rather: 'We will have the capability to lead innovation and possess competitive advantages in major manufacturing areas, and will develop advanced technology and industrial systems.'[3] That is to say, if all goes well, China would be competitive, not dominant, in some sectors, not most or all. However, there is little detail about how even this might be achieved.

The policy principally revolves around numerical targets such as levels of R & D spending per unit of GDP or the numbers of patents per unit of operating revenue in each sector. Chinese spending on R & D, at 2.1 per cent of GDP is half that of South Korea and well below Japan's 3.5 per cent, Germany's 2.9 per cent and the US 2.8 per cent.[4] Because China's per capita GDP is around 15 per cent to 25 per cent of those countries, its per capita R & D spend is tiny. However, the biggest problem may not be quantity of spending, but what this money achieves.

The starting point for Chinese technological development is essentially the same as for any other Third World society – scientific backwardness in most areas. As Liu Yadong, editor-in-chief of *Science and Technology Daily*, which is supervised by the Ministry of Science and Technology, stated, 'The large gap in science and technology between China and developed countries in the West, including the US, should be common knowledge'.[5]

As outlined, not all R & D is equal. Typically, research is of a higher level than development – the latter being modification of existing technology. Wang Zhigang, China's science and technology minister, for example, regards 'basic research' as 'the source of all technological innovation'. He says this is a 'weakness of China's science and technology sector'.[6] Of China's total R & D spend, only 5 per cent goes to basic research, compared to 15 per cent in the United States.

However, these are not problems that can be fixed simply by adjusting policy settings. According to Zeng Fang, a delegate to the Chinese People's Political Consultative Conference, '[t]he difficulty' is finding 'the right talent that can direct funds into projects that can produce genuine innovation and fresh knowledge – that is why most [private sector technology] funding goes on applications'.[7] The *South China Morning Post* reported Zeng Fang as arguing 'the major challenge for the private sector is talent, not money when it comes to investing in basic research'.[8] According to Leng, 'these included a lack of theoretical scientific knowledge, a skills deficit in some areas'.[9]

The problems run deeper than development of the scientific community. They concern the social development and organisation of the whole economy and society. According to Scott Kennedy, 'the efficiency and quality of Chinese producers are highly uneven, and multiple challenges need to be overcome in a short amount of time if China is to avoid being squeezed by both newly emerging low-cost producers and more effectively cooperate and compete with advanced industrialized economies'.[10] Xin Guobin, vice-minister of industry and information technology, concurs: 'We are still decades behind the developed countries, and the road to building a strong manufacturing country is long.'[11]

Lašinskas points out that MIC-2025 is inspired by Germany's industrial development policy, called *Industry 4.0*. The term '4.0' refers to industrial adoption of cyber-physical systems. However, Lašinskas suggests China cannot adopt level '4.0' industrial systems because most Chinese industry remains at the level of 'Industry 2.0' – manual assembly lines. The next step would be 'Industry 3.0' – the adoption of robots and automation.[12]

The problem is not only slow speed of development or starting from well behind but also imperialist monopoly over the highest technology. As outlined, the basis of this monopoly is imperialism's ability to produce new technology – negating the efficacy of any Chinese advance. According to Shanker – a research analyst in electronics and semiconductors – 'it will be difficult for China to innovate in the technological space within such a short span of time and make Chinese industries independent'.[13] Kennedy thinks 'it's a guarantee that MNCs will be needed to provide critical components, technology, and management for this plan is to work'.[14]

A key reason for the negative assessment of so many China and industry specialists is that they see MIC-2025 as a rerun of previous upgrading attempts. In nanotechnology, Cao et al. note that 'China included nanotechnology as one of four science mega-programs in its Medium and Long-Term Plan for the Development of Science and Technology (2006–2020)',[15] the forerunner to MIC-2025. However,

> the commercialization side of nanotechnology has not been as impressive as its tangible success in publishing, patenting, and the creation of nanotechnology-oriented science parks … reform of China's [science and technology] system launched in the mid-1980s aimed to tackle this problem, but the outcome thus far has been mixed at best.[16]

Taking the example of robotics, weakness in technology development was worked around, in one instance, by purchasing it – Midea Group's purchase of German robotics maker, Kuka. However, the opportunities for even this workaround are rapidly closing with the US trade war: 'Midea was trying, like many other Chinese companies, to develop their own industrial robotics products. This went on for a number of years, but the quality of systems was not comparable to what was being produced in Europe and Japan.'[17] There is robotics manufacturing in China, but like other sectors, robotics is divided into high- and low-end producers and high- and low-end labour processes within each product. According to Pang, an analyst with ING bank, Chinese robots 'are like robots that are used in packaging or logistics'. They are so low tech, according to Pang, that, 'robotics makers, they could be thinking, maybe Vietnam is a better choice after all [to locate production]. Hence they're cutting down on capital expenditure' in China.[18]

The overall pattern is that the more determined and deeper any Chinese foray into high technology, the more it can proceed only with greater dependence on foreign technological inputs. In the sectors where Chinese capital appears to be attempting some sort of direct confrontation with imperialist monopolies, such as aerospace and 5G, this is carried out in practice by the importation of advanced components – and hence the reproduction of the same old First World – Third World labour division, albeit branded as 'made in China'.

The Commercial Aircraft Corporation of China

One area of MIC-2025 that is sometimes touted as a success story is the Chinese state's push to start commercial aerospace production. This is organised through the Commercial Aircraft Corporation of China (COMAC), which is headquartered in Shanghai and directly controlled by China's cabinet. COMAC was established in 2008 and has so far invested around $10 billion to develop a mid-sized passenger jet – the C919 – with the aim of competing with the global duopoly of Boeing and Airbus in mid-sized jets. The SOE's enormous investment includes facilities and personnel spread over 110 buildings.

The first test flight of a C919 prototype took place three years behind schedule in May 2017, while the second prototype was tested a further three months behind schedule in December 2017.[19] It is not due to fly commercially until 2021. This compares to monthly production of twenty commercial planes at Airbus's Chinese assembly plant and Boeing's 2016 sales to China of 116 aircraft. The C919 uses long-established technologies and cannot match the performance of Boeing and Airbus's mid-sized commercial planes already in operation, let alone of their next-generation planes under development. For example, the C919's range is around two-thirds of Airbus's equivalent A320.

The C919 project relies on collaboration with US industrial giants GE and Honeywell for many of its high-technology components. The *New York Times* reports that, 'in addition to the avionics, GE has also collaborated on the engines, while Honeywell is providing auxiliary power systems, wheels, brakes, fly-by-wire controls and navigation equipment'. The paper reported that 'Honeywell expects $15 billion in sales to the C919 program during its 20 or more years of production'.[20] Thus, even if the Chinese cabinet were successful in establishing an international competitor to Boeing and Airbus in some of their low-end markets, this will not guarantee that most of the profits from the aircraft's sales will stay in China.

The C919, with a maximum seating configuration of 190, does not attempt to compete with Boeing and Airbus's larger and more profitable wide-bodied planes, but with the common narrow-bodied Boeing 737 and Airbus A320. Notably, Brazil's Embraer has produced dual-purpose commercial and military aircraft since the late 1960s – though its commercial aircraft business has suffered many years of losses.

By May 2020 COMAC had received 815 orders for the C919–781 domestic and 34 from overseas.[21] GE, which stands to gain from involvement in the project, has ordered twenty. If such a trend were to continue, COMAC might begin to look like an aerospace version of other large, hardly profitable, domestically oriented non-monopolistic monopolies.

COMAC is not the first but the latest attempt by the Chinese state to start commercial aircraft construction. The Shanghai Aviation Industrial Company (SAIC) designed and built three prototypes of the Shanghai Y-10 between 1970 and 1980 that aimed to compete with the Boeing 707. Using Pratt and Whitney (United Technologies) engines, the Y-10 was tested in the air for 170 hours before the programme was abandoned in 1984.[22]

Between 1986 and 1993, 34 MD82/83 aircraft were assembled in Shanghai by McDonnell Douglas. In 1992 McDonnell Douglas and Aviation Industries China (AVIC) established a joint venture to produce the MD90 aircraft based on existing McDonnel Douglas technology. However, after just two planes could be assembled, the programme was cancelled in 1997 by McDonnell Douglas's new owner – Boeing.[23]

AVIC then went on to itself develop the ARJ21, a small, regional jet that closely resembles the earlier MD80/90. The ARJ21 was expected to have its first flight in 2006, with commercial operations by 2008. By 2010 it had two hundred orders. However, as of mid-2019, there were still only eleven of the planes in commercial operation.[24] While there are plans to expand production, this is hardly threatening to imperialism. The first MD80 (not the Chinese version) was launched by Swissair in 1980.

Huawei and imperialist monopoly over microchips

The telecommunications equipment and consumer electronics maker Huawei is – or was – widely touted as a Chinese technological success story – until the US Department of Commerce, leveraging US technological dominance, blew up that image with sanctions beginning in 2019. Huawei was China's most successful international company. With sales of $108 billion and profits of $8.8 billion by 2018, it had become one of the largest companies in China and the world. Huawei was perhaps the only major Chinese MNC competing as a peer in high-value global markets. When in May 2019 the US Department of Commerce added Huawei to its 'entities list', prohibiting US firms from supplying it (without departmental permission), the company became a test case at the apex of Chinese technological development. The struggle around Huawei and the broader struggle around microchips illustrates most clearly the nature and degree of imperialist technological domination.

Under the 2019 sanctions, Huawei was prohibited from offering Google applications such as Gmail, Google Maps and Play Store on its phones, and from purchasing US- and British-designed microprocessing chips needed to produce phones and telecommunications equipment. The attack did not come without warning. It repeated a similar attack on China's number two telecommunications company – ZTE – one year earlier.

In May 2018 ZTE announced it was shutting its factories just weeks after the Department of Commerce (DoC) placed it under sanctions for alleged violation of other US-imposed sanctions – those on Iran. ZTE had 74,000 employees at the time and – like Huawei – its business spanned telecommunications equipment and consumer electronics. *Forbes* reported that ZTE confirmed it would shut down because 'most of its products use American technologies, from high-end 5G equipment to low-end Android smartphones, and that it will be close to impossible for ZTE to redesign new products around the U.S. tech ban'.[25] Trump ultimately rescinded the ZTE ban as part of the broader US–China trade negotiations – bringing ZTE back to life. This came after a personal appeal from Chinese president Xi Jinping. ZTE agreed in July 2018 to pay $1 billion in fines and allow increased US regulatory scrutiny as part of the deal.

One year later Huawei was hit with its own DoC bans, supposedly due to the 'national security' threat the company's equipment is said to pose to the United States. Like ZTE, Huawei faced the loss of critical US-based high-tech suppliers, without which it could not keep producing high-end phones or 5G equipment. Prior to the ban, Huawei had purchased roughly $11 billion in US components and services from 1,200 suppliers in 2018.[26] Leading microchip companies Intel, Qualcomm, Xilinix, Broadcom, Infineon and

ARM all suspended business with Huawei following the announcement. Google also announced suspension of Huawei's access to future Android operating system updates. Huawei could still use the open-source version of Android on its phones, but not Google applications. This made it harder to sell high-priced phones, especially outside China.

Huawei's phones relied for their primary microchips on both the US-based market leader Qualcomm and Huawei's fully owned subsidiary HiSilicon, which was established in 2004 and is based in China. HiSilicon is a chip *designer* that outsources production to specialist companies – or 'foundries'.

Sourcing part of its chip design needs from HiSilicon perhaps made Huawei less directly dependent than ZTE on US suppliers. However, HiSilicon is itself dependent on foreign technology to produce its chip designs. In particular, it is dependent on ARM, the UK-based provider, and California-based software companies Synopsys and Cadence, which are used to produce the blueprints for circuits.[27] Referring to the 2019 sanctions, Blaber commented: 'ARM is the foundation of Huawei's smartphone chip designs, so this is an insurmountable obstacle for Huawei … They're not going to be able to easily replace these parts with new, in-house designs – the semiconductor industry in China is nascent.'[28] The same bottleneck around microchips appears in both phones and 5G network equipment (that is, in both of the key planks of Huawei's business). Yang of the *Financial Times* reported:

> When it comes to telecoms equipment such as mobile masts, Huawei relies on logic chips called field-programmable gate arrays (FPGAs) made by US company Xilinx. The other major FPGA suppliers, Intel's Altera and Lattice Semiconductor, are also US companies … Analysts reckon China is more than 10 years behind in designing high-end logic chips of the kind used in Huawei's switches and routers.[29]

In their article 'American Threat to Huawei's Chip Maker Shows Chinese Tech Isn't Self-Sufficient', *Wall Street Journal* business writers Kubota and Strumpf suggested at the time that, 'while other chip [producers] and HiSilicon's suppliers shift to future versions of ARM technology or products from the software companies, the U.S. blacklisting will leave HiSilicon stuck with older tools, hindering its ability to compete on the frontiers of chip design and extending the time it takes to develop its products'.[30] This is how things transpired for a while. In its high-end phones, Huawei was able to swap Qualcomm chips for its proprietary Kirin chipsets designed by its subsidiary, HiSilicon, and manufactured by Taiwan Semiconductor Manufacturing Co. – the largest chip manufacturer in the world. However, in August 2020, the DoC passed new sanctions, closing these loopholes.

Since then, no company anywhere in the world can sell semiconductors, including their designs, to Huawei if these were produced using US software or equipment.[31]

According to the *Financial Times*, 'Given the dominance of US tools in certain segments of chip making, the new trade rule amounted to a blanket ban on any chip sales to Huawei.' The article quotes Credit Suisse researcher Manish Nigam who argues: 'We believe this step to significantly (almost completely) curtail Huawei's ability to source any semiconductor from anyone.'[32]

In response, Huawei is reportedly planning to build its own semiconductor fabrication plant in Shanghai to replace the imported specialised chips it needs for its telecommunications equipment business when its stockpile runs out.[33] The planned factory will initially produce 45 nano meter (nm) grade chips, a standard that has been in commercial production for fifteen years. After that, it is supposed to progress to 20 nm chips by late 2022. If successful, these could be used for Huawei's 5G equipment, but not smartphones.

Mark Li, a semiconductor analyst, told the *Financial Times* that mobile base stations would 'ideally be made on 14 nm or more advanced process technology' but 'using 28 nm was possible'. The *Financial Times* journalists argued that 'Chinese producers could tolerate higher costs and operational inefficiencies than their offshore competitors'.[34] Li notes that 'such a facility would most likely run on a combination of equipment from different Chinese suppliers such as AMEC and Naura, plus some used foreign tools which they can find in the [used equipment] market'.[35] Without US supplied logic chips, Huawei may still be able supply 5G network equipment to Chinese and other Third World markets, but these systems will deliver second-rate performance and require more labour to service. Such equipment is hardly likely to penetrate far into the most lucrative First World markets – unless massively subsidised.

While Taiwan Semiconductor did most high-end chips, much of the fabrication of Huawei's less advanced chips – such as for lower-end phones – was contracted to the largest Chinese mainland contract chip maker, the Semiconductor Manufacturer International Corporation (SMIC). Now, under the sanctions, the future of Huawei's phone handset and consumer electronics business appears to turn, in part, on SMIC's capabilities. Perhaps for that reason the DoC extended similar sanctions to SMIC in September 2020.

SMIC, established in 2000, is a global low-end chip manufacturer. Prior to the sanctions it manufactured basic chips cheaply for both the Chinese and international market. Even this low-end production is completely reliant on foreign technology. The *only* commercially available technology for the manufacture of advanced chips is something called extreme ultra-violet (EUV) lithographic machinery, owned and distributed by the Dutch global monopoly ASML. The company supplies these lithographic machines to leading chip manufacturers Taiwan Semiconductor and Samsung. It is blocked from supplying its newest machines to SMIC and instead sells older models on the mainland.[36]

Now, to meet increased demand for high-end chips caused by the sanctions, SMIC is forced to try to rapidly upgrade its facilities while simultaneously trying to replace foreign equipment and services that it has lost access to due to sanctions. It is also trying to upgrade from a low starting base. *Bloomberg Intelligence* analyst Charles Shum reports that SMIC would need to double its R & D spend over the coming years to prevent the technological gap between it and Taiwan Semiconductor and Samsung from widening.[37]

The semiconductor industry is divided into three basic segments. These are ranked according to the level of technology involved. The first is R & D, design and software. Second is manufacturing and third is testing and assembly. SMIC, currently sits at the low-end of the middle segment – manufacturing.

Taiwan Semiconductor and Samsung are producing chips printed with 7 nm circuits. The most advanced SMIC production is 14 nm. 'This isn't the first time either' that SMIC is behind, 'the Chinese foundry was four years behind Taiwan Semiconductor for the 65 nm, 40 nm, 28 nm, and 14 nm nodes'.[38] In this crucial arena, China has been attempting to strengthen its domestic production for decades. As Addison wrote, 'In the 1990s billions of yuan were invested into new semiconductor fabrication lines using technology (legitimately, in this case) transferred from foreign chipmakers, only to find that these "wafer fabs" – that can take two years to build from scratch – were outdated on day one because the state of the art had moved on.'[39] China for many years has been the world's largest electronics assembly point. Last year it imported around $300 billion worth of semiconductors – more than any other country. Given the industry has also been given state backing for decades, China might therefore be expected to have developed large successful companies in this space. SMIC, which had revenues of $3.1 billion in 2019, is the largest.

That compares to $34.6 billion revenue for Taiwan Semiconductor, $10.3 billion for Tokyo Electron, $23.2 billion for SK Hynix (South Korea) and $55.7 Billion for Samsung Electronics Co. There are, in addition, four companies in Germany, Switzerland and the Netherlands each with revenues of $8.8 to $13.2 billion. In the United States eleven companies each had higher sales than China's largest. Most of these are many times larger, such as Micron Technology ($20.3 billion), Qualcomm (19.6 billion) and

Broadcom ($22.6 billion). Intel ($72 billion) alone had sales thirty-three times greater than SMIC, which is now twenty years old.

It is not that Huawei or other Chinese capitalists will be unable to produce smartphones, 5G equipment or other 'technology' goods without inputs from the United States and other First World countries, they can still do that. What the sanctions show is China's inability to do so quickly and at the highest level, and therefore competitively at the highest level of the world market, the monopolistic part of the market, where super-profits are made. Short of earning such super-profits, Chinese companies cannot generate from their market activities the profits needed to make the necessary investments to create more super-profits.

How can China respond to US economic attacks?

Another highly revealing angle to view the trade war is by examining China's response to US aggression. At least within the productive sector, this can only be described as weak. Notably, there have been no Chinese moves that involve withholding *Chinese* technology. We could expect a rising peer competitor to US imperialism would have developed *some* technological monopolies of its own, if not yet on the scale or complexity of the United States, Europe or Japan. However, the Chinese response to US technology bans has not involved technology bans at all. China has implemented trade tariffs in response to earlier and more severe US tariffs. No Chinese technology response seems possible.

The voluminous online chatter about possible responses China could make has not come up with a single example of a technology ban that China could plausibly announce. Instead, what is mentioned are hypothetical bans on purchasing certain US products, Chinese sale of US Treasury notes, a ban on Chinese exports of rare earth minerals and Chinese state regulatory obstruction or sabotage of US companies invested in China.

Besides rare earths, none of these are even productive monopolies, let alone technological. The speculated embargo on rare earths did provide a sound bite to the rising China commentaries. However, the Chinese monopoly in this sphere is not because 'rare earths' are actually rare. For example, they are quite abundant in the United States, Australia and Japan. The United States was the dominant rare earths supplier until the 1980s. More recent Chinese monopoly in the sector resulted from Chinese capital's willingness to tolerate – for far lower returns than acceptable in the imperialist countries – the severe environmental (and likely health) impacts of mining and processing the minerals. Now, in the context of the trade war, sources are being developed once again in the United States and elsewhere.

Responding to US attacks, President Xi Jinping urged Chinese people to prepare for difficulties that he likened to a 'new Long March' – hardly an optimistic outlook.

Does historical precedent suggest China threatens imperialism?

Capitalism's transition from British to US hegemony was neither smooth, uncontested, nor quick, despite Britain being far outstripped economically by its larger and more advanced rivals well before the politico-military crises began. It seems inconceivable that the same imperialist ruling classes would fight two world wars to divide the spoils of British decline, but then, for the past three decades, sit on their hands (and missiles) watching their collective hegemony eroded by China without waging any sort of coherent struggle, only to be awoken by Donald Trump!

Overcoming British hegemony required Germany and the United States to independently revolutionise the means of production in profound and far-reaching ways. This involved the electrification of industry, the development of new chemical industries that could replace natural production of raw materials and the development of mass automotive assembly, the combustion engine and the production line.

It also took place as a part of the capitalist transition from free competition to monopoly. British early industrial power had been achieved in capitalism's pre-monopoly stage. For this reason, its capitalist structure embodied earlier and lower forms of organisation.[40] German and US ascent, by contrast, initiated capitalism's monopoly stage and its associated organisational forms. The scale of investment required for these new industries was beyond the reach of individual capitalists. It required capitalist combination in trusts, cartels and joint stock companies, the merger of banks with each other and of giant banks with giant industry in order to achieve the required scale of finance.[41]

The slower, haphazard and partial uptake of new productive techniques in Britain – owing to its still pre-monopoly class structure – gifted US and German capitalists an extended period of far higher labour productivity than Britain. On that basis they could also secure *consistent super-profits* that were reinvested in further productive improvements and expansion.[42] None of these conditions or advantages are today present in China, which, by contrast, has a *lower labour productivity* than the United States and other imperialist states.

Electrification was not only a new 'leading sector' in the later nineteenth century (i.e. new, rapidly expanding and highly profitable), but it also revolutionised the industrial production process as a whole. As electricity came on board, factories were forced to replace antiquated steam engines and their associated cumbersome and inflexible propulsion assembly with electrical cabling fitted to electrical machinery. Commercial-scale production of chemicals and recycling of industrial waste played a similarly disruptive role as they revolutionised the production of raw materials and industrial inputs. Mass auto production completely transformed economic geography, allowing whole new territories to be brought under intensified exploitation. The scale and technical sophistication of the new apparatus demanded the adoption of scientific management – 'Taylorism'.

As Schumpeter observed, 'In capitalist reality [decisive competition is that which comes] from the new commodity, the new technology, the new source of supply, the new type of organisation ... competition which commands a decisive cost or quality advantage and which strikes not at the margins of the profits and the outposts of existing firms but at their foundations and their very lives.'[43] China's supposed rise has occurred not on the basis of breaking up or remaking the world division of labour but integration into an existing imperialist-dominated labour division, initially under the auspices of the World Trade Organisation. The present trade war was not started by China and China seeks to end it. US attacks on China are a one-sided affair. While China is forced to respond to US aggression, its policy is to seek to normalise trade and investment relations.

To believe that Chinese capital's ability to carry out long, established production processes is a challenge to the status quo, we must believe that historical materialism – which asserts the need for revolutionary transformation – does not apply to the sphere of economic development. Nor, therefore, could it be said to apply to social development in its most important sense. To accept that China is rising through an evolutionary process of capitalist development, we need to put Marx's method to one side and embrace instead Warren's 'Marxist' version of Rostow. If China were to return to a socialist development path – which some argue is possible under CCP rule – this would extinguish the operation of the capitalist law of value, along with the associated limitations capitalist society imposes on social development. Yet to fight the might of the imperialist countries on a socialist basis is not possible while the social system in China remains geared to enriching the Chinese billionaires, nor while working people are excluded from full and democratic participation in directing and leading that struggle. Nor can such a project succeed in the long term without the support and collaboration of working people in the richest and most developed countries – that is, without revolutions in other countries. Most of all, in the United States.

Notes

1 State Council [of China], *Made in China 2025* (2015), 7 July, p. 4.

2 State Council, *Made in China 2025*, p. 3.

3 State Council, *Made in China 2025*, p. 8.

4 F. Tang, 'Made in China 2025? Not Unless It Starts Spending More Money, Lawmaker Says', *South China Morning Post* (2018), 10 December.

5 Quoted in A. Lee, 'China's Plans to Dominate Hi-Tech Sector with "Made in China 2025" Plan Hit a Stumbling Block as US Trade War Takes Its Toll', *South China Morning Post* (2019), 22 January.

6 Jing et al., 'China Calls on Private Sector'.

7 Jing et al., 'China Calls On Private Sector'.

8 Jing et al., 'China Calls On Private Sector'.

9 S. Leng, 'China Must Stop Fooling Itself It Is a World Leader in Science and Technology, Magazine Editor Says', *South China Morning Post* (2018), 26 June.

10 S. Kennedy, 'Made in China 2025', *Center For Strategic and International Studies* (2015), 1 June, www.csis.org/analysis/made-china-2025.

11 Cited in I. Deng, 'China's AI industry Gets the Most Funding, But Lags the US in Key Talent, Says Tsinghua', *South China Morning Post* (2018), 17 July.

12 Cited in S. Ward-Foxton, 'Made in China 2025: Make or Break for Europe?' *Electronic Engineering Times* (2017), 25 July.

13 Cited in Ward-Foxton, 'Made in China 2025'.

14 Kennedy, 'Made in China 2025'.

15 C. Cao, R. Appelbaum and R. Parker, 'Research Is High and the Market Is Far Away: Commercialization of Nanotechnology in China', *Technology in Society*, 35 (2013), 55.

16 Cao et al., 'Research Is High', p. 56. See also L. Brandt and E. Thun, 'The Fight for the Middle: Upgrading, Competition, and Industrial Development in China', *World Development*, 38:11 (2010), 1555–74.

17 Cited in Ward-Foxton, 'Made in China 2025'.

18 Lee, 'China's Plans'.

19 Reuters [World News], 'Second Prototype of China's C919 Jet Conducts Test Flight: State TV' (2017), 17 December.

20 Bradsher, 'China's New Jetliner'.

21 C. Zhou, 'Roll-Out of China's Home-Grown Passenger Jet Still Up in the Air as US Tech Restrictions Expected to Persist Under Joe Biden', *South China Morning Post* (2020), 15 November.

22 Nolan, *Is China Buying the World?* p. 129.

23 Nolan, *Is China Buying the World?* p. 127.

24 J. Yang, 'ARJ21 Starts Commercial Operation with 2nd Operator', *Shine* (2019), 26 July.

25 J. B. Su, 'China's ZTE Shuts Down After U.S. Tech Ban Over Iran Sales', *Forbes* (2018), 9 May.

26 *Financial Times* [staff] 'Huawei Warns Ban Set to Hurt 1,200 US Suppliers' (2019), 29 May.

27 Y. Kubota and D. Strumpf, 'American Threat to Huawei's Chip Maker Shows Chinese Tech Isn't Self-Sufficient', *Wall Street Journal* (2019), 2 June; *The Economist*, 'The Technology Industry Is Rife with Bottlenecks' (2019), 6 June.

28 Cited in D. Lee, 'Huawei: ARM Memo Tells Staff to Stop Working with China's Tech Giant', *BBC* (2019), 22 May.

29 Y. Yang, 'How Trump Blacklisting Affects the Inside of a Huawei Smartphone', *Financial Times* (2019), 2 June.

30 Kubota and Strumpf, 'Chinese Tech Isn't Self-Sufficient'.

31 K. Hille, E. White and K. Inagaki, 'Chip and Phone Supply Chain Shaken as Huawei Faces Mortal Threat', *Financial Times* (2020), August 18.

32 Hille et al., 'Chip and Phone Supply Chain Shaken'.

33 K. Hille, Y. Yang and Q. Liu, 'Huawei Develops Plan for Chip Plant to Help Beat US Sanctions', *Financial Times* (2020), 1 November.

34 Hille et al., 'Huawei Develops Plan for Chip Plant'.

35 Hille et al., 'Huawei Develops Plan for Chip Plant'.

36 A. Alper, T. Sterling and S. Nellis, 'Trump Administration Pressed Dutch Hard to Cancel China Chip-Equipment Sale: Sources', *Reuters* (2020), 6 January.

37 A. Crawford, D. Wu, C. Murphy and I. King, 'The U.S.–China Conflict Over Chips Is About to Get Uglier', *Bloomberg* (2020), 22 October.

38 H. Jonnalagadda, 'SMIC: Everything You Need to Know About China's Answer to TSMC', *androidcentral* (2020), 6 August.

39 C. Addison, 'China Reliant on US Core Technology for Some Time, But So Is the World: America's Unassailable Lead in Semiconductor Manufacturing Is the Dividend from Over 50 Years of Research and Development', *South China Morning Post* (2018), 4 July.

40 Wood, *Empire of Capital*, p. 124.

41 Lenin, *Imperialism*, chap. 1; Schwartz, *States Versus Markets*, p. 153.

42 British capital was eventually forced, particularly in preparation for war against Germany and afterwards, also to adopt monopoly forms of organisation. See Schwartz, *States Versus Markets*, pp. 120–1, 153.

43 Schumpeter, *Capitalism, Socialism and Democracy*, p. 84; Schwartz, *States Versus Markets*, p. 282. By contrast, Japanese innovations in the 1970s, such as lean production or just-in-time inventory, achieved a more advanced organisation of existing technologies. As such, they were fairly easily replicated by Japan's rivals and helped Japan to catch up to but not surpass US and European competitors.

Conclusion

The neoliberal period reconfirmed the global polarisation inherent in the imperialist system. It also made the basic mechanism of Third World exploitation – unequal exchange – explicit and hence easier to explain and demonstrate. It has shown Lenin's theory of monopoly finance capital is a basically accurate application, not negation, of Marx's labour theory of value. For this reason his theory was able to anticipate how the rich countries – more than a hundred years after the first inter-imperialist world war – reproduce their dominance through monopolistic dominance of the labour process. By applying Lenin's theory, the book was able to arrive at a concrete, simple and empirically verifiable outline of the economic foundation of contemporary imperialism.

The global polarisation in income documented in Chapter 1 was shown to be a function of the polarisation of the world division of labour. The polarised division of labour flows from the polarisation of capital into competing monopoly and non-monopoly parts. The polarisation of world states between rich and poor, developed and differently developed (i.e. into monopoly and non-monopoly countries) reflects this same polarisation of capital at the heart of the economic process.

The concept of non-monopoly capital and elaboration of its role and relationship to monopoly capital may appear original in a contemporary context. However, the concept flows easily from Lenin's concept of monopoly finance capital. As a form of *capitalist property*, monopoly finance capital must ultimately rely on commodity production for the market and hence can never create a world where all production is monopolised. Lenin made explicit his own view of the inevitable continuation under monopoly capitalism of the category of non-monopoly capital – this was correct. In the neoliberal period non-monopoly capitalist production was greatly expanded, closely integrated into the global division of labour and systematically drawn into production for the world market. It was thoroughly integrated into the global production networks dominated by the monopolist groups.

During the First World War Lenin not only anticipated the Second World War, but also the period of inter-imperialist 'peace' that would follow it – that period has now extended for seventy years. He also anticipated the basic character of the global economy: imperialist exploitation of the poor countries. While Lenin could hardly have anticipated the precise form this exploitation might take in our time, his theory of monopoly finance capital left us with the framework with which it has been possible to most fully explain the forms that did eventuate.

Lenin's theory emphasises the labour process as the primary arena of monopoly competition. Once this is recognised, it becomes apparent that competition must proceed in large extent along lines parallel to the forms of competition outlined by Marx in *Capital* (albeit with modifications). For this reason, Marx's law of value – his basic theory of capitalist development – which proceeds via capitalist competition, is not nullified but only conditioned by capitalist monopoly. The latter is also a form of capitalist competition – its highest form. Competition becomes monopoly competition. Value, which in Marx's theory is distributed via competition on the market, is under monopoly conditions distributed through monopoly competition that still occurs on the capitalist market and will continue to, so long as capitalism remains.

It is this conditioning of Marx's law – in accordance with the principles detailed in Lenin's monopoly finance capital – that has made possible the concrete application of the law of value to the international economy in the neoliberal period. If its application has been inadequate in this book, it at least shows in what direction a more systematic application is possible.

Marxists have long contended that satisfactory application of Marx's law of value to the international economy has not yet been achieved. At the same time, it is commonly held that no satisfactory, contemporary Marxist theory of imperialism exists. Few imagined what the neoliberal period proved in practice: the resolution of both theoretical problems lay in the fusion of Marx's law of value with Lenin's *Imperialism* and his theory of monopoly finance capital. In other words, Lenin's theory stands as a scientific application of Marx's law of value to capitalism's monopoly stage.

It has been shown that Lenin's work applies the most concrete aspects of Marx's study of capitalism – especially Marx's concept of capitalism's 'highest stage'. Lenin's application of Marx's highest stage involves analysis of the relationship between the changes in the social labour process and the new forms of capitalist property relations brought about by these changes. His development of this conceptual framework takes place, explicitly, within the bounds of capitalist commodity production. Applying Marx's *Capital* in this way is how Lenin's theory of 'monopoly finance capital' actualises Marx's labour theory of value in the modern, monopoly capitalist era.

Marx argued in 1868 that 'science consists precisely in demonstrating how the law of value asserts itself'.[1] Despite the clamouring to condemn his work, it seems Lenin – who lived through the change from free competition to monopoly, and led a workers' revolution out of the ensuing crisis – may have something to say about that after all.

What Lenin's work produces, as shown, is something that closely describes contemporary conditions: the concept of monopoly and non-monopoly capital. Monopoly finance capital in the imperialist states can be described as 'monopoly' due to its monopolistic dominance of the global labour process. Non-monopoly capital is deprived of access to the higher levels of the labour process and can dominate only its lower sphere, which, because it is easily reproduced, cannot be monopolised.

Differentiating between monopoly and non-monopoly is theoretically superior to other available theoretical concepts aimed at explaining the global polarisation, because it is able simultaneously to explain the general forms of development of capitalist commodity production in the Third World, the different dynamic of its development in the imperialist world and the relationship between the two poles. That is, it characterises the economies of the Third World with reference to the inner life of their own societies while at the same time explaining the conditioning of those societies by their situation in imperialist capitalism as whole, including in relation to the imperialist economies. Likewise, it explains the imperialist economies on the basis of their own internal economic and social life and their different (opposite) situation in imperialist capitalism as whole, and by their relation to the Third World. In short, the monopoly–non-monopoly theory gives a concrete characterisation of the internal economic life of both the imperialist and Third World poles of the system and concretely characterises the relationship between the poles *on that basis*.

The other 'binary' explanations or descriptions – the North–South divide, semi-colonial versus imperial, metropolis and satellite and core and periphery – relate only to the Third World's relationship with the imperialist economies and cannot give an adequate characterisation of the internal dynamic of each pole or the relationship of the internal development to the external.

The monopoly versus non-monopoly concept allows for recognition that non-monopoly economies can expand their commodity production, sometimes quite rapidly, but this expansion is of a specific character. It is the expansion of non-monopoly production that, by definition, ultimately remains subordinate to monopoly capital. Hence the concept also provides an integrated explanation of the two principal concrete dynamics characteristic of the neoliberal period of history – rapid expansion in parts of the Third World, combined with the continued subjugation by imperialism of the Third World as a whole.

The theory of monopoly and non-monopoly capital – or we can alter-natively call it Lenin's theory of 'monopoly finance capital' because the monopoly–non-monopoly relationship is a subordinate part of Lenin's framework as a whole – paints a fundamentally bleak picture of the pros-pects for economic and social development of the majority of the world's people (that is, for the Third World poor majority) within the imperialist system. Bleaker, that is, than the picture painted by Rostow, Warren or the contemporary rising China crowd, Marxist or not. These thinkers can see the capitalist expansion in the poor countries – but not its relationship to capitalist expansion in the imperialist states. Nor therefore can they see how this non-monopoly Third World capital (and Third World labour too) is subject to monopoly domination.

Once we remove the perception that China's current technological level in relation to imperialism is a temporary phase within a long march to dom-inance, it becomes clear how devastatingly imperialism has plundered China and the Third World as a whole in the neoliberal period and continues to do so. The painful burdens on Chinese workers, the poisoning of Chinese soil, air and waterways, the grand-scale dispossession of farmers, separation of working parents from their children, the suicides, the days, weeks and whole working lives forfeited to sewing machines and assembly lines, the humiliations, injuries, industrial deaths, needlessly wasted human talents and energies and the countless other injustices and crimes inflicted on the Chinese working class have all supposedly been in pursuit of development.

Once it is realised these sacrifices are not really in aid of Chinese capital-ism's coming global triumph – and hence sacrifices to ameliorate the future suffering by Chinese working people – it becomes apparent they are the sacrifices required of China's current 'success'. Its success merely as a Third World capitalist society par excellence. They are the sacrifices of its fight to win the dubious privilege of becoming the number one provider of cheap inputs to the imperialist economies; the cheap, efficient supplier of the most toxic and laborious products that secure returns too low for monopoly cap-ital to bother with. China's sacrifices are those not of a Third World society suffering a horrible end to its exploitation – they represent horror without end. Yet China is the feted success story to be emulated by other, weaker, Third World societies. In other words, Chinese working people's sacrifice is the *best* that the immense majority of humanity can aspire too – so long as we keep living in a system of capitalist imperialism. Having already devel-oped on a world scale, no other form of capitalism is now possible.

The only path for the working-poor majority is to defeat the imperi-alist system, something that will require cooperation, solidarity and trust between working people across borders. Yet the surest way to destroy the trust of Chinese and Third World workers, or fail to win it, is if workers and the Left inside the imperialist states continue to swallow the imperialist propaganda that China is a rising imperialist power: that the imperialist oppression of China is merely competition among equals. It is not. The Chinese working class knows it is not. The imperialist world's workers, so far, do not. The sooner the centrality of imperialist exploitation of China and the Third World are recognised by Marxists and others on the First World Left, the sooner the Left can start fighting within our own working classes for a perspective of building international solidarity among working people.

Note

1 K. Marx, 'Marx to Ludwig Kugelmann in Hanover' [Letter, 1868], in *Selected Correspondence* (Moscow, Progress, 1975), marxists.org/archive/marx/works/1868/letters/68_07_11-abs.htm.

Bibliography

Abi-Habib, Maria, 'How China Got Sri Lanka to Cough Up a Port', *New York Times*, 25 June 2018.

Achcar, Gilbert, 'Rethinking Imperialism: Past, Present and Future', *International Socialism*, vol. 2, no. 126, 2010.

Addison, Craig, 'China Reliant on US Core Technology for Some Time, But So Is the World: America's Unassailable Lead in Semiconductor Manufacturing Is the Dividend from Over 50 Years of Research and Development', *South China Morning Post*, 4 July 2018.

Adkins, Daniel Casey, 'The Future China–U.S. Competition and Democratic Socialism', *Washington Socialist*, February 2018.

Ahmad, Aijaz, 'Imperialism of Our Time', *Socialist Register*, vol. 40, 2004, pp. 43–62.

Alper, Alexandra, Sterling, Toby and Nellis, Stephen, 'Trump Administration Pressed Dutch Hard to Cancel China Chip-Equipment Sale', *Reuters*, 6 January 2020.

Amin, Samir, *Unequal Development: An Essay on the Social Formations of Peripheral Capitalism*, Sussex, Harvester, 1976.

Amin, Samir, 'Globalization and Capitalism's Second Belle Epoque', *Radical Philosophy Review*, vol. 5, no. 1–2, 2002, pp. 86–95.

Amin, Samir, *The Law of Worldwide Value*, New York, Monthly Review, 2010.

Amin, Samir, 'Contemporary Imperialism', *Monthly Review*, vol. 67, no. 3, 2015.

Amsden, Alice, H., *The Rise of 'The Rest': Challenges to the West from Late-Industrializing Economies*, Oxford, Oxford University Press, 2001.

Andersson, Jan Otto, *Studies in the Theory of Unequal Exchange Between Nations*, Turku, Åbo Akademi, 1976.

Anievas, Alexander (ed.), *Marxism and World Politics*, New York, Taylor and Francis, 2012.

Ariff, Mohammed and Hill, Hal, *Export-Oriented Industrialisation: The ASEAN Experience*, Sydney, Allen and Unwin, 1985.

Arrighi, Giovanni, 'Hegemony Unravelling – 1', *New Left Review*, no. 32, 2005.

Arrighi, Giovanni, Silver, Beverly J. and Brewer, Benjamin D., 'Industrial Convergence, Globalization, and the Persistence of the North–South Divide', *Studies in Comparative International Development*, vol. 38, no. 1, 2003, pp. 3–31.

Ashman, Sam, 'Symposium on David Harvey's *The New Imperialism*: Editorial Introduction', *Historical Materialism*, vol. 14, no. 4, 2006, pp. 3–7.

Bailey, Geoff, 'Accumulation by Dispossession: A Critical Assessment', *International Socialist Review*, no. 95, 2014/15.

Bannon, Stephen (dir.) *Generation Zero* [documentary]. New York, Citizens United, released 5 February 2010.

Baran, Paul A., *The Political Economy of Growth* [1957], New York, Monthly Review, 1973.

Baran, Paul A. and Sweezy, Paul M., *Monopoly Capital: An Essay on the American Economic and Social Order*, New York, Monthly Review, 1966.

Barone, Charles A., *Marxist Thought on Imperialism: Survey and Critique*, London, Macmillan, 1985.

Barrat-Brown, Michael, *Essays on Imperialism*, Nottingham, Spokesman, 1972.

Barrigos, Rebecca, 'The Neoliberal Transformation of Higher Education', *Marxist Left Review*, no. 6, 2013.

Bauer, Otto, *The Question of Nationalities and Social Democracy* [1907], Minneapolis, University of Minnesota, 2000.

Baumol, William J., 'Macroeconomics of Unbalanced Growth: The Anatomy of Urban Crisis', *American Economic Review*, vol. 57, no. 3, 1967, pp. 415–26.

Bieler, Andreas and Morton, Adam D., 'Axis of Evil or Access to Diesel? Spaces of New Imperialism and the Iraq War', *Historical Materialism*, vol. 23, no. 2, 2015, pp. 94–130.

Block, Fred and Keller, Mathew, R., 'Where Do Innovations Come from? Transformations in the US Economy, 1970–2006', *Socio-Economic Review*, vol. 7, no. 3, 2009, pp. 459–83.

Bond, Patrick and Garcia, Ana (eds), *BRICS: An Anti-Capitalist Critique*, Chicago, Haymarket, 2015.

Boron, Atilio, A., *Empire and Imperialism: A Critical Reading of Michael Hardt and Antonio Negri*, London, Zed, 2005.

Bose, Prasenjit, ' "New" Imperialism? On Globalisation and Nation-States', *Historical Materialism*, vol. 15, no. 3, 2007, pp. 95–120.

Boston Consulting Group, 'Reshoring of Manufacturing to the US Gains Momentum', 10 December 2015, www.bcg.com/publications/2015/reshoring-of-manufacturing-to-the-us-gains-momentum.

Bowden, Brett, *The Empire of Civilization: The Evolution of an Imperial Idea*, Chicago, University of Chicago Press, 2009.

Bradsher, Keith, 'China's New Jetliner, the COMAC C919, Takes Flight for First Time', *New York Times*, 5 May 2017.

Brandt, Loren and Rawsky, Thomas, G. (eds), *China's Great Economic Transformation*, New York, Cambridge University Press, 2008.

Brandt, Loren and Thun, Eric, 'The Fight for the Middle: Upgrading, Competition, and Industrial Development in China', *World Development*, vol. 38, no. 11, 2010, pp. 1555–74.

Braverman, Harry, *Labor and Monopoly Capital: The Degradation of Work in the Twentieth Century* [1974], New York, Monthly Review, 1998.

Brenner, Robert, *The Boom and the Bubble: The US in the World Economy*, London, Verso, 2002.

Bresser-Pereira, Luiz Carlos, 'The Rise of Middle Class and Middle Management in Brazil', *Journal of Inter-American Studies*, vol. 4, no. 3, 1962, pp. 313–26.

Brewer, Anthony, *Marxist Theories of Imperialism: A Critical Survey* [1980], London, Routledge and Kegan Paul, 1990.

Brolin, John, *The Bias of the World: Theories of Unequal Exchange in History*, PhD thesis, Finland, Lund University, 2007.

Bukharin, Nikolai, *Toward a Theory of the Imperialist State* [1915], New York, M. E. Sharpe, 1982, marxists.org/archive/bukharin/works/1915/state.htm.

Bukharin, Nikolai, *Imperialism and World Economy* [1915–17], London, Martin Lawrence, n.d., marxists.org/archive/bukharin/works/1917/imperial/.

Bureau of Economic Analysis, 'U.S. Net International Investment Position First Quarter 2017, Year 2016, and Annual Update', *US Department of Commerce*, 28 June 2017.

Callinicos, Alex, *The New Mandarins of American Power: The Bush Administration's Plans for the World*, Cambridge, UK, Polity, 2003.

Callinicos, Alex, *Imperialism and Global Political Economy*, Cambridge, UK, Polity, 2009.

Callinicos, Alex, 'The Multiple Crises of Imperialism', *International Socialism*, vol. 2, no. 144, 2014.

Callinicos, Alex, 'Fighting the Last War', *International Socialism*, vol. 2. no. 147, 2015.

Cao, Cong, Appelbaum, Richard P. and Parker, Rachel, 'Research Is High and the Market Is Far Away: Commercialization of Nanotechnology in China', *Technology in Society*, vol. 35, no. 1, 2013, pp. 55–64.

Carr, Edward H., *What Is History?* London, Penguin, 1961.

Cattaneo, Olivier, Gereffi Gary and Staritz, Cornelia (eds), *Global Value Chains in a Post-Crisis World: A Development Perspective*, Washington, DC, World Bank, 2010.

Chamberlin, Edward H., *The Theory of Monopolistic Competition: A Reorientation of the Theory of Value* [1933], Cambridge MA, Harvard University Press, 1969.

Chandra, Pratyush, Ghosh, Anuradha and Kumar, Ravi, *The Politics of Imperialism and Counterstrategies*, Delhi, Aakar, 2004.

Chen, Wenjie, Dollar, David and Tang, Heiwai, 'China's Direct Investment in Africa: Reality Versus Myth', *Brookings*, 3 September 2015.

Chenery, Holis B., 'Industrialization and Growth: The Experience of Large Countries', *World Bank Staff Working Paper No. SWP 539*, 1982.

Chenery, Holis B., Robinson, S. and Syrquin, M., *Industrialization and Growth: A Comparative Study*, New York, World Bank and Oxford University Press, 1986.

Chesnais, François, 'The Economic Foundations of Contemporary Imperialism', *Historical Materialism*, vol. 15, no. 3, 2007, pp. 121–42.

Chibber, Vivek, *Locked in Place: State-Building and Late Industrialization in India*. Princeton, NJ, Princeton University Press, 2003.

Chibber, Vivek, 'Capital Outbound', *New Left Review*, no. 36, 2005.

Chilcote, Ronald M. (ed.), *The Political Economy of Imperialism: Critical Appraisals*, New York, Kluwer, 1999.

Chilcote, Ronald M. (ed.), *Imperialism: Theoretical Directions*, Amherst, NY, Humanity, 2000.

Chomsky, Noam, 'State and Corp' [interview], *Znet Germany*, 18 May 2005.

Clarke, Renfrey and Annis, Roger, 'The Myth of "Russian Imperialism": In Defence of Lenin's Analyses', *Links: International Journal of Socialist Renewal*, 29 February 2016.

Clelland, Donald A., 'The Core of the Apple: Degrees of Monopoly and Dark Value in Global Commodity Chains', *Journal of World-Systems Research*, vol. 20, no. 1, 2015, pp. 82–111.

Cliff, Tony, *Lenin 2: All Power to the Soviets* [1976], Chicago, Haymarket, 2004.

Cope, Zak, 'Global Wage Scaling and Left Ideology: A Critique of Charles Post on the "Labour Aristocracy"' *Research in Political Economy*, vol. 28, 2013, pp. 89–129.

Cope, Zak, *Divided World Divided Class, Global Political Economy and the Stratification of Labour Under Capitalism* [2012], Montreal, Kersplebedeb, 2015.

Crawford, Alan, Wu, Debby, Murphy, Colum and King, Ian, 'The U.S.–China Conflict Over Chips Is About to Get Uglier', *Bloomberg*, 22 October 2020.

Credit Suisse, *Global Wealth Report 2016*, Zurich, Credit Suisse, 2016.

Daalder, Ivo H. and Lindsay, James M., 'American Empire, Not "If" But "What Kind"', *New York Times*, 10 May 2003.

D'Amato, Paul, 'Imperialism and the State: Why McDonalds Needs McDonnell Douglas', *International Socialist Review*, no. 17, 2001.

Day, Richard B. and Gaido, Daniel (eds), *Discovering Imperialism: Social Democracy to World War I*, Chicago, Haymarket, 2012.

De Jong, Alex, *Imperialism Today* [class guide for Fourth International Training School], New York, Fourth International, 2013.

Delizo, Rasti, 'US Imperialist Aggression in the Early 21st Century', *Links: International Journal of Socialist Renewal*, 27 November 2010.

Deng, Iris, 'China's AI industry Gets the Most Funding, But Lags the US in Key Talent, Says Tsinghua', *South China Morning Post*, 17 July 2018.

Devlin, Kat, 'Americans Leery of China as Trump Prepares to Meet Xi at G20', *Pew Research*, 30 November 2018.

Dhanani, Shafiq, *Indonesia: Strategy for Manufacturing Competitiveness*, vol. 2, *Main Report*, Jakarta, United Nations Industrial Development Organization, 2000.

Dieter, Ernst, *A New Geography of Knowledge in the Electronics Industry? Asia's Role in Global Innovation Networks*, Policy Studies, No. 54, Honolulu, HI, East-West Center, 2009.

Dieter, Ernst, 'China's Bold Strategy for Semiconductors – Zero-Sum Game or Catalyst for Cooperation?' *East-West Center Working Paper IEGS No. 9*, 2016.

Dobbs, Steve, 'Centenary of Lenin's Theory of Imperialism: A Reply To Pete Glover', *Marxist World*, April 2017.

Dowling, Joshua, 'Ford GT Supercar Gets Hi-Tech Wheels Made by Geelong Company Carbon Revolution', *news.com.au*, 16 May 2016.

Duménil, Gerard and Lévy, Dominique, *The Crisis of Neoliberalism*, Cambridge, MA, Harvard University Press, 2011.

Dussel Peters, Enrique, 'GCCs and Development: A Conceptual and Empirical Review', *Competition and Change*, vol. 12, no. 1, 2008, pp. 11–27.

Dussel Peters, Enrique and Yanez, Anibal, 'Marx's Economic Manuscripts of 1861–63 and the "Concept" of Dependency', *Latin American Perspectives*, vol. 17, no. 2, 1990, pp. 62–101.

Eatwell, John, Milgate, Murray and Newman, Peter (eds), *Marxian Economics*, Basingstoke, Palgrave Macmillan, 1990.

eMarketer, 'US Digital Ad Spending to Top $37 Billion in 2012 as Market Consolidates', 20 September 2012.

Emmanuel, Arghiri, *Unequal Exchange: A Study of Imperialism in Trade*, New York and London, Monthly Review, 1972.

Emmanuel, Arghiri, 'White-Settler Colonialism and the Myth of Investment Imperialism', *New Left Review*, no. 73, 1972, pp. 35–67.

Fieldhouse, David K., ' "Imperialism": An Historiographical Revision', *Economic History Review*, vol. 14, no. 2, 1961, pp. 187–396.

Financial Times [staff] 'Huawei Warns Ban Set to Hurt 1,200 US Suppliers', 29 May 2019.

Fine, Ben, 'Debating the New Imperialism', *Historical Materialism*, vol. 14, no. 4, 2006, pp. 133–56.

Fisher, Max and Carlsen, Audrey, 'How China Is Challenging American Dominance in Asia', *New York Times*, 9 March 2018.

Forbes, 'Global 2000', 2019, forbes.com/global2000/list/.

Fortune, 'Global 500', 2017, fortune.com/global500/2018/.

Foster, John Bellamy, 'Monopoly Capital at the Turn of the Millennium', *Monthly Review*, vol. 51, no. 11, 2000.

Foster, John Bellamy, 'January 2004' [Editorial note], *Monthly Review*, vol. 55, no. 8, 2004.

Foster, John Bellamy, 'Monopoly-Finance Capital', *Monthly Review*, vol. 58, no. 7, 2006.

Foster, John Bellamy, 'The Financialization of Capitalism', *Monthly Review*, vol. 58, no. 11, 2007.

Foster, John Bellamy, 'The Imperialist World System: Paul Baran's Political Economy of Growth After Fifty Years', *Monthly Review*, vol. 59, no. 1, 2007.

Foster, John Bellamy, 'The Age of Monopoly-Finance Capital', *Monthly Review*, vol. 61, no. 9, 2010.

Foster, John Bellamy, 'The Financialization of Accumulation', *Monthly Review*, vol. 62, no. 5, 2010.

Foster, John Bellamy, 'The New Imperialism of Globalized Monopoly-Finance Capital', *Monthly Review*, vol. 67, no. 3, 2015.

Foster, John Bellamy, 'Monopoly Capital at the Half-Century Mark', *Monthly Review*, vol. 68, no. 3, 2016.

Foster, John Bellamy, 'Late Imperialism: Fifty Years After Harry Magdoff's The Age of Imperialism', *Monthly Review*, vol. 71, no. 3, 2019.

Foster, John Bellamy and McChesney, Robert W., *The Endless Crisis: How Monopoly-Finance Capital Produces Stagnation and Upheaval from the USA to China*, New York, Monthly Review, 2012.

Foster, John Bellamy, McChesney, Robert W. and Jonna, R. Jamil, 'Monopoly and Competition in Twenty-First-Century Capitalism', *Monthly Review*, vol. 62, no. 11, 2011.

Foster, John Bellamy, McChesney, Robert. W. and Jonna, R. Jamil, 'The Global Reserve Army of Labor and the New Imperialism', *Monthly Review*, vol. 63, no. 6, 2011.

Frank, Andre G., *Capitalism and Underdevelopment in Latin America: Historical Studies of Chile and Brazil* [1967], New York, Monthly Review, 2009.

Freeman, Alan, 'Ernest Mandel's Contribution to Economic Dynamics', *MPRA Paper No. 64974*, University of Manitoba, November 1996.

Freeman, Alan, 'The Poverty of Statistics and the Statistics of Poverty, *Third World Quarterly*, vol. 30, no. 8, 2009, pp. 1427–48.

Freeman, Richard, *The Great Doubling: The Challenge of the New Global Labor Market* [unpublished manuscript], Berkeley, University of California Press, 2006.

Friedman, Thomas, 'Manifesto for a Fast World', *New York Times Magazine*, 28 March 1999.

Friedman, Thomas, *The World Is Flat*, New York, Picador/Farrar, Straus and Giroux, 2005.

Fuchs, Christian, 'Critical Globalization Studies and the New Imperialism', *Critical Sociology*, vol. 36, no. 6, 2010, pp. 839–67.

Gasper, Phil, 'Imperialism: The Highest Stage of Capitalism', *Socialist Worker (US)*, no. 686, 2008.

Gasper, Phil, 'Imperialism: Lenin and Bukharin' [speech presented at the Socialism 2008 Conference, Chicago], 2008, www.youtube.com/watch?v=kWRrd8I1gUU.

Gasper, Phil, 'Obama, Imperialism and Capitalism', *International Socialist Review*, no. 78, 2011.

Ge, Dongsheng and Fujimoto, Takahiro, 'Quasi-Open Product Architecture and Technological Lock-In: An Exploratory Study on the Chinese Motorcycle Industry', *Annals of Business Administrative Science*, no. 3, 2004, pp. 15–24.

Gereffi, Gary, 'Development Models and Industrial Upgrading in China and Mexico', *European Sociological Review*, vol. 25, no. 1, 2009, pp. 37–51.

Gereffi, Gary, 'Global Value Chains in a Post-Washington Consensus World', *Review of International Political Economy*, vol. 21, no. 1, 2014, pp. 9–37.

Gereffi, Gary, Humphrey, John and Sturgeon, Timothy, 'The Governance of Global Value Chains', *Review of International Political Economy*, vol. 12, no. 1, 2005, pp. 78–104.

Gereffi, Gary and Korzeniewicz, Miguel (eds), *Commodity Chains and Global Capitalism*, Westport, CT, Praeger, 1994.

Ghosh, Jayati, 'The Creation of the Next Imperialism: The Institutional Architecture', *Monthly Review*, vol. 67, no. 3, 2015.

Goldstein, Walter, 'The Multi-National Corporation: A Challenge To Contemporary Socialism', *Socialist Register*, vol. 11, 1974, pp. 279–301.

Gopal, Balakrishna (ed.), *Debating Empire*, London and New York, Verso, 2003.

Grossman, Henryk, *The Law of Accumulation and Breakdown of the Capitalist System: Being Also a Theory of Crises* [1929], translated and abridged by Jairus Banaji, London, Pluto, 1991, marxists.org/archive/grossman/1929/breakdown/.

Guerin, Daniel, *Fascism and Big Business* [1939], New York, Pathfinder, 1973.

Guevara, Ernesto and Deutschmann, David, *Che Guevara Reader*, Melbourne and New York, Ocean Press, 2003, marxists.org/archive/guevara/1961/04/09.htm.

Hardt, Michael and Negri, Antonio, *Empire*, Cambridge, MA, Harvard University Press, 2000.

Harman, Chris, 'Imperialism, East and West', *Socialist Review*, no. 2, 1980, pp. 21–3, marxists.org/archive/harman/1980/03/monetarism.htm.

Harman, Chris, *Explaining The Crisis: A Marxist Reappraisal*, London, Bookmarks, 1984.

Harman, Chris, 'The State and Capitalism Today', *International Socialism*, vol. 2, no. 51, summer 1991, pp. 3–54.

Harman, Chris, 'Analysing Imperialism', *International Socialism*, vol. 2, no. 99, summer 2003, marxists.org/archive/harman/2003/xx/imperialism.htm.

Harman, Chris, 'China's Economy and Europe's Crisis', *International Socialism*, vol. 2, no. 109, winter 2006.

Harman, Chris, *Zombie Capitalism: Global Crisis and the Relevance of Marx*, Chicago, Haymarket, 2009.

Harris, Jerry, 'Emerging Third World Powers: China, India and Brazil', *Race and Class*, vol. 46, no. 3, 2005, pp. 7–27.

Harris, Nigel, *The End of the Third World: Newly Industrializing Countries and the Decline of an Ideology*, London, Penguin, 1987.

Hart-Landsberg, Martin and Burkett, Paul, 'China and the Dynamics of Transnational Accumulation: Causes and Consequences of Global Restructuring', *Historical Materialism*, vol. 14, no. 3, 2006, pp. 3–43.

Harvey, David, *The Limits to Capital*, Oxford, Basil Blackwell, 1982.

Harvey, David, *The New Imperialism*, New York, Oxford University Press, 2003.

Harvey, David, 'The "New" Imperialism: Accumulation By Dispossession', *Socialist Register*, vol. 40, 2004, pp. 63–87.

Harvey, David, *A Brief History of Neoliberalism*, New York, Oxford University Press, 2007.

Harvey, David, *Seventeen Contradictions and the End of Capitalism*, New York, Oxford University Press, 2014.

Heintz, James, 'Low-Wage Manufacturing and Global Commodity Chains: A Model in the Unequal Exchange Tradition', *Cambridge Journal of Economics*, vol. 30, no. 4, 2006, pp. 507–20.

Higginbottom, Andy, 'Imperialist Rent in Practice and Theory', *Globalizations*, vol. 11, no. 1, 2014, pp. 23–33.

Hilferding, Rudolph, *Finance Capital: A Study of the Latest Phase of Capitalist Development* [1910], [edited by Tom Bottomore], London, Routledge and Kegan Paul, 1981, marxists.org/archive/hilferding/1910/finkap/ch15.htm.

Hille, Kathrin, White, Edward and Inagaki, Kana, 'Chip and Phone Supply Chain Shaken as Huawei Faces Mortal Threat', *Financial Times*, 18 August 2020.

Hille, Kathrin, White, Edward and Inagaki, Kana, 'Huawei Develops Plan for Chip Plant to Help Beat US Sanctions', *Financial Times*, 1 November 2020.

Hillman, Jonathan, *China's Belt and Road is Full of Holes*, Washington, DC, Center for Strategic and International Studies, 2018.

Hobson, John A., *Imperialism: A Study*, London, James Pott, 1902.

Hopkins, Terence K. and Wallerstein, Immanuel, 'Commodity Chains in the World-Economy Prior to 1800', *Review*, vol. 10, no. 1, 1986, pp. 157–70.

Horowitz, David, *Imperialism and Revolution*, London, Allen Lane, 1969.

Howard, Michael C. and King, John E., *A History of Marxian Economics*, vol. 1, *1883–1929*, London, Macmillan, 1989.

Howard, Michael C. and King, John E, *A History of Marxian Economics*, vol. 2, *1929–1990*, London, Macmillan, 1992.

Howe, Gary Nigel, 'Dependency Theory, Imperialism, and the Production of Surplus Value on a World Scale', *Latin American Perspectives*, vol. 8, no. 3–4, 1981, pp. 82–102.

Huang, Yiping and Wang, Bijun, 'From the Asian Miracle to an Asian Century? Economic Transformation in the 2000s and Prospects for the 2010s', *The Australian Economy in the 2000s* [conference proceedings] (Sydney, Reserve Bank of Australia), 2011, pp. 7–35.

Huawei, 'Research and Development' [corporate publicity material], 2018, www.huawei.com/uk/corporate-information/research-development.

Hung, Ho-fung, 'America's Head Servant? The PRC's Dilemma in the Global Crisis', *New Left Review*, no. 60, 2009.

Hung, Ho-fung, 'Sinomania: Global Crisis, China's Crisis?' *Socialist Register*, vol. 48, 2012, pp. 217–34.

Hung, Ho-fung, *The China Boom: Why China Will Not Rule the World*, New York, Columbia University Press, 2015.

Hymer, Stephen H., 'The Internationalization of Capital', *Journal of Economic Issues*, vol. 6, no. 1, 1972, pp. 91–111.

Ignatieff, Michael, 'The American Empire: The Burden', *New York Times Magazine*, 5 January 2003.

India Infoline, 'Tata Motors Domestic Sales Up 58% in Nov.', 1 December 2017, www.indiainfoline.com/article/capital-market-hot-pursuit/tata-motors-picks-momentum-on-strong-sales-in-nov-117120400024_1.html.

India Infoline, 'Why Stock at 52 Weeks Low May Not Make a Value Buy?' 1 December 2017, www.indiainfoline.com/article/news-top-story/why-52-week-low-stocks-might-not-make-a-value-buy-indiainfoline-117120100512_1.html.

Itoh, Makoto, 'Unequal Exchange Reconsidered in Our Age of Globalization' [talk presented at the Rebellious Macroeconomics: Marx, Keynes and Crotty Conference, Amherst, MA, Political Economy Research Institute], October 2007.

Japan News/Yomiuri, 'Japanese Steelmakers Prioritize High-Grade Production in Glut', *Guam Daily Post*, 31 January 2017.

Jing, Meng, Chen, Celia and Cai, Jane, 'China Calls on Private Sector to Beef Up Investment in Basic Science as It Seeks to Become Tech Powerhouse', *South China Morning Post*, 11 March 2019.

Jones, Lee, 'China's Belt and Road Initiative Is a Mess, Not a Master Plan', *Foreign Policy*, 9 October 2020.

Jones, Lee and Hameiri, Shahar, 'Debunking the Myth of "Debt-Trap Diplomacy": How Recipient Countries Shape China's Belt and Road Initiative', *Chatham House*, 19 August 2020.

Jonnalagadda, Harish, 'SMIC: Everything You Need to Know About China's Answer to TSMC', *androidcentral*, 6 August 2020.

Kautsky, Karl, *The Social Revolution*, unknown location, Charles Kerr, 1903, marxists.org/archive/kautsky/1902/socrev/.

Kay, Cristobal, *Latin American Theories of Development and Underdevelopment*, London and New York, Routledge, 1989.

Kelly, Gordon, 'How Google Used Motorola To Smack Down Samsung – Twice', *Forbes*, 10 February 2014.

Kennedy, Paul, *The Rise and Fall of the Great Powers: Economic Change and Military Conflict from 1500 to 2000*, London, Vintage, 1989.

Kennedy, Scott, 'Made in China 2025', *Center For Strategic and International Studies*, 1 June 2015, www.csis.org/analysis/made-china-2025.

Kidron, Michael, 'Imperialism, Highest Stage But One', *International Socialism*, vol. 1, no. 9, summer 1962.

Kidron, Michael, 'International Capitalism', *International Socialism*, vol. 1, no. 20, spring 1964–65.

Kiely, Ray, *Rethinking Imperialism*, London, Palgrave, 2010.

Kiernan, Victor G., *Marxism and Imperialism*, London, Edward Arnold, 1974.

King, Samuel T., 'Lenin's Theory of Imperialism: A Defence of Its Relevance in the 21st Century', *Marxist Left Review*, no. 8, winter 2014.

King, Samuel T., *Lenin's Theory of Imperialism Today: The Global Divide between Monopoly and non-Monopoly Capital*, PhD thesis, Melbourne, Victoria University, 2018.

Kitching, Gavin, 'The Theory of Imperialism and its Consequences', *Middle East Research and Information Project (MERIP) Reports*, no. MER100/101, 1981, pp. 36–42.

Klein, Matthew C., 'China's Household Debt Problem', *Financial Times*, 7 March 2018.

Krugman, Paul, *The Age of Diminishing Expectations: US Economic Policies in the 1990s*, Cambridge MA, MIT Press, 1997.

Kubota, Yoko and Strumpf, Dan, 'American Threat to Huawei's Chip Maker Shows Chinese Tech Isn't Self-Sufficient', *Wall Street Journal*, 2 June 2019.

Kueh, Y. Y., *China's New Industrialisation Strategy: Was Chairman Mao Really Necessary?* Cheltenham, Edward Elgar, 2008.

Kynge, James, Mitchell, Tom and Massoudi, Arash, 'M & A: China's World of Debt', *Financial Times*, 12 February 2016.

Lall, Sanjaya, 'The Technological Structure and Performance of Developing Country Manufactured Exports, 1985–1998', *QEH Working Paper Series*, no. 44, 2000.

Lane, Max, *Unfinished Nation: Indonesia Before and After Suharto*, London and New York, Verso, 2008.

Lauesen, Torkil and Cope, Zak, 'Imperialism and the Transformation of Values into Prices', *Monthly Review*, vol. 67, no. 3, 2015.

Lee, Amanda, 'China's Plans to Dominate Hi-Tech Sector with "Made in China 2025" Plan Hit a Stumbling Block as US Trade War Takes Its Toll', *South China Morning Post*, 22 January, 2019.

Lee, Amanda, 'China Will Need More Than 35 Years to Upgrade to Hi-Tech Manufacturing Industry, Study Finds', *South China Morning Post*, 19 July 2019.

Lee, Dave, 'Huawei: ARM Memo Tells Staff to Stop Working with China's Tech Giant', *BBC*, 22 May 2019.

Lees, Jonathan, 'Growing Wealth Inequality Reaching Breaking Point', *Socialist Appeal*, 4 December 2017.

Lees, Josh, 'Australian Imperialism in an Era of US–China Tensions', *Red Flag*, 8 August 2019.

Leng, Sidney, 'China Must Stop Fooling Itself It Is a World Leader in Science and Technology, Magazine Editor Says', *South China Morning Post*, 26 June 2018.

Lenin, Vladimir I., *The Development of Capitalism in Russia: The Process of the Formation of a Home Market for Large-Scale Industry* [1899], vol. 3, *Collected Works*, Moscow, Progress, 1960, pp. 21–608, marxists.org/archive/lenin/works/1899/devel/.

Lenin, Vladimir I., *Imperialism: The Highest Stage of Capitalism* [1917], vol. 1, *Selected Works*, Moscow, Progress, 1963, pp. 634–731, marxists.org/archive/lenin/works/1916/imp-hsc.

Lenin, Vladimir I., *A Caricature of Marxism and Imperialist Economism* [1916–17], vol. 23, *Collected Works*, Moscow, Progress, 1964, pp. 28–76, marxists.org/archive/lenin/works/1916/carimarx/.

Lenin, Vladimir I., *Imperialism and the Right of Nations to Self-Determination* [1914], vol. 20, *Collected Works*, Moscow, Progress, 1964, pp. 393–454, marxists.org/archive/lenin/works/1914/self-det/index.htm.

Lenin, Vladimir I., *The Position and Tasks of the Socialist International* [1914], vol. 21, *Collected Works*, Moscow, Progress, 1964, pp. 35–41, marxists.org/archive/lenin/works/1914/oct/x01.htm.

Lenin, Vladimir. I., *Revision of the Party Programme* [1917], vol. 26, *Collected Works*, Moscow, Progress, 1964, pp. 149–78, marxists.org/archive/lenin/works/1917/oct/06.htm.

Lenin, Vladimir I., *The State and Revolution* [1917], vol. 25, *Collected Works*, Moscow, Progress, 1964, pp. 385–497, marxists.org/archive/lenin/works/1917/staterev/.

Lenin, Vladimir I., *Theses: The Socialist Revolution and the Right of Nations to Self-Determination* [1916], vol. 22, *Collected Works*, Moscow, Progress, 1964, pp. 143–56, marxists.org/archive/lenin/works/1916/jan/x01.htm.

Lenin, Vladimir I., *The New Economic Policy and the Tasks of the Political Education Departments: Report to the Second All-Russia Congress of Political Education Departments, October 17, 1921*, vol. 33, *Collected Works*, Moscow, Progress, 1965, pp. 60–79, marxists.org/archive/lenin/works/1921/oct/17.htm.

Lenin, Vladimir I., *'Last Testament' Letters to the Congress* [1923], vol. 36, *Collected Works*, Moscow, Progress, 1966, pp. 593–611, marxists.org/archive/lenin/works/1922/dec/testamnt/index.htm.

Lenin, Vladimir I., *Report of the Commission on the National and Colonial Questions* [1920], vol. 31, *Collected Works*, Moscow, Progress, 1966, pp. 213–63, marxists.org/archive/lenin/works/1920/jul/x03.htm.

Lenin, Vladimir I., *Notebooks on Imperialism* [1916], vol. 39, *Collected Works*, Moscow, Progress, 1968, marxists.org/archive/lenin/works/cw/volume39.htm.

Lenin, Vladimir I., *The Revolutionary Proletariat and the Right of Nations to Self-Determination* [1915], vol. 21, *Collected Works*, Moscow, Progress, 1974, pp. 407–14, marxists.org/archive/lenin/works/1915/oct/16.htm.

Lenin, Vladimir I., *Imperialism: The Highest Stage of Capitalism* [1917] [introduction by Doug Lorimer], Sydney, Resistance, 1999.

Lewis, Tom, 'Marxism and Nationalism', *International Socialist Review*, no. 13, 2000.

Long, Zhiming, Herrera Rémy and Andréani, Tony, 'On the Nature of the Chinese Economic System', *Monthly Review*, vol. 72, no. 5, 1 October 2018.

Lorimer, Doug, *Imperialism in the 21st Century: War, Neo-Liberalism and Globalisation*, Sydney, Resistance, 2002.

Lorimer, Doug, 'Capitalist Economic Crisis and Finance Capital' [talk presented at the RSP Marxist Education Conference], 2–5 January 2010, sa.org.au/node/3979.

Love, Joseph L., 'Raul Prebisch and the Origins of the Doctrine of Unequal Exchange', *Latin American Research Review*, vol. 15, no. 3, 1980, pp. 45–72.

McDonough, Terrence, 'Lenin, Imperialism, and the Stages of Capitalist Development', *Science and Society*, vol. 59, no. 3, 1995, pp. 339–67.

McMichael, Philip, Petras, James and Rhodes, Robert R., 'Imperialism and the Contradictions of Development', *New Left Review*, no. 85, 1974.

McNally, David, 'Understanding Imperialism: Old and New Dominion', *Against the Current*, no. 117, 2005.

McNally, David, 'From Financial Crisis to World-Slump: Accumulation, Financialisation and the Global Slowdown', *Historical Materialism*, vol. 17, no. 2, 2009, pp. 35–83.

Magdoff, Harry and Foster, John Bellamy (ed.), *Imperialism Without Colonies*, New York, Monthly Review, 2003.

Mahbubani, Kishore, 'While America Slept: How the United States botched China's rise', *Foreign Policy*, 27 February 2013.

Mallaby, Sabastian, 'The Reluctant Imperialist: Terrorism, Failed States, and the Case for American Empire', *Foreign Affairs*, vol. 81, no. 2, 2002.

Mandel, Ernest, *Marxist Economic Theory*, New York, Merlin, 1968.

Mandel, Ernest, *Late Capitalism* [1972], London, Verso, 1978.

Mandel, Ernest, *The Meaning of the Second World War*, London, Verso, 1986.

Marshall, Alexander, 'Lenin's Imperialism Nearly 100 Years on: An Outdated Paradigm?' *Journal of Socialist Theory*, vol. 42, no. 3, 2014, pp. 317–33.

Martin, William G. (ed.), *Semiperipheral States in the World Economy*, New York, Greenwood, 1990.

Marx, Karl, 'Revolution in China and In Europe', *New York Daily Tribune*, 14 June 1853, marxists.org/archive/marx/works/1853/06/14.htm.

Marx, Karl, 'The British Rule in India', *New York Daily Tribune*, 25 June 1853, marxists.org/archive/marx/works/1853/06/25.htm.

Marx, Karl, 'Future Results of British Rule in India', *New York Daily Tribune*, 8 August 1853, marxists.catbull.com/archive/marx/works/1853/07/22.htm.

Marx, Karl, *The Poverty of Philosophy: Answer to the Philosophy of Poverty by M. Proudhon* [1847], Moscow, Progress, 1955, marxists.org/archive/marx/works/1847/poverty-philosophy.

Marx, Karl, *The Process of Circulation of Capital*, vol. 2, *Capital: A Critique of Political Economy* [1893], edited by Engels Frederick, Moscow, Progress, 1956, marxists.org/archive/marx/works/1885-c2.

Marx, Karl, *Grundrisse: Foundations of the Critique of Political Economy* [1857–61], London, Penguin, 1973, marxists.org/archive/marx/works/download/Marx_Grundrisse.pdf.

Marx, Karl, *A Contribution to the Critique of Political Economy* [1859], Moscow, Progress, 1977, marxists.org/archive/marx/works/1859/critique-pol-economy/preface.htm.

Marx, Karl, *A Critique of Political Economy*, vol. 1, *Capital: A Critique of Political Economy* [1867], Moscow, Progress, n.d., marxists.org/archive/marx/works/1867-c1.

Marx, Karl, *The Process of Capitalist Production as a Whole*, vol. 3, *Capital: A Critique of Political Economy* [1894], edited by Engels, Frederick, New York, International Publishers, n.d., marxists.org/archive/marx/works/1894-c3.

Marx, Karl and Engels, Frederick, *Manifesto of the Communist Party* [1848], vol. 1, *Selected Works*, Moscow, Progress, 1969, pp. 98–137, marxists.org/archive/marx/works/1848/communist-manifesto.

Milanovic, Branko, 'Is "Neo-Imperialism" the Only Path to Development?' *Globalinequality*, 18 May 2017.

Milberg, William, 'Shifting Sources and Uses of Profits: Sustaining US Financialization with Global Value Chains', *Economy and Society*, vol. 37, no. 3, 2008, pp. 420–51.

Milberg, William and Winkler, Deborah, *Outsourcing Economics: Global Value Chains in Capital Development*, New York, Cambridge University Press, 2013.

Milios, John and Sotiropoulos, Dimitris P., *Rethinking Imperialism A Study of Capitalist Rule*, London and New York, Palgrave Macmillan, 2009.

Mohandesi, Salar, 'The Specificity of Imperialism', *Viewpoint Magazine*, no. 6, 2018.

Narayan, John and Sealey-Huggins, Leon, 'Whatever Happened to the Idea of Imperialism?' *Third World Quarterly*, vol. 38, no. 11, 2017, pp. 2387–95.

Nell, Edward J. (ed.), *Growth, Profits and Property*, Cambridge, UK, Cambridge University Press, 1980.

Nolan, Peter, *Is China Buying the World?* Cambridge, UK, Polity, 2012.

Nolan, Peter and Zhang, Jin, 'Global Competition After the Financial Crisis', *New Left Review*, no. 64, 2010.

Norfield, Tony, *The City: London and the Global Power of Finance*, London and New York, Verso, 2016.

Norfield, Tony, 'Finance and the Imperialist World Today' [interview by Philip Ferguson], *Redline*, 29 February 2016.

Owen, Roger and Sutcliffe, Bob (eds), *Studies in the Theory of Imperialism* [1972], London, Longman, 1978.

Paget, Roger K. (ed. and trans.), *Indonesia Accuses! Sukarno's Defence Oration in the Political Trial of 1930*, New York, Oxford University Press, 1975.

Palloix, Christian, 'The Self Expansion of Capital on a World Scale', *Review of Radical Political Economics*, vol. 9, no. 2, 1977, pp. 1–28.

Panitch, Leo, 'Rethinking Marxism and Imperialism for the Twenty-first Century', *New Labour Forum*, vol. 23, no. 2, 2014, pp. 22–8.

Panitch, Leo and Gindin, Sam, 'Global Capitalism and American Empire', *Socialist Register*, vol. 40, 2004.

Panitch, Leo and Gindin, Sam, *The Making of Global Capitalism: The Political Economy of the American Empire*, London and New York, Verso, 2013.

Panitch, Leo and Leys, Colin (eds), *The New Imperial Challenge: Socialist Register*, vol. 40, London, Merlin, 2004.

Panitch, Leo and Leys, Colin (eds), *The Empire Reloaded: Socialist Register*, vol. 41, London, Merlin, 2005.

Park, Barry, 'Australia Takes Lead on Lightweight Car Technology', *Wheels Magazine*, 21 November 2017.

Patnaik, Prabhat, 'Whatever Has Happened to Imperialism?' *Social Scientist*, vol. 18, no. 6/7, 1990, pp. 73–6.

Patnaik, Prabhat, 'Notes on Contemporary Imperialism', *Monthly Review Online*, 20 December 2010, mrzine.monthlyreview.org/2010/patnaik201210.html.

Patnaik, Utsa and Patnaik, Prabhat, 'Imperialism in the Era of Globalization', *Monthly Review*, vol. 67, no. 3, 2015.

Patnaik, Utsa and Patnaik, Prabhat, *A Theory of Imperialism*, New York, Columbia University Press, 2017.

Patsoura, Louis, *Marx in Context*, New York, iUniverse, 2005.

Perdue, Jon B., *The War of All the People: The Nexus of Latin American Radicalism and Middle Eastern Terrorism*, St Louis, MO, Potomac, 2012.

Petras, James, 'Rising and Declining Economic Powers: The Sino–US Conflict Deepens', *Journal of Contemporary Asia*, vol. 41, no. 1, 2011, pp. 117–37.

Petras, James and Veltmeyer, Henry, 'Imperialism and Capitalism: Rethinking an Intimate Relationship', *Global Research*, 16 December 2015.

Petras, James and Veltmeyer, Henry, *Imperialism and Capitalism in the Twenty-First Century: A System in Crisis* [2013], New York, Routledge, 2016.

Politi, James, Wong, Sue-Lin and Edgecliffe-Johnson, Andrew, 'US Companies Step Up Response to Donald Trump's China Ultimatum', *Financial Times*, 23 May 2019.

Potter, Ben, 'Skilled Manufacturing Labour Has Edge Over US', *Financial Review*, 14 November 2016.

Pradella, Lucia, 'Imperialism and Capitalist Development in Marx's Capital', Historical Materialism, vol. 21, no. 2, 2013, pp. 117–47.

Prashad, Vijay, *The Poorer Nations: A Possible History of the Global South*, London, Verso, 2014.

Probsting, Michael, *The Great Robbery of the South: Continuity and Changes in the Super-Exploitation of the Semi-Colonial World by Monopoly Capital. Consequences for the Marxist Theory of Imperialism*, Vienna, Revolutionary Communist International Tendency, 2013.

Probsting, Michael, 'China's Emergence as an Imperialist Power', *New Politics*, vol. 15, no. 57, summer 2014.

Reinert, Erik, *How the Rich Countries Got Rich … And Why the Poor Countries Stay Poor*, London, Constable and Robinson, 2007.

Renton, David (ed.), *Marx on Globalisation*, London, Lawrence and Wishart, 2001.

Reshoring Initiative, *Reshoring Initiative 2016 Data Report: The Tide Has Turned*, 9 May 2017, http://reshorenow.org/content/pdf/Reshoring_Initiative_2016_Data_Report.pdf.

Reuters [Staff], 'Nigeria's 10-Year Bonds Yield Fall to 11-Month Low on Liquidity', *Reuters*, 17 October, 2015.

Reuters [World News], 'Second Prototype of China's C919 Jet Conducts Test Flight: State TV', *Reuters*, 17 December 2017.

Riddell, John (ed.), *The Communist International in Lenin's Time: Workers of the World and Oppressed Peoples, Unite! Proceedings and Documents of the Second Congress, 1920* [1920], New York, Pathfinder, 1991.

Roberts, Michael, 'Banking: Business as Usual', *Michael Roberts Blog*, 7, January 2013, https://thenextrecession.wordpress.com/2013/01/07/banking-business-as-usual/.

Roberts, Michael, 'China: A Weird Beast', *Michael Roberts Blog*, 17 September 2015, https://thenextrecession.wordpress.com/2015/09/17/china-a-weird-beast/.

Roberts, Michael, *The Long Depression: Marxism and the Global Crisis of Capitalism*, Chicago, Haymarket, 2016.

Roberts, Michael, 'Puerto Rico: When It Rains, It Pours', *Michael Roberts Blog*, 17 October 2017, https://thenextrecession.wordpress.com/2017/10/17/puerto-rico-when-it-rains-it-pours/.

Roberts, Michael, 'Xi Takes Full Control of China's FUture', *Michael Roberts Blog*, 25 October 2017, https://thenextrecession.wordpress.com/2017/10/25/xi-takes-full-control-of-chinas-future/.

Robinson, William I., *Global Capitalism and the Crisis of Humanity*, New York, Cambridge University Press, 2014.

Rostow, Walt W., *Stages of Economic Growth: A Non-Communist Manifesto*, New York, Cambridge University Press, 1960.

Rowthorn, Robert and Ramaswany, Ramana, 'Deindustrialization: Causes and Implications', *IMF Working Paper (WP/97/42)*, 1997.

Roxborough, Ian, *Theories of Underdevelopment*, London, Macmillan, 1979.

Sakellaropoulos, Spyros and Panagiotis, Sotiris, 'From Territorial to Nonterritorial Capitalist Imperialism: Lenin and the Possibility of a Marxist Theory of Imperialism', *Rethinking Marxism*, vol. 27, no. 1, 2015, pp. 95–106.

Sargent, John F., Esworthy, Robert, Harris, Laurie A., Johnson, Judith A., Monke, Jim, Morgan, Daniel and Upton Harold F., *Federal Research and Development Funding: FY2017*, Washington, DC, Congressional Research Service, 2017, https://fas.org/sgp/crs/misc/R44516.pdf.

Saull, Richard, 'Rethinking Hegemony: Uneven Development, Historical Blocs, and the World Economic Crisis', *International Studies Quarterly*, vol. 56, no. 2, 2012, pp. 323–38.

Schumpeter, Joseph, *Capitalism, Socialism and Democracy* [1942], New York, Taylor and Francis, 2003.

Schwartz, Herman M., *States Versus Markets: The Emergence of a Global Economy*, Basingstoke, Palgrave Macmillan, 2000.

Schwartz, Herman M., 'Dependency or Institutions? Economic Geography, Causal Mechanisms, and Logic in the Understanding of Development', *Studies in Comparative International Development*, vol. 42, no. 1, 2007, pp. 115–35.

Schwartz, Herman M., *Subprime Nation: American Power, Global Capital, and the Housing Bubble*, New York, Cornell University Press, 2009.

Schwarzenberg, Andres B., 'U.S.–China Investment Ties: Overview and Nos for Congress', *Congressional Research Service*, 7 August 2017.

Scissors, Derek, 'Chinese Investments in the United States', *AEI*, 2020, aei.org/china-tracker-home.

Screpanti, Ernesto, *Global Imperialism and the Great Crisis: The Uncertain Future of Capitalism*, New York, Monthly Review, 2014.

Sekiguchi, Waichi, 'Huawei to Set Up R & D Base in Tokyo', *Nikkei Asian Review*, 26 November 2016.

Selwyn, Benjamin, 'Trotsky, Gerschenkron and the Political Economy of Late Capitalist Development', *Economy and Society*, vol. 40, no. 3, 2011, pp. 421–50.

Selwyn, Benjamin, 'Commodity Chains, Creative Destruction and Global Inequality: A Class Analysis', *Journal of Economic Geography*, vol. 15, no. 2, 2014, pp. 253–74.

Semmel, Bernard, 'On [Arrighi's] "The Geometry of Imperialism"', *New Left Review*, no. 118, 1979.

Shaikh, Anwar, *Capitalism: Competition, Conflict, Crises*, New York, Oxford University Press, 2016.

Sirkin, Harold L., Zinser, Michael, Hohner, Doug and Rose, Justin, 'U.S. Manufacturing Nears the Tipping Point: Which Industries, Why, and How Much?' *BCG*, 22 March 2012, www.bcg.com/publications/2012/manufacturing-supply-chain-management-us-manufacturing-nears-the-tipping-point.

Smith, Ashley, 'Obama's New Imperialist Strategy', *International Socialist Review*, no. 83, 2012.

Smith, Ashley, 'US imperialism's Pivot to Asia', *International Socialist Review*, no. 88, 2013.

Smith, Ashley, 'Deal or No Deal, the Rivalry Between the US and China Will Intensify', *Truth Out*, 22 May 2019.

Smith, John, *Imperialism and the Globalisation of Production*, PhD thesis, Sheffield, University of Sheffield, 2010.

Smith, John, 'Imperialism and the Law of Value', *Global Discourse*, vol. 2, no. 1, 2011, pp. 1–36.

Smith, John, 'Imperialism in the Twenty-First Century', *Monthly Review*, vol. 67, no. 3, 2015.

Smith, John, *Imperialism in the Twenty-First Century: Globalization, Super-Exploitation and Capitalism's Final Crisis*, New York, Monthly Review, 2016.

Somel, Cem, 'Surplus Allocation and Development under Global Capitalism', *ERC Working Papers in Economics 5/5*, 2005, pp. 1–32.

Song Loong, Melissa, 'Greece Takes Rain Check After Savage Equity Sell-Off', *Reuters*, 6 February 2018.

Starosta, Guido, 'Global Commodity Chains and the Marxian Law of Value', *Antipode*, vol. 42, no. 2, 2010, pp. 433–65.

Starrs, Sean, 'American Economic Power Hasn't Declined – It Globalized! Summoning the Data and Taking Globalization Seriously', *International Studies Quarterly*, vol. 57, no. 4, 2013, pp. 817–30.

Starrs, Sean, 'The Chimera of Global Convergence', *New Left Review*, no. 87, 2014.

Starrs, Sean, 'China's Rise Is Designed in America, Assembled in China', *China's World*, vol. 2, no. 2, 2015, pp. 9–20.

State Council [of China], *Made in China 2025*, 7 July, 2015.

Steil, Benn and Smith, Emma, 'China's Exorbitant Detriment, Mirror Image of America's Exorbitant Privilege, Is Costing It Dearly', *Council on Foreign Relations* [blog], 17 April 2017, www.cfr.org/blog/chinas-exorbitant-detriment-mirror-image-americas-exorbitant-privilege-costing-it-dearly.

Steinbeck, John, *The Grapes of Wrath* [Introduction by Robert DeMott], New York, Penguin, 1992.

Steinfeld, Edward S., 'Chinese Enterprise Development and the Challenge of Global Integration', *MIT Special Working Paper Series No. 02-001*, 2002.

Steinfeld, Edward S., 'China's Shallow Integration: Networked Production and the New Challenges for Late Industrialization', *World Development*, vol. 32, no. 11, 2004, pp. 1971–87.

Steinfeld, Edward, S., *Playing Our Game: Why China's Rise Doesn't Threaten the West*, New York, Oxford University Press, 2010.

Sturgeon, Timothy J., 'From Commodity Chains to Value Chains: Interdisciplinary Theory Building in an Age of Globalization', *Industry Studies Association Working Paper Series No. 2008-02*, 2008.

Sturgeon, Timothy, van Biesebroeck, Joannes and Gereffi, Gary, 'Value Chains, Networks and Clusters: Reframing the Global Automotive Industry', *Journal of Economic Geography*, vol. 8, no. 3, 2008, pp. 297–321.

Su, Jean Baptiste, 'China's ZTE Shuts Down After U.S. Tech Ban Over Iran Sales', *Forbes*, 9 May 2018.

Sutton, Alex, 'Towards an Open Marxist Theory of Imperialism', *Capital and Class*, vol. 37, no. 2, 2013, pp. 217–37.

Suwandi, Intan, 'Labor-Value Commodity Chains, The Hidden Abode of Global Production', *Monthly Review*, vol. 71, no. 3, 2019.

Suwandi, Intan, *Value Chains: The New Economic Imperialism*, New York, Monthly Review, 2019.

Suwandi, Intan and Foster, John Bellamy, 'Multinational Corporations and the Globalization of Monopoly Capital: From the 1960s to the Present', *Monthly Review*, vol. 68, no. 3, 2016.

Sweezy, Paul, M., *The Theory of Capitalist Development* [1942], New York, Monthly Review, 1970.

Sweezy, Paul, M., 'The Triumph of Finance Capital', *Monthly Review*, vol. 46, no. 2, 1994.

Tang, Frank, 'Ten Years On, Where to Now for China's Sovereign Wealth Fund?' *South China Morning Post*, 27 August 2017.

Tang, Frank, 'Made in China 2025? Not Unless It Starts Spending More Money, Lawmaker Says', *South China Morning Post*, 10 December 2018.

Tang, Frank, 'China Ignoring US Demand for Trade War Reform by Reinforcing State-Directed Economic Model', *South China Morning Post*, 13 July 2019.

Tett, Gillian, 'Executives Take a Quiet Turn Away from Globalisation', *Financial Times*, 2 June 2017.

The Economist [Editorial], 'The Headwinds Return', 13 September 2014.

The Economist, 'Great Leap Backward: Capacity Cuts in China Fuel a Commodity Rally and a Debate', 7 September 2017.

The Economist, 'The Technology Industry Is Rife with Bottlenecks', 6 June 2019.

Tokatli, Nebahat, 'Toward a Better Understanding of the Apparel Industry: A critique of the Upgrading Literature' [2012], *Journal of Economic Geography*, vol. 13, no. 6, 2013, pp. 993–1011.

Trotsky, Leon, *Ninety Years of the Communist Manifesto* [1938], New York, Fourth International, 1948, marxists.org/archive/trotsky/1937/10/90manifesto.htm.

United Nations Conference on Trade and Development (UNCTAD), *World Investment Report 2013: Global Value Chains: Investment and Trade for Development*, New York and Geneva, UNCTAD, 2013.

United Nations Conference on Trade and Development (UNCTAD), *Trade and Development Report, 2016: Structural Transformation for Inclusive and Sustained Growth*, New York and Geneva, UNCTAD, 2016.

United Nations Conference on Trade and Development (UNCTAD), *Trade and Development Report 2017: Beyond Austerity: Towards a Global New Deal*, New York and Geneva, UNCTAD, 2017.

United Nations Conference on Trade and Development (UNCTAD), *World Investment Report 2017: Investment and the Digital Economy*, New York and Geneva, UNCTAD, 2017.

United Nations Conference on Trade and Development (UNCTAD), *Trade and Development Report 2020: From Global Pandemic to Prosperity for All: Avoiding Another Lost Decade*, New York and Geneva, UNCTAD, 2020.

United Nations Conference on Trade and Development (UNCTAD), *World Investment Report 2020: International Production Beyond the Pandemic*, New York and Geneva, UNCTAD, 2020.

United Nations Department of Economic and Social Affairs: Population Division, *World Population Prospects, the 2015 Revision: Key Findings and Advanced Tables*, New York, United Nations Department of Economic and Social Affairs, 2015.

United Nations Industrial Development Organization (UNIDO), *Industrial Development Report 2013: Sustaining Employment Growth – The Role of Manufacturing and Structural Change*, Vienna, UNIDO, 2013.

United Nations Statistical Division, 'Statistics Division', 2018, unstats.un.org.

US Bureau of Labor Statistics, 'All Employees, Manufacturing [MANEMP]', *FRED: Economic Data*, 2020, fred.stlouisfed.org/series/MANEMP.

Vernon, Raymond, 'International Investment and Trade in the Product Cycle', *Quarterly Journal of Economics*, vol. 80, 1966, pp. 190–207.

Vine, David, 'Where in the World Is the U.S. Military?' *Politico*, July/August 2015.

Wallerstein, Immanuel, *Decline of American Power: The U.S. in a Chaotic World*, New York, New Press, 2003.

Ward-Foxton, Sally, 'Made in China 2025: Make or Break for Europe?' *Electronic Engineering Times*, 25 July 2017.

Warren, Bill, 'Imperialism and Capitalist Industrialization', *New Left Review*, no. 81, 1973.

Warren, Bill, *Imperialism: Pioneer of Capitalism*, London, New Left, 1980.

Weaver, Frederick S., 'The Limits of Inerrant Marxism' [Review of Imperialism: Pioneer of Capitalism by Bill Warren], *Latin American Perspectives*, vol. 13, no. 4, autumn 1986, pp. 100–7.

Webb, Quentin, 'Broken Record', *Reuters*, 17 February 2016.

Weiniger, Patrick, 'Understanding Imperialism: A Reply to Sam King', *Marxist Left Review*, no. 9, 2014.

Williams, Sam, 'Is Russia Imperialist?' *A Critique of Crisis Theory*, 2014, https://critiqueofcrisistheory.wordpress.com/is-russia-imperialist/.

Willoughby, John, *Capitalist Imperialism, Crisis and the State*, London, Harwood, 1986.

Willoughby, John, 'Evaluating the Leninist Theory of Imperialism', *Science and Society*, vol. 59, no. 3, 1995, pp. 320–38.

Wong, Edward, 'U.S. Versus China: A New Era of Great Power Competition, but Without Boundaries', *New York Times*, 26 June 2019.

Woo, Wing Thye and Hong, Chang, 'Indonesia's Economic Performance in Comparative Perspective: A New Policy Framework for 2049', *Bulletin of Indonesian Economic Studies*, vol. 46, no. 1, 2010, pp. 33–64.

Wood, Ellen Meiksins, *Empire of Capital*, London and New York, Verso, 2005.

World Bank Data Team, 'New Country Classifications By Income Level', *Data Blog*, 7 January 2016, blogs.worldbank.org/opendata/new-country-classifications-2016.

World Bank, 'DataBank', 2017, databank.worldbank.org.

World Bank, 'DataBank', 2018, databank.worldbank.org.

Yang, Jian, 'ARJ21 Starts Commercial Operation with 2nd Operator', *Shine*, 26 July 2019.

Yang, Yuan, 'How Trump Blacklisting Affects the Inside of a Huawei Smartphone', *Financial Times*, 2 June 2019.

Yates, Michael, 'Measuring Global Inequality', *Monthly Review*, vol. 68, no. 6, 2016.

Zarembka, Paul, 'Lenin as Economist of Production: A Ricardian Step Backwards', *Science and Society*, vol. 67, no. 3, fall 2003, pp. 276–302.

Zavareei, Hassan, A., 'Industry and Trade in Some Developing Countries: A Comparative Study', *Science and Society*, vol. 39, no. 4, 1975–6.

Zhou, Cissy, 'Roll-Out of China's Home-Grown Passenger Jet Still Up in the Air as US Tech Restrictions Expected to Persist Under Joe Biden', *South China Morning Post*, 15 November 2020.

Index

EU authorised representative for GPSR:
Easy Access System Europe, Mustamäe tee 50,
10621 Tallinn, Estonia
gpsr.requests@easproject.com